...didn't [illegible] was expecting the [illegible] from [illegible]
all he said was "damn", gave me a high five
and I walked out smiling.

That proposed evidence [illegible]
caused damage to valuable [illegible]
equipment but there was [illegible] no one [illegible]
of his responsibility as a [illegible]
photographer Danny Lyon, [illegible]
the beautiful and talented wife of [illegible]
Allender the [illegible] children had
made [illegible] ballo[illegible] [illegible] [illegible]
pack complete with a bag for [illegible]
Bob [illegible] and myself. Fortunately
he was able to [illegible] [illegible] and spent
most of my time there too. We caught
a fish in a [illegible] and [illegible] never
[illegible] had my first tasted a
southern fried catfish and the incredible
flavor of raw oysters on the half shell.
The next day we visited some of the
nearby projects as a [illegible] my first
glimpsed of the beauties of the black
belt country. After photographing a
burnt cross in front of the [illegible] Batesville
Freedom House, I started back to
Atlanta. Before [illegible] [illegible] we [illegible]
stopped to take a picture of
the Welcome to Mississippi sign which
we needed for the next issue of the
Student Voice.
The next morning we received a
frantic call from our friends of
[illegible] chapter in New York. A shipment
of posters using some of Danny's most
memorable photos and others had
not arrived. [illegible] enclosed a big [illegible]

Soul on Rice: A Debbie Lou [illegible]

ENEMY ALIEN

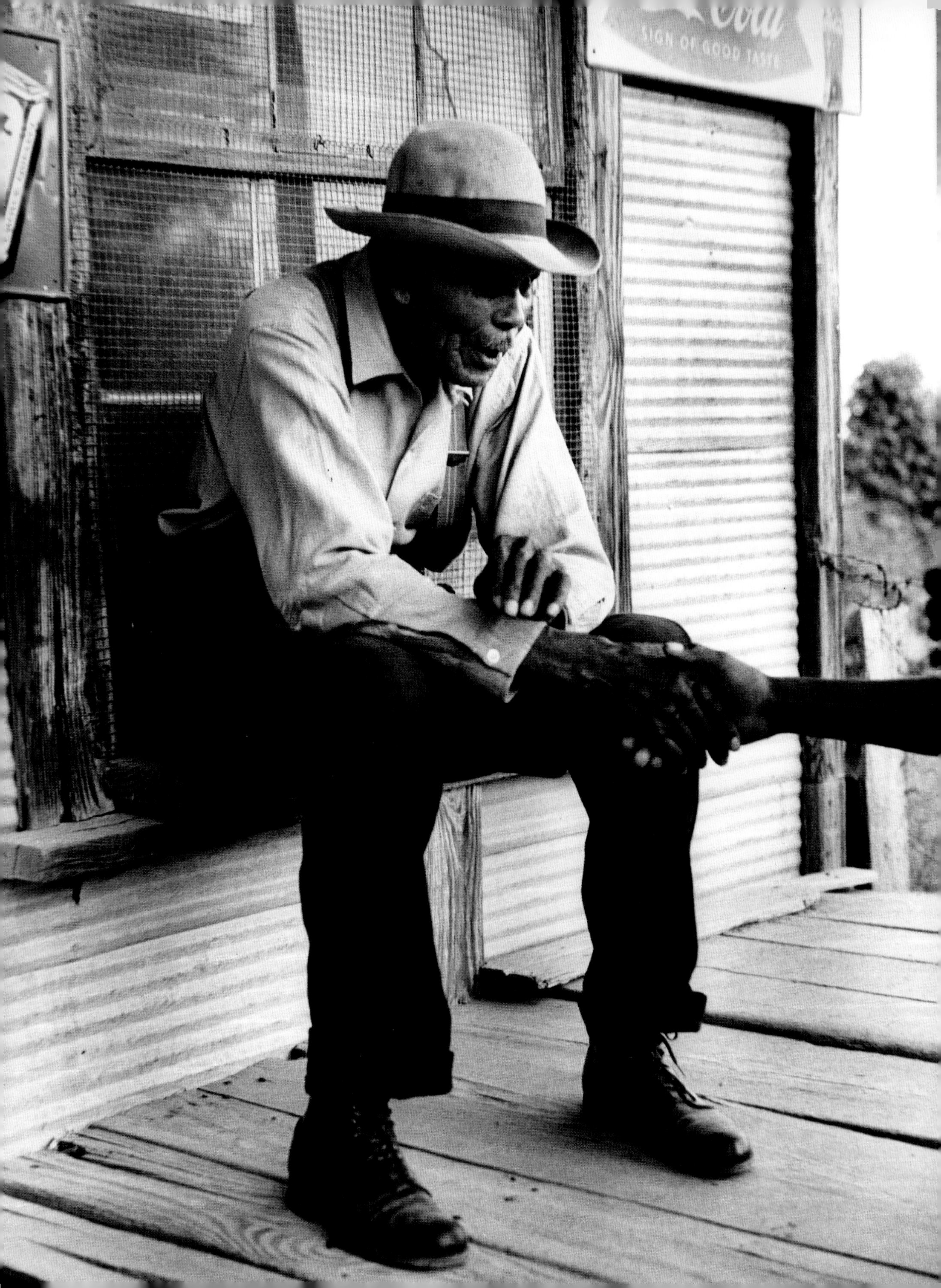
Cola
SIGN OF GOOD TASTE

ENEMY ALIEN TAMIO WAKAYAMA

Vancouver Artgallery

Figure.1
Vancouver / Berkeley

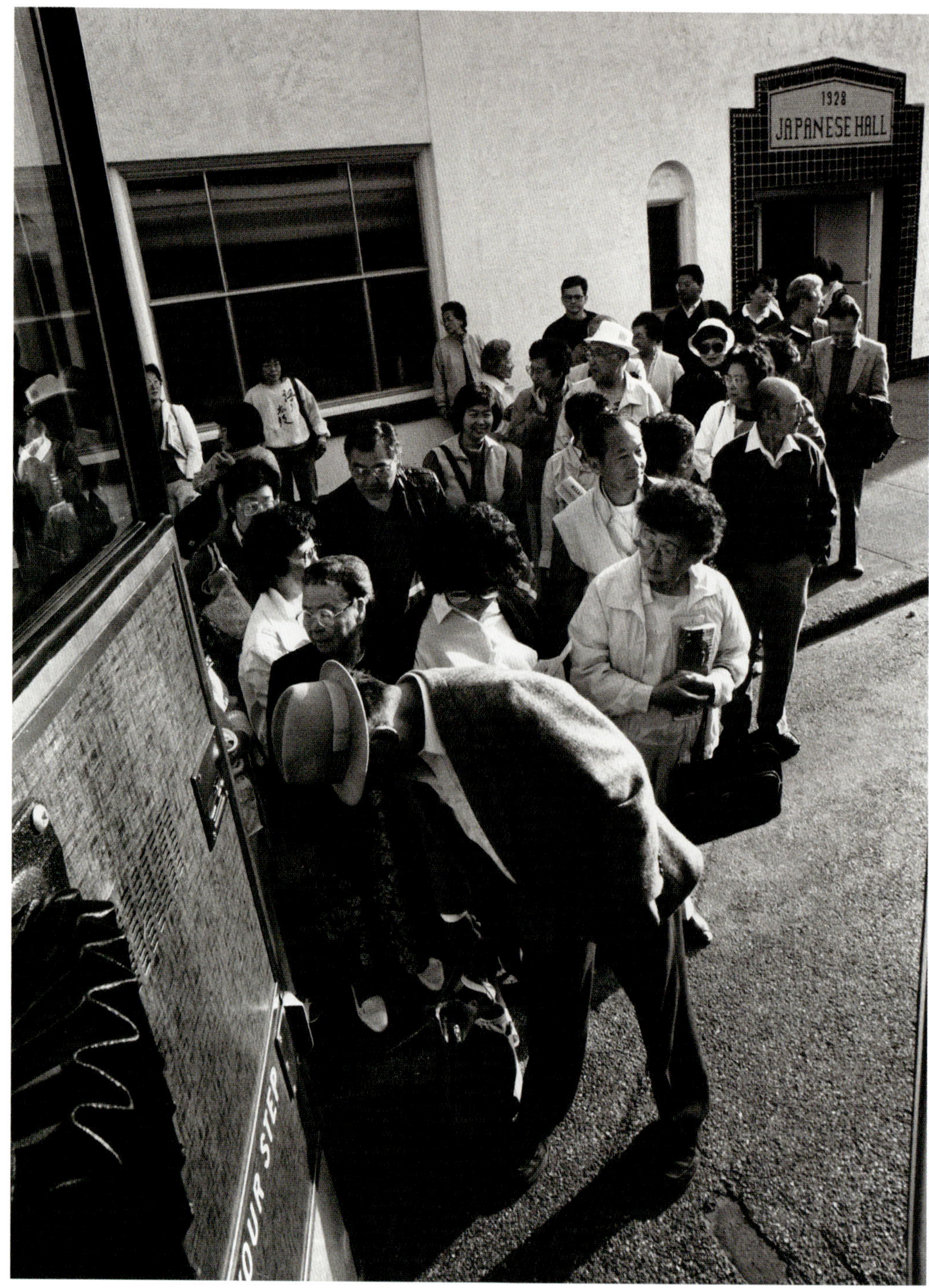

National Association of Japanese Canadians (NAJC) bus tour of the wartime internment camps, Vancouver, British Columbia, May 1987

FOREWORD

THE VANCOUVER ART GALLERY has a significant history of exhibiting photography in all its forms. Among our earliest exhibitions were *B.C. Mountaineering Club Photographic Exhibition* (February 1932) and a solo presentation of the renowned modernist photographer John Vanderpant (May 1932)—the second artist to be feted with a solo show in the Gallery's history. Located in a city known for contemporary photo-based work, our collection and programming reflect the history of local production within a global context. In the last decade, we have organized and hosted in-depth presentations of the work of photographers Cindy Sherman, Vikky Alexander, Elad Lassry, Stephen Shore, Walker Evans, Harry Callahan, Stephen Waddell and Christos Dikeakos. *Enemy Alien: Tamio Wakayama* is conceived as part of our ongoing commitment to exploring the photographic medium while contributing to global dialogues on its aesthetic, material and conceptual possibilities.

Enemy Alien represents the most significant presentation of photographer Tamio Wakayama's work to date and features examples from important bodies of work that span his more than fifty-year career. Wakayama—who was born just months before the Japanese attack on Pearl Harbor—was part of the community of twenty-two thousand Japanese Canadians who were declared to be Enemy Aliens, dispossessed of their property and placed in remote internment camps in the interior of British Columbia and sugar beet farms in the Prairie provinces. Deeply affected by these formative years, Wakayama would spend the rest of his life working tirelessly to document community history and activism, and to tell stories with his lens.

With no formal training, Wakayama fell into photography when he was handed a camera when he began volunteering with the Student Nonviolent Coordinating Committee (SNCC) in the American South in 1963. His biography is truly the stuff of a Hollywood film, and we are thrilled to be posthumously publishing his captivating autobiography, *Soul on Rice*, in this volume. *Soul on Rice* recounts Wakayama's work with SNCC in Georgia, Mississippi and Alabama during the Civil Rights Movement; documenting everyday life in parts of Canada, Japan and Cuba, including Indigenous communities in Saskatchewan and the Doukhobors in Eastern British Columbia; and his photographic practice in Vancouver capturing Japanese Canadian culture and the Redress Movement. It is an enthralling read.

The *Enemy Alien* exhibition and publication were many years in the making. We would like to acknowledge Senior Curator Diana Freundl who developed this project from a germ of an idea that emerged in a casual conversation with artist Cindy Mochizuki more than five years ago and oversaw its evolution. We thank Diana for her dedication to realizing this significant exhibition of Wakayama's work. Guest Curator Paul Wong first met Tamio Wakayama in the late 1970s and would later feature Wakayama's work in his influential curatorial projects *Yellow Peril: New World Asians* (1988) and *Yellow Peril: Reconsidered* (1990–91). We were thrilled when Paul agreed to work with us on this project, and he influenced every aspect through his insight, energy and creativity. It would not have been possible to realize it without his immense efforts, and we thank him as well for his sharp introduction to this volume. We would also like to recognize Mayumi Takasaki—Tamio's partner for forty years—for her support of *Enemy Alien* since its infancy. Mayumi's generosity and knowledge shaped all aspects of the exhibition and publication. We thank her for her partnership throughout this lengthy process and for contributing her voice and astute observations to this publication. Cindy Mochizuki's documentary *Between Pictures: The Lens of Tamio Wakayama* (2024) is featured as an important component of the *Enemy Alien* exhibition. We are grateful to Cindy for allowing us to screen the film and for sharing her extensive research.

A project of this scale requires the contribution of many, and we would like to thank the dedicated and hardworking staff at the Gallery for all their immense efforts to bring *Enemy Alien* to life. Former Curatorial Assistant Joanne So Jeong Chung spent countless hours at Paul's studio combing through Wakayama's archive and providing order to Paul's working process. She was instrumental in the project's early stages. Photographers Ian Lefebvre and Brian Howell documented and organized more than three hundred prints, and Registrars Amber McBride and Jaclyn Pollock tracked the myriad details.

Director of Publishing & Content Strategy Stephanie Rebick worked closely with our partners at Figure 1 Publishing to produce this volume. We thank Stephanie, our Editor Michael Leyne and Managing

Editor Lara Smith for their oversight. Debbie Cheung, who first worked with Paul on the *Occupying Chinatown* (2021) book project, provided a thoughtful design that captured Wakayama's ethos. We extend our gratitude to the Gallery's Board of Trustees for their enthusiasm for this project.

Finally we would like to thank Tamio Wakayama for the incredible legacy that he has left us. His shrewd eye and keen ability to tell stories through photographs produced a rich archive that will be of immense value for generations to come. His innate understanding of the importance of documenting and preserving community is truly inspirational.

Sirish Rao and Eva Respini
Interim Co-CEOs, Vancouver Art Gallery

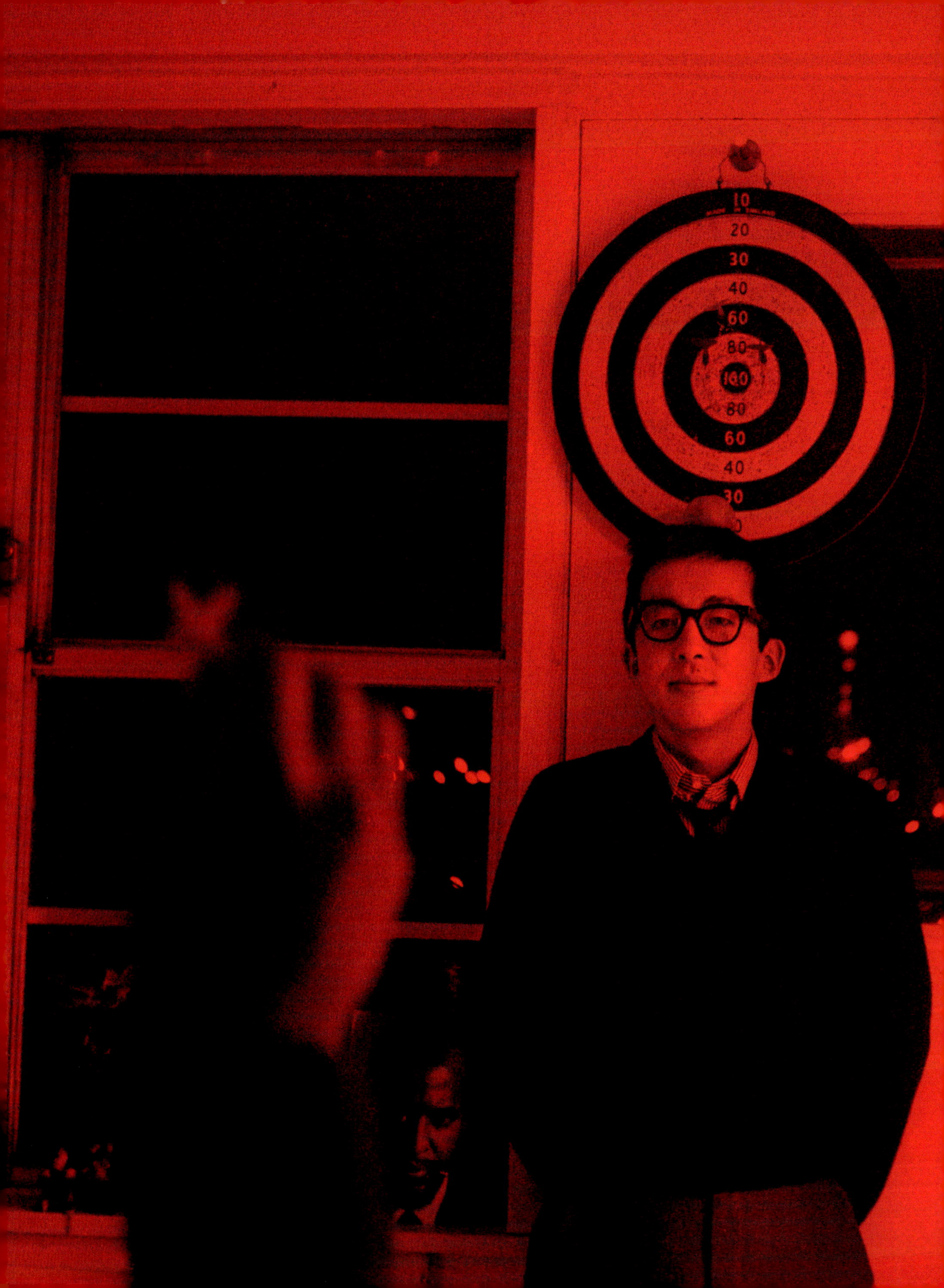

ENEMY ALIEN: TAMIO WAKAYAMA

Paul Wong

ENEMY ALIEN: TAMIO WAKAYAMA is the first comprehensive exploration of the photography of Tamio Wakayama, tracing his remarkable journey as a social justice activist and photographer from the 1960s to the 1990s. The story is told mostly through his own words and his black and white photographs.

My connection to the Japanese Canadian community goes back to the 1970s when I was a co-founding director of the Satellite Video Exchange Society (est. 1973). This non-profit, artist-led organization—formerly known as Video Inn and now rebranded as the VIVO Media Arts Centre—was located at 261 Powell Street in the heart of what was Little Tokyo before the removal and internment of all Japanese Canadians from the West Coast during WWII. We occupied the ground floor, and the basement—a former Japanese-style bath house—was used by the landlord for storage.

We were a ragtag collective of artists and activists sharing equipment, space and knowledge to explore radical new ways of telling our own stories through experimental documentary and video art. We created a new model of media democracy for those not represented in mainstream culture. We were acutely aware of the history of the impoverished and neglected area where we were situated. Among the social service agencies, Christian missions, second hand stores and rooming houses were a few signs of the neighbourhood's vibrant history as a centre for Japanese Canadian life: Language Aid (a multilingual service agency), Aki Restaurant (where I was first introduced to sushi), the Japanese Buddhist church and the Japanese Language School (where I attended punk concerts in the auditorium).

I can recall participating in the first Powell Street Festival in 1977—Video Inn set up a viewing tent in Oppenheimer Park and showed tapes. I attend the two-day festival annually—it is the best and longest running community festival in the city. For almost fifty years, it has stayed true to its roots and remains a place to gather and celebrate the resilience and survival of the Japanese Canadian community. I can't remember when I first met or became aware of Tamio. I would run into him at the Powell Street Festival as he was wandering the grounds with cameras strapped to his body. He was totally immersed in his community.

In 1988 I included Tamio's work in *Yellow Peril: New World Asians*, an exhibition that I curated for the Chisenhale Gallery in London, UK. The exhibition featured sixteen Asian Canadian lens-based artists. The Black Arts Movement had emerged in England in the 1980s, which addressed issues of racism and decolonization and the effects of living in what was once the centre of the British Empire. Within that context *Yellow Peril* was seen as peculiar—photography and video were exported from a former colony and presented as an import in what had been the centre of imperial power. The artists were not viewed as marginalized— they were instead seen as serious artists at the forefront of Canadian art.

I developed this project into *Yellow Peril: Reconsidered*, which featured twenty-five artists and toured across Canada between 1990 and 1991. The exhibition and book generated a lot of attention and controversy, acceptance and resistance. Tamio's contribution to the exhibition included *Furasato* (hometown)—a text panel—and seventeen photographs from the 1960s, 70s and 80s. In some ways, it was the precursor to what is being presented in more depth here. It is shocking that it would take thirty-five years from *Yellow Peril* to finally arrive at this long overdue attention and recognition that Tamio's work deserves.

In 1992 I was invited by Tamio to curate *Kikyō: Coming Home to Powell Street*—an exhibition and book project he had initiated that focused on photographs documenting the first fifteen years of the Powell Street Festival. *Kikyō* is a metaphorical and spiritual journey, a return from exile. Interwoven with the black and white photographs are texts gathered from Japanese Canadians, which collectively provide a powerful and sobering counterpoint to a shameful past. We spent months working together discussing every photo and text, as well as his introduction and my afterword. Many of these photographs are included in this book—images of celebration interwoven with those depicting the Japanese Canadian community's struggle for redress.

Given my experience working with Tamio and knowledge of his practice, I was invited by the Vancouver Art Gallery in 2022 to curate this retrospective exhibition. To facilitate my research, we moved his archive to my Chinatown studio in the fall of 2023—a five-minute walk from the home he had shared with Mayumi for more than forty years. Vancouver Art Gallery Curatorial Assistant Joanne So Jeong Chung and I devoted a year to combing through the archive of contact sheets,

TO MALE ENEMY ALIENS
NOTICE

Under date of February 2nd, 1942, the Honourable the Minister of National Defence with the concurrence of the Minister of Justice gave public notice defining an area of British Columbia, as described below, to be a protected area after the 31st day of January, 1942; that is to say, that area of the Province of British Columbia, including all islands, west of a line described hereunder:-

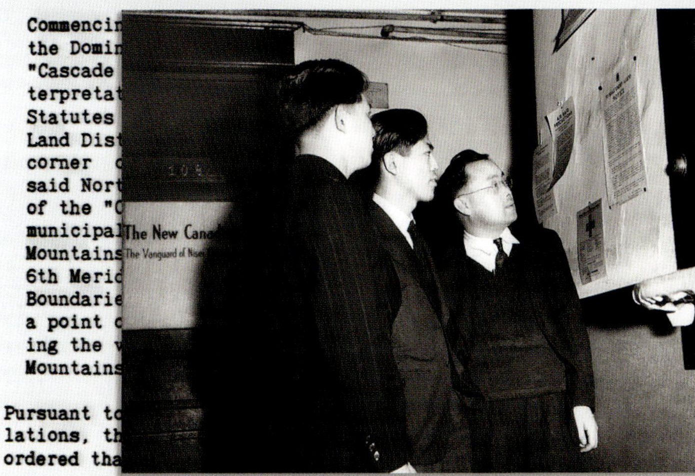

Commencing ... between the Domin... of the "Cascade ... of the Interpretat... Revised Statutes ... 5, Coast Land Dist... Northwest corner ... South to said Nort... oned line of the "C... village municipal... "Cascade Mountains ... st of the 6th Merid... Southerly Boundarie... of, being a point ... surrounding the v... "Cascade Mountains

Pursuant to ... ada Regulations, th... ry, 1942, ordered tha...

1. All male Enemy Aliens of the ages of 18 years to 45 years, inclusive, shall leave the protected area hereinbefore referred to on or before the 1st day of April, 1942;

2. That, subject to the provisions of paragraph No. 1 of this Order, no Enemy Alien shall, after the date of this order, enter, leave or return to such protected area except with the permission of the Commissioner of the Royal Canadian Mounted Police Force, or an Officer of that Force designated by the Commissioner to act for him in this respect;

3. That no Enemy Alien shall have in his possession or use, while in such protected area, any camera, radio transmitter, radio shortwave receiving set, firearm, ammunition, or explosive.

S.T. WOOD (Commissioner)
Royal Canadian Mounted Police.

OTTAWA, February 7, 1942.

TO BE POSTED IN A CONSPICUOUS PLACE

Composite: Notice to male "enemy aliens," February 7, 1942; Three men reading the evacuation notice, Vancouver, British Columbia, 1942

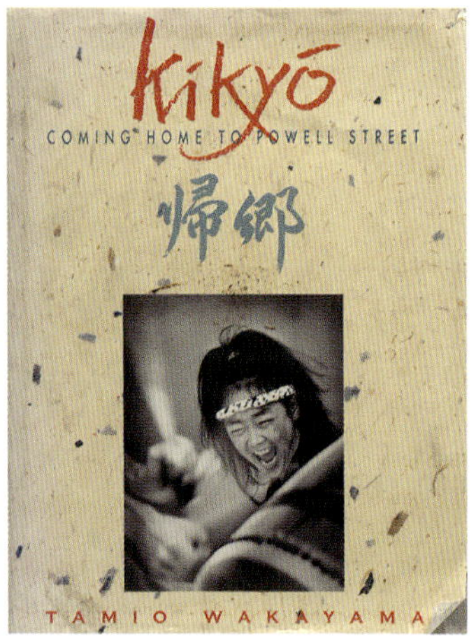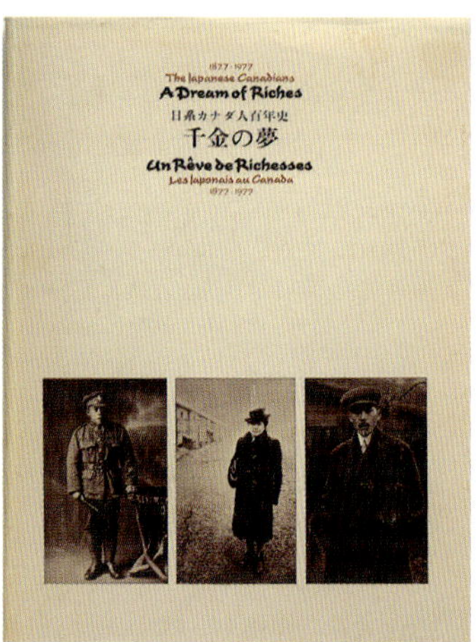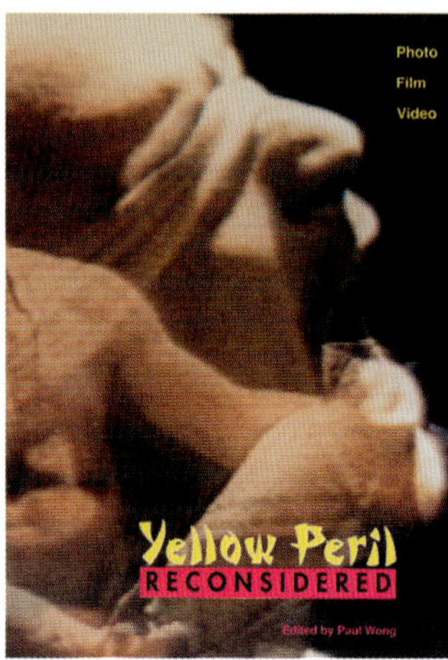

Book covers of *Kikyō: Coming Home to Powell Street* (1992); *A Dream of Riches: The Japanese Canadians, 1877–1977* (1978); *Yellow Peril: Reconsidered* (1990)

negatives and prints. We spent months looking through the pictures documenting the Student Nonviolent Coordinating Committee's (SNCC) activities. These negatives and contact sheets have remained stored in the original SNCC file folders and envelopes for sixty years—it was a privilege to handle, examine, learn and play with these incredible documents of an extraordinary time. Prior to this research, my knowledge of the Civil Rights Movement in general, and SNCC specifically, was vague at best.

The archive included a portfolio of printed photographs. Over the years, many of these images were featured in publications and group exhibitions related to the Civil Rights Movement. I wanted to better understand these prints by seeing what was on either side of the frames, what preceded them on the contact sheets, what happened on the days before and those that followed.

Using the memoir as our guide, we were able to identify and select photos that best illustrated Tamio's writing. It was a slow process; we were frequently distracted by attempts to identify subjects, locations and events, which we researched online and in other publications. It was exciting to learn more about this fascinating time and so many of the key people in the Movement.

My work with the archive also revealed Tamio as an individual with eclectic interests. His trajectory after his time in the Deep South was the prototypical 1960s experience—embrace of New Left causes, stints as an anti-war and political activist, wandering Canada, the US, Cuba and Japan in search of meaning, and experimentations with alternative lifestyles.

Editing the collection frame by frame, I have taken curatorial and editorial licence in some cases by selecting a different frame than what Tamio had chosen and printed.

He did not shoot pictures intended for gallery or museum exhibitions. He was a photojournalist; he took pictures that were intended for publications, newspapers, community bulletins and posters.

Through this project, we gained intimate insight into his practice—how he framed a shot, what lens he favoured and how he would crop and print in the darkroom. With that knowledge, we worked closely with expert photographer Brian Howell to digitize the negatives and make prints. Of the hundred photographs selected for the Black Belt South section of the exhibition, seventy have never been printed. I can only hope that the photographs reproduced in this book would have met with Tamio's approval.

The image reproduced at the beginning of this essay is a rare photograph of Tamio taken during his time with SNCC; what is even rarer is that this is a staged photograph. Captured in New York in 1964—removed from the troubles in the Deep South—the images on this contact sheet depict Tamio and others relaxed and at play at a friend's apartment. With a smirk on his face and an apple precariously balanced on his head, Tamio is shown standing in front of a dart board. A blurred hand holding a dart is visible on the left-hand side of the picture. This hand belongs to Len Chandler—renowned folk singer and Civil Rights activist who performed alongside Joan Baez and Bob Dylan at the March on Washington for Jobs and Freedom in August 1963. Tamio watched that event—which featured Dr. Martin Luther King's "I Have a Dream" speech—on television and was motivated by the words of John Lewis to drive from Southern Ontario to volunteer with SNCC in Atlanta. The photo was likely taken by Bob Fletcher, a SNCC photographer with whom Tamio felt a great affinity.

This is Tamio Wakayama's journey—from a place of hatred to a place of acceptance and peace of self.

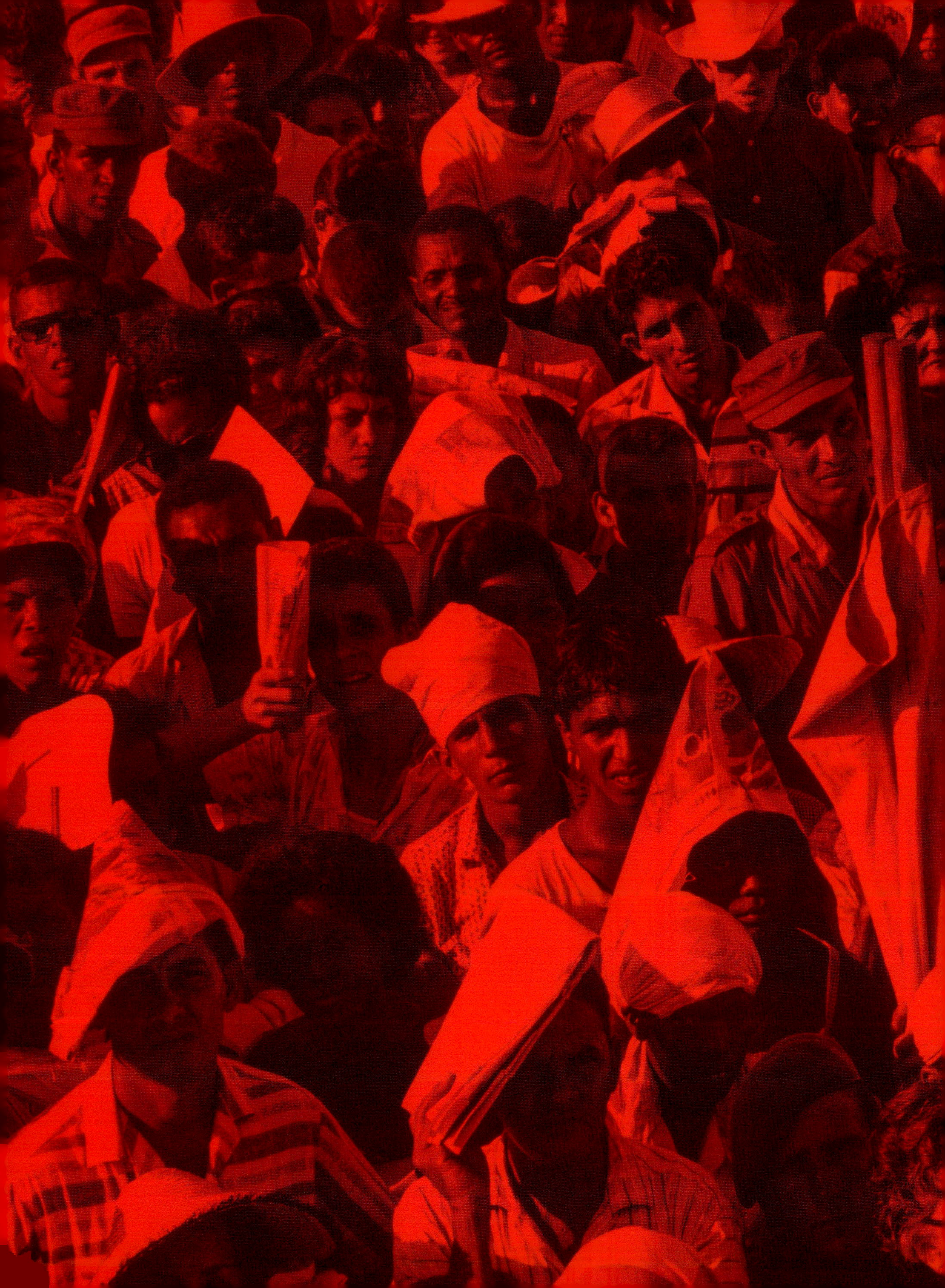

TAMIO WAKAYAMA: A REVOLUTION OF THE SELF

Eva Respini

THE FIRST TIME I encountered the work of photographer and activist Tamio Wakayama was in the Chinatown studio of artist Paul Wong. Paul had known Wakayama since the 1970s and firmly believed his work deserved more recognition. Paul walked me through the impressive range of Wakayama's output—which he had meticulously organized by series—starting with his foundational work documenting racial segregation in the American South during the Civil Rights Movement and ending with his lyrical and emotive images capturing Vancouver's Powell Street Festival in the late 1970s. Paul recounted Wakayama's fascinating life story: his family forced into a Japanese Canadian internment camp during World War II (a deeply shameful history still not fully recognized in North America) and his subsequent call to activism in the US South followed by a journey of self-discovery, which included making pictures on reservations and of urban blight in Canada, living in Japan, and eventually focusing his lens to give voice and image to Japanese Canadian communities. Despite having worked as a photography curator at the Museum of Modern Art, New York, for many years, I had never heard of Wakayama and sheepishly attributed my ignorance to being new to Canada. However, as I started discussing Wakayama's work with members of the artistic community both in Canada and beyond, I realized that the work is not deeply known, nor has it travelled widely. Paul was right: the work needs to be seen.

As much as Wakayama's work needs to be seen, it also needs to be contextualized within photography's history. His pictures are in dialogue with photographers of the Civil Rights era, but also with those beyond the Movement, including Walker Evans, Eikoh Hosoe, Dorothea Lange and Daido Moriyama. Wakayama did not attend school to become a photographer. He learned his métier on the go, and from one of the best—Danny Lyon, an important figure in the rise of documentary photography in the US in the 1960s. Wakayama's partner Mayumi Takasaki recalled that he was more interested in content than technique or style.[1] Yet his work is full of lyricism and artistry. Despite Wakayama's focus on subject matter, the more I looked at his work, I could not help thinking how it might be considered within the rich and varied photographic traditions.[2] This essay attempts to draw a loose constellation of image-makers around Wakayama. He was likely unaware of the photographers addressed in this essay (at least early on in his career).[3] Nevertheless, these links are vital to situate Wakayama's practice within a larger history of photography.

***

The Civil Rights Movement birthed Wakayama as a photographer, but his sense of social justice was forged as a child. After the bombing of Pearl Harbor, Wakayama's family was uprooted from their coastal life in Western Canada and herded into internment camps for Japanese Canadians in the inhospitable interior of British Columbia. They were branded Enemy Aliens, a term Wakayama would later use as a battle cry in his career. After the War, many Japanese Canadians were forcibly deported to Japan, but Wakayama's family escaped that fate and relocated, once again, to Chatham, an underserved rural community in Southern Ontario that had been the terminus of the Underground Railroad. Wakayama recalls: "The sudden uprooting and incarceration was an appalling tragedy but we, the children of the dispossessed, know the greater damage to our individual and collective psyche occurred in the lonely years of exile."[4] These early experiences would form Wakayama's moral compass and his convictions as a photographer.

Few photographs of Canadian and American Japanese internment camps exist, a notable exception being Dorothea Lange's pictures of Northern Californian camps. Although her photographs had been commissioned by the US Office of War Information—which enlisted photographers to document American life during wartime—they were never made public by the Office. Lange's pictures go beyond the brief to document and are incisive images that show a human dimension to this brutal moment. To make her photograph of the children of the Weill public school (1942) (fig. 1), Lange positioned herself at the eye-level of her subjects as the children dutifully held their hands over their chests to recite the Pledge of Allegiance. Lange captured the girls' earnestness and humanity on the eve of their imprisonment. As activist and historian Julie Ault wrote, Lange succeeded in putting a face to "a pivotal moment of the threshold of demoralisation."[5] Wakayama's pictures taken for the Student Nonviolent Coordinating Committee (SNCC) similarly focused on intimate moments pregnant with meaning within the larger stories of racial segregation. In *Holding hands before the bus leaves for Mississippi Freedom*

Summer, Oxford, Ohio (1964) (p. 93), for example, he captures a moving gesture that communicates the human story with tenderness and intimacy.

Lange is part of a rich history of photographers of the American West, which also includes those known for their fine art practices, such as Edward Weston and Ansel Adams. But the chasm between so-called documentary pictures and those made under the mantle of fine art was not that wide, as photographers needed to make a living and often accepted assignments from commercial outlets and magazines. Adams, along with Lange, was commissioned in 1944 by *Fortune* magazine to document the wartime economy in Richmond, California, which produced many images of Japanese Americans. Wakayama was likely not aware of Lange or Adams' images of Japanese Americans, but he was aware of the West Coast photographic tradition: "I had always admired the brilliant American photographer Edward Weston, who I felt had striven to express the essence of human sexuality and sensuality. His nude studies, although beautiful, were only partially successful; it was in his disturbing photographs of such mundane objects as a green pepper or a seashell that he fully realized his vision. Though as a Movement photographer I'd always been disdainful of art for art's sake, I decided to explore the classic genre of the nude."[6] (See examples of Wakayama's nude studies on pp. 194–96, 266–70.)

Wakayama's formation as a photographer happened during the Civil Rights Movement in the American South. Already aware of racial segregation as a young adult, he was moved by images of activists in the South, and in September 1963, drove to Birmingham, Alabama, to help the cause. He began running errands for SNCC and was quickly promoted to taking photographs for the organization under the mentorship of legendary photographer Danny Lyon. Wakayama recalls: "Danny Lyon thought I had a good eye that I should try to develop through photography, and he even offered to lend me his spare Nikon F mounted with the incredibly fast and razor-sharp 105 mm NIKKOR lens."[7]

Lyon's New Journalism espoused that a photographer become immersed in their subject matter, an active participant rather than a cool, journalistic observer. As historian Steven Kasher argued: "The great photographs of the movement were

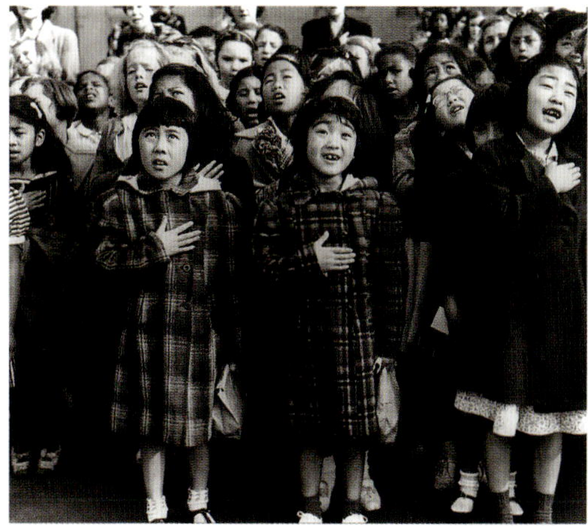

FIGURE 1 Dorothea Lange, San Francisco, Calif., April 1942 – Children of the Weill public school, from the so-called international settlement, shown in a flag pledge ceremony. Some of them are evacuees of Japanese ancestry who will be housed in War Relocation Authority centres for the duration, 1942.

crafted with urgent passion—for their own time and for the future."[8] Lyon's most successful images—such as one taken during the 1963 March on Washington (fig. 2)—are predicated on trust and his ability to access the centre of the Movement's activity. Similarly, Wakayama used his position within the Movement to capture moments of intimacy in the everyday—such as the joy of child's play in *Boys playing in Vine City, Atlanta, Georgia ("Super Snick")*, July 7, 1964 (cover)—alongside incisive and emotionally charged moments depicting violence as in *Burnt cross at Freedom School, Pascagoula, Mississippi* (1964) (pp. 120–21). Wakayama was drawn to the medium for the immediacy of representation and did not think of himself as an artist. "There was a sense pervading that period that not only were we a part of history, but we were history itself," Wakayama wrote.[9] Even though he strove to chronicle the moment, his pictures nevertheless are aesthetically considered and persuasive as artworks.

Wakayama's output also included pictures of vernacular signage and architecture that give a sense of place and living conditions. His 1964 images of a family of sharecroppers at home in Ruleville, Mississippi (pp. 112–13), are some of the rarer interior shots he made during this time period. These images of labourers in modest dwellings documenting harsh living conditions are reminiscent of Walker Evans' pictures of sharecroppers in the American Dust Bowl in the 1930s (fig. 3). Wakayama was likely aware of Evans,[10] and perhaps his precise vison

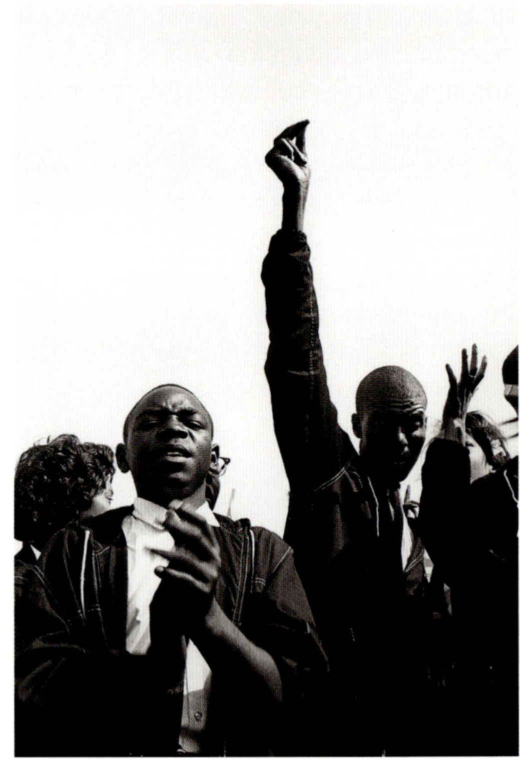

FIGURE 2 Danny Lyon, *The March on Washington, Washington, DC, August 28, 1963*

was imparted on Wakayama at this time. His pictures taken after his return to Canada, on the James Smith Reserve in Saskatchewan in 1965 (pp. 138–39, 141) for example, similarly consider architecture, landscape and personal dwellings as crucial components of storytelling.

The Movement fuelled Wakayama's desire to explore and define his own identity. "For a young, naive Japanese Canadian seeking to re-create his identity," he wrote, "the moment was especially luminous, for the black revolution was, in essence, a revolution of self."[11] After his stint documenting the Civil Rights Movement, Wakayama lived in Japan, a contemplative time when he travelled the country—interested in both ancient and new cultures—and absorbed the cultural upheavals of the post-war period. He made streetscapes and landscapes that were more experimental than his work with SNCC. Wakayama's images underscore the contrast between tradition and modernity, as exemplified in *Covered auto at a temple, Tokyo, Japan, 1969–70* (p. 216) and pictures of modern American ads on the streets of Japan (pp. 202–5). His focus on those juxtapositions recalls Daido Moriyama's gritty and indelible images of post-war Japan, which similarly captured the poetry of contrasts and the tension of a nation coming to terms with its history in a new post-war reality (fig. 4). Ultimately Wakayama felt like a stranger in Japan and returned to Canada—he recalled his time in Japan as "the bridge to home."[12]

Back in Canada, Wakayama became involved in the burgeoning Japanese Canadian Redress Movement, and once again used his camera to tell stories from within. Perhaps his most lyrical works depict the Powell Street Festival, which Wakayama documented in depth from its

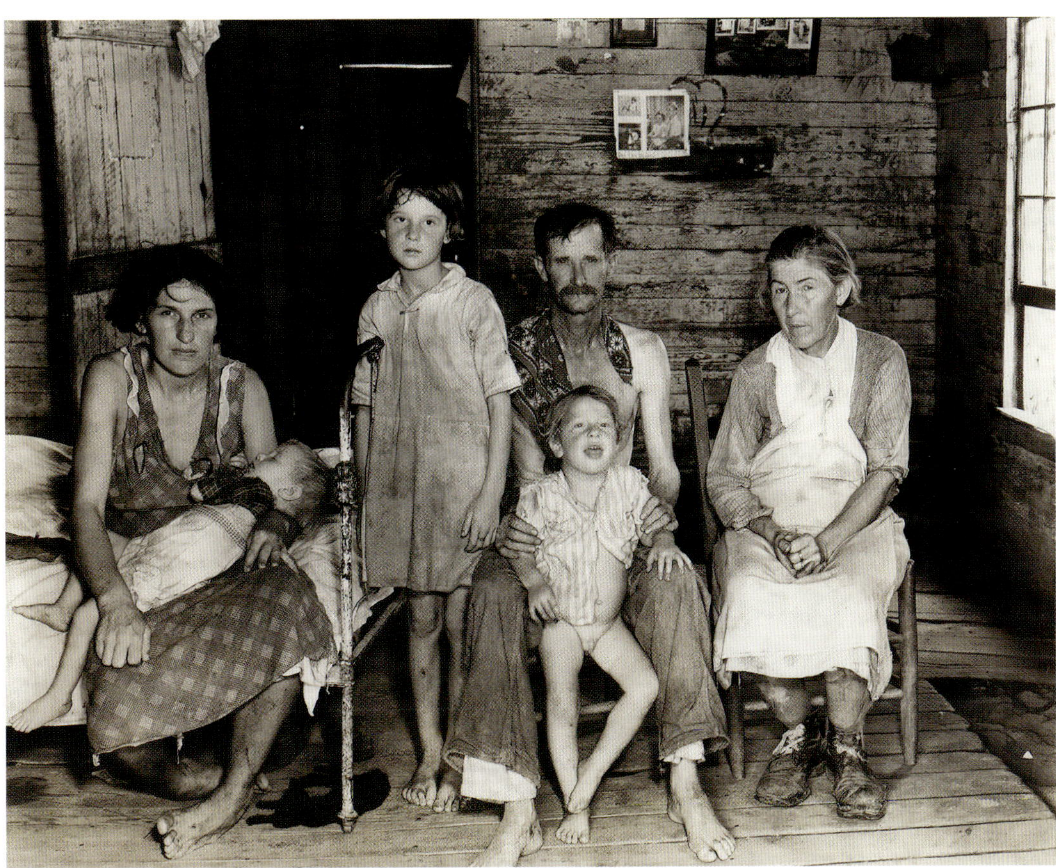

FIGURE 3 Walker Evans, *Sharecropper's Family, Hale County, Alabama*, March 1936

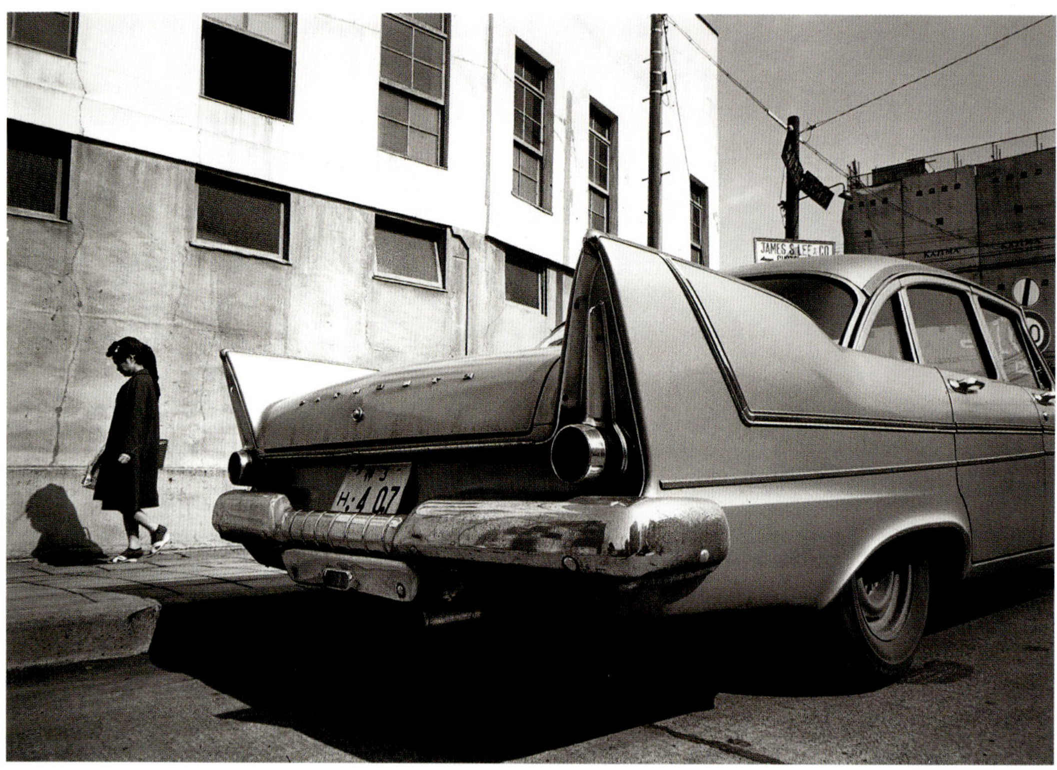

FIGURE 4 Daido Moriyama, *Yokosuka, Kanagawa*, 1965

founding in 1977. He captured images of traditional dancers and musicians with great emotional resonance and intensity. Wakayama described these pictures as more than mere documents: "the images… have had to venture beyond the limits of documentary photography to find their proper home in the realm of metaphor and myth."[13] The sense of mythmaking is clear in the close-up of performer Linda Uyehara Hoffman—member of the Katari Taiko ensemble—her face captured at the full range of expression, bringing the viewer into the heart of the performance (p. 224). The intensity of these pictures recalls the work of Eikoh Hosoe and his collaborations with Butoh dancers Tatsumi Hijikata and Kazuo Ohno. Hosoe's famous pictures made with Hijikata in 1965 occupy a space between live performance and still photography, and explore the indelible relationship between Japan's mythical past and present. Wakayama's images, and indeed the Powell Street Festival itself, also bridged that gap between past and present, and facilitated, as Wakayama wrote, "the re-creation of community."[14]

The pictures Wakayama made throughout his career challenged conventional notions of what socially engaged photography should be and could do. Made with incredible conviction, his photographs tell stories with dignity and humanity, inspiring a call to action. This book accompanies the first exhibition of Wakayama's work in a major museum, and as such, will bring more visibility to his work. The intent with a museum platform, and this volume, is to allow the work to travel wider and reach new audiences, and for Wakayama to find his rightful place within photography's canon.

ENDNOTES

1   Mayumi Takasaki, email to author on January 4, 2025.

2   Most of the published writing on Wakayama focuses on his Civil Rights and Powell Street Festival pictures. I am indebted to Wakayama's own writing: "Tamio Wakayama," in *This Light of Ours: Activist Photographers of the Civil Rights Movement*, ed. Leslie G. Kelen (Jackson: University Press of Mississippi, 2011); "Tamio Wakayama," in *Yellow Peril: Reconsidered*, ed. Paul Wong (Vancouver: On Edge, 1990); and *Kikyō: Coming Home to Powell Street* (Madeira Park, BC: Harbour Publishing, 1992). As well as the following essays: Jade Ferguson, "'This is our Alabama': Racial Segregation, Discrimination, and Violence in Tamio Wakayama's Signs of Life," *The Global South* 9, no. 1 (Spring 2015); Greg Robinson, "Way Down in Egypt Land / Tamio Wakayama, Civil Rights Photographer," in *The Unknown Great: Stories of Japanese Americans at the Margins of History* (Seattle: University of Washington Press, 2023).

3   Takasaki, email to author on January 4, 2025.

4   Tamio Wakayama, *Kikyō: Coming Home to Powell Street* (Madeira Park, BC: Harbour Publishing, 1992), 9.

5   Julie Ault, "Just About to Step into the Bus for the Assembly Center, San Francisco," in *Dorothea Lange: Words & Pictures*, ed. Sarah Hermanson Meister (New York: The Museum of Modern Art, 2019), 93.

6   Tamio Wakayama, *Soul on Rice*, 171.

7   Wakayama, *Soul on Rice*, 81.

8   Steven Kasher, *The Civil Rights Movement: A Photographic History, 1954–1968* (New York: Abbeville Press, 1996), 17.

9   Tamio Wakayama, "Tamio Wakayama," in *This Light of Ours: Activist Photographers of the Civil Rights Movement*, ed. Leslie G. Kelen (Jackson: University Press of Mississippi, 2011), 210.

10 Conversation with Paul Wong, November 2024.

11 Wakayama, *Kikyō: Coming Home to Powell Street*, 10.

12 Tamio Wakayama, "Tamio Wakayama," in *Yellow Peril: Reconsidered*, ed. Paul Wong (Vancouver: On Edge, 1990), 47.

13 Wakayama, *Kikyō: Coming Home to Powell Street*, 13.

14 Wakayama, *Yellow Peril: Reconsidered*, 47.

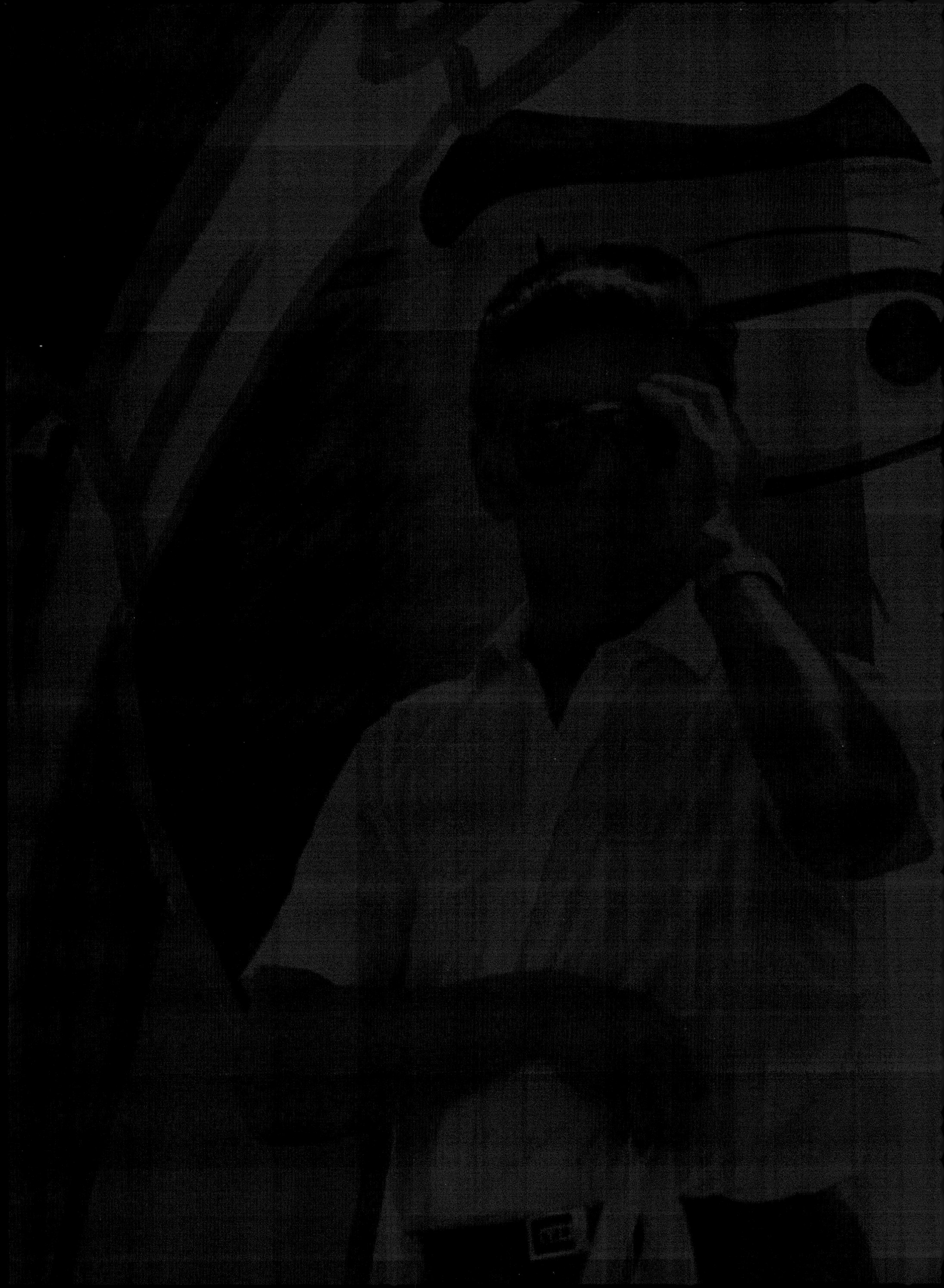

SOUL ON RICE

Tamio Wakayama

EDITOR'S NOTE

TAMIO WAKAYAMA *wrote the first draft of* Soul on Rice *by hand beginning in 1986. The afterword was added in 2008 after the election of Barack Obama.* Soul on Rice *reflects the author's recollections of events and conversations, and some dialogue was recreated from his memory. At the time of his passing in 2018, Tamio had been looking to publish his memoir and had in fact sent an unedited manuscript to the University of Mississippi Press for review. Unfortunately he did not receive a response prior to his death. While we can feel confident that we are honouring Tamio's wishes in bringing his words and memories to a larger audience, we did face a number of difficult choices when preparing the text for publication in the absence of a living author to consult. As a first step, we worked with Linda Uyehara Hoffman—an important member of the Japanese Canadian community who is featured in a photo on page 224—as a preliminary editor and reader. She knew Tamio very well and could retain his voice in any necessary edits. Curator Paul Wong also took creative licence to shorten the text in some cases to increase readability. He elected not to publish the prologue. We also copyedited lightly throughout for clarity and intended meaning, and fixed typos and grammatical inconsistencies.*

As Soul on Rice *was written nearly forty years ago, it contains some language and word choices that may be offensive to contemporary sensibilities. After considerable discussion, in most cases, we opted to retain this language in the absence of an opportunity to review alternatives with the author. The language is also authentic to the period being described and helps to convey the charged and very dangerous atmosphere of the 1960s. In a few instances we did make the decision to subtly adjust the language.*

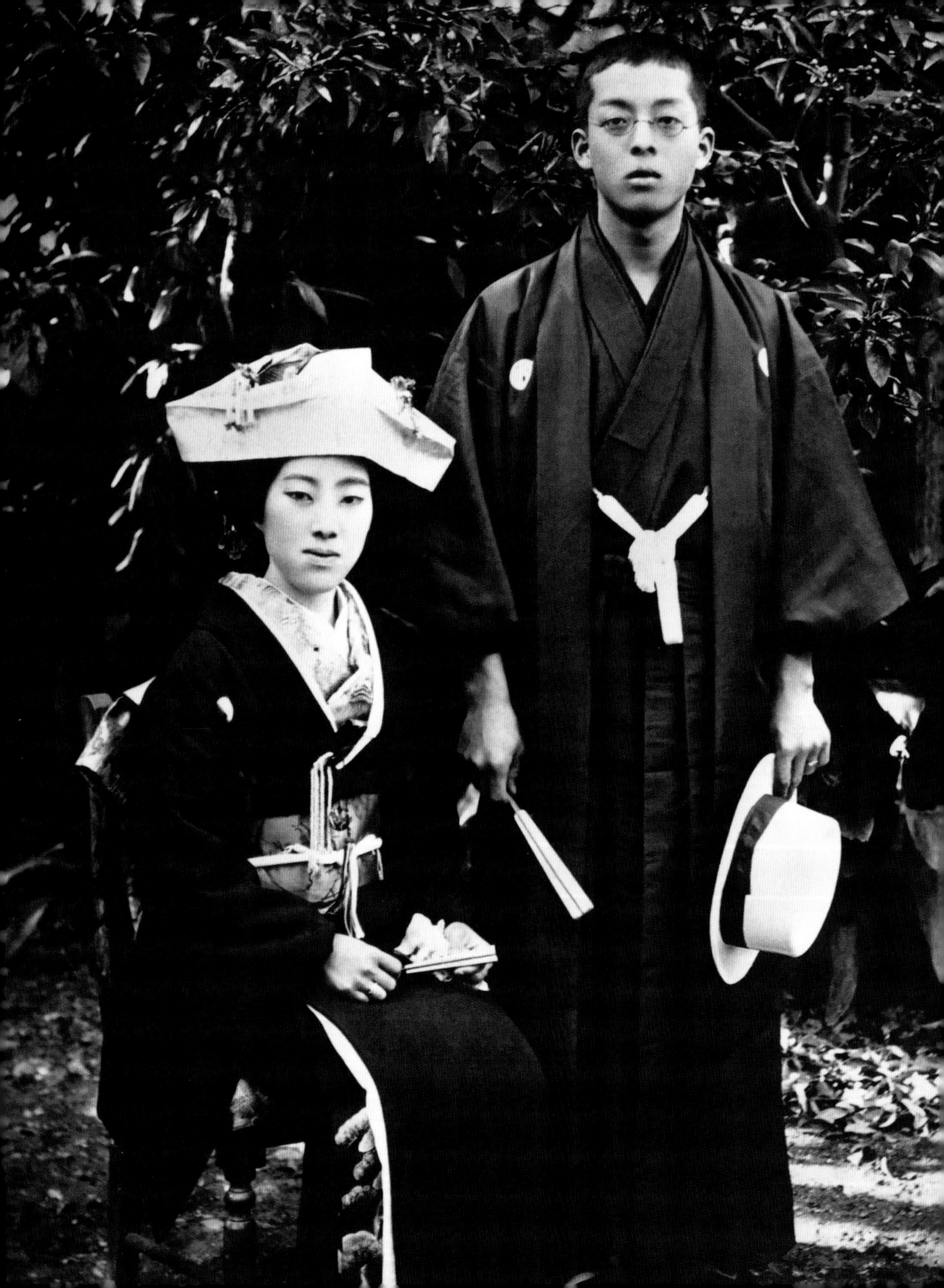

1

HOME WAS A SMALL, ramshackle house situated at the bottom of our town's Black ghetto. Chatham, a small community in the rich farmlands of Southwestern Ontario, was once a terminus of the Underground Railroad, and within a short walk from our home stood two gospel churches with historic markers planted in front to memorialize the heroic sojourn of runaway slaves. The squalor and abject poverty of our neighbourhood was sorry proof that the descendants of those runaways had fared no better than their African American brothers. Chatham was also the final destination of my family after our forced exodus from the West Coast.

For my father, the journey began in 1921 when he emigrated to Canada from Shiida, a small, impoverished fishing village in Fukuoka Prefecture, located in the northeast quadrant of Japan's southernmost island of Kyushu. He spent the early years working in the virgin rain forests of British Columbia, and despite the gruelling work and bitter racism of the times, he saw enough promise in the New World to bring over my mother, grandparents and several aunts, uncles and cousins. The added energies of the new arrivals enabled our family to purchase, in a remarkably short time, an old farmhouse and several acres of untamed bush near the sawmill town of Port Hammond in the Fraser Valley. After the back-breaking labour of clearing the land, they lovingly cultivated garden beds, which, over the coming years, were to provide not only sustenance but also much-needed capital for our rapidly growing clan.

Tamio's parents, Kinu and Kokichi Wakayama, Shiida, Fukuoka, Japan, c. 1915

The family was dominated by my grandfather, a typical Meiji-era patriarch who ruled with a tight iron fist—abusive toward the women and exploitive of the menfolk's labour. My father struggled to escape his dominance, and eventually, with money scrimped from seasonal work in the nearby sawmill and logging camps, he bought his own property and began to realize his dream of riches.

In our family album is a fading print of our West Coast home, a boxy, two-storey wooden structure with the saving elegance of two ivory columns supporting an overhanging balcony. Its location on a busy corner of the Dewdney Trunk Road, the main artery leading to the bright lights of nearby Vancouver and its burgeoning *Nikkei* (people of Japanese ancestry) settlement of Little Tokyo, was ideally suited to service the growing community of immigrants who were arriving in a steady stream from Fukuoka. The first floor of our home was devoted to the family business: in the spacious front room, a long service counter and rows of shelves were stacked with canned goods and fresh produce; in the back, a kitchen was crammed with huge vats for the steaming of creamy blocks of tofu. The second floor provided slightly crowded but comfortable living quarters for our family, which had, by then, grown with the addition of three more children. I was to be the fifth and final offspring.

As the year 1941 was coming to an end, my family began to prepare for a special *Shogatsu* (New Year's) celebration to mark the prosperity of our communal farm and my father's booming business. That spring, the rickety old flatbed truck, which my father loaded up twice a week to make his round of deliveries to the nearby farms, had been replaced by his pride and joy: a brand-new Ford pickup truck. Of all the suffering that was to follow, the loss of his prized pickup was the one injustice that my father could never forgive. The joyful anticipation of the holidays came to an abrupt end on December 7 with the fearful news that an armada of the Imperial Japanese navy had attacked the United States naval base at Pearl Harbor, and once Canada joined its American ally in declaring war on Japan, the fate of over twenty-two thousand Nikkei living along the coast of British Columbia was sealed.

Two months later, my mother, with my siblings trailing behind, carried me in her arms into the cavernous agricultural buildings of Hastings Park, the site of Vancouver's annual fair. My father, who had found seasonal work at a lumber camp near Revelstoke, was still trapped beyond the hundred-mile restricted zone, and my mother never quite forgave

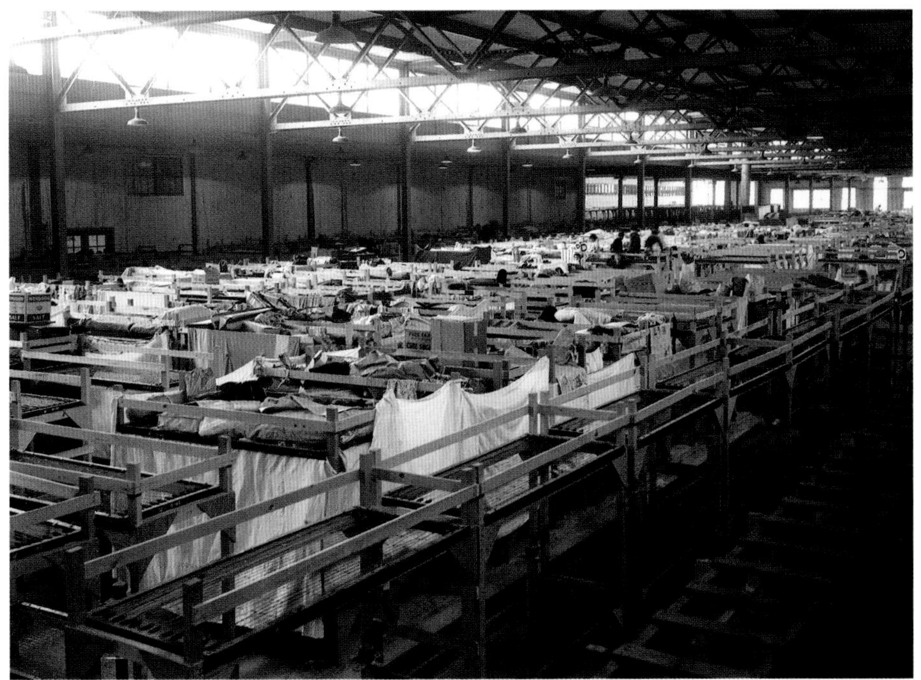

him for leaving her alone to face the trauma of the uprooting. Our home for the next three months was a fetid cattle stall with only a thin blanket hastily strung up to provide some semblance of privacy.

We shared these crowded quarters with nearly four thousand other Nikkei who had been rounded up from their coastal homes to await the completion of numerous internment camps in the BC interior. Earlier, our family possessions—tools, furniture, household goods, priceless heirlooms brought from Japan, the new Ford pickup—had been sold at fire sale prices; our home and land in the Fraser Valley was placed in trust with the Custodian of Enemy Property but was later sold, without my parents' knowledge, to pay for our wartime incarceration.

In the spring, we were moved to Tashme, the largest of the camps, located just east of the town of Hope. We were fortunate in finding accommodations in the large barn, which, although crowded, had the warmth and security of solid construction and a communal kitchen. All the other families suffered the war years in uninsulated nine-by-twelve-foot shacks built hastily from green wood, which offered little protection against the winter's bitter cold and heavy snowfalls. I remember almost nothing of the camps, but my older brother Peter Hiroshi, on a recent visit to Tashme—now a vacation resort centre—

Leonard Frank, Women and Children's Dormitory, Hastings Park, Vancouver, British Columbia, May 13, 1942 vividly recalled the old firehall, the communal *ofuro* (bathhouse), the dining hall, the houses where his playmates lived and the mountain creek in which he almost drowned.

When World War II ended with the atomic bombing of Hiroshima and Nagasaki, Canada had had enough of its Nikkei citizens and made a concerted and often devious effort to deport them all to Japan; the only other alternative was to settle east of the Rockies. Tired and disillusioned, my grandparents returned to their homeland while the rest of the clan began our eastern migration. After an extended stopover in New Denver, a small town nestled in the awesome beauty of the Kootenay Valley, we continued on to Winnipeg. Since it was one of the few Canadian centres that had not imposed an outright ban on the exiled Nikkei, my Uncle Yoshimaru and his family decided to try their fortunes in that prairie city. My family and that of my other uncle, Mitsuo, reboarded the train, and after two days' travel, we found ourselves on the shores of Lake Erie. We were greeted there by our sponsor, an old family friend who had found work on one of the orchard and onion farms that dot the rich black soil of Erie's shoreline. After a year helping in the fields, my parents had saved enough money to make their final move to nearby Chatham.

I can still picture my father standing on the front lawn of our new home, carefully counting out hundred-dollar bills into the hand of our kindly Mormon neighbour, who had bravely gone against the prevailing winds by selling to a Japanese. Although our house, complete with a two-seater outhouse, was tiny and worn, we were one of the more fortunate families; my mother's closest friends, the Nagaos, and their four children were living in an abandoned chicken coop. About the only work available to the Nikkei men was at Darling, a nearby factory that processed the carcasses of diseased farm animals into tanning hides and fertilizer. On windless days, the belching smokestack of Darling would blanket the town with its foul stench, and McGregor Creek, a stone's throw from our backyard, was almost always covered with a thick, grey coat of scum from all the effluent poured in by both Darling and an adjacent chemical plant. My father worked in the basement of Darling. I only visited his workplace once, when my mother sent me to deliver dinner to my father, who had to work an extra shift.

With the bento tucked in my backpack, I pedalled to the factory, where I walked down a narrow stairway to enter the dim basement, lit only by a string of naked light bulbs. Stacks of dripping hides sand-wiched between layers of coarse salt rose from a floor awash with a

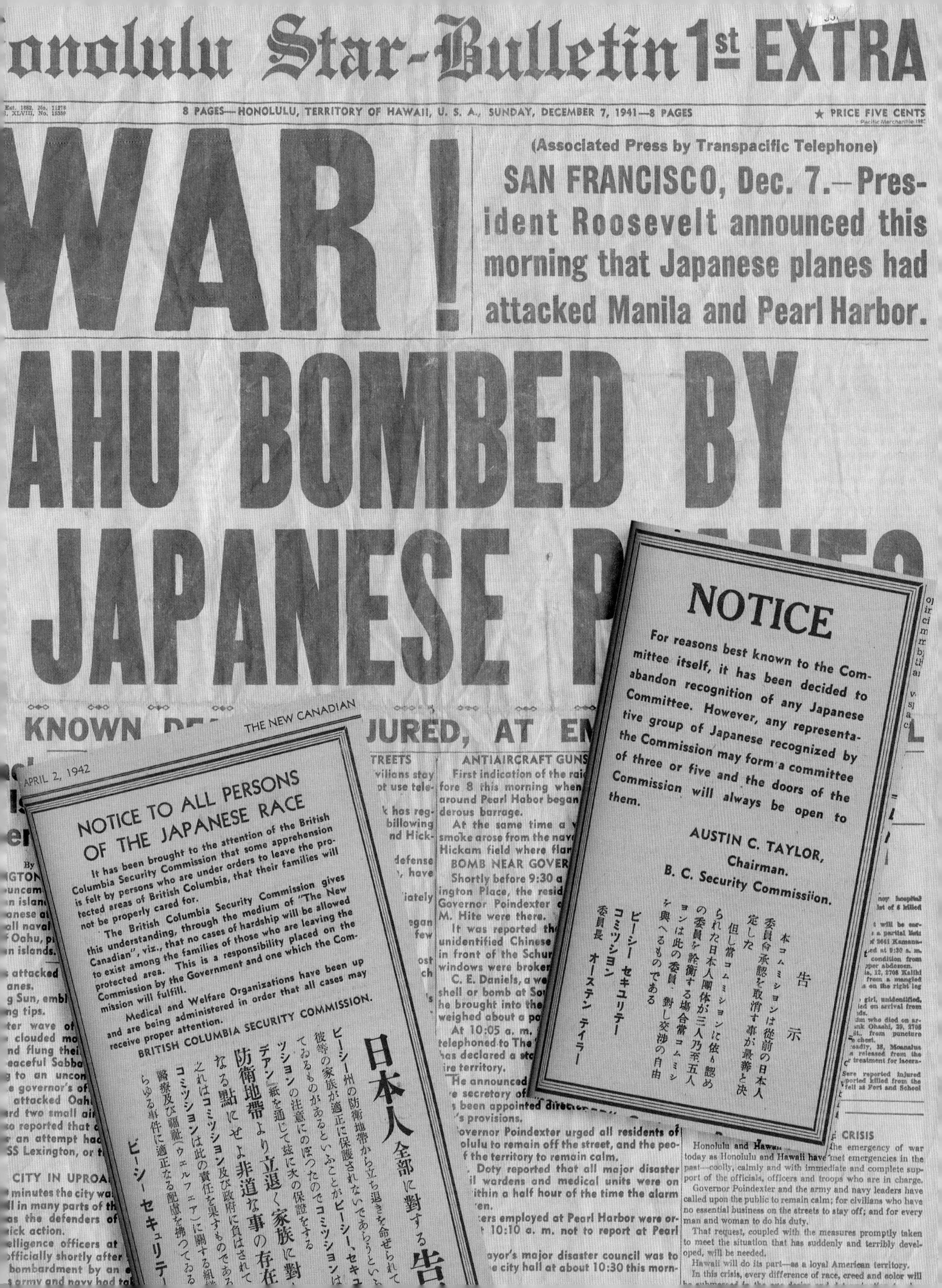

Honolulu Star-Bulletin 1ˢᵗ EXTRA

Est. 1882. No. 11218
J. XLVIII, No. 15350

8 PAGES—HONOLULU, TERRITORY OF HAWAII, U.S.A., SUNDAY, DECEMBER 7, 1941—8 PAGES

★ PRICE FIVE CENTS
Pacific Merchantile 192.

WAR!

AHU BOMBED BY JAPANESE P...

(Associated Press by Transpacific Telephone)

SAN FRANCISCO, Dec. 7.—President Roosevelt announced this morning that Japanese planes had attacked Manila and Pearl Harbor.

KNOWN DEA... JURED, AT EM... ...L

THE NEW CANADIAN

APRIL 2, 1942

NOTICE TO ALL PERSONS OF THE JAPANESE RACE

It has been brought to the attention of the British Columbia Security Commission that some apprehension is felt by persons who are under orders to leave the protected areas of British Columbia, that their families will not be properly cared for.

The British Columbia Security Commission gives this understanding, through the medium of "The New Canadian", viz., that no cases of hardship will be allowed to exist among the families of those who are leaving the protected area. This is a responsibility placed on the Commission by the Government and one which the Commission will fulfill.

Medical and Welfare Organizations have been up and are being administered in order that all cases may receive proper attention.

BRITISH COLUMBIA SECURITY COMMISSION.

日本人全部に對する告示

ビーシー州の防衛地帯から立ち退きを命ぜられてある日本人、彼等の家族が適正に保護されないであらうといふことがビーシー、セキユリテアン『紙を通じて茲に次の保證をするコミッションの注意にのぼつたのでコミッションは此の委員、對し交渉の自由ヶ與へるものである

それはコミッション及び政府に負はされなる點にせよ非道な事の存在防衛地帯より立退く家族に對しコミッションは此の責任を果すものであらゆる事件に適正なる配慮を拂つてゐる醫療及び福祉（ウエルフエア）に關する

ビーシー セキユリテー コミッション

NOTICE

For reasons best known to the Committee itself, it has been decided to abandon recognition of any Japanese Committee. However, any representative group of Japanese recognized by the Commission may form a committee of three or five and the doors of the Commission will always be open to them.

AUSTIN C. TAYLOR,
Chairman.
B. C. Security Commissiion.

告示

本コムミションは従前の日本人に定した

委員命承認を取消す事が最善と決

但し當コムミションに依り認められた日本人團体が三人乃至五人の委員を詮衡する塲合當コミションは此の委員、對し交渉の自由ヶ與へるものである

ビーシー セキユリテー コミッション
委員長 オーステン テイラー

TREETS

vilians stay ...ot use tele... ...k has reg... ...billowing ...nd Hick... ...defense ..., have ...iately ...egan few ...ost ...ch ...'s

ANTIAIRCRAFT GUNS...

First indication of the rai... ...fore 8 this morning when ...around Pearl Habor began ...derous barrage.

At the same time a v... smoke arose from the nav... Hickam field where flam...

BOMB NEAR GOVER...

Shortly before 9:30 a... ...ington Place, the resid... Governor Poindexter ...M. Hite were there.

It was reported th... unidentified Chinese ...in front of the Schur... windows were broker...

C. E. Daniels, a we... shell or bomb at Sou... he brought into the... weighed about a po...

At 10:05 a.m.,... telephoned to The... ...has declared a st... ...ire territory.

He announced ...re secretary of... ...s been appointed direct... ...'s provisions.

...overnor Poindexter urged all residents of ...olulu to remain off the street, and the peo... ...f the territory to remain calm.

...Doty reported that all major disaster ...l wardens and medical units were on ...ithin a half hour of the time the alarm ...en.

...ers employed at Pearl Harbor were or... ...10:10 a.m. not to report at Pearl

...ayor's major disaster council was to ...e city hall at about 10:30 this morn...

...CRISIS

Honolulu and Hawai... the emergency of war today as Honolulu and Hawaii have met emergencies in the past—coolly, calmly and with immediate and complete support of the officials, officers and troops who are in charge.

Governor Poindexter and the army and navy leaders have called upon the public to remain calm; for civilians who have no essential business on the streets to stay off; and for every man and woman to do his duty.

That request, coupled with the measures promptly taken to meet the situation that has suddenly and terribly developed, will be needed.

Hawaii will do its part—as a loyal American territory.

In this crisis, every difference of race, creed and color wil...

By ...IGTON... ...uncem... ...n island... ...anese at... ...all naval... ...f Oahu, p... ...n islands.

...s attacked ...anes. ...g Sun, embl... ...ng tips.

...ter wave of ...clouded mo... ...nd flung thei... ...eaceful Sabba... ...g to an uncon... ...e governor's of... ...attacked Oah... ...rd two small air... ...o reported that ... ...e an attempt had... ...SS Lexington, or t...

CITY IN UPROA...

...minutes the city wa... ...l in many parts of th... ...as the defenders of... ...ick action. ...elligence officers at... ...fficially shortly after... ...bombardment by an ... ...navy had tak...

mixture of brine, blood, hair and offal. The concrete walls, weeping moisture, were splattered with the same grisly mosaic. But the overriding reality was the stench, penetrating and mesmerizing in its intensity. My father walked in from a back room with a long, bloody knife in one hand and stood before me dressed all in black, with a thick, encrusted rubber apron hanging down to the tops of his gumboots. He looked so small and spent, as if his life force was swirling down the drain with all the other refuse. I handed him his dinner and fled out the door, for had I stayed a second longer, I would have added my vomit to the filth of that room.

He died late one winter night coming home from yet another late shift. A car filled with drunken teenagers smashed into his bicycle, killing him instantly. The image I retain of my father is that of a stern and silent man, frugal even beyond the necessity of the times. When we, his unruly children, were very bad, he would suffocate us with a futon; early on I learned the trick of struggling mightily and caterwauling my abject apologies and promises to reform only after I had created a sufficient air passage. And once, in the dead of night at our Fraser Valley home, he had lowered my brother in a wooden bucket down into our well for the unpardonable sin of having dinner at a friend's house without his permission. The times my father and I shared normal father-son activities were so rare as to be memorable: bicycle trips at dusk to the local drive-in to catch the latest Tarzan movie; an evening with our eyes glued to the TV set, watching the formidable Rocky Marciano pummel his way to a heavyweight championship; a fishing expedition to McGregor Creek, where I caught a large carp that had miraculously survived its polluted environment—he was about to throw it back when I insisted we take it home to show mother, who would, of course, cook it for dinner; we did bring it back, but my father wisely buried the carp for compost in his immaculate garden. As I write these words, I realize that I am now the same age as my father when he died. Lately, at odd moments while flipping through the leisure section of the *Vancouver Sun*, I have imagined the two of us on the waters off Winter Harbour, reeling in a forty-pound chinook salmon, or strolling up Granville Street to catch the latest cinematic reincarnation of Tarzan.

My father died at the height of our private war, the age-old struggle of the rebellious teenager breaking free from parental dominance, and with his sudden passing I was robbed forever of the opportunity to tell him that I have finally come to understand the magnificence of his courage in rising those many mornings to enter that hellish basement so that we could seek and live a better life.

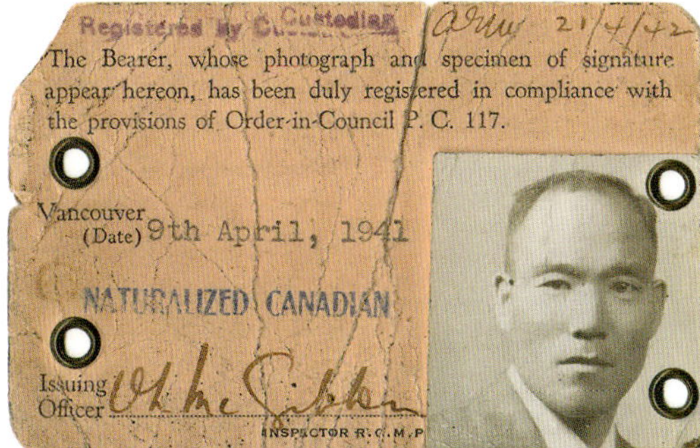

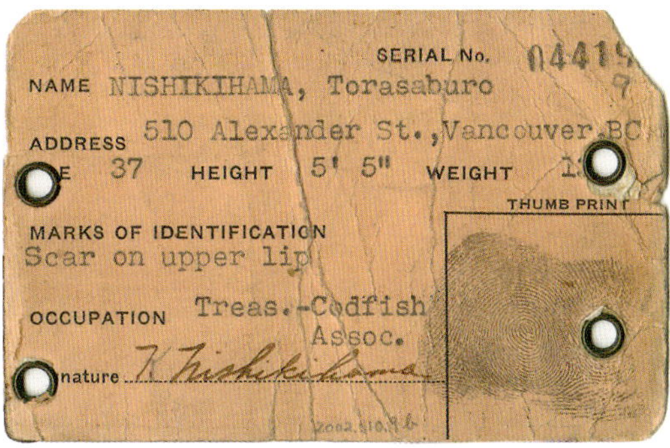

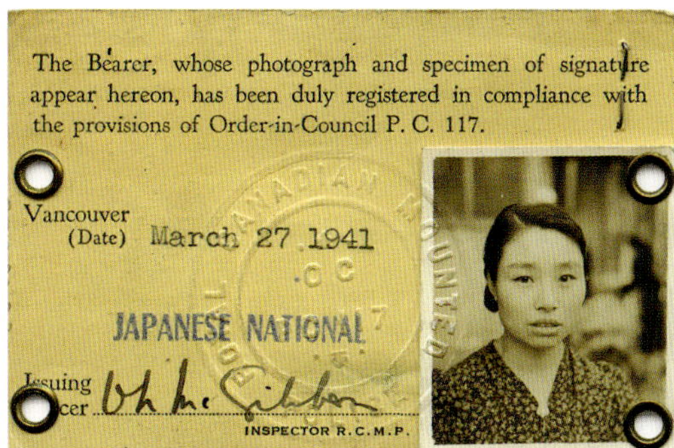

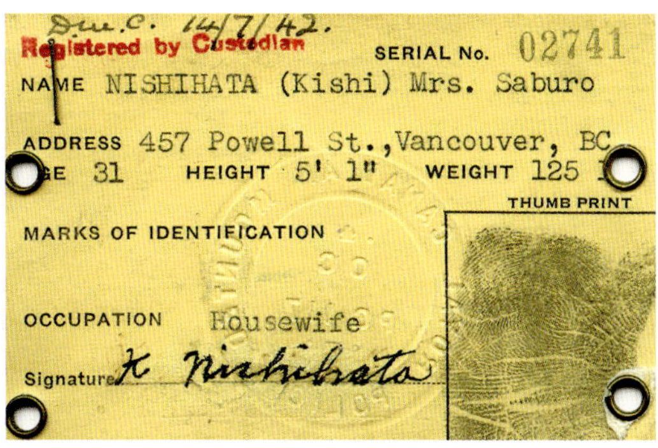

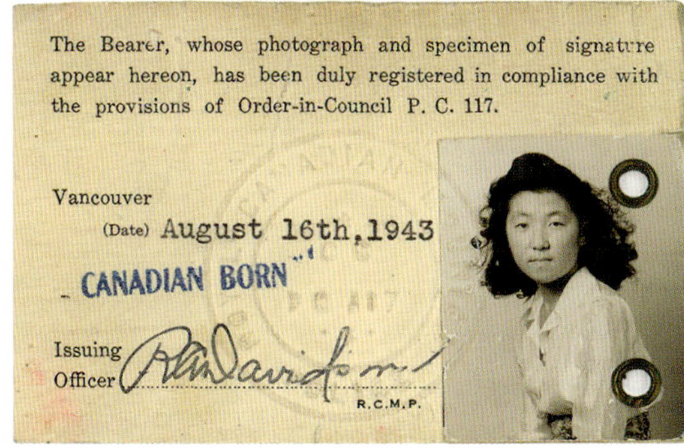

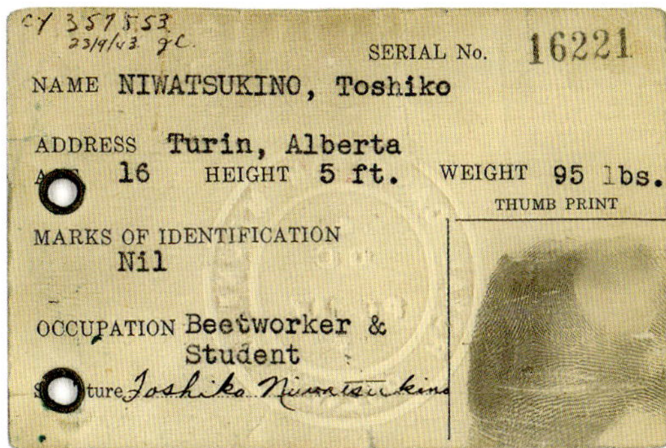

Registration cards for Torasaburo Nishikihama and Mrs. Saburo Nishihata (Kishi), 1941, and Toshiko Niwatsukino, 1943

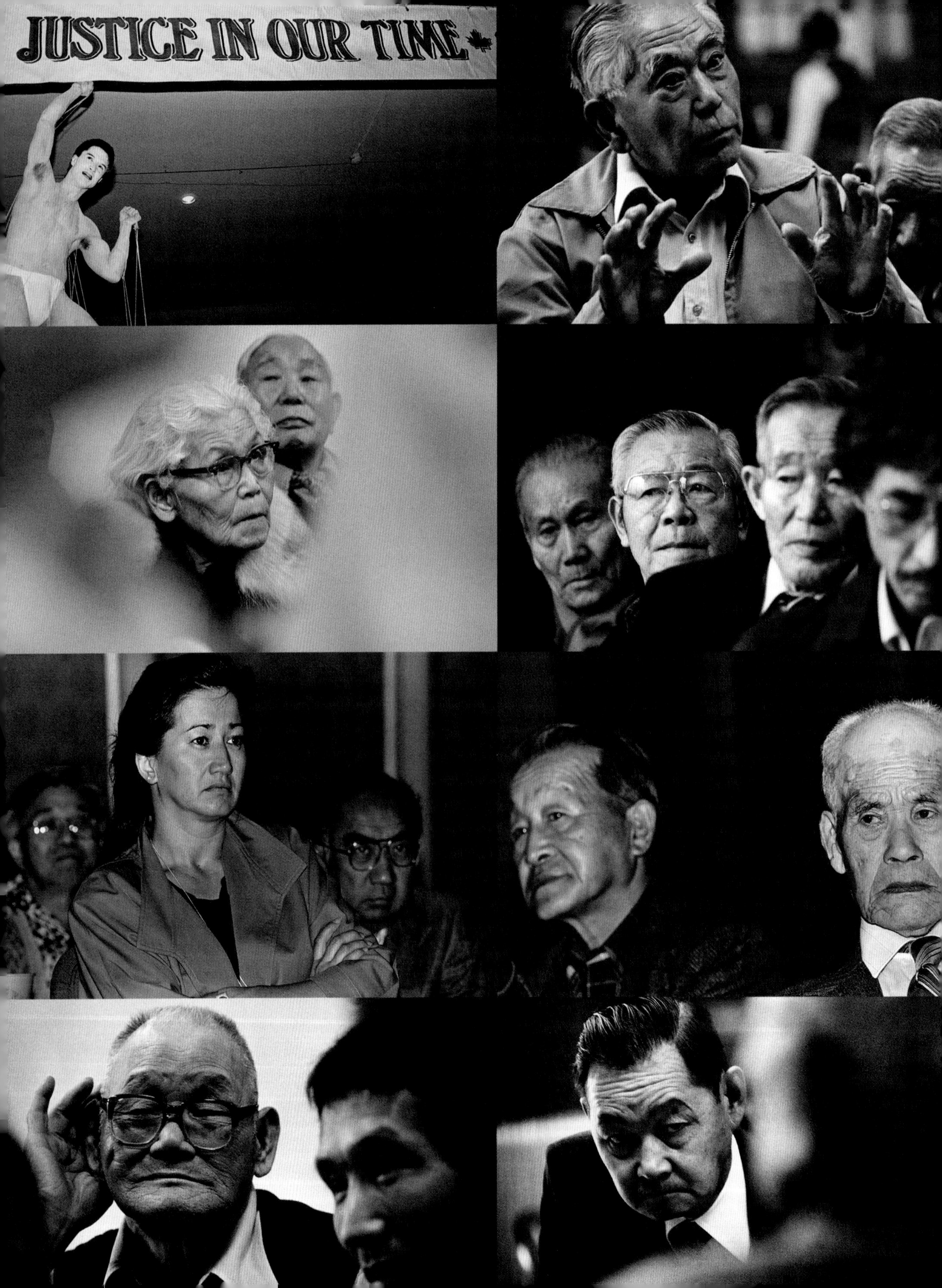
JUSTICE IN OUR TIME

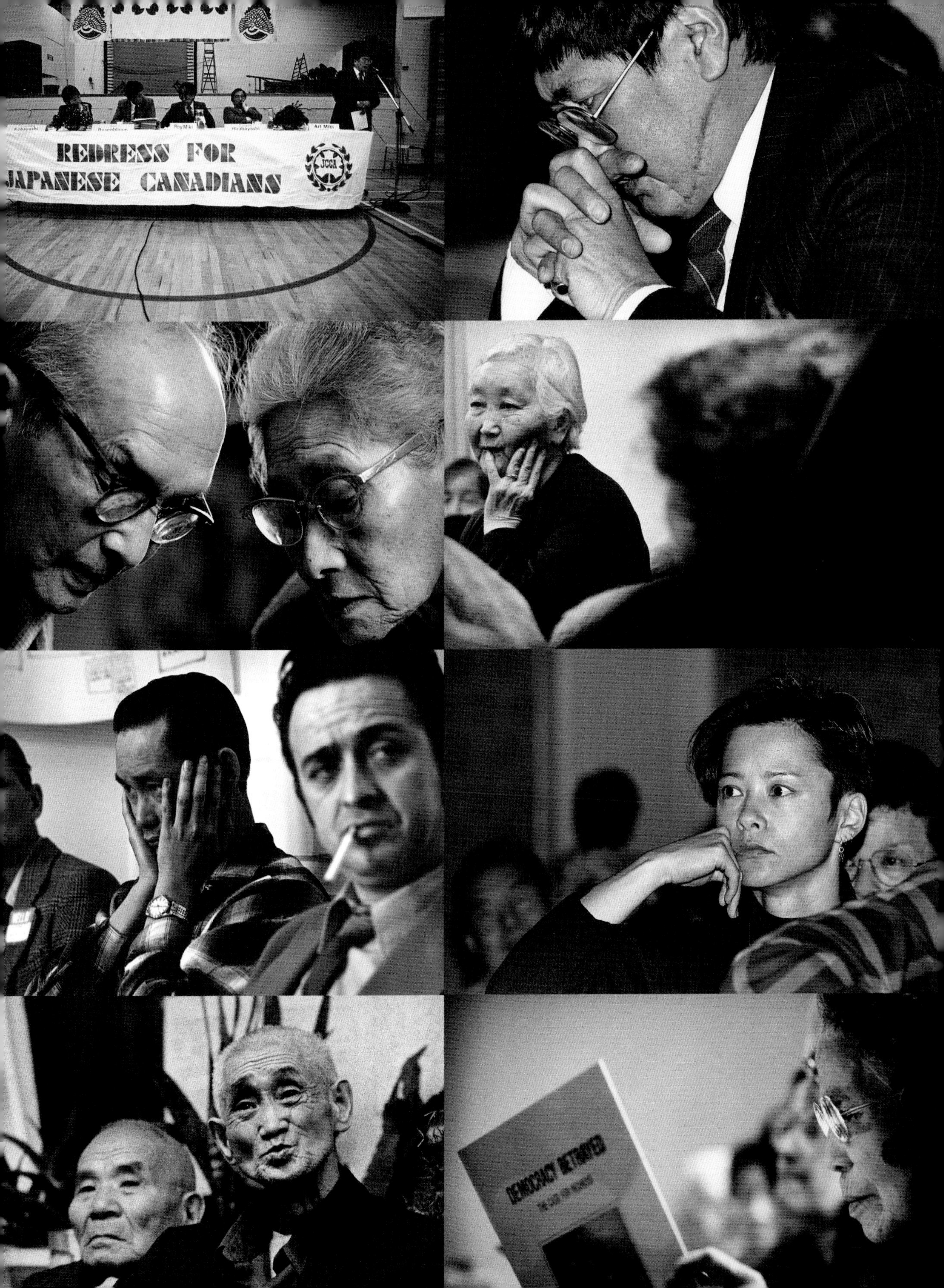

Kobayashi
Rosenbloom
Roy Miki
Hirabayashi
Art Miki
REDRESS FOR JAPANESE CANADIANS
JCCA
DEMOCRACY BETRAYED

PREVIOUS SPREAD

P.36 LEFT TO RIGHT, TOP TO BOTTOM

Jay Hirabayashi of Kokoro Dance, Japanese Language School, Vancouver, British Columbia, April 1988; Redress Symposium, Japanese Language School, Vancouver, British Columbia, August 1983; Tonari Gumi senior, Vancouver, British Columbia, November 29, 1975; National Association of Japanese Canadians (NAJC) release of the Redress brief, "Democracy Betrayed: The Case for Redress," Japanese Language School, Vancouver, British Columbia, November 21, 1984; Homecoming '92, Hotel Vancouver, Vancouver, British Columbia, October 9–10, 1992; Homecoming '92, Hotel Vancouver, Vancouver, British Columbia, October 9–10, 1992; Mr. Hamada, Redress Symposium, Japanese Language School, Vancouver, British Columbia, August 1983; Yosh Arai, Redress Symposium, Japanese Language School, Vancouver, British Columbia, August 1983

P.37 LEFT TO RIGHT, TOP TO BOTTOM

Redress Forum, Steveston Community Centre, Richmond, British Columbia, February 24, 1985; Art Miki, house party at Roy Miki's house after the Redress Conference, Vancouver, British Columbia, February 23, 1985; Mr. and Mrs. Sato at home, Vancouver, British Columbia, March 6, 1976; Tea party for NDP candidates running in the provincial election, Tonari Gumi, Vancouver, British Columbia, November 29, 1975; Members at a Strathcona Property Owners and Tenants Association (SPOTA) meeting, Vancouver, British Columbia, March 1975; Homecoming '92, Hotel Vancouver, Vancouver, British Columbia, October 9–10, 1992; Tea party for NDP candidates running in the provincial election, Tonari Gumi, Vancouver, British Columbia, November 29, 1975; National Association of Japanese Canadians (NAJC) release of the Redress brief, "Democracy Betrayed: The Case for Redress," Japanese Language School, Vancouver, British Columbia, November 21, 1984

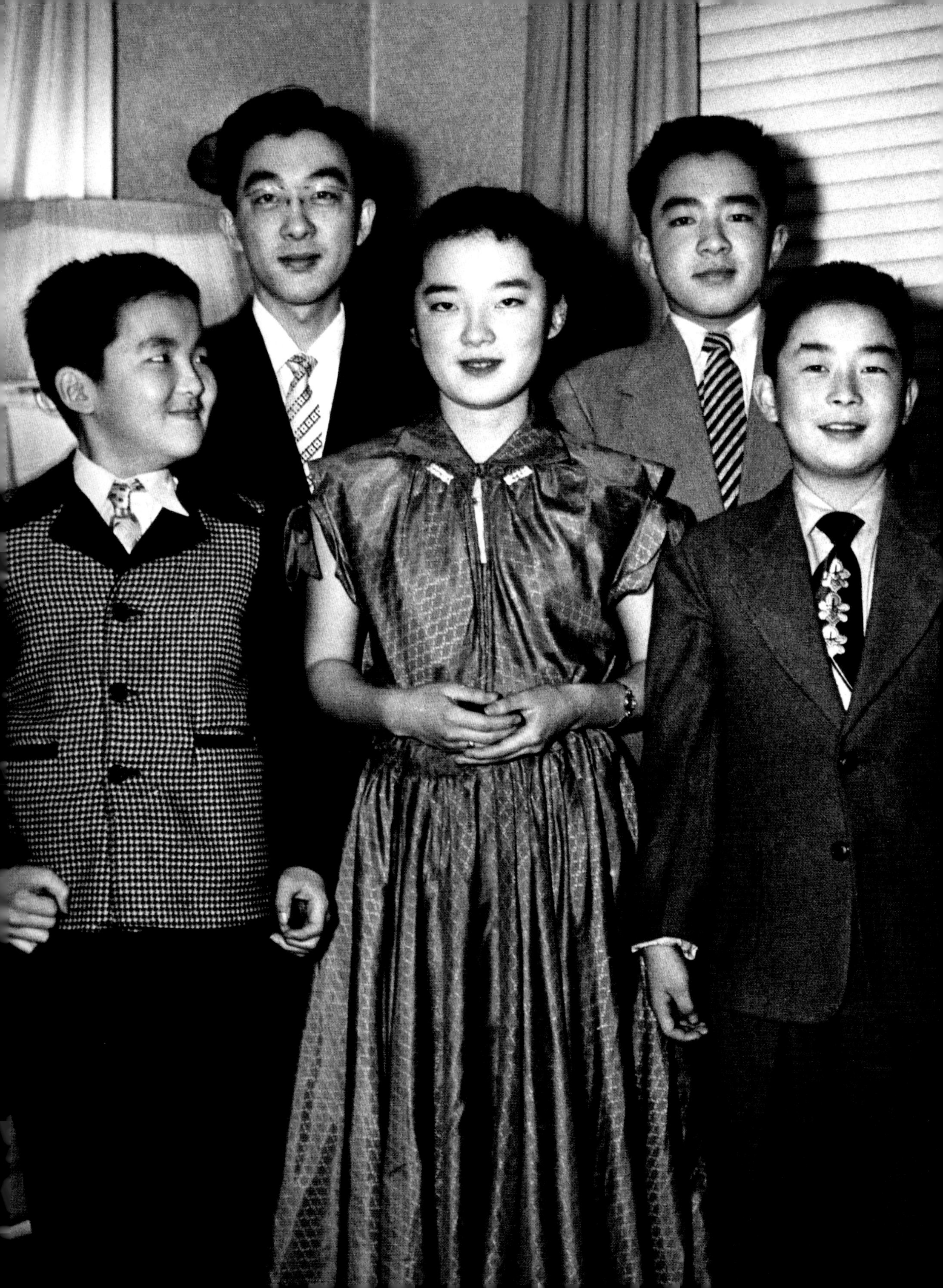

THE HISTORIC EYE IS transfixed by the war years and the sheer spectacle of an entire community uprooted, dispossessed and strewn across a vast and hostile landscape, but I believe it was in the years immediately following the closing of the camps that we, the outcast Nikkei, suffered the most damage. With our vibrant and nurturing pre-war communities only a distant memory, we went eastward bearing the brand of "Enemy Alien" and settled where we could as tiny, isolated islands in a sea of fear and hatred. We, the Nisei (second-generation Japanese Canadians), felt the most betrayed, for we were Canadian-born, and running the gauntlet of state-sanctioned racism in such places as Taber, Winnipeg, Toronto or Chatham was to leave permanent scars on our young psyches.

When we entered the schools of our new communities, we were alone to face our first, prolonged encounter with the daunting white world. I used to dread the first day of school, when we would be called upon to say aloud our fathers' names. With mounting anxiety, I would await the moment when I would have to interrupt the envied litany of William, Thomas and Robert with the tortured syllables of my father's name, Kokichi. One year the pressure became too great, and I blurted out, "My father's name is Tom, just like me." With a knowing half smile, the stout and kindly Mrs. Chapman continued on to the next name. Mrs. Blackburn, the fierce and moustached teacher of my fourth year, was not so kind, and on Remembrance Day, after an angry diatribe against the treacherous Japanese and their cowardly sneak attack on Pearl

Tamio Wakayama,
Masami Wakayama,
Rumi Wakayama,
Hiroshi Wakayama
and Jim Abe,
Chatham, Ontario,
c. 1960–63

Harbor, she called upon me to recite the poem "In Flanders Fields" by John McCrae. I barely made it beyond the first line before I froze with the shame and embarrassment of the moment.

Later in the year, just before the Christmas holidays, our school would hold its annual open house, an event that I would carefully hide from my parents. But one year, my mother learned of it from a neighbour and insisted we go. I tried to lead her unobtrusively through the minefield of white respectability, but my mother, this alien presence who spoke no English, felt it her duty to greet my homeroom teacher. Grabbing her arm, I almost pushed her to a nearby wall lined with neatly printed rows of ABCs, but at the moment of turning, I caught in her eye a brief reflection of such utter pain that its memory shames me to this day.

One day I was visiting the home of the Nishizakis when I overheard the oldest son, Jack, who had a black belt in judo, telling his brothers how he was attacked, on his first day at a new job, by three white workers and how he managed to blunt their violence with an intricate series of deft moves. Going to and from school, I had my own battles, which were fought with less skill and even less glory. My allies in this uneven struggle were my Nisei and Black friends from the neighbourhood, and on Saturdays, to celebrate the survival of yet another week, we would venture downtown and, with our orders of greasy fish and chips wrapped in newspaper, enter one or the other of Chatham's two theatres. Our favourites were the Bowery Boys, Bud Abbott and Lou Costello, Lash LaRue, Hopalong Cassidy and the singing cowboys, Roy Rogers and Gene Autry. Unfortunately, the second feature of the double bill was too often one of the war movies churned out by Hollywood in a seemingly endless celluloid stream. In the titanic clash of good versus evil, good was the iconic figure of John Wayne: tall, handsome, stalwart, white. Evil was the Jap: short and whippet thin with beady black eyes squinting through thick granny glasses; a thin, pencil-line moustache atop protruding lips and predatory buck teeth. I desperately wanted to be John Wayne, but the image that kept appearing in my mirror was that of an Enemy Alien. One afternoon, my Nisei friends and I were watching a stark drama involving the tortured lives of British and American women caught in a Japanese prison camp, and in one horrific scene, in which Claudette Colbert is nearly raped by a sadistic guard, my friend Keibo leaped up from his seat and dashed out of the theatre, screaming, "Japs, Japs, Japs!" J-A-P: three simple letters, the initials of my boyhood agony.

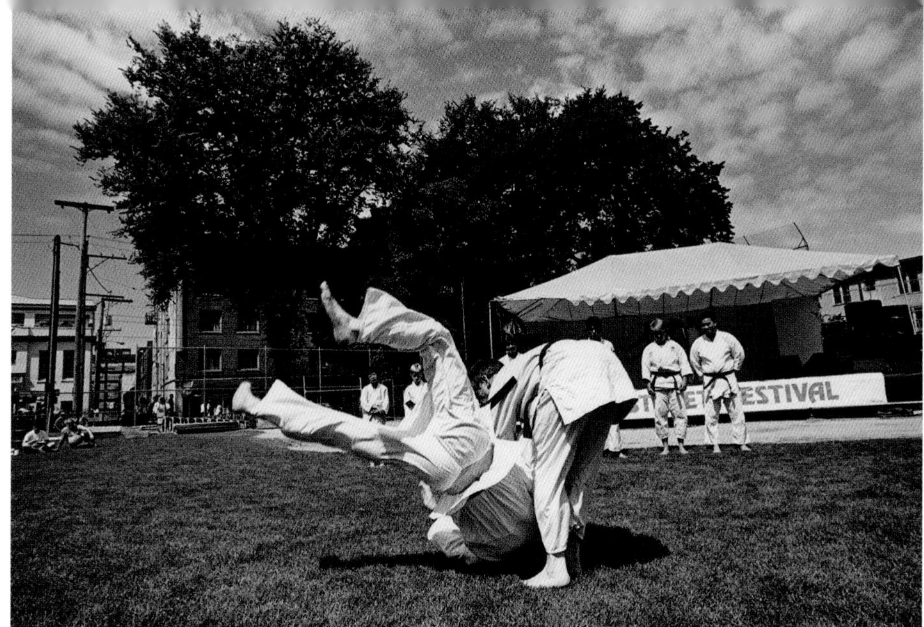

Despite the pain and humiliation, there was much joy, for the lush topography of our new home was the magical land of my boyhood years. We swam in the deep-blue ponds of the nearby Cornwall brickworks and poled our rafts through the endlessly fascinating ecology of tadpoles, frogs, turtles, snakes and brightly coloured birds, elusive targets for our homemade slingshots. For more challenging aquatic adventures, we went to the deeper waters of the Thames River and the clear pools of the more distant rock quarries. One hot summer day, four of us hastily packed provisions for our lunch and pedalled to the nearest quarry. After a bracing swim, we built a huge bonfire to heat our oversized can of Libby's pork and beans, but no one had remembered to bring an opener. We threw it into the fire to heat up while we pondered a solution to our dilemma. Suddenly there was a loud bang, and the only pork and beans we ate that day was scraped from our faces, hair and clothes.

Around the corner from our house lived Mr. Baba, a shipwright, who one year built a tiny, perfect boat for his children, and I was invited to come along for its launch at Mitchell's Bay. I proudly learned to row that day and, on the way home, experienced my first heavenly taste of a hamburger. With a tin can and wood scraps from the boatyard, Baba-san once built me an exact replica of a Tommy gun, which was my favourite toy until I entered the mad-scientist phase of my boyhood. One desultory Sunday morning threatened by rain clouds, I sterilized an empty mayonnaise jar and half filled it with precisely measured quantities of every substance I could find in our kitchen and bathroom. In our garage, I lit a match to the solution, but instead of the expected

Judo demonstration,
Powell Street Festival,
Vancouver, British Columbia,
July 31, 1988

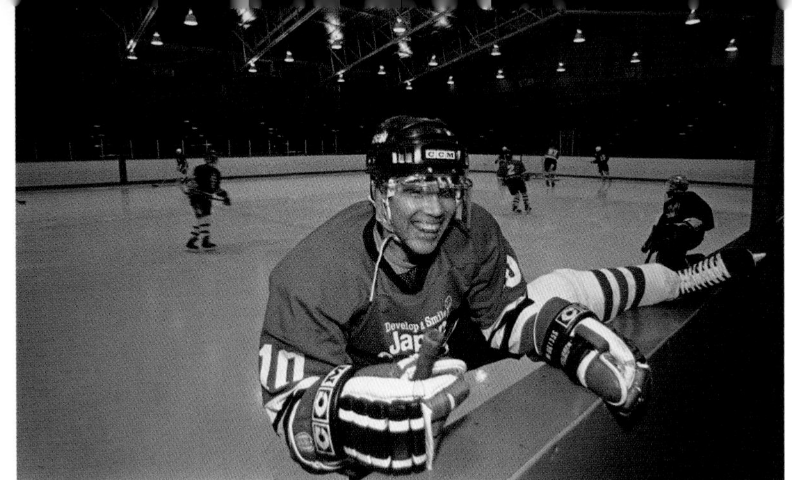

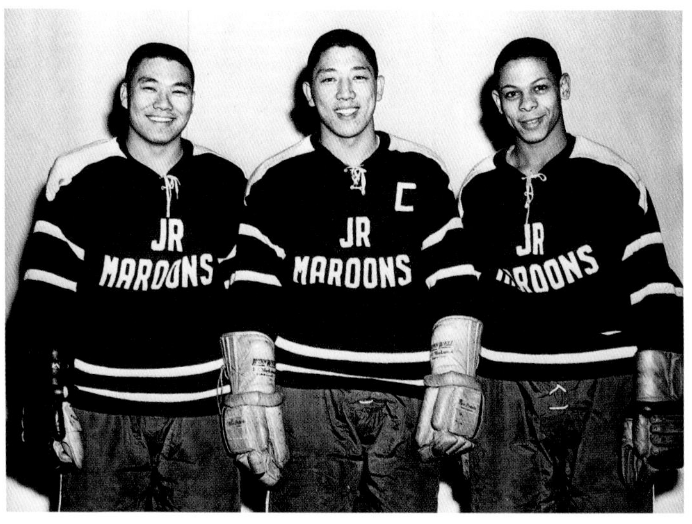

earth-shattering chemical reaction, there was only a small yellow flame undulating between wisps of indifferent white smoke. Sensing the need for a more active catalyst, I carefully tipped a glass quart jar of gasoline into the mixture and nearly panicked in the ensuing explosion. I dashed into the house, and after mumbling to my parents something about how thirsty I was from the day's heat, I dashed out again with a glass of water. After the third or fourth glass, my parents became suspicious, and eventually, with more appropriate buckets of water, they managed to save the garage. My father brought out the futon that day.

In winter, the focus of our world became hockey. On weekends, we would trudge along the banks of McGregor Creek, and, far beyond the polluting factories, where the waters ran widest, we would shovel off deep layers of snow for our impromptu arena. Racing furiously up the ice, we saw ourselves as the legendary Rocket Richard, eyes blazing,

44

fierce in our determination to score the winning goal for our first Stanley Cup. The best amongst us were the Wakabayashi brothers: one would be drafted by the Detroit Red Wings; both would go to Japan to prepare their diminutive teams to compete for Olympic gold.

As the rampant hostility that greeted our arrival gradually faded in the warm sun of the passing years, the Nikkei of Chatham, like a hardy perennial that takes root in the harshest soil, began to reassert their cultural life. The venue for our communal rebirth was the Masonic Temple, a white and stately building managed by the avuncular Mr. Dougherty, walrus-like with his portly frame and bushy moustache. On Nisei Nights, with the sweet music of the Glenn Miller Band echoing through the hall, we would dip and swirl in our best imitations of Fred and Ginger. The grandest night of all was the annual *keirokai*, when the entire community would gather to honour its elders. Once the mounds of sushi, chow mein and teriyaki chicken were devoured, the evening's entertainment would begin: children screeching on violins and singing ancient songs of dragonflies; the raucous skits of the Nisei and the more serious drama of the Issei (first-generation Japanese immigrants born in Japan before World War II), redolent with hints of Kabuki and Noh; and finally, the oldest amongst us would stand and walk proudly to the podium to receive commemorative china plates with the eyes of Queen Elizabeth peering benignly through strokes of calligraphic kanji brushed by my father's steady hand. In the weeks before the event, my father, the resident artist of our community, would devote every spare moment to preparing props and scenery and, with mounds of horsehair reeking of the Darling factory, fashioning the flowing headdresses for the play.

My fondest memories are of the holidays that brought each year of my boyhood to a joyous end. We had the best of both worlds, for we celebrated Christmas with all the trimmings—the tree, the turkey dinner and, best of all, the I-can't-wait-to-see presents (a Daisy pump-action BB gun once made me the envy of our neighbourhood), and then, on December 26, the entire family would spring into action to prepare for Shogatsu, the most intense and protracted celebration in my parents' homeland. One day there would appear in our charred garage, as if by magic, a bushel basket brimming with fat, shiny, BC Red Delicious apples, and not one but two whole cases of pop: precious and rare as any fine French wine. New Year's Eve was the one day in the year that my father took over the kitchen. With sprigs of holly, cuttings of pine, flowers and

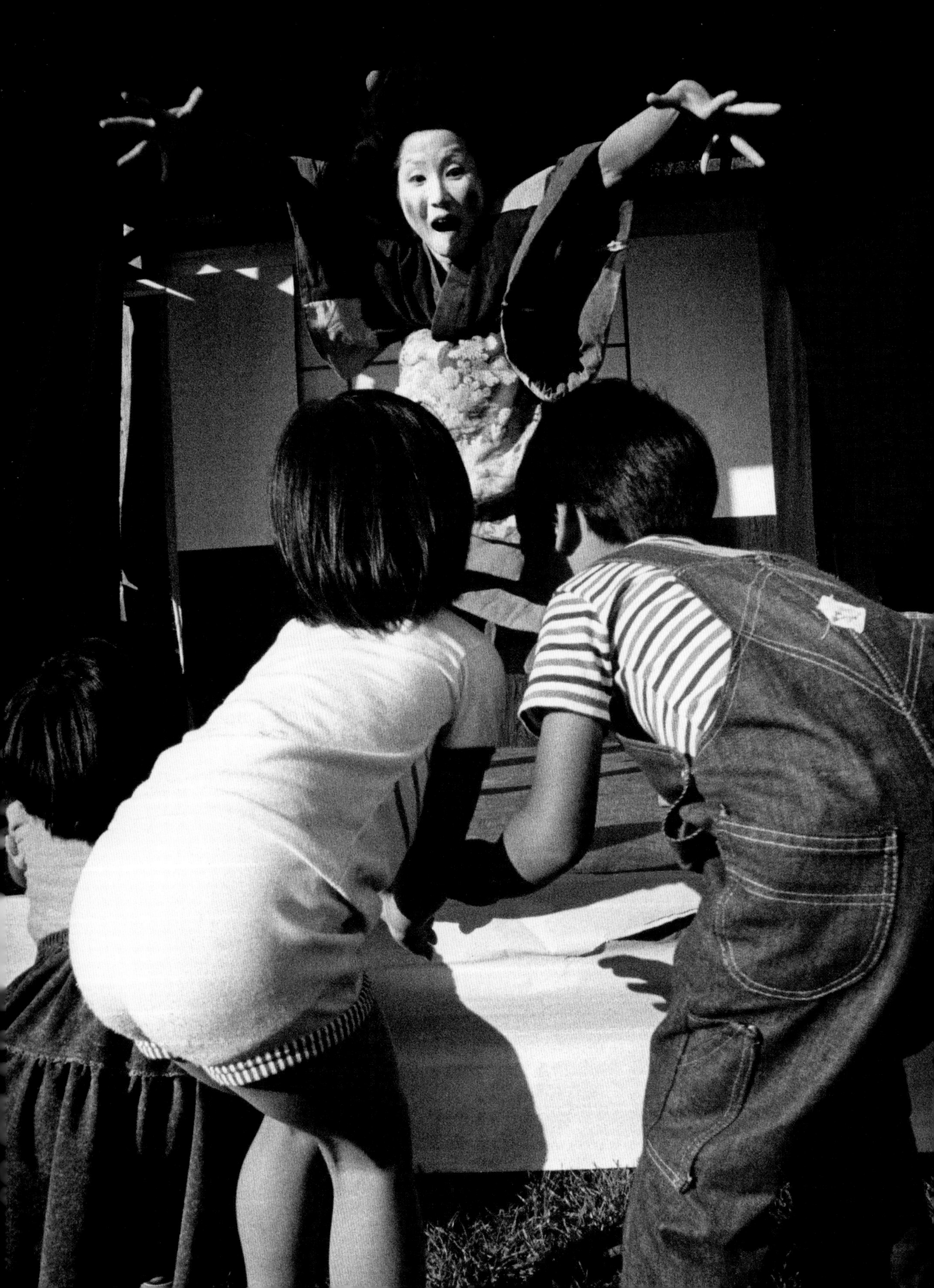

animals delicately carved from carrots and daikon, he would prepare the many delicacies, specially ordered from Toronto, to create the beautiful plates of *osechi ryori*. After a light supper, we would haul out the wooden mallets and two-foot-tall round, cut long ago from a stout tree. My mother, reduced to the role of sous-chef, would tend two huge pots that would eventually steam the entire ten-pound bag of sweet sticky rice. When the first batch was ready, she would dump the plump pearls of grain into the hollowed-out depression in the wooden round. With my father counting cadence in singsong Japanese, we would begin pounding the rice, and once the grains began to come together, he would drop to his knees. In between each beat, his hands would dart in and out like pistons, either slapping the glutinous mound with lubricating cold water or stretching and pulling it, exposing fresh areas for pounding. It was a potentially lethal syncopation, for had I or my brothers missed a stroke, we could easily have ruined my father's hand. After several hours of exhausting work and, thankfully, no accidents, we had our mochi, without which no Shogatsu is ever complete. At midnight the whole family would gather at the table to slurp steaming bowls of *toshikoshi soba*, fully believing that the long buckwheat noodles did indeed hold the promise of long life.

The next morning, after a late brunch of *ozoni*—the traditional first meal of Shogatsu—and a final inspection of the table loaded with tall bottles of sake, wine and Canadian rye standing like sentries over the culinary treasures, my father would go out the door to begin his round of visits. My two older brothers would soon follow, but I was still too young and would spend the day with my mother and sister greeting the parade of visitors. The first to arrive was usually Matsuda-san. My mother would greet him at the door, and in an ancient ritual that seemed to last forever, they would bow incessantly and repeat the endless catechism

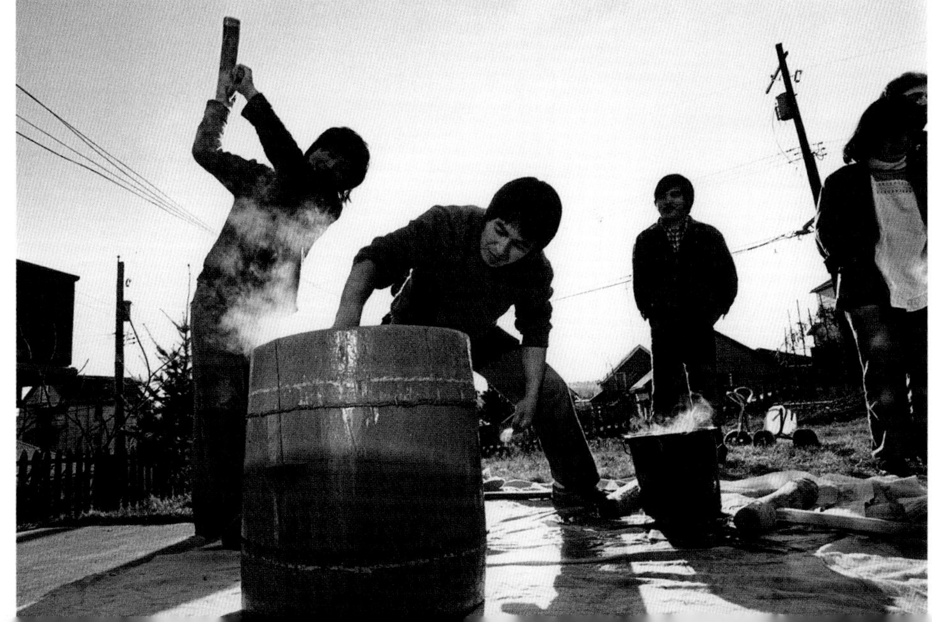

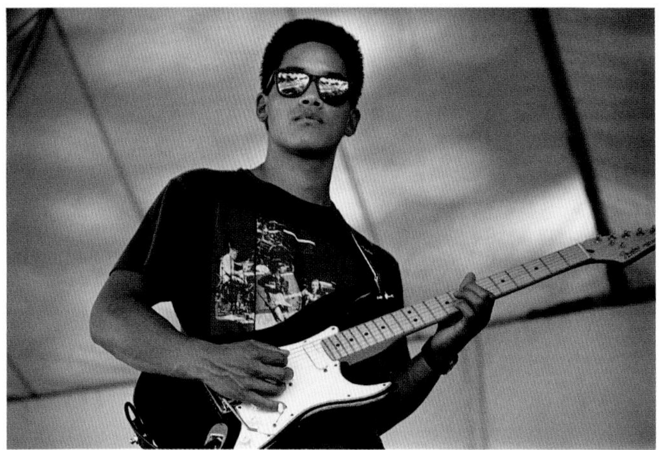

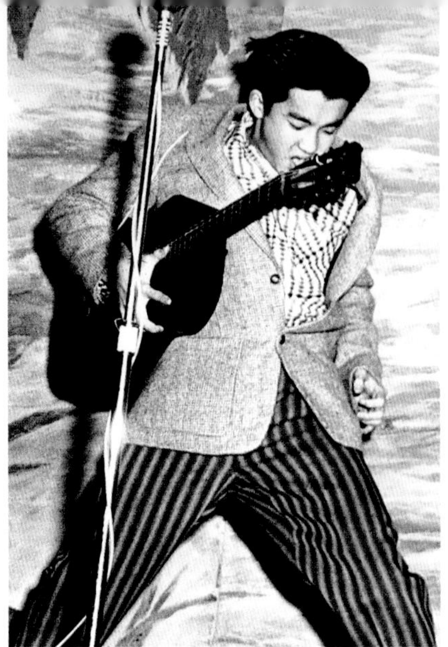

of a Shogatsu greeting with sibilant intakes of the morning air. Finally, my mother would seat our guest at the table and pour him a shot of rye. While he drank and sampled our fare, they would discuss the events of the past year. After a short while, Matsuda-san would rise and, after more bows, continue on to the next house. The Issei tended to make their rounds individually while the Nisei went in different age groups. We eagerly awaited the tumultuous arrival of the youngest group.

In my twelfth or thirteenth year, my father casually mentioned one night after dinner that I might think about joining the boys on New Year's. It was one of my proudest moments, for this was a Nikkei rite of passage as joyous as any bar mitzvah. I woke early that Shogatsu morning to eagerly await the arrival of my peers. We were more like an army of storm troopers, descending upon each house with shouts of "Happy New Year" and hugs and kisses for our hosts. After a toast to the house, we entertained the women and ourselves with ribald jokes, outrageous insults, off-key renditions of the hit parade and sentimental ballads in our mutilated Japanese, and the grand finale: an impeccable Elvis impersonation by Joe Matsuda. Our mission accomplished, we stumbled out the door to attack the next house. In the first two years, before I wisely learned to switch to Pepsi, I never made it beyond the fourth or fifth home, but I made up for it with the ability to truly savour the delicacies of Shogatsu. The recognized master of the Japanese culinary arts was Mrs. Mori, and the memory of her plump, perfectly cooked tiger prawns and exquisitely flavoured *kazunoko*, seen only at this one time of the year, still resonates along my palate.

As the day wore on, the songs became more slurred, the Elvis impersonation less precise, and our numbers dwindled as more and more fell to the hail of rye-and-beer bullets. In the evening, the army of celebrants, along with their womenfolk, would reform at one of the larger homes to nibble on leftovers and quietly discuss who had been the most outrageous that day. Finally, when the last straggler appeared, bleary-eyed, from a few hours of sleep at one of the houses along our route, we awarded the annual prize to the one who had made it standing to the end of the day's march; no mean feat, since there well over thirty homes visited that New Year's Day.

There was much to celebrate in those days, much to be grateful for. But every now and then, the ugly face of racism would appear like a thief in the night to snatch away our hard-won victories and remind us that we were prisoners still shackled to our Enemy Alienness.

In my final year of public school, the comely face of Shirley Sharpe had awoken our prepubescent lust. One day at recess, I was occupying a urinal in the boy's washroom when George Murphy, a tough Irish kid and my chief rival for the fair hand of our dream girl, walked in and took the stall adjacent to mine. Glancing over his shoulder, he said, "I don't know why you're so interested in Shirley, because you can't ever marry her." He said this calmly, without anger or malice, a simple recitation of a natural and immutable law, like "the sun will rise tomorrow in the east." And much later, I learned from Jerry Cummings, my high school friend and roommate in my second year of college, that it really was true—they don't want us to marry their sisters.

Baseball has long been an important part of Nikkei life. It began in the pre-war settlement of Vancouver's Little Tokyo, when the legendary Asahi team brought much glory to their beleaguered community. It continued in Chatham with the formation of the Nisei softball team, and, using the same brand of "small" ball (key bunts and singles coupled with lightning speed) and the powerful windmill arms of the Seki twins, they too won their fair share of championships. One night, under the floodlights of Tecumseh Park, our gang from the east side turned out in force for the final game of the season. We were engaged in a spirited but friendly heckling battle with the opposition when one blonde and buxom teenager fired back, "Why don't you dirty Japs go back where you came from?" We were silenced. The dreaded J-bomb had been dropped.

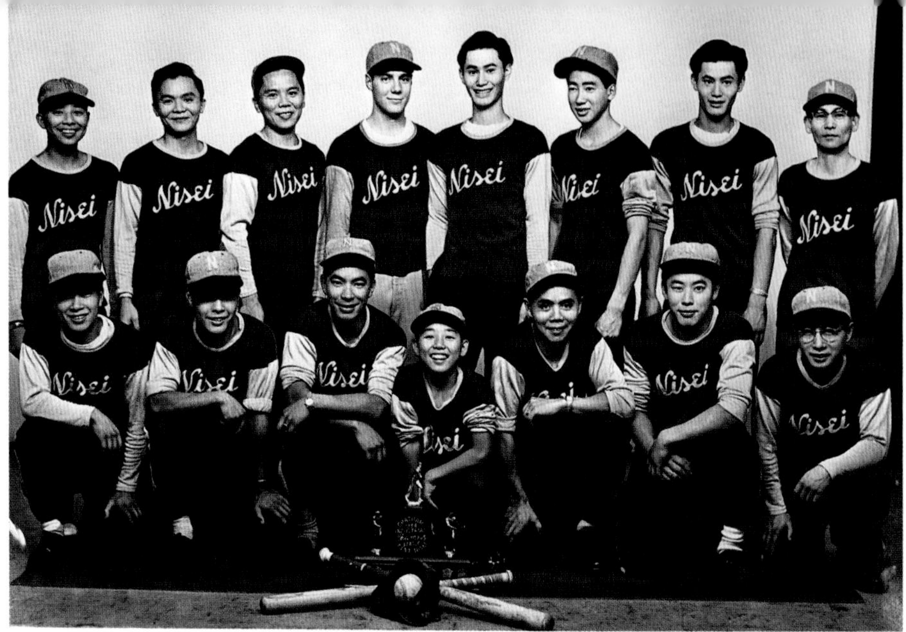

Racism, in its most absurd form, struck again to tarnish my crowning moment. In my final year of high school, I was appointed commander-in-chief of our cadet corps. Once a year in the spring, the entire student body would turn out fully uniformed for the Passing Out parade. I was resplendent that day in black boots spit polished to a mirror finish, spotless white spats over tartan hose tops, MacGregor kilt with ceremonial horsehair sporran, gleaming claymore clipped to Sam Browne belt, red sash emphasizing the clean lines of blue doublet, and red-tasselled blue bonnet precisely creased by my white-gloved hands. My troops had assembled and were awaiting my orders. I began to march over the freshly mown grass of Tecumseh Park when a grizzled, red-nosed descendant of the tribes that had once battled on these plains looked up from his seat in the bleachers and, in a voice hoarse from too many bottles of cheap red wine, snorted, just loud enough for the front ranks to hear, "Goddamn chink!"

My boyhood years were a kaleidoscope of joy and pain, and Chatham was a brutal yet wondrous boot camp for the coming wars.

Unknown photographer,
Nisei Industrial League
Softball Champions,
Chatham, Ontario, 1954

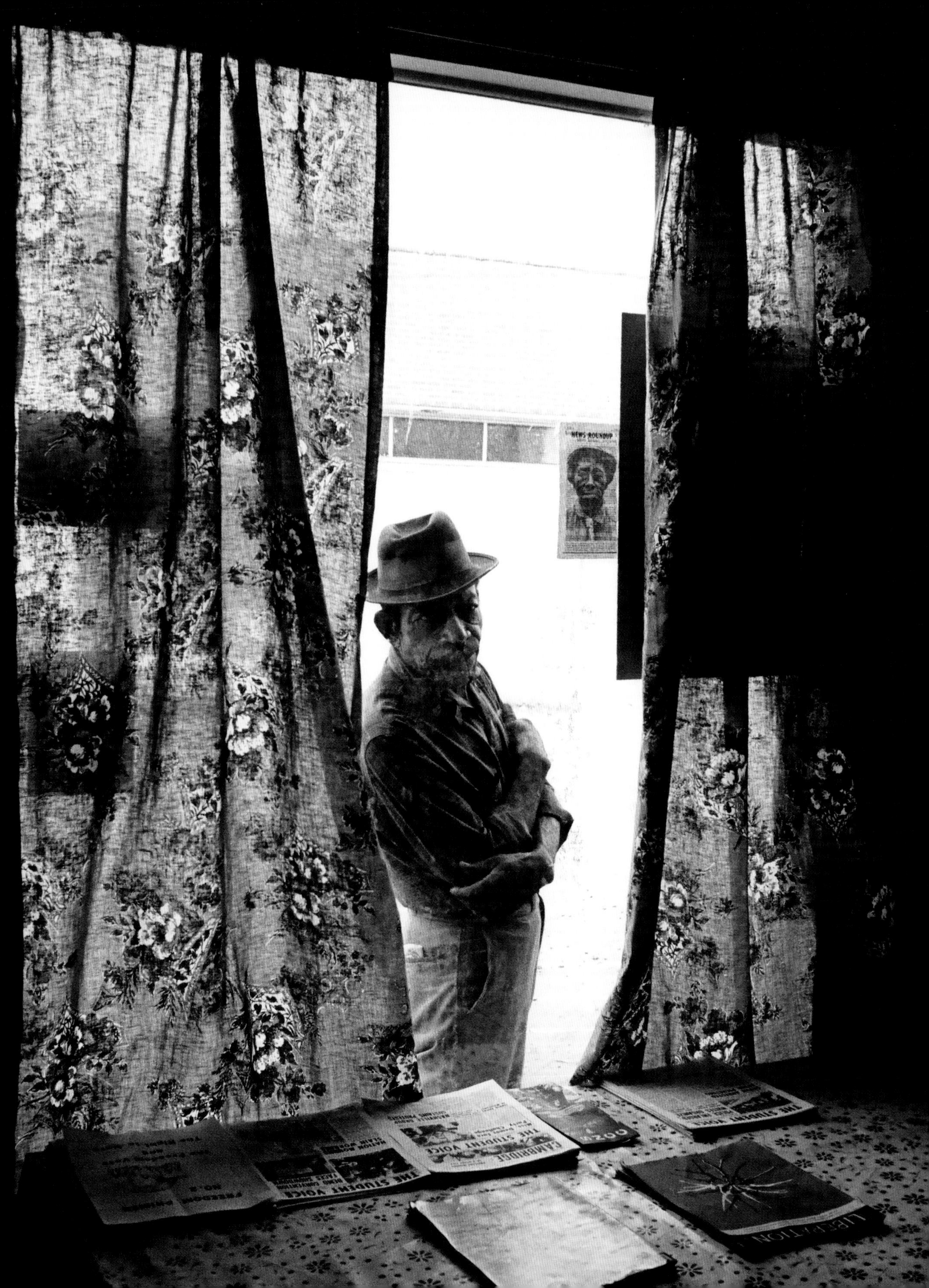

NEWS ROUNDUP
THE STUDENT VOICE
THE STUDENT VOICE
CAMBRIDGE
FREEDOM
GOZA
LIBERATION

3

WHEN I RETURNED FROM university, there were only my mother and me living at home. My father had died four years earlier, and my siblings were off pursuing careers or starting their own families. My mother sensed my unhappiness but thankfully said nothing, and even if I had wanted to have a consoling mother-son conversation, it was no longer possible, for we had long ago lost the ability to verbally communicate. My mother still spoke almost no English, while, in my eagerness to assimilate, I had carelessly discarded my Japanese.

I was fortunate that summer in landing one of the most sought-after student jobs in the city. With $850 borrowed from my mother, I purchased a blue '58 Volkswagen Beetle, which enabled me to become a crop tester for Libby's. It was a pleasant job, driving around all day to the many farms contracted by Libby's to supply their large canning plant in Chatham. My duties were simple enough: walk to the four corners and centre of a field to gather samples of peas or corn and take them to the lab in nearby Wallaceburg, where they would be tested to determine their suitability for harvest. The pay was not great, but the generous mileage allowance made for a princely total.

One of the great side benefits of the job was that all the surrounding farmlands became a free and open market for my mother and me. One day on my travels, I spotted a small field dotted with lush heads of cabbage, one of my favourite foods. Surrounding the field were several large

Man peeking in the window of Freedom House with a SNCC *Student Voice* newsletter visible on the table, Winstonville, Mississippi, c. December 1964

signs with bold, red lettering warning that the area had been recently sprayed with a deadly insecticide, but I assumed a careful washing would eliminate any problems. I came out with a sackful of cabbages. The next day, when I brought my morning samples into the lab, I casually mentioned to the manager my earlier visit to the cabbage patch.

"Oh, you must mean the Hudson farm on Number 16 Road. We went in there about a week ago to apply that new systemic poison we've been experimenting with."

"What's systemic mean, and how deadly is it?"

"Well, unlike a regular insecticide that you spray directly on the plant, a systemic poison is introduced into the soil, where it's absorbed through the plant's root system. It's supposed to leach completely out by the time the crop is ready to be harvested. This new chemical is pretty powerful stuff; one of the Hudson boys walked through the field the day after we went in, and he passed out in his truck. Damn lucky he wasn't in an accident."

I made a hasty exit, jumped in the car and sped back to Chatham in record time. As I entered our back door, my mother was contentedly slicing up half a head of cabbage for my lunch; the other half, neatly cored and quartered, was ready to go into the *tsukemono* pickle pot. With a mumbled apology, I gathered up all the pieces, dumped them into the sack with the remaining heads of cabbage and tossed all of the contaminated produce into McGregor Creek.

With my mind clouded by heartbreak and longing for my ex-girlfriend Natasha, I went through that summer lurching from one near disaster to another. One day I walked into a forty-acre field of peas to gather my last sample of the day. The area was heavily infested by deer flies and horseflies, and, as usual, I was shirtless. As I stooped down to gather my first sample, they began to attack like an angry squadron of dive-bombers. I tried swatting them away with my burlap sack, but that only increased the fury of their attack. With their iridescent green heads glinting in the sun and the sound of their wings a constant, maddening drone on the hot, humid air, they circled and circled and circled, and every now and then, one would dive in to take an agonizingly painful bite of my arm. As I fled in near hysteria to my car, I realized the awful truth of the tales that I had heard of people who had got lost in the bush at the height of the insect season and come out alive but with their sanity shattered. I slammed the door shut, squashed the four or five flies that had managed to sneak in, and drove furiously away. By

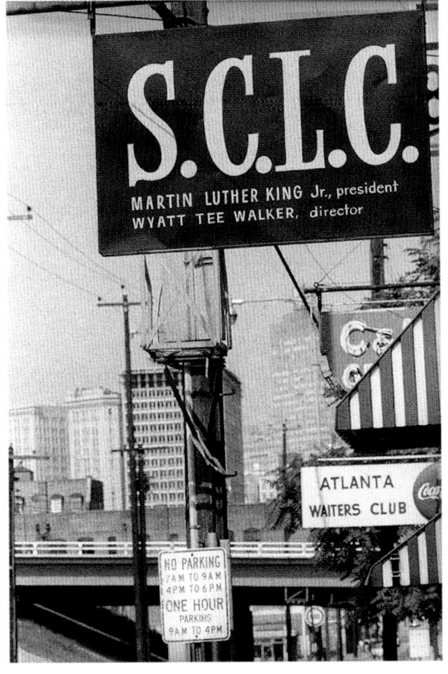

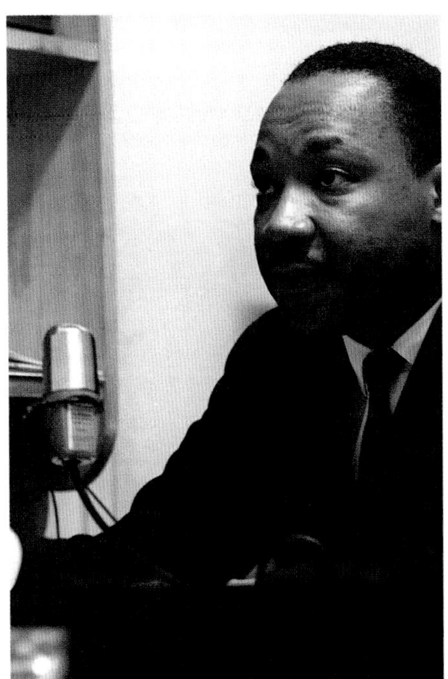

the time I arrived in Wallaceburg, my right arm had swollen to twice its normal size, and one of the lab workers had to drive me to the emergency ward, where I spent the night recovering from shock and a high fever.

There was only one beacon of light that managed to pierce through my deep depression. Throughout the summer of 1963, I had been following, with growing intensity, the spectacle of the Civil Rights Movement that had erupted across the Southern States. I remember one evening in particular when I turned on the TV to witness a compelling drama unfolding at a lunch counter in Danville, Virginia. Like the eye of a hurricane, a group of Black and white students, about my age, sat calmly at the forbidden counter, while all around them raged the winds of racial violence and hatred. Their faces remained unchanged even when Coke and raw eggs were poured over their heads, and when a student was shoved to the floor, he simply stood up and took his seat again. They were a powerful presence that day, and in some deep but unnamed part of me, I understood the essence of their struggle.

Later that summer, I watched the historic March on Washington: well over a quarter million people gathered at the nation's capital to demand "jobs and freedom" for Black America. Along with millions of other viewers around the world, I was swept away by the mellifluous

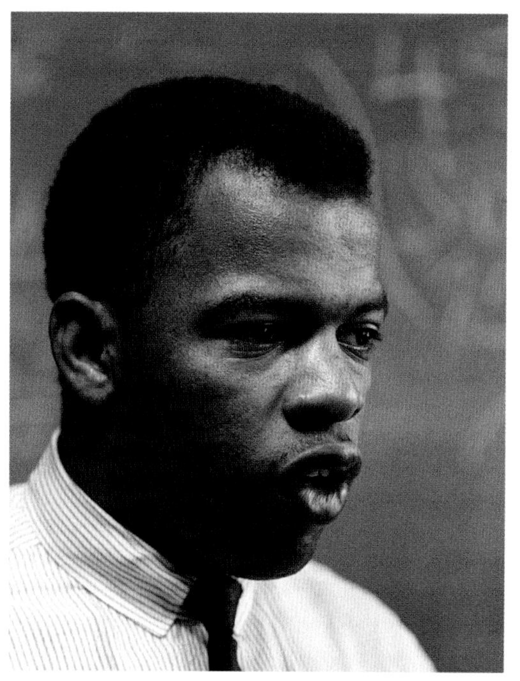

"dream" rhetoric of Martin Luther King Jr., but it was the rough, uncompromising words of John Lewis, the young, battle-scarred chairman of the Student Nonviolent Coordinating Committee, that were to remain with me: "We are involved in a serious social revolution. By and large, politicians who build their careers on immoral compromise and allow themselves an open forum of political, economic and social exploitation dominate American politics... What political leader can stand up and say, 'My party is a party of principles'? The party of Kennedy is also the party of Eastland. The party of Javits is also the party of Goldwater. Where is our party?"

And where, I wondered, is my own rightful place in this monolithic white world? These thoughts awoke in me the distant hope that perhaps, within this Black movement for freedom, I could locate the matrix of my own liberation.

As the summer was coming to an end, I announced to my mother that I had worked hard and wanted to take a short vacation to the States before returning to complete my final year of university. On the second Saturday in September, I loaded my sleeping bag and a backpack into the Beetle, hugged my mother goodbye, and drove south. I had no plan, knew no one, had made no contacts. Up until then, the furthest I had roamed was the occasional excursion to the bright lights of Toronto, but I sensed that once I crossed the bridge from Windsor to Detroit, there would be no turning back.

Late that first evening, I had neared the Kentucky border and decided to stop for the night at the next highway rest station; wishing to preserve my meagre stash of traveller's cheques, my bed would be the cramped back seat of the Volks. I pulled into a truck stop for my final meal of the day and, after dinner, found a washroom where I could wash up for the night. As I went to grab a paper towel, I was stopped cold by the sight of an oblong box dispensing three kinds of condoms. For someone from the cold and repressed climate of the North Country, this was truly a wondrous sight. I was reminded of one night in my

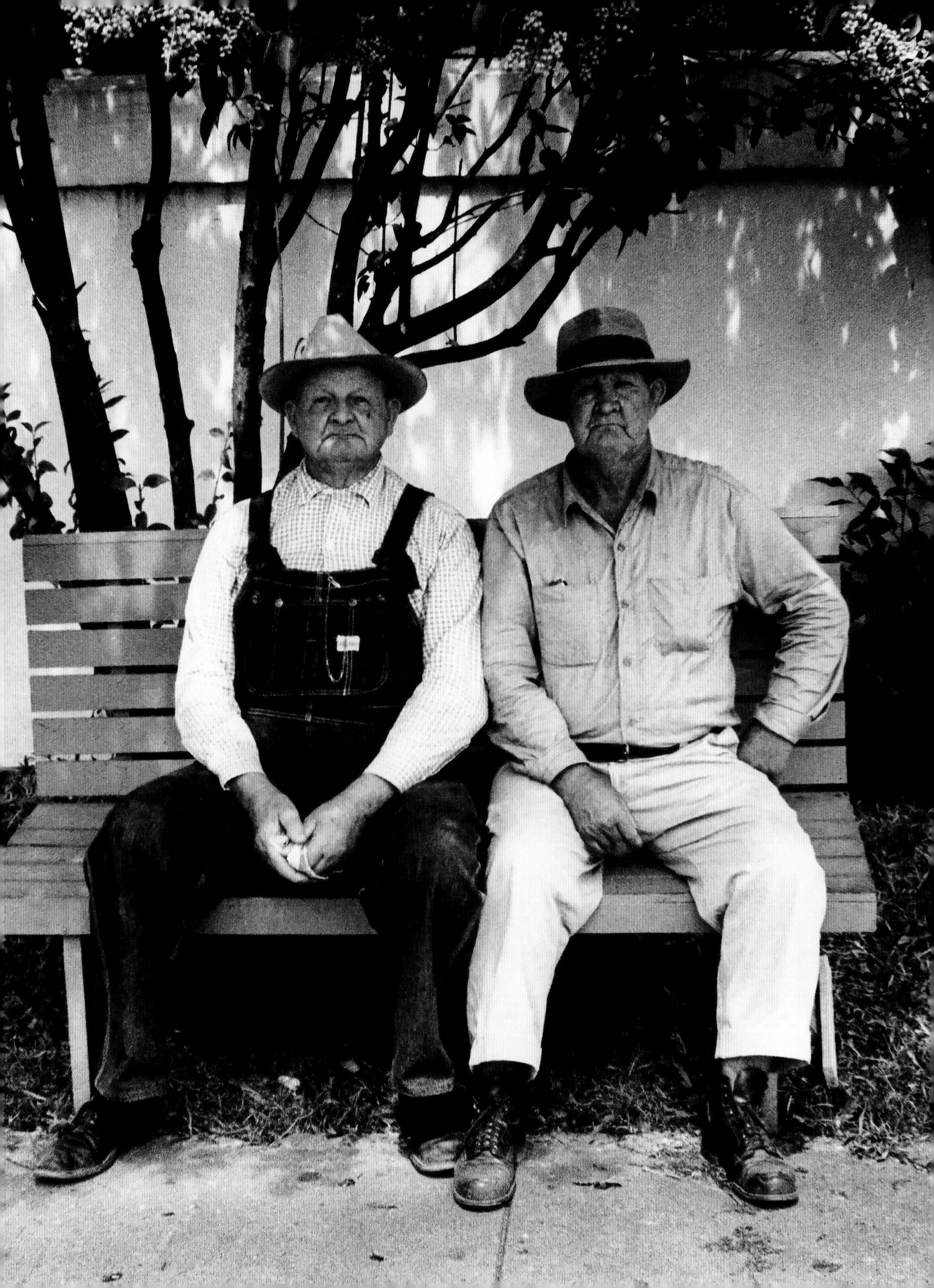

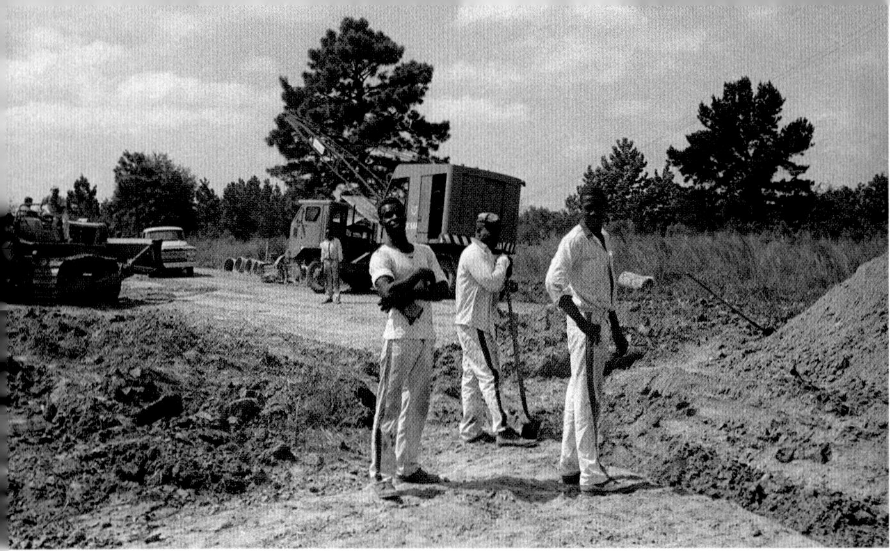

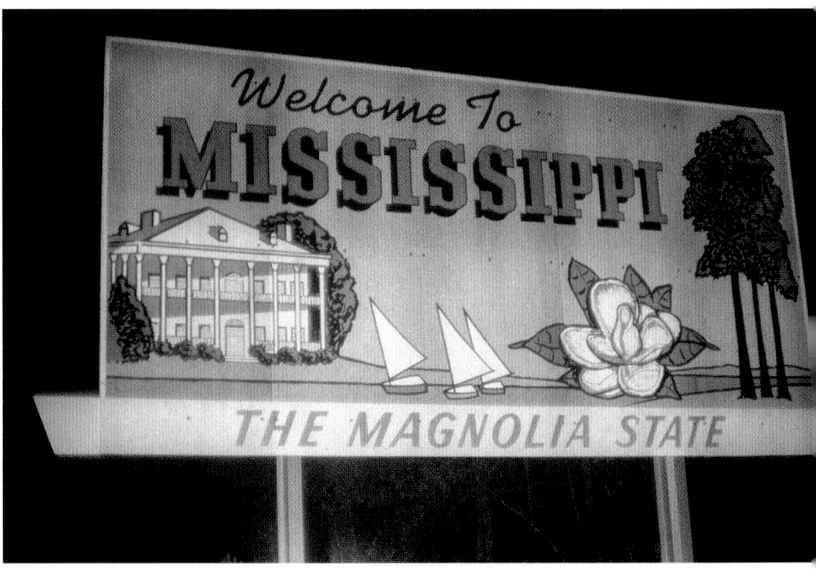

first year of university, when my roommate Herb Kikuta, who was even more sexually frustrated than me, decided it was imperative we venture out and buy some condoms. It wasn't that we were in immediate need of them—far from it—there was only the vague hope that the mere possession of this sexual talisman would somehow hasten the loss of our virginity. So late that night, we drove to a remote drugstore, and after a losing coin toss, I went in to make the purchase. I amassed a sizable mound of unneeded chewing gum, soap, razor blades, pens and toothpaste before working up the nerve to ask for a box of safes. With a knowing smirk, the elderly druggist threw the box onto the pile, and after paying for the goods, I fled out the door like a thief. But now I was in America, the land of the free, where anyone could walk into a public facility and buy condoms to his heart's content—they must be doing it in the streets. My sexual experience had been limited to occasional stolen kisses on various dance floors and one night of true heat when four of us snuck into the basement of Gloria Vincent's home. Gloria, or Milky as she was longingly called, was the beautiful and voluptuous cinnamon-coloured siren of our high school. While Don Wakabayashi, the oldest and the most experienced of us, plied Milky with artful kisses, Mas, Keibo and I worked like three frenzied monkeys, clutching and grabbing any luscious body part we could get our greedy hands on. I left the washroom with the happy thought that the condom machine was a sure harbinger of the opening of new sensual vistas.

By late morning of the second day, I had reached Nashville, Tennessee, and for lack of anything better to do, I went on a sightseeing tour of the imposing complex of state capital buildings; but I was, and still am, an indifferent tourist. I soon grew tired of climbing up and down the stairs, and besides, if you've seen one magnificent building, you've seen them all. I returned to the car and wondered what I was doing so far away from home. Thoughts of turning back were crossing my mind when the lamentation of the Grand Ole Opry on the car radio was interrupted by a news bulletin: earlier that morning, a bomb had exploded in the basement of the 16th Street Baptist Church in Birmingham, Alabama, killing four young Black girls who had been attending Bible classes. I had arrived in the South on Birmingham Sunday. After checking my map, I saw that the city was a two-hundred-mile straight shot down Interstate 65.

Several hours later, I crossed the border into Alabama and pulled into a large Gulf station for a much-needed pit stop for both me and my car. After a bracing cup of coffee, I followed the washroom signs to the rear of the restaurant, where I confronted the first of many existential dilemmas. On opposite sides of the narrow corridor were two doors: one marked "Colored," the other "White."

I finally reached Birmingham in the early evening. Exhausted from hours of driving and a near-sleepless night jack-knifed in the back of the car, I missed the downtown exit and found myself lost in a residential neighbourhood. The streets were filled with people milling around, and when I had to stop at an intersection, I was immediately surrounded by a crowd of angry Black youth brandishing a variety of weapons. When they peered through the windshield and failed to see a Black face, they began shouting and rocking the Beetle. I realized I couldn't outrun the situation, so I slowly got out of the car, and in the momentary confusion created by the appearance of a face that, although not Black, was not entirely white either, I stammered out a hurried explanation: I was a student from Canada on my way to Mexico for a vacation and had got lost looking for the downtown YMCA. After expressing my outrage at the bombing and my condolences for the death of the four girls, they set me on the right path with the added advice to get to my lodgings quickly, for this was not a night to be wandering the streets of Birmingham.

Eventually I found myself driving down one of the main thorough-fares of the city, a wide, tree-lined boulevard that I thought bore a remarkable resemblance to Toronto's stately University Avenue. The illusion of familiarity was soon shattered by an army jeep that came careening around a corner. The top of the vehicle looked like a steel picket fence with the profusion of antennae and fixed bayonets, and in the seats were crammed four young soldiers with grim faces peer-ing resolutely from under camouflage-covered helmets. As I continued down the street, I began to notice other disturbing anomalies—this metropolis, in the early hours of a pleasantly warm summer's evening with a soft southern breeze gently stirring the trees, was practically deserted. This was definitely not Toronto, for the sidewalks were almost bereft of strolling pedestrians. Mine was about the only vehicle on the street, the stores and restaurants were mostly dark and shuttered, the neon lights of the theatre marquees were unlit and unmoving. Since I hadn't eaten yet, I was desperate for some food and coffee. When I finally spotted a small establishment with its lights blazing and doors open, I parked the car and walked in only to discover that it was a news-paper and magazine kiosk with a long shoeshine stand. The obese white owner stood sprawling against the stand and, in a voice muffled by a fat cigar stuck in his porcine mouth, asked his two shoeshine boys, "Well boys, what you all gonna do now?"

The workers kept looking at the floor, and finally the older of the two ebony teenagers mumbled, without looking up, "Don't know boss. Mebbe we goin' to go out and kill."

As I was returning to my car, I heard, from across the street, the voice of a newspaper street vendor loudly proclaiming the morning's tragedy. An older, prosperous-looking white couple came walking by. As the wife veered off to check out the headlines, her husband gently grabbed her arm to pull her away from the awful news, and after a slight nod of his silvery patrician head, they continued walking up the street.

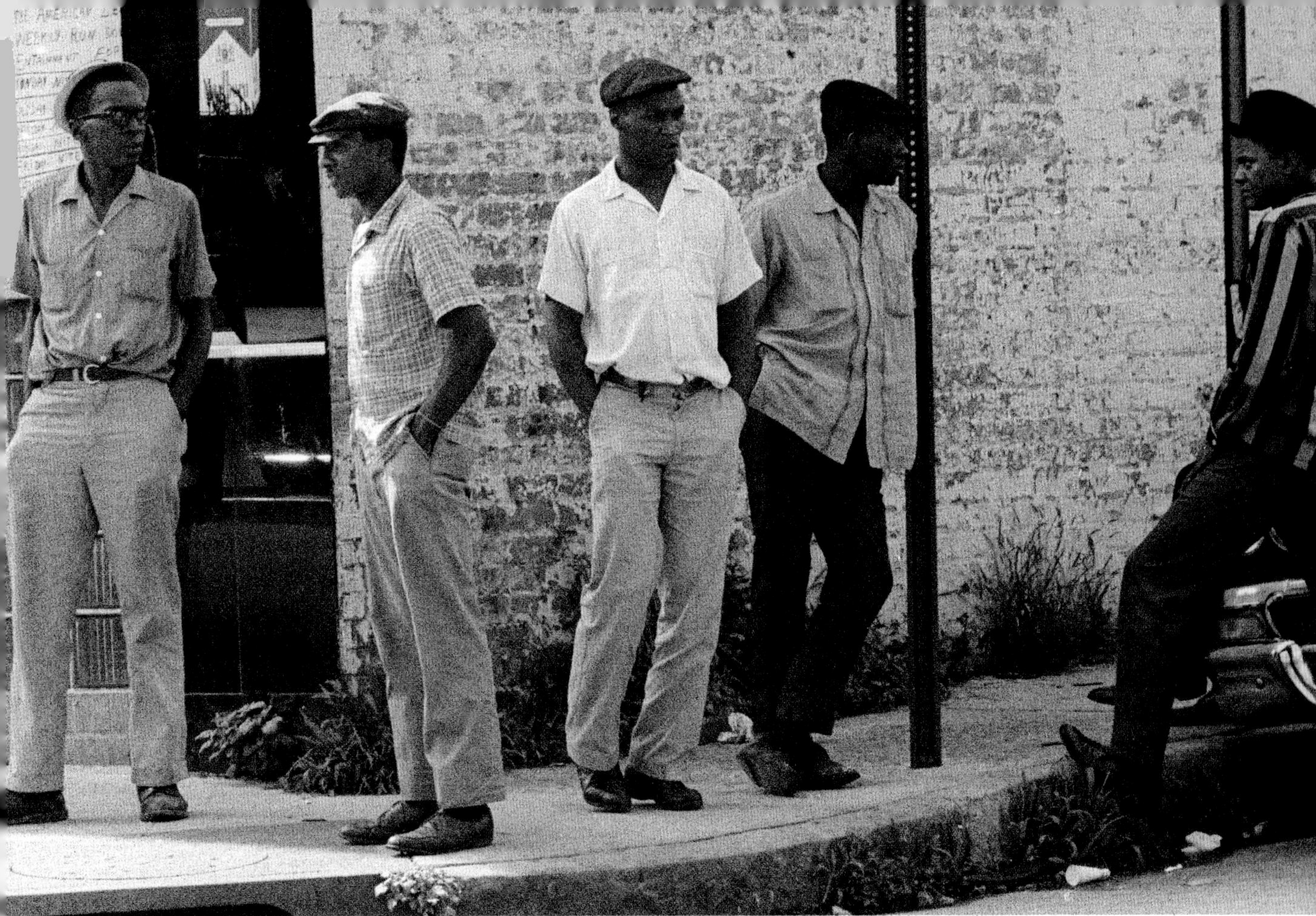

I was determined to satisfy my hunger and was rewarded several blocks later by the lights of a small restaurant radiating from a side street. I rounded the corner and parked behind a pickup truck emblazoned with Confederate flags and bumper stickers heralding the arrival of white supremacy. As I entered, my stomach growled at the tantalizing odour of barbecue ribs smoking on the open grill. Sitting at tables scattered around the small room were four men who, to my eyes, looked very Black and very large, and as I took a stool at the empty counter, I could feel their eyes boring into my back. I ordered a cup of coffee and scanned the large menu on the wall. The room was deathly silent. When I noticed the counter helper, a tall, dark youth, curiously eyeing my crimson pack of Du Mauriers, I shoved the pack toward him and said, "Try one. They're Canadian cigarettes, quite a bit different from your American brands." In return he slipped me one of his Lucky Strikes, and this exchange of smokes broke the ice. Soon the apparent owner of the restaurant, a middle-aged, scholarly looking man, came over to refill my cup and struck up a conversation, and for the next hour and a half,

Atlanta, Georgia,
July 1964

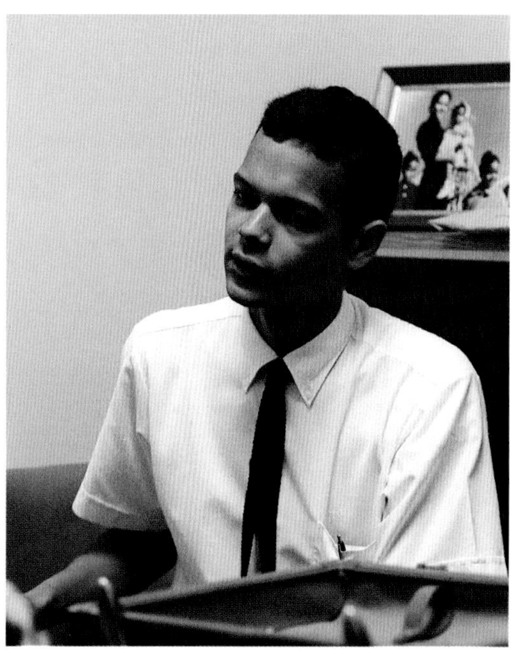

while I wolfed down a huge plate of savoury ribs and sipped at my bottomless cup of coffee, he told me what it was like to be Black and living in the Deep South. At the end of this nightmarish account of repression and daily humiliations that could so easily lead to violence and death, he offered me some sage advice: "Well I thank y'all for comin' down here, but I think you should get back in your car and go back home. You can tell all your people in Canada that what's happening in the South is all very, very real. The beatings, jailings and lynchings, they be happening now, and they be happening for a long time. But you be careful leaving, 'cause the Klan are keeping a careful eye on this place since we're about the only place open this night. That pickup you parked behind probably belongs to one of them, and when you get out of town, they just might pull you over to check you out, and God knows what could happen." I paid my bill and thanked him profusely, but before leaving, I managed to secure one more vital piece of information: the name and location of the A.G. Gaston Motel, the de facto headquarters of the Movement.

I made it without harm to the YMCA, and after I checked in, a decrepit, white-haired bellboy, wheezing with the effort of carrying my light backpack, escorted me to my room. As we rode the elevator up to my floor, he looked up at me with his tired, sad eyes and said, "It's not always like this." I went to bed and fell asleep to the sound of sirens and gunfire.

The next morning, after breakfast, I drove over to the motel named after its owner, A.G. Gaston: one of the few Black millionaires and a staunch supporter of the Movement. Since his motel was not only a gathering point for the Movement but also the only desegregated facility in the city, it had been a favourite target for Klan bombings. The lobby was filled with Movement leaders and workers who had been arriving in a steady stream from all parts of the South and across the nation. Most of them were the young, dungaree-clad workers of the Student Nonviolent Coordinating Committee (SNCC, or *Snick,* as I was to later learn) who

Julian Bond at the Southern Christian Leadership Conference (SCLC) office, Atlanta, Georgia, July 1964

had come in from their desegregation and voter registration projects in Alabama, Georgia and Mississippi. I spotted their chairman, John Lewis, and went over to tell him how much I had been moved by his speech at the March on Washington. Of all the people I met in the Movement, John best exemplifies the true spirt of Gandhian non-violence. There was a gentle, almost childlike quality to the man, which belied the supreme courage and iron will that sustained him through a number of vicious beatings in demonstrations and in the famous Freedom Rides of 1961, when his bus was attacked by an angry mob at the Montgomery depot. That morning, I received the full benefit of his generous spirit, for he seemed genuinely interested in who I was and took some time so we could reach some understanding of each other's lives. At the end of a lengthy conversation, he suggested I carry on to Atlanta to visit Snick headquarters, and later he introduced me to his good friend Julian Bond, the handsome, honey-voiced director of communications, and some of the other Snick workers.

I spent the remainder of my time in Birmingham at the motel. Initially, I felt and undoubtedly looked totally out of place, and I shall always be grateful to Annie Pearl Avery, a young but seasoned veteran of the Movement in Birmingham, who took me under her wing. She made sure I met her fellow workers and had enough to eat from the buckets of fried chicken, collard greens, potato salad and buttermilk biscuits brought over by volunteers from one of the churches, and she left each night only after I was assured of a bed, or at least floor space, in one of the rooms rented by Snick. Soon after teaming up with Annie Pearl, one of the Snick workers came over and told me to be careful, for it was rumoured that she had become a bit unstable after a particularly savage beating in the Birmingham jail. And in fact, Annie Pearl was often quite abrasive, but with me she always took the role of the kind and caring older sister.

Annie Pearl and I went together to the funeral for Denise McNair, Cynthia Wesley and Addie Mae Collins, three of the girls killed in the church bombing; a private ceremony was held for the fourth victim, Carole Robertson. On our way to the church, we got lost in an upscale residential area, and I looked to my right to ask directions from Annie Pearl, but she had disappeared. Looking down, I spotted this tough veteran of the freedom wars scrunched under the dash of the car.

"Annie Pearl, what the hell you doing down there?"

"Tom, we is in whitey territory, and if they catch my Black ass in this car with you, we could be in a whole lot of trouble, so get us out of here as fast as you can."

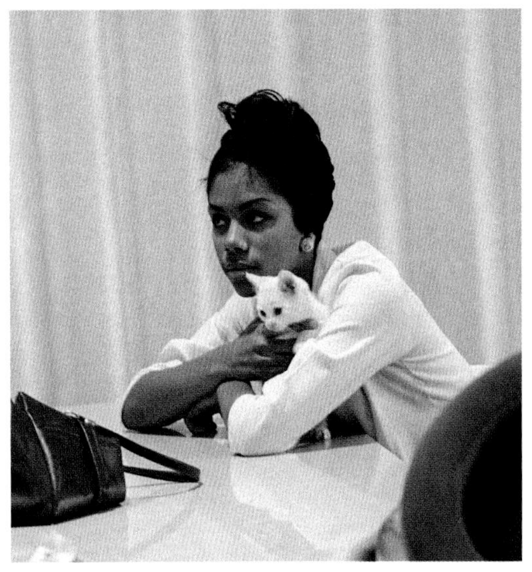

I floored the accelerator, and after manoeuvring through the heavily patrolled streets, we made it to the church on time. The church was overflowing with a crowd of three thousand mourners, but I managed to squeeze in using press credentials leftover from a summer job working as bureau correspondent for the *London Free Press*. Martin Luther King Jr. led a contingent of eight hundred pastors, both white and Black, and for the first time, I was able to personally witness the commanding presence and riveting oratory of this remarkable leader. Near the end of the ceremony, one of the mothers of the slain girls was overcome with grief and threw her body over the small casket while loudly bewailing the death of her innocent child.

After the service, one of the elderly deacons of the church came over to talk with Annie Pearl. After introductions were made, he said to me in a somewhat embarrassed voice, "I guess you're not used to seeing all this weepin' and wailin' we Black people do in our churches." I replied that such grief was understandable and that I wasn't totally unfamiliar with the church service since I had grown up in a Black neighbourhood. And indeed, I had once attended services at the Methodist church around the corner and half a block up from our house in Chatham. In a highly unique situation for the times, an Issei man, who was a friend of my parents, had married a stunningly beautiful Black woman, and through that union he somehow became an itinerant preacher for the Methodist church. He was scheduled to lead the service one Sunday and asked my mother to attend. I went with her, and I can still remember sitting on the wooden bench, watching my mother, this diminutive Japanese lady who had grown up with the sombre rituals of Shinto and Buddhism, desperately trying to keep up with the raucous rhythms of the gospel choir.

The next day I offered a ride to anyone returning to Snick headquarters. After Julian Bond, James Forman (SNCC executive secretary) and Danny Lyon (their brilliant young photographer) piled into the car, I drove off for Atlanta. After we crossed over into Georgia, I went to pass

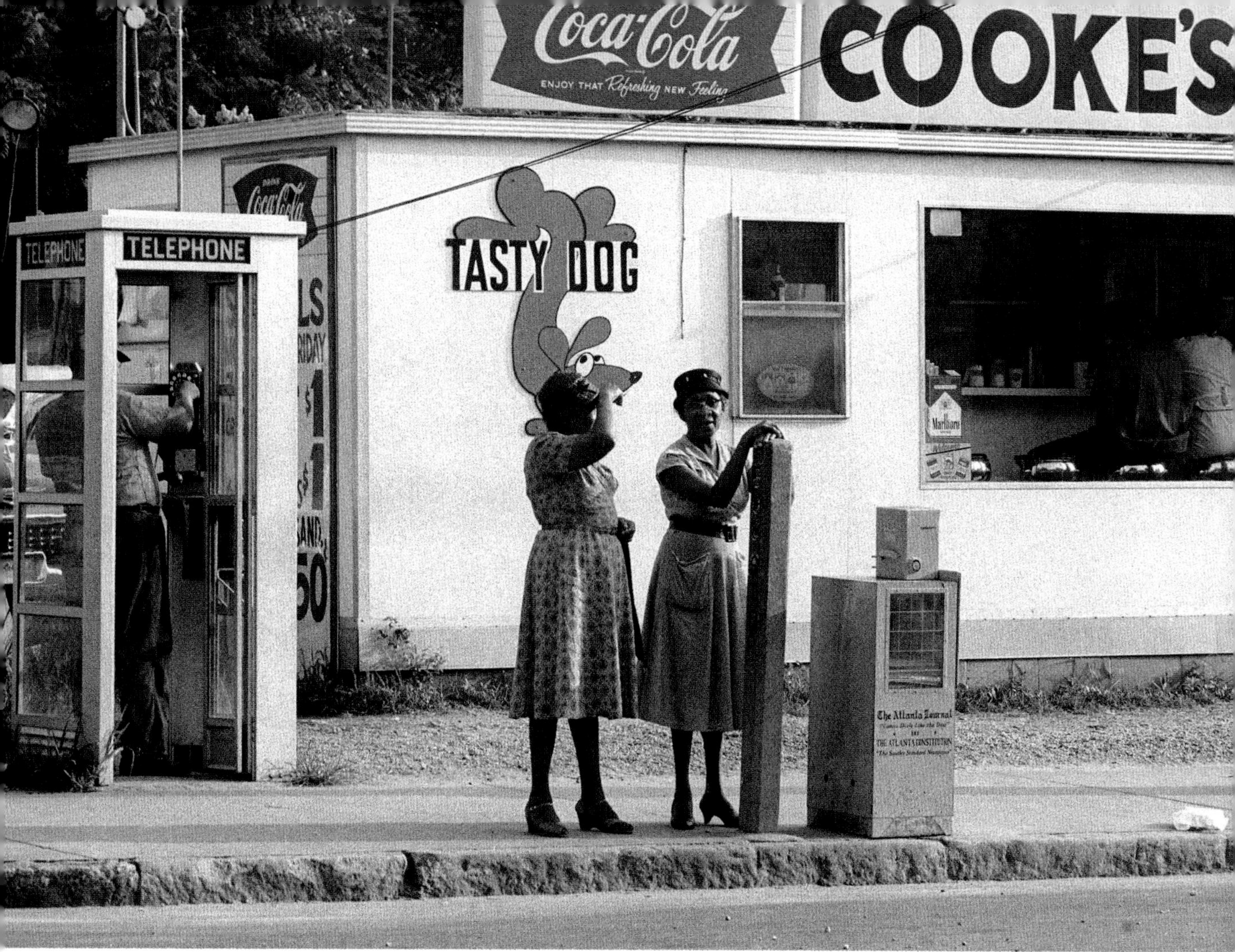

a slow-moving farm truck, but I wasn't used to the lethargy of the fully loaded Volks and barely managed to tuck in front of the truck before a sixteen wheeler came whooshing by in the opposite lane. Killing off the leadership of a major Civil Rights organization would not have been a good way to begin my career as a freedom fighter.

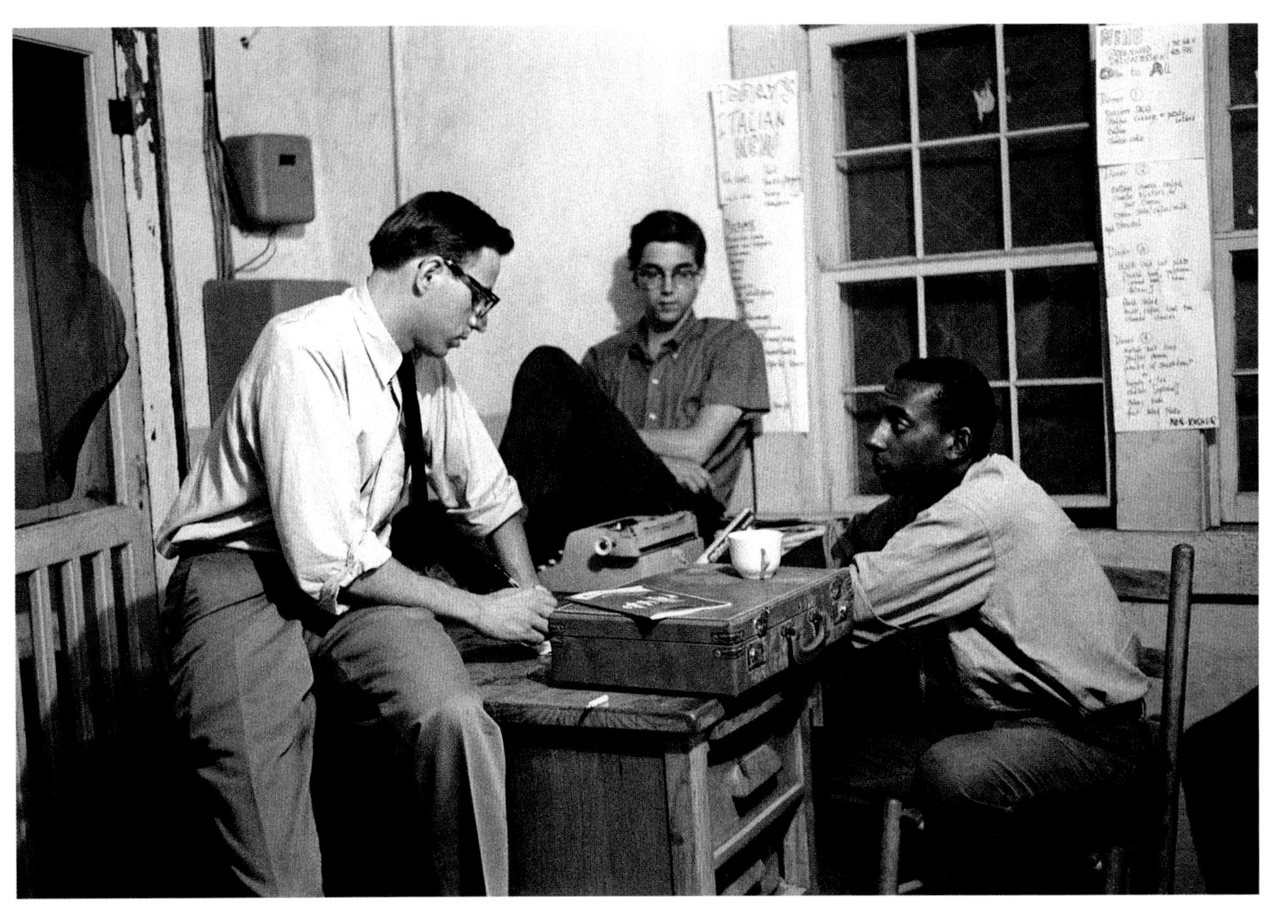

 Mississippi Freedom Democratic Party (MFDP)/SNCC office, Greenwood, Mississippi, August 1964

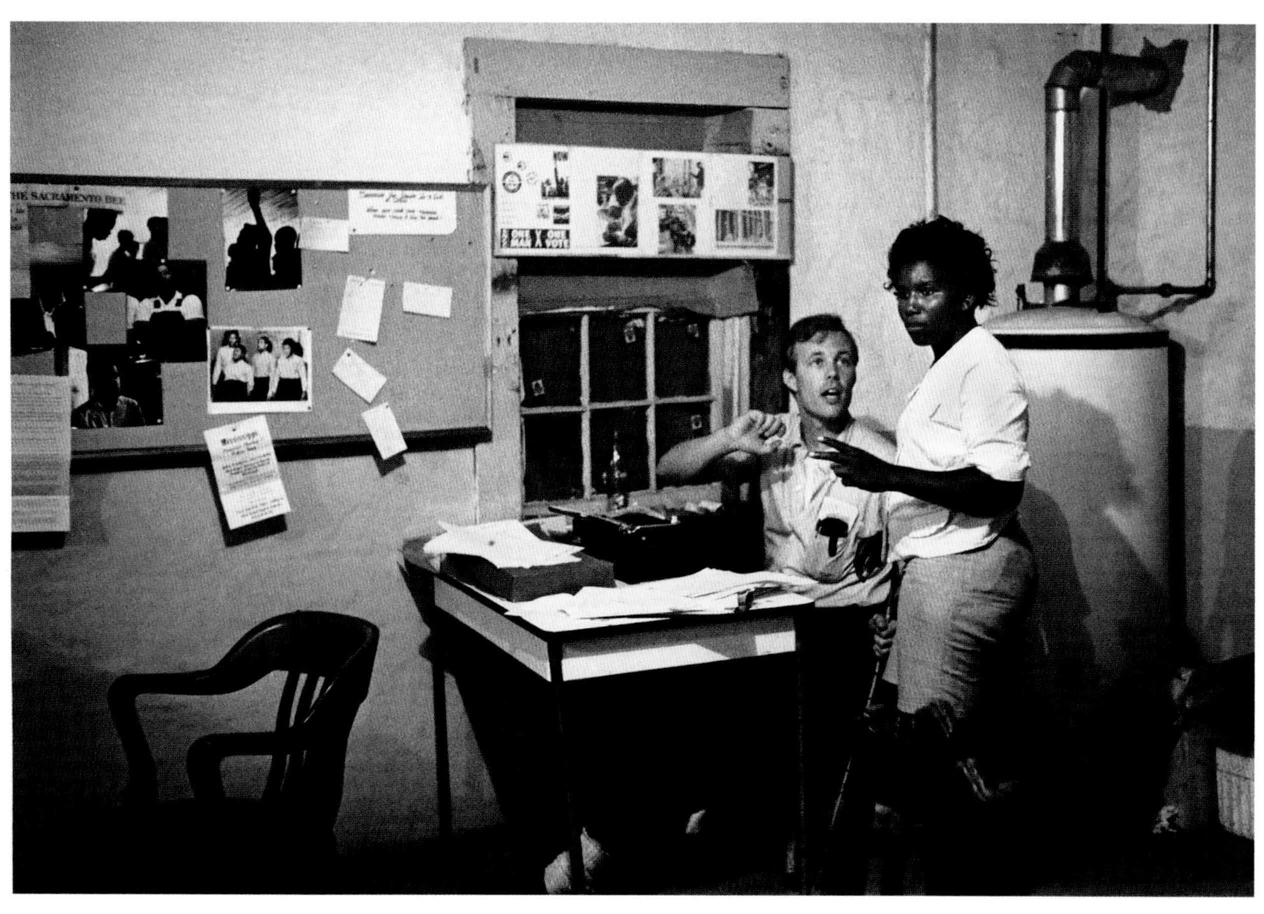

SNCC staff in Council of Federated Organizations (COFO)/SNCC office, Greenwood, Mississippi, August 2, 1964

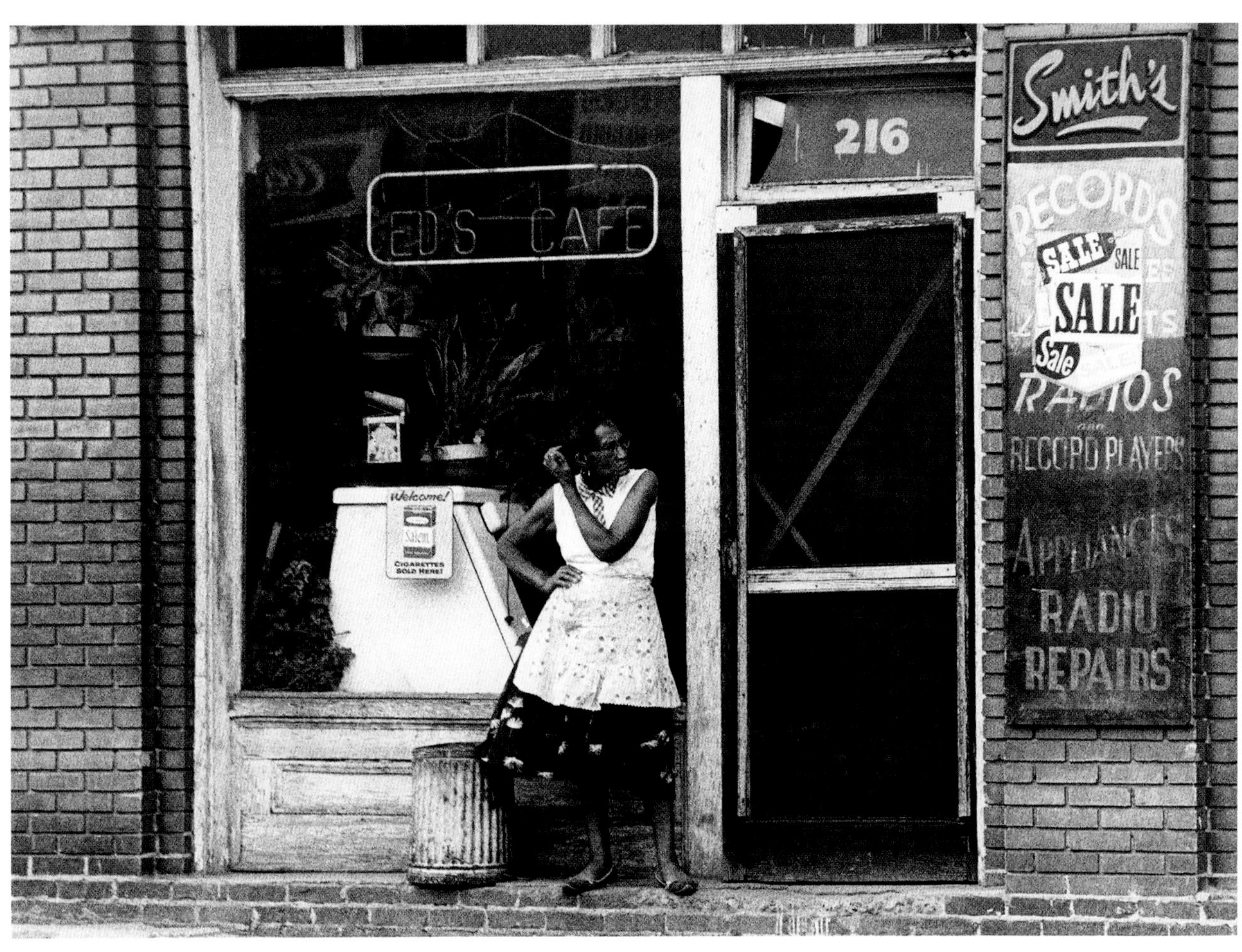

Vine City area store, Atlanta, Georgia, July 7, 1964

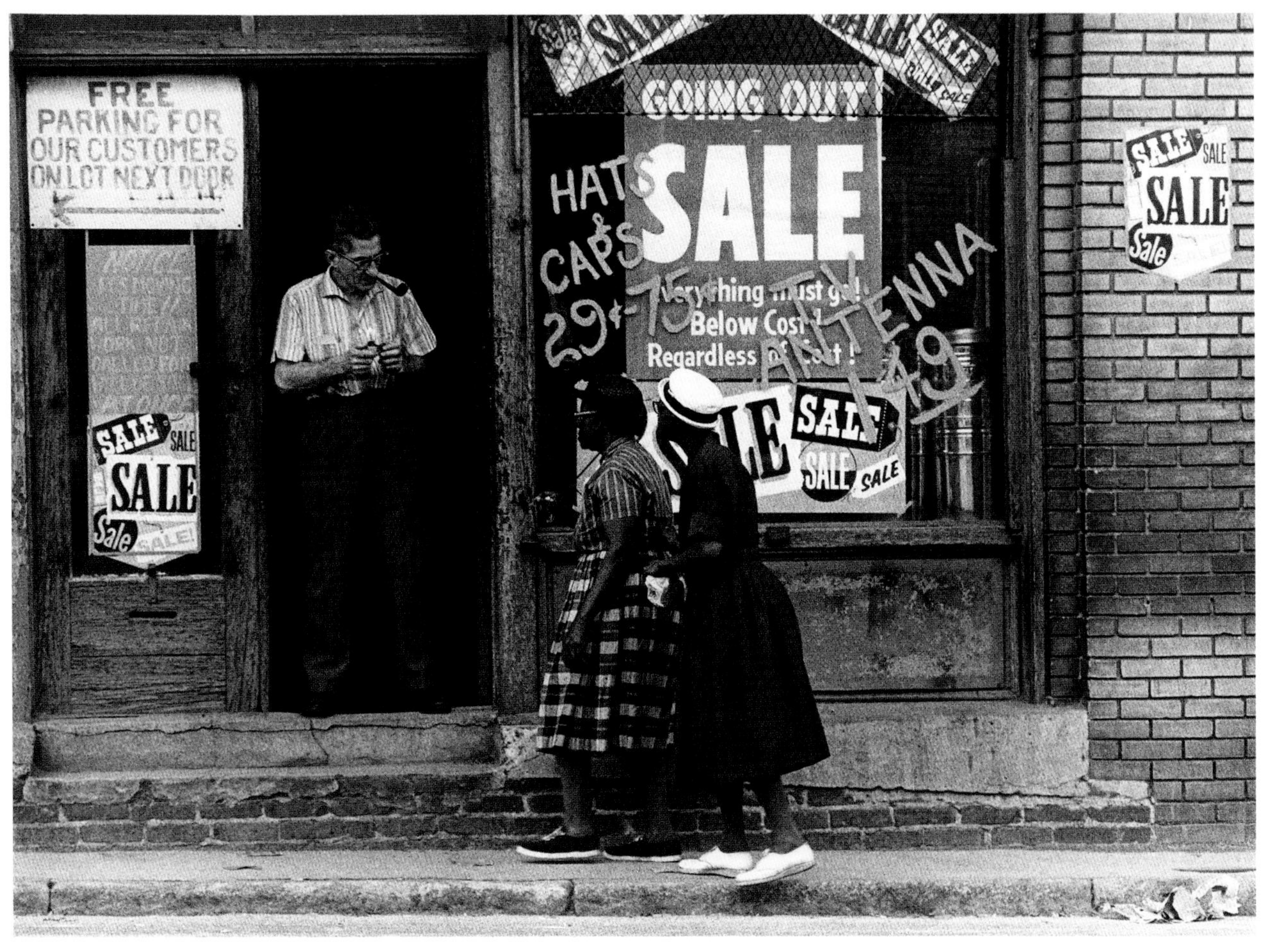

Vine City area store, Atlanta, Georgia, July 7, 1964

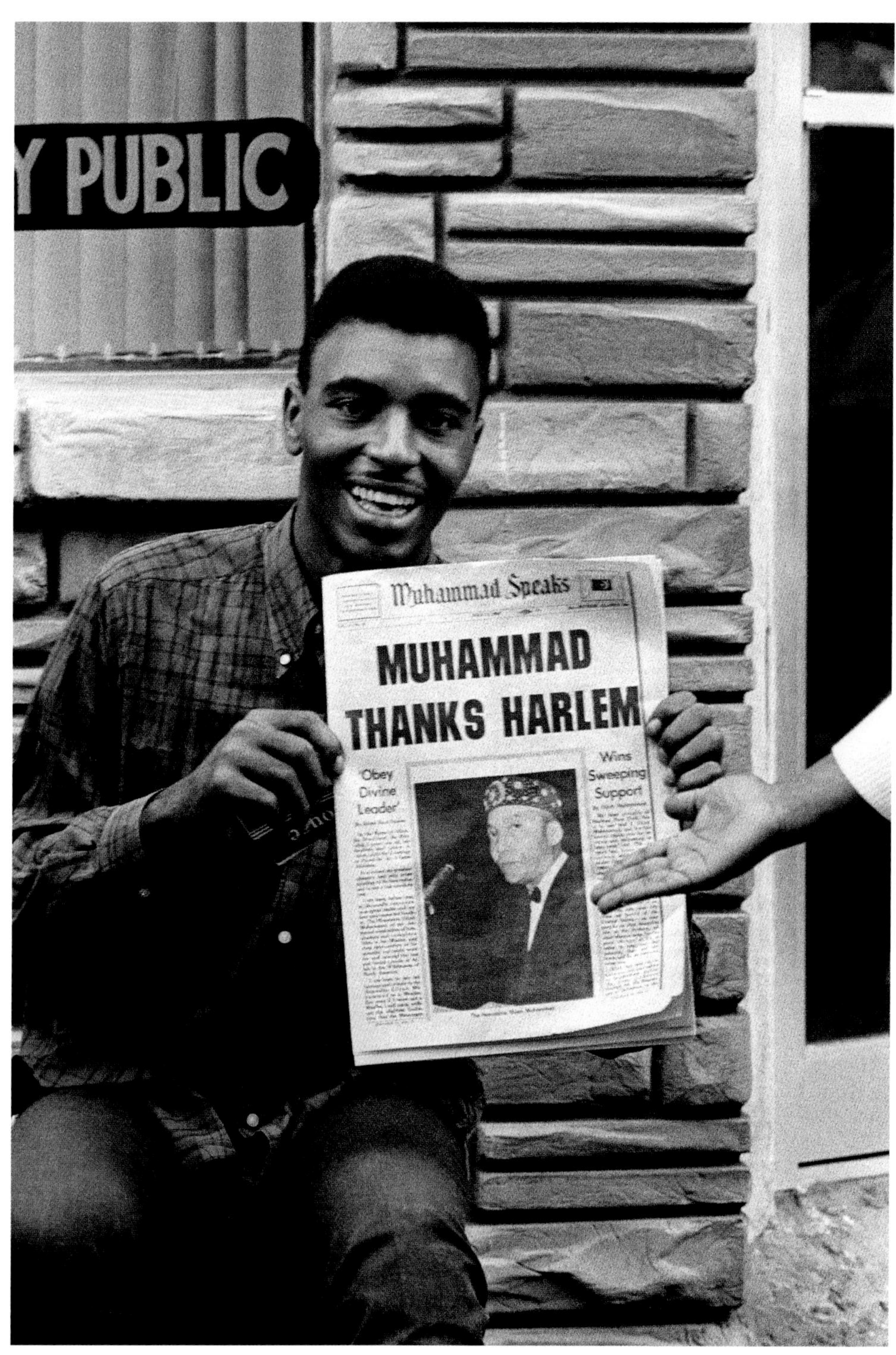

Vine City, Atlanta, Georgia, July 1964

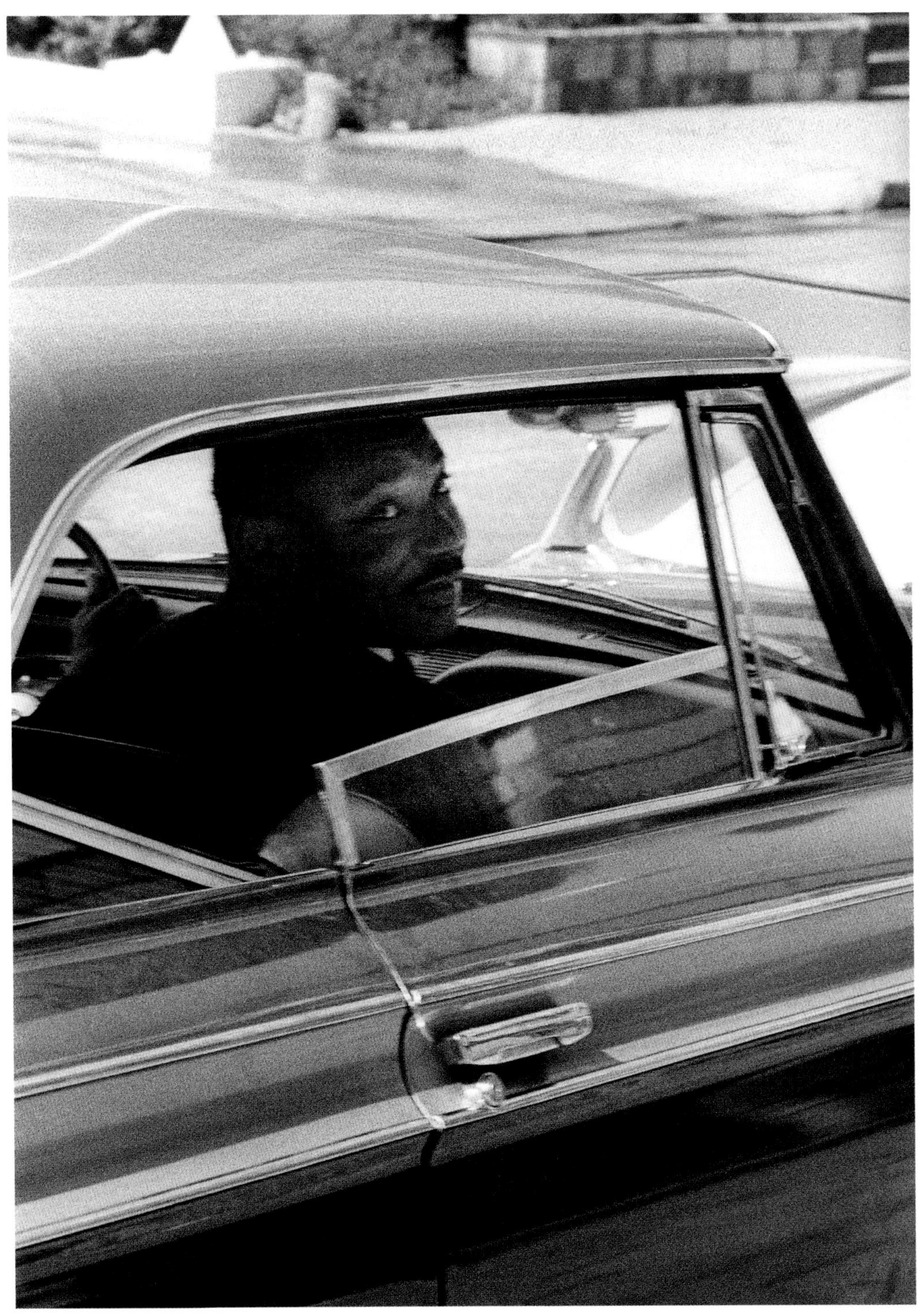

Martin Luther King Jr. outside the Southern Christian Leadership Conference (SCLC) office, Atlanta, Georgia, July 1964

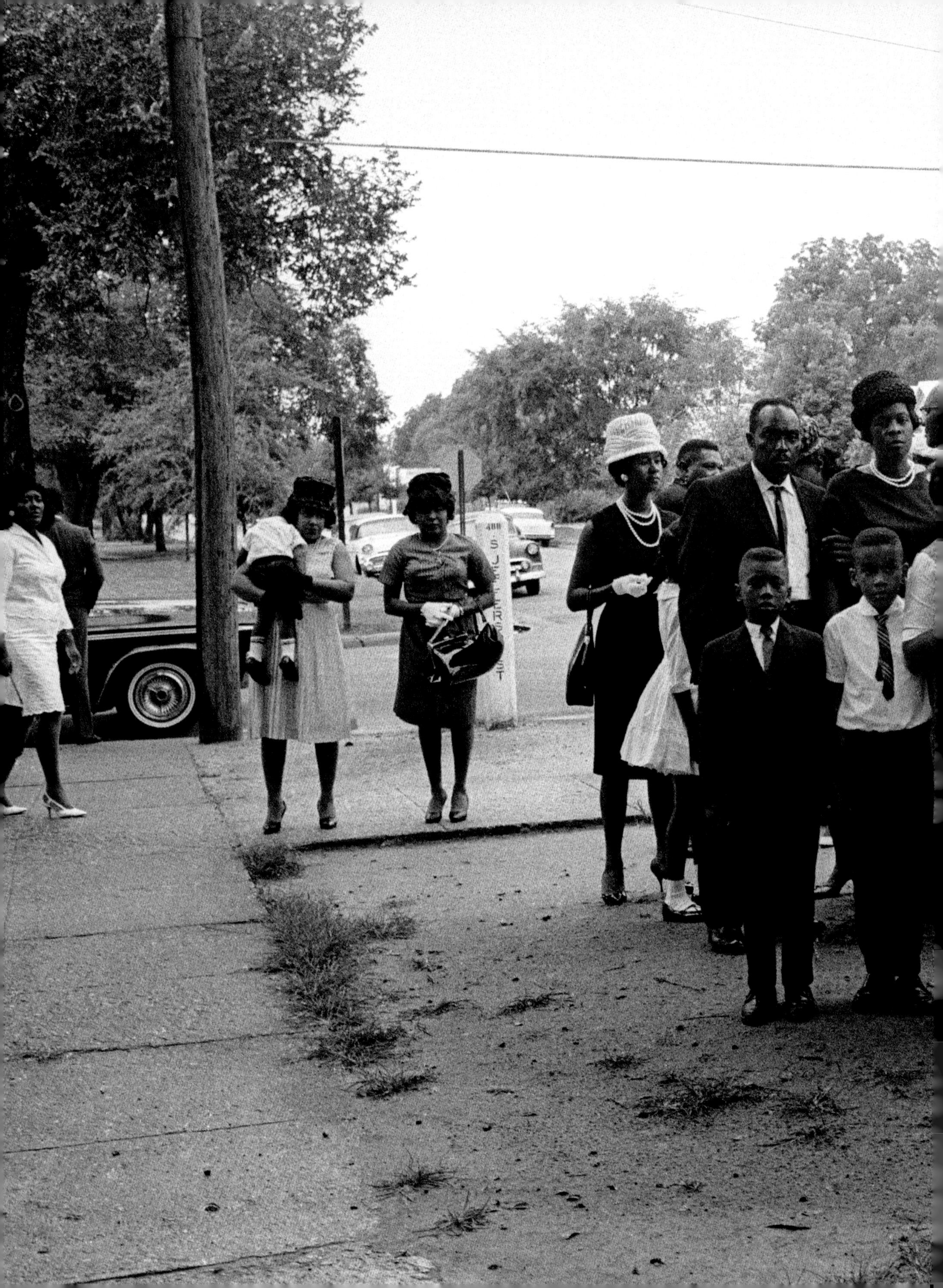
400
S JUBER ST

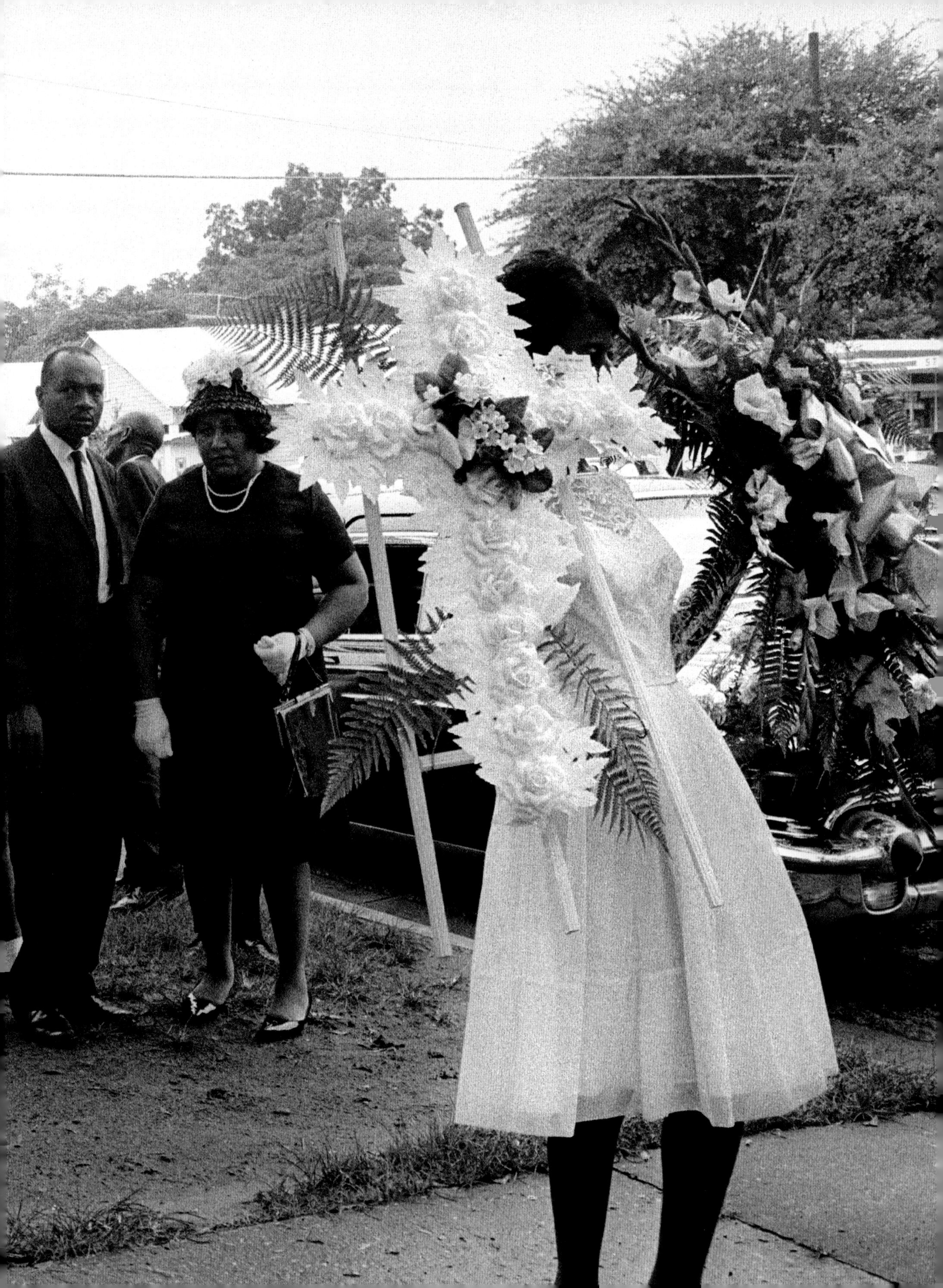

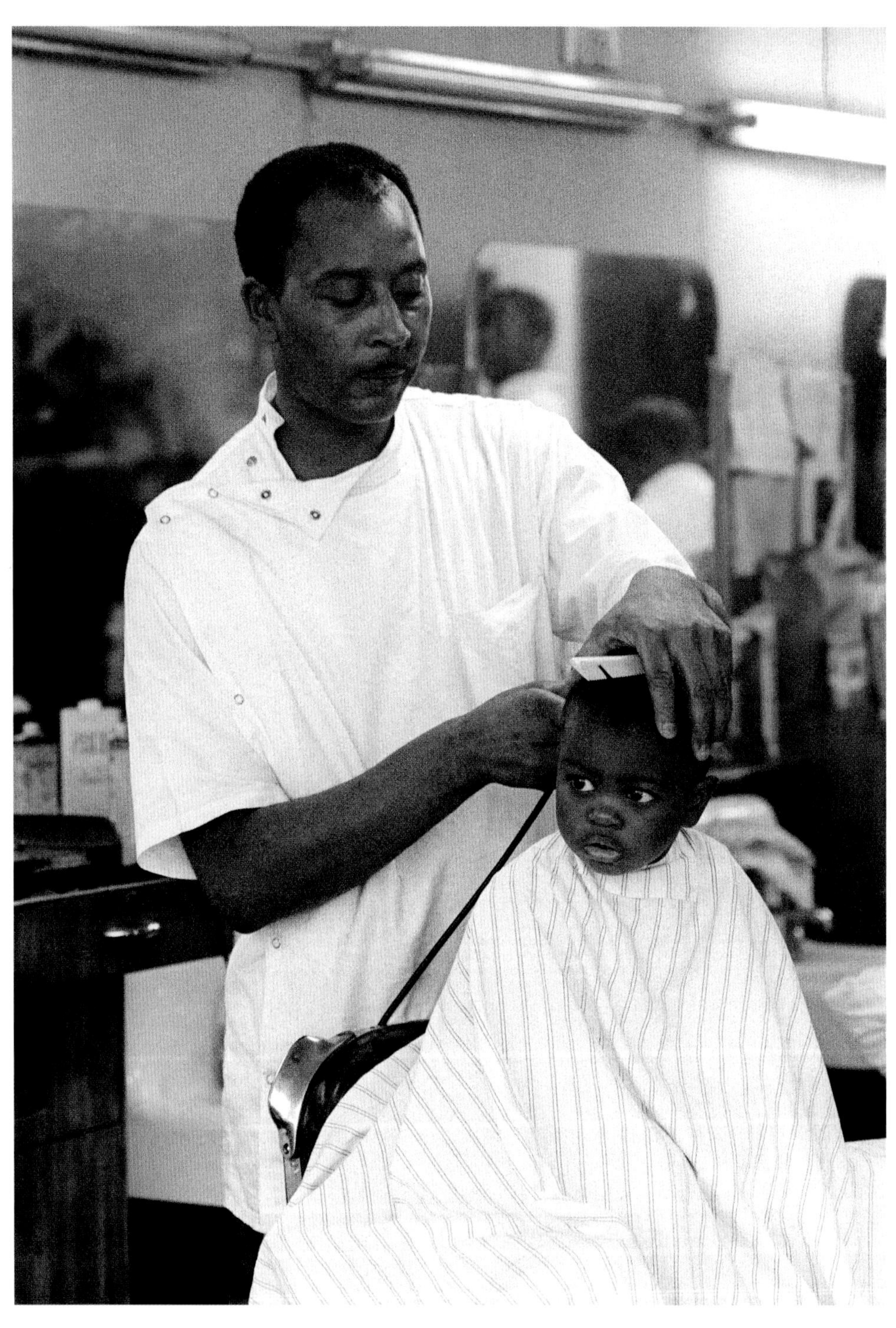

PREVIOUS SPREAD Funeral for Wilmont Jones, who was shot by police, Albany, Georgia, July 1964
Barbershop below the SNCC office, Atlanta, Georgia, July 1964

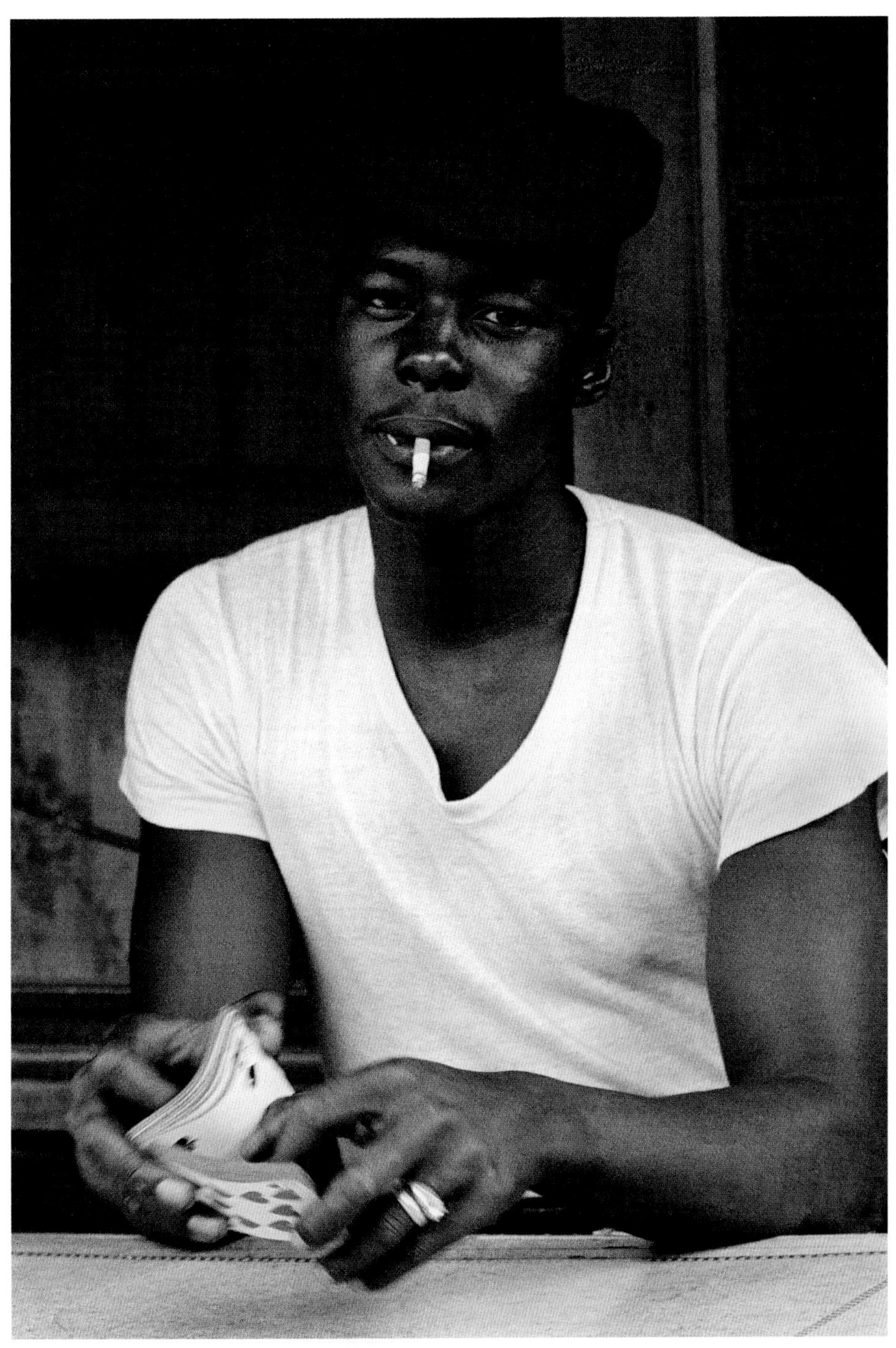

Vine City, Atlanta, Georgia, July 1964

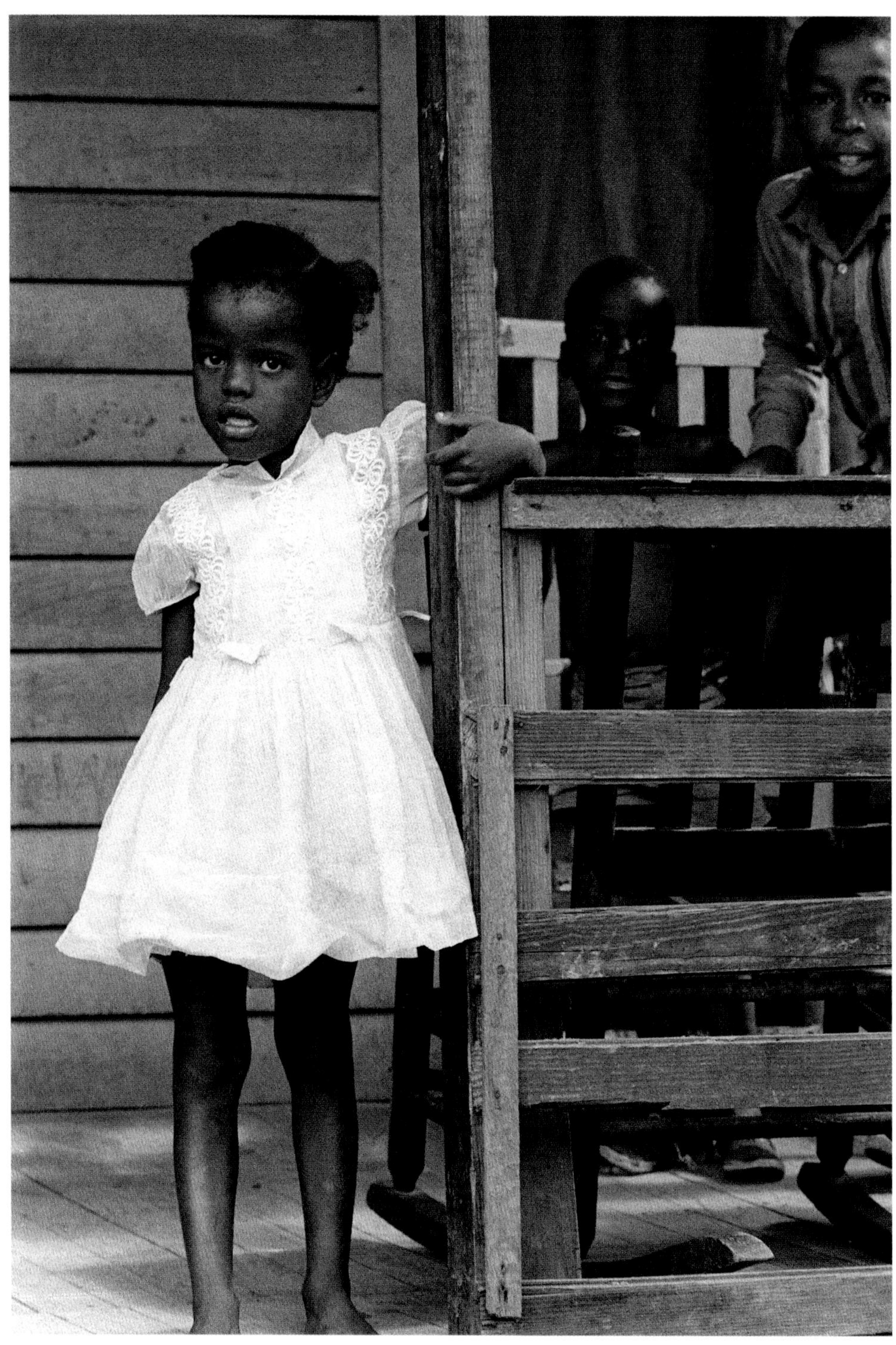

Atlanta, Georgia, July 1964

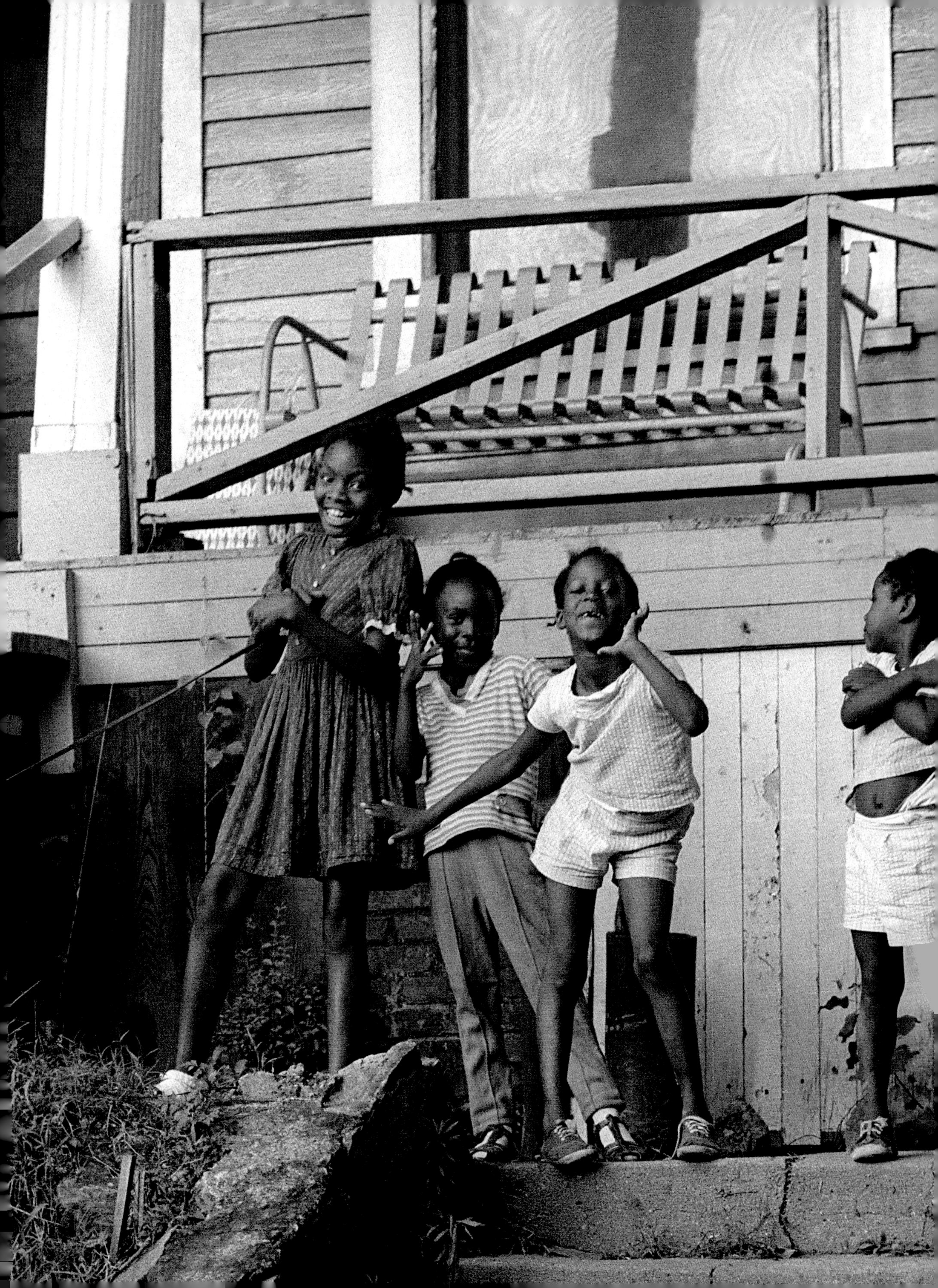

4

WE ARRIVED IN ATLANTA in the early evening and went directly to Snick headquarters. Julian and Danny went home while Forman and I climbed the stairs to the second-storey office at 8½ Raymond Street, a rather plain building clad in dirty grey stucco with a barbershop occupying the first floor.

James Forman was a big man, a gruff pipe smoker with a towering intellect that made him one of the most respected strategists in the Movement. But he was not one to suffer fools gladly, and with his arsenal of sneers, scowls and exasperated sighs, he could be quite intimidating. As a test of my worthiness, he ordered me to sweep up and take out the garbage while he finished up some work. When both our tasks were completed, he said I could spend the night sleeping on the ratty office couch. In exchange, I offered to drive him home. On the way there, he looked over at me, and in a voice dripping with scorn, he asked, "What are you, man, one of them humanitarians?" Refusing to be intimidated, I made up a nonsensical reply: "No sir, I'm a Sokuseki Buddhist," and was rewarded by perplexed silence that lasted all the way to his home.

The next morning, I was awakened by the arrival of the office staff, a fairly even mixture of Black and white students who had left their campuses in various parts of the nation to come work for Snick. I was the only Asian, but my presence wasn't particularly startling, for they were used to strange people suddenly appearing on their doorsteps, and for

Atlanta, Georgia,
July 1964

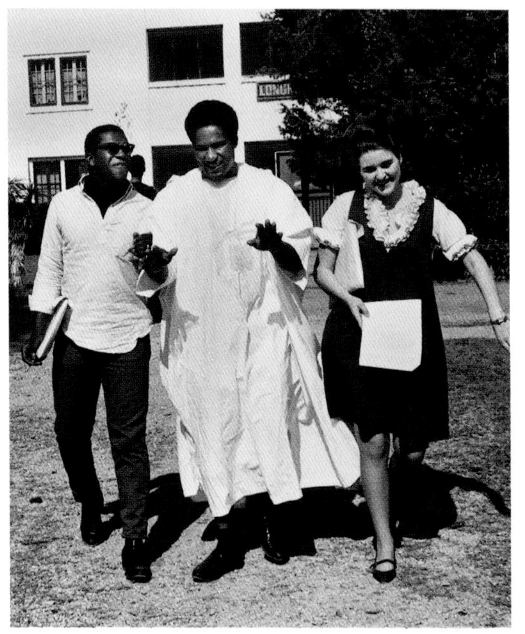

Chuck McDew,
James Forman and
Constancia Dinky Romilly
at the Waveland retreat,
SNCC staff meeting,
Waveland, Mississippi,
November 1964

the most part they were friendly and welcoming. Over the following days, I tried to make myself as useful as possible, continuing with a nightly cleanup of the office and, during the day, using my car as a delivery and chauffeur service. Snick, the youngest and smallest of the national Civil Rights organizations, was constantly in financial crisis, so my Beetle was a welcome asset. But this advantage was threatened one morning when I discovered that someone had stolen both of my front seats. Fortunately I was able to locate a set at a distant auto wrecker, and after hauling in a cardboard box filled with copies of the *Student Voice*, the Snick newsletter, to serve as a replacement seat, I started off on the long and harrowing trip. Each time I came to a stop, the box would slide forward, crushing my arms against the steering wheel, and I had to be careful accelerating because the box would slide right back. I made it to the wrecker's safely, and with the installation of the seats, I was back in business.

After about a week, Forman took pity on me and offered to put me up at the Snick apartment on Gordon Road, which was rented primarily for John Lewis and Danny Lyon, but since they were out travelling most of the time, the apartment was used more as a Freedom House for itinerant Snick field agents. I suspect part of the motivation for this kind offer was the rank odour emanating from my body after a week living in the office, which had no bathing facilities. I moved my meagre belongings into the apartment, which was furnished with only the bare necessities: a mattress on the floor, a dilapidated couch, a kitchen table with a set of rickety chairs that probably came from the Salvation Army. On the floor of one of the bedrooms was an enlarger, trays and an array of chemical bottles, which Danny would lug into the tiny bathroom to set up his makeshift darkroom. I got to spend a fair amount of time with John Lewis, who once told me he had always wanted to be a preacher, and as a boy, growing up on the farm in Pike County, Alabama, he would go out to the hen house and practice his sermons in front of the chickens. As Snick chairman, John was the public face of the organization, and in the preparation for his many speeches, I became a surrogate for the family chickens.

Snick was engaged in a massive campaign to desegregate restaurants in Atlanta's downtown core. The city jail was rapidly filling up with demonstrators and Snick office staff. More bodies were needed, so it was decided Snick would stage a mass rally on the nearby campuses of Morehouse and Spelman colleges. There was no one left in the production department to produce the necessary rally flyers, so I went in to see what I could do. I came across a powerful image, taken by Forman at an earlier sit-in, of an obese Klansman in full regalia—white sheet and tall, pointed hood—glaring menacingly out the window of a lunch counter. On the Vari-Typer, I punched out two captions in thirty-six-point bold—THE FACE OF ATLANTA and HELP CHANGE IT—and sandwiched them between the tight headshot of the Klansman. The rally was a huge success, and everybody loved the flyer. Danny Lyon thought I had a good eye that I should try to develop through photography, and he even offered to lend me his spare Nikon F mounted with the incredibly fast and razor-sharp 105 mm NIKKOR lens.

I went with Danny and some of the office staff to a sit-in at Leb's, a rather upscale restaurant in the heart of the city, and as we arranged ourselves around the corner, the enraged owner came out and screamed at us to get out. Danny went ballistic and yelled back, "How can you do this? You're a Jew like me. Don't you remember the camps? You're no better than a Nazi." It was the only time I saw Danny—who, to my mind, produced the most compelling images of the Civil Rights Movement—blow his photographic cool.

My role in Snick was expanding. Thankfully I had been excused from my janitorial duties, and although my services as a driver were still in constant demand, more and more of my time was spent in the production office helping to produce the *Student Voice* through layout, proofreading and writing the occasional article. I'd been with Snick over a month before working up the nerve to speak up at a staff meeting. I said I had limited resources to maintain myself and my car, and I didn't mind using any of it on Snick business, but lately I'd felt that people were taking advantage of me by asking me to drive them on errands that were strictly personal, like going to the hairdressers or picking up a six-pack of beer. At the end of the meeting, the executive not only instituted a business-only policy for my car but also put me on the payroll with a modest allowance for car expenses, which was a godsend,

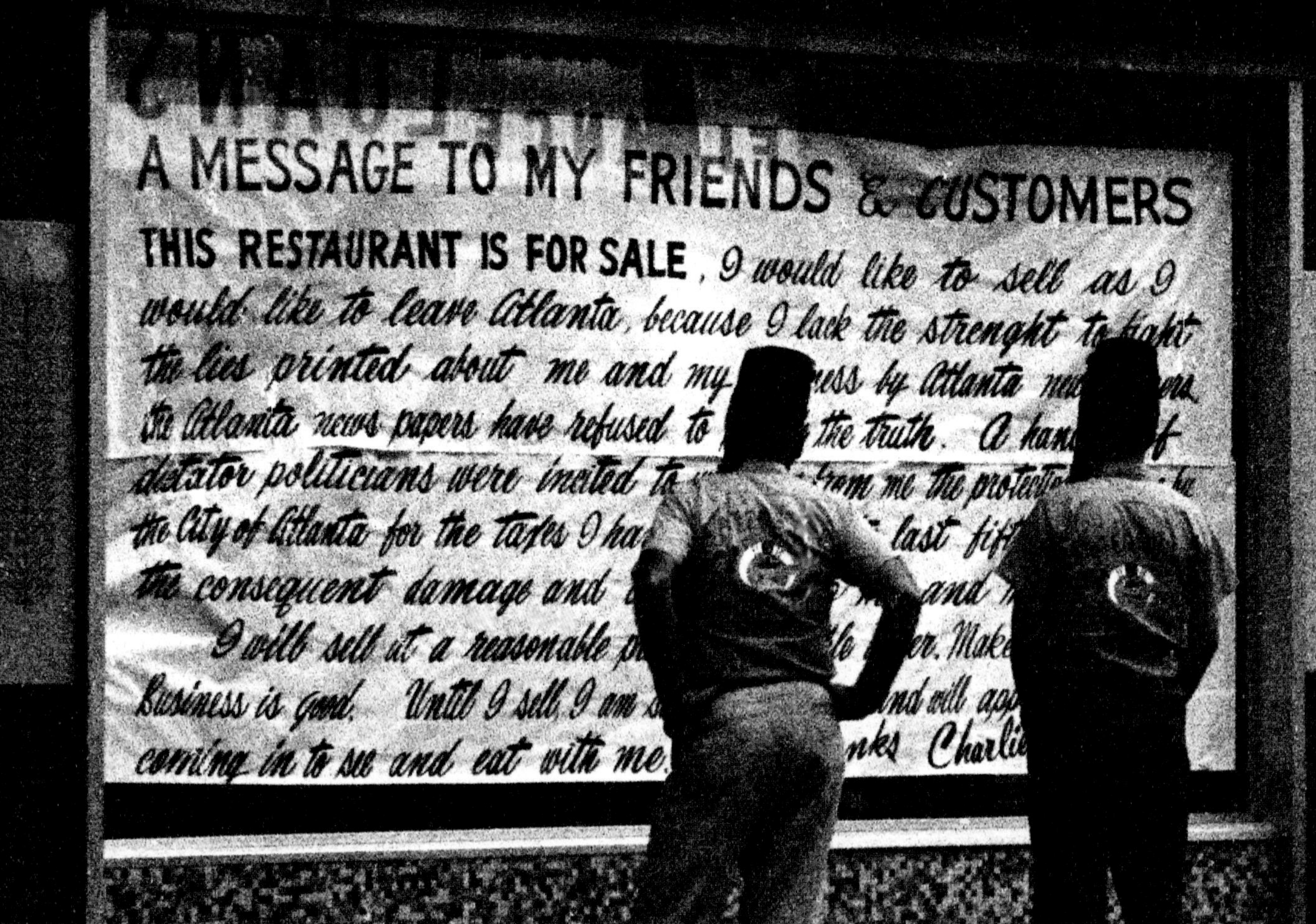

ABOVE AND FACING
Signage after SNCC sit-in at Leb's Restaurant, Atlanta, Georgia, July 1964

since the money I had earned in the summer was nearly gone. Given the chronic cash flow problem, there were occasions when the weekly stipend of twenty-five dollars couldn't be paid, but we were never in danger of starving; in lean times, local church groups would bring over buckets of tasty Southern dishes. I was now officially a Snick staff member and part of a dynamic movement that was reshaping America. It was one of my proudest moments.

In late November, I decided to return home for the holidays to finally face my mother and my older siblings, for whom I undoubtedly had caused a great deal of worry. It was a surprisingly pleasant visit, and the expected anger and harsh condemnations never materialized. Of course they were curious about my adventures and wanted to know why I had gone south to join the Movement, but I couldn't provide an answer, for I wasn't too sure myself what had brought on this sudden change.

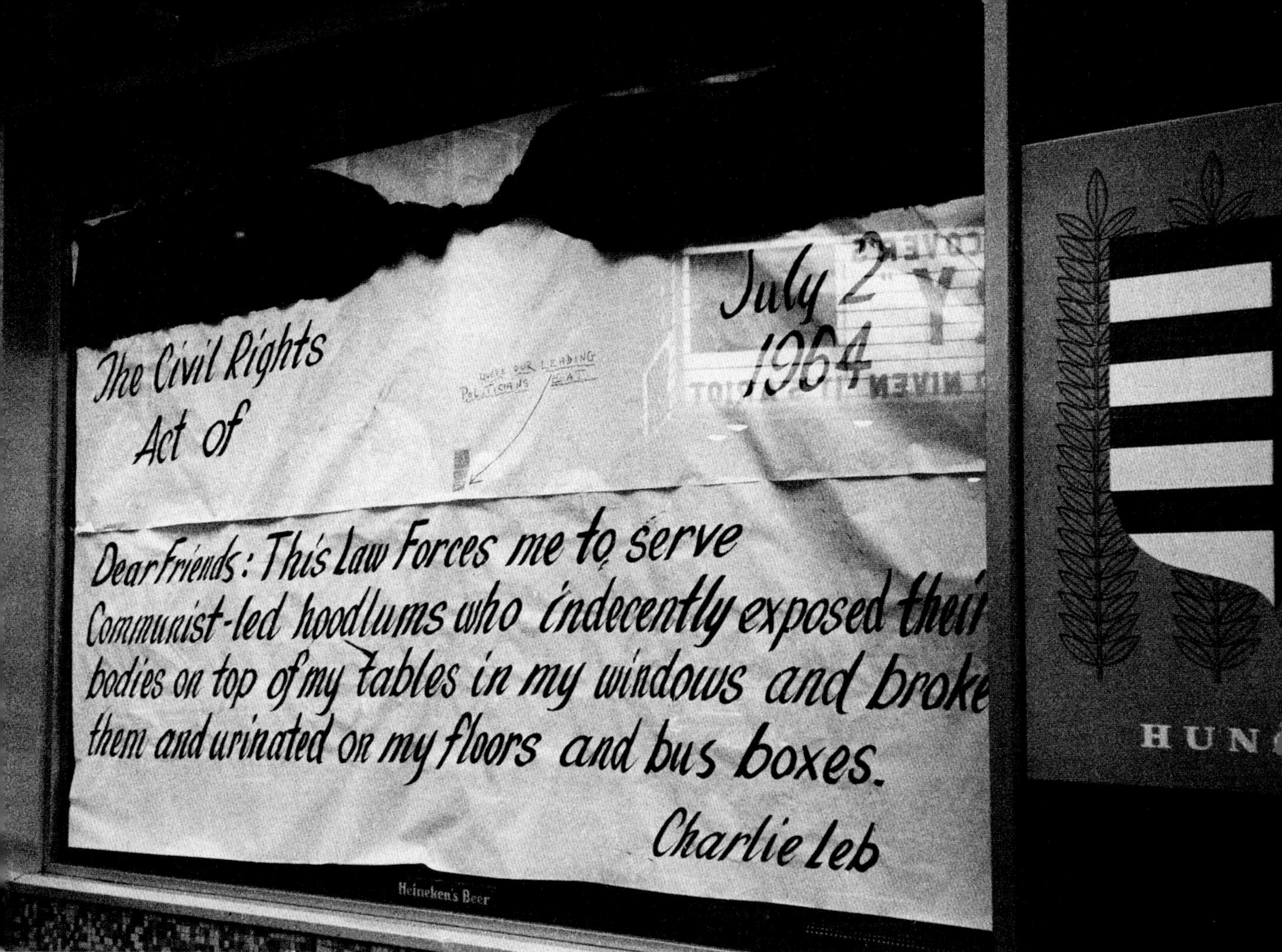

Even old Mr. Matsuda, on his yearly New Year's Day visit, opined that what I was doing was good but that I should also seriously think about my future. That seemed to be the general consensus. I think everyone thought I would soon come to my senses, finish university and go on to bring credit to our family and community.

One of my reasons for returning home was to organize Friends of Snick chapters on Canadian campuses, so before the holidays, I had driven up to London to enlist the help of some old friends at Western University. I saw Natasha. My feelings for her still ran deep, but it wasn't with the same sense of desperation and inadequacy. I still had miles to go on my journey, but I wasn't quite the same person as when we last met. With my mission accomplished, I continued north to Toronto. As I entered the city, I learned via the car radio that President Kennedy had been shot and killed in Dallas, Texas. I immediately stopped to call my

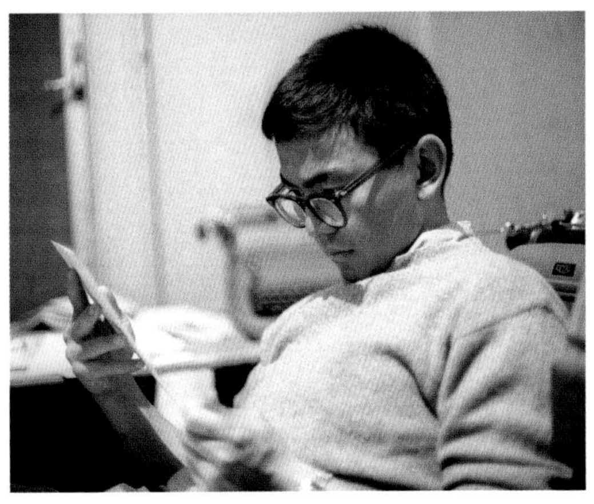

cousin Tosh and spent the rest of the day glued to her TV set. Sam Shirah, a veteran white worker from the South, once told me that he was on the campus of Ole Miss when the Kennedy assassination was announced, and the students stood up and cheered. I spent the next few days talking to members of the Student Union for Peace Action (SUPA), a national organization of political activists that was to play an important role in my future. After they agreed to do their best to support Snick, I drove to Chatham for the holiday season with my mother, and in January I headed off once again for Atlanta.

When I arrived at Snick headquarters, I found out that I was no longer the only Asian in the Movement. Ed Nakawatase, a Sansei (a child of Nisei parents; the third generation) originally from Seabrook, New Jersey, had arrived. Initially I was a bit resentful at the loss of my unique status, but he turned out to be a total delight, incredibly well-read with a wry, often hilarious world view, and we soon became good friends. Brother Ed is a shining example of Nikkei upbringing: self-effacing, courteous and scrupulously honest (a true credit to his race, as some would say). He worked with Julian in the communications office, and when we had a WATS line installed (a new service whereby we paid one flat fee for unlimited long distance calls), Brother Ed was assigned as its operator.

We had devised a system to take maximum advantage of this service: if you were James Forman in Jackson, Mississippi, you would place a person-to-person collect call to Julian Bond in Atlanta. The Snick WATS operator would say that Mr. Bond was out of office but would return the call if Mr. Forman cared to leave a number. The message would be handed to Julian, who would call Forman on the WATS line. A simple-enough system, but when Brother Ed picked up the phone, he would break out in a cold sweat, turn red and, after much hemming and hawing, thrust the phone into Julian's hand. This task was obviously too stressful for Brother Ed, who had been genetically programmed to always tell the truth. It was costing us too much money, so he was assigned other duties.

Ed Nakawatase
at the SNCC office,
Atlanta, Georgia,
October 1964

Snick's programs had expanded greatly, and to meet the new needs, we rented the adjacent building to use as a Freedom House for itinerant field agents and to house the new A.B. Dick printing press. Despite a vehement protest from the female staff—the feminist movement was still in its infancy—we converted the ladies' washroom into a darkroom. Mark Suckle, a carrot-top worker from Philadelphia, was placed in charge of the expanded production office while I took over the darkroom. Mark had never operated an offset printing press, just as I had never worked in a darkroom, but youthful confidence and a learn-as-you-go attitude were two of the larger engines that powered the Movement. Mark, Brother Ed, James Bond—Julian's rotund younger brother—and I hung out together. Whenever we received our weekly cheque, we would drive downtown to desegrated Shoney's for a fattening treat of big hamburgers, onions rings and thick milkshakes, or else we would walk around the corner from our office to Barbecue Heaven, a dingy and incredibly filthy hole-in-the-wall that served the best ribs I've ever eaten. One night we went to see the first of the Pink Panther series, with Peter Sellers as the hilarious Inspector Clouseau, and for days after we would greet each other with "Is that a minkey on your shoulder?" or else either Ed or I would suddenly leap out with a karate chop in imitation of Cato, the attack-dog Japanese houseboy.

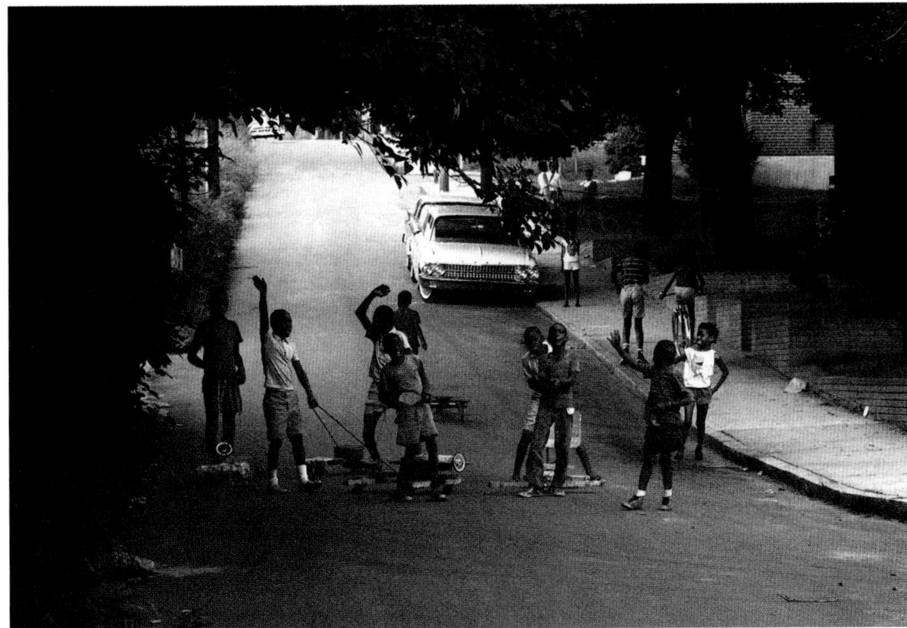

Atlanta, Georgia,
September 1964

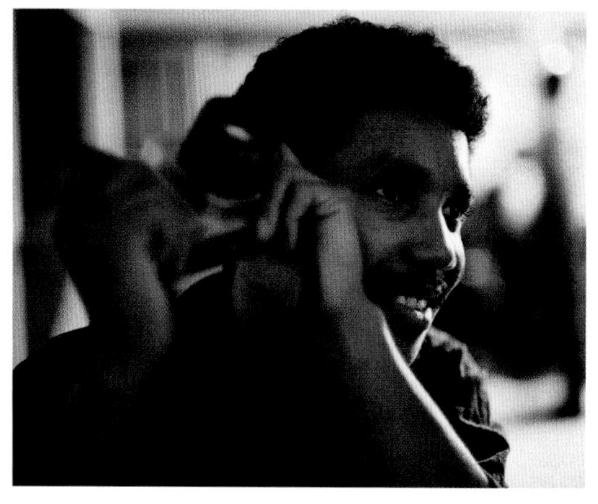

But there was little time for leisure activities since Snick was gearing up for the Freedom Summer of 1964, an ambitious program to recruit volunteers from across the country to work on a variety of initiatives in Mississippi: voter registration drives, Freedom Schools for underprivileged children, literacy programs, legal and medical services, a documentary photography project and even developmental theatre in the Delta. Although there was a desperate need for volunteers, the underlying hope was that the presence of so many students from white, middle-class families would finally force the federal government to protect Civil Rights workers who had been under constant attack by the white power structure.

Matt Herron and his gracious wife Jeannine came over from New Orleans to administer the Southern Documentary Project, whose objective was to train young photographers to record the events of the summer. An administrative, processing and distribution centre would operate out of Snick headquarters, and I was asked to stay in Atlanta. Although I was desperate to be out shooting in the field, I couldn't really say no, since priority was given to aspiring Black photographers; besides, I was the only one with any experience in the darkroom even though my knowledge was, at best, rudimentary. One of these young photographers was Bob Fletcher, a cinnamon-coloured volunteer from Detroit. When we first met, I felt an immediate affinity with this gentle soul, not only because of his grace but also because he was of the same diminutive stature as myself. As his wife Marilyn once said, we were like two yellow peas in a pod.

In preparation for the summer, Snick held a weekend retreat at the lovely, isolated campus of Tougaloo College, nestled in the rich farmlands outside of Jackson, Mississippi. On the final day of the retreat, we crowded into a hot auditorium to hear a chilling tale from the Reverend Ed King, a white minister at the college and a veteran of the Civil Rights Movement. As a white man fighting for a Black cause, he was especially hated by the Klan, which had placed him near the top of their hit list. One night he was driving his two guests, visiting professors from a university in India, back to their hotel in Jackson. Just as he cleared the

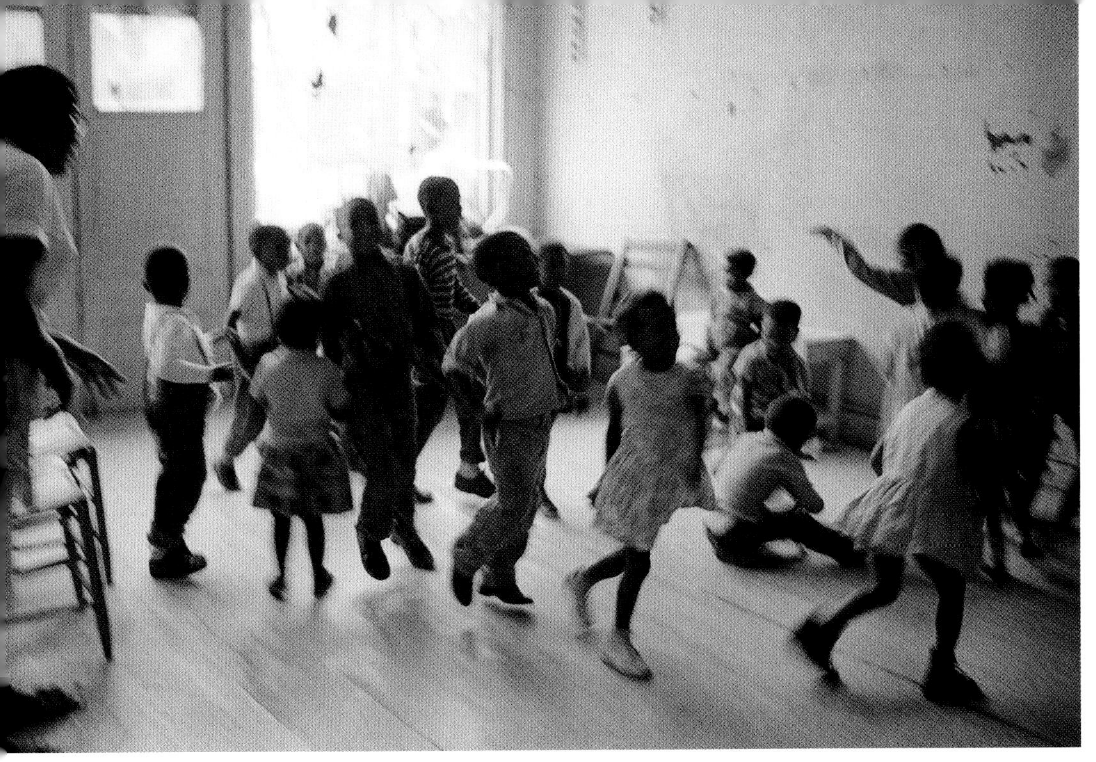

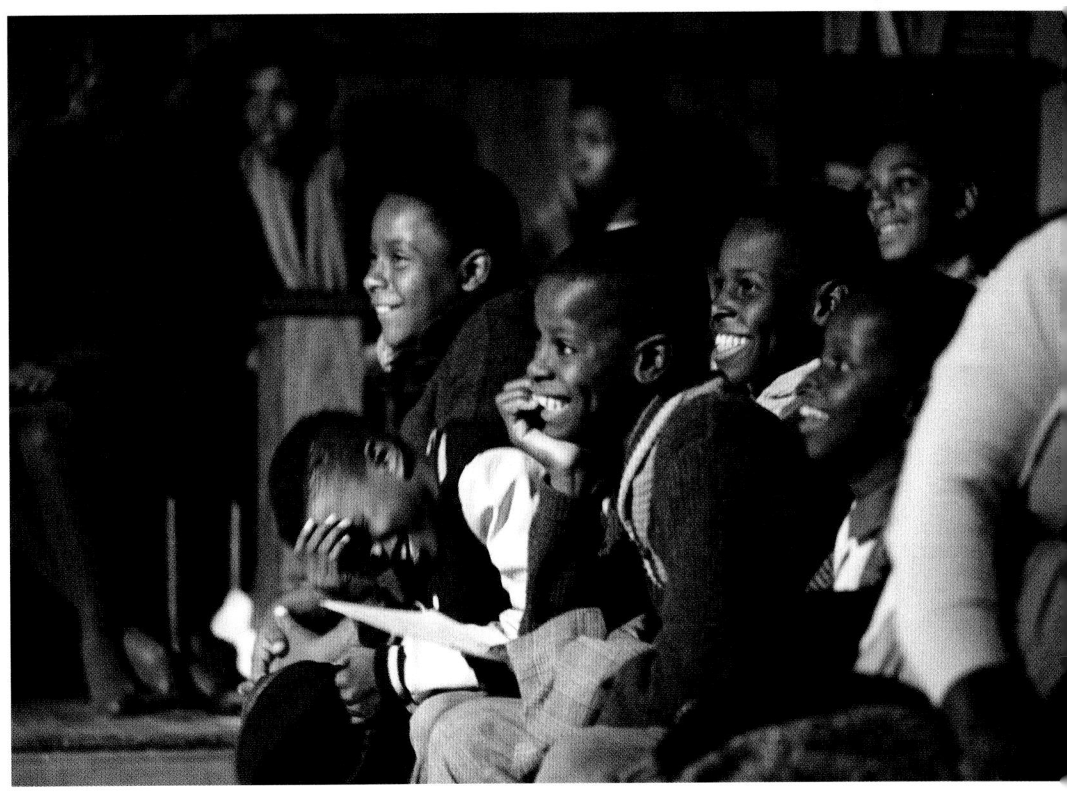

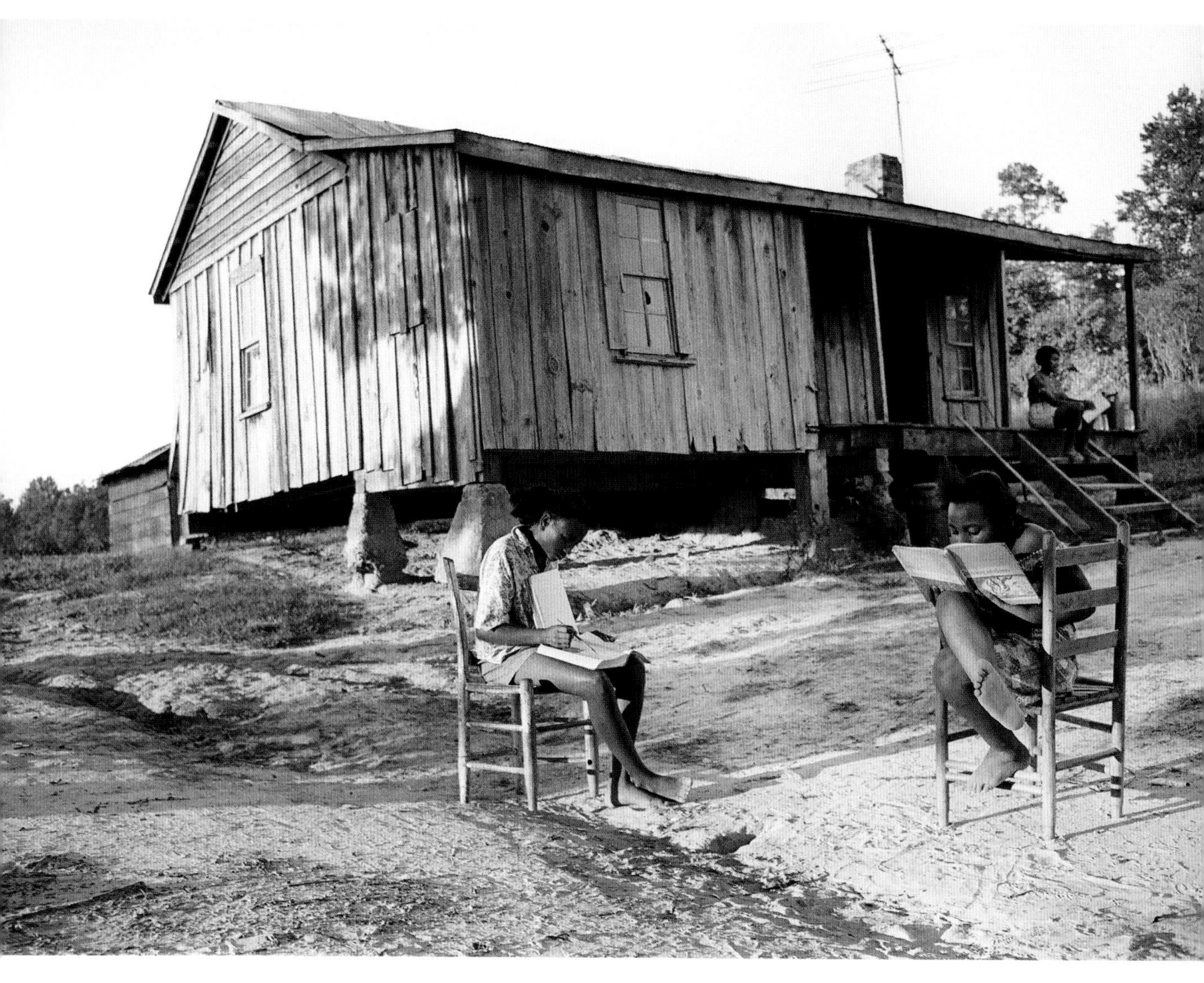

campus gates, he was forced to stop when two pickup trucks suddenly appeared out of the darkness. The triumphant Klansmen in the trucks, brandishing a variety of weapons, ordered the "n***** lover" out of the car. Rev. King had spent enough time in the South to know that his life was about to end, but just as he reached for the door handle, a heavily accented but distinct voice piped out from the back seat, "I want all of you to know that I and my colleague are guests of your American State Department, and if any harm is done to us, my government will lodge an immediate protest. To avoid international embarrassment, your government will be forced to use every resource to hunt you down and bring you to justice." This warning was met by further verbal abuse, but just as the Klansmen were about to force the men from the car, one Klansman interjected with a cautionary note. After much argument, that one dissenting voice of reason—or perhaps greater cowardice—won out, and Rev. King and his guests were allowed to continue on their way.

The retreat ended on that horrific note, and we piled into our cars to head back to work. In my car that day were myself, Bob Fletcher, Betty Garmen—a tall, white Snick office staffer who always reminded me of a librarian—and Prathia Hall—a beautiful, robust Black woman from Philadelphia who, as rumour had it, was the inspiration for Martin Luther King Jr.'s "I Have a Dream" speech. We were a veritable United Nations on wheels, which made us potential targets in a white Mississippi that was bracing for the onslaught of "outside agitators." I must have been distracted by the potential danger and the resonances of Rev. King's story, for I inadvertently turned onto an exit ramp for the freeway and, as luck would have it, almost collided with a state police patrol car. The officer told me to pull over and get out of the car. I jumped out and Fletcher, who was sporting a modest Afro, exited from the passenger side to provide moral support, but the officer shouted, "Hey fuzzy head, get your Black ass back in the car." Mindful of Rev. King's story, I was determined to push my foreign status for all it was worth, and when I reached the officer, I said, "I'm really sorry sir, it was a dumb mistake, but as a foreigner I'm not used to your road system. Here is my driver's licence from Ontario, Canada, and my registration, also from Ontario, Canada." All during my litany of Canada this and foreign that, he refused to look up from his writing of the citation. Finally his eyes lifted, and after a long, menacing stare, he asked, "What are you, boy?" I replied, "Officer, I am a foreign correspondent, and this is my press card from the *London Free Press* in Ontario, Canada" (an outdated souvenir from a summer job two years ago). With an exasperated sigh, he again asked, "No, boy, I mean, what are you?" I knew what he was getting at, so I replied, "Well, officer, I am a Canadian citizen of Japanese descent." After a dismissive grunt, he said, "You a Jap, eh? I thought we got rid of all you sons of bitches in the last big war. Now you get back in that little car and follow me." I dutifully obeyed, and we started to get really nervous when he turned onto a side road and started to drive into the dreaded backcountry. After eating his dust for a few miles, we stopped in front of a modest house where a woman, who we assumed was his wife, was waving to him from the doorway. He went in, and for a brief moment we discussed hightailing it out of there, but I knew he would hear our car pulling away. In a chase, my puny four cylinders would be no match for his big V8, and I didn't want to give him any excuse to reach for the heavy artillery mounted on his gun rack. After about five minutes, he came back, and we resumed our journey. It finally ended at the nearest courthouse, where a judge fined me an exorbitant amount. As we were leaving, he said, "Canada, eh? I hear it's a beautiful country. Sure would like to visit there someday. Y'all come back soon, ya hear?" I went out the door, muttering to myself, "My friend, I would love to get you alone on my home turf." The atmosphere in our car was quite subdued on our drive back to Atlanta.

Freedom Summer '64 was rapidly approaching. In Mississippi the campaign would be under the aegis of the Council of Federated Organizations, but manned primarily by Snick and Congress of Racial Equality (CORE) staff. The recruiting campaign had proved successful with nearly a thousand volunteers already signed up—three-quarters of them were white and half were women. In mid-June we drove up to the bucolic campus of the Western College for Women in Oxford, Ohio, for a two-week orientation session to prepare volunteers for their entry into the South. With Snick and CORE workers playing the role of brutal policemen or violent rednecks, mock sessions of sit-ins or courthouse confrontations were staged to train volunteers in the techniques of non-violence. We knew that Mississippi was going to turn into a war zone, so Snick set up a photo booth in a small room on campus, and over the course of the orientation session, with a Nikon specially rigged to hold a one hundred feet of Tri-X film, we made sure to take an ID mug shot of everyone who would be going south.

At the midpoint in the orientation session, after the first group of volunteers had left by bus for Mississippi, we received news that three civil

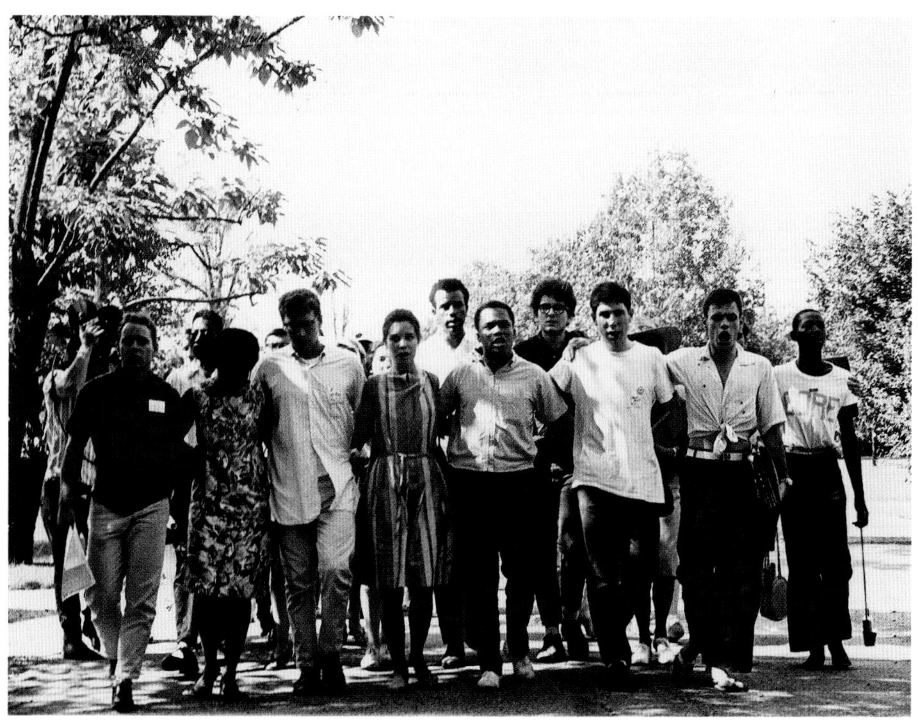

rights workers were reported missing in Neshoba County. After a desperate search, the local project members discovered that Deputy Sheriff Cecil Ray Price had arrested the three while they were driving in their blue Ford station wagon. They were then taken to the jail in the nearby town of Philadelphia, fined twenty dollars for speeding and released later that evening. They hadn't been heard from since, and when a blue Ford station wagon was pulled from a swamp outside of Philadelphia two days later, we knew they were dead.

Back in Oxford, Ohio, news of the missing workers cast a pall over the orientation session. None felt the loss more deeply than Bob Moses. He spent that morning sitting silently on the cafeteria steps, staring into space. Later that day, he spoke at a hastily called staff meeting.

Bob began to speak, and you had to listen carefully, for he always spoke slowly and ever so softly with never a hint of bombast. His words, punctuated by long moments of silence, came even more slowly that day, as he agonized over their moral right to send so many good young people into the killing zone of Mississippi. Into the last of his silences, a voice, like a pebble dropped into a still pond, began to sing, and soon everyone in the room joined hands and added their voices to the

Solidarity march
after learning of three
missing and presumed
slain Civil Rights
workers in Mississippi,
Oxford, Ohio,
June 22–27, 1964

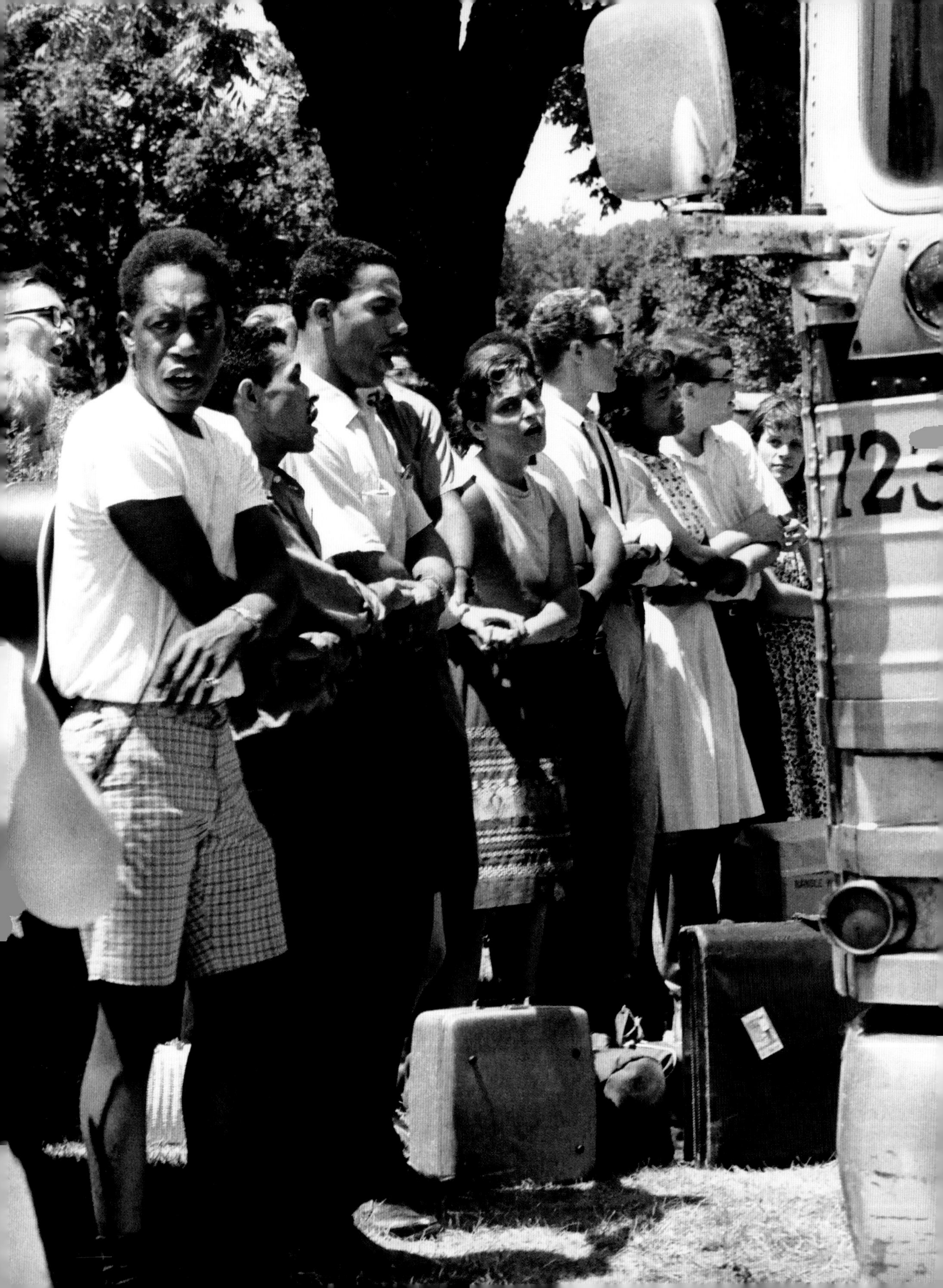

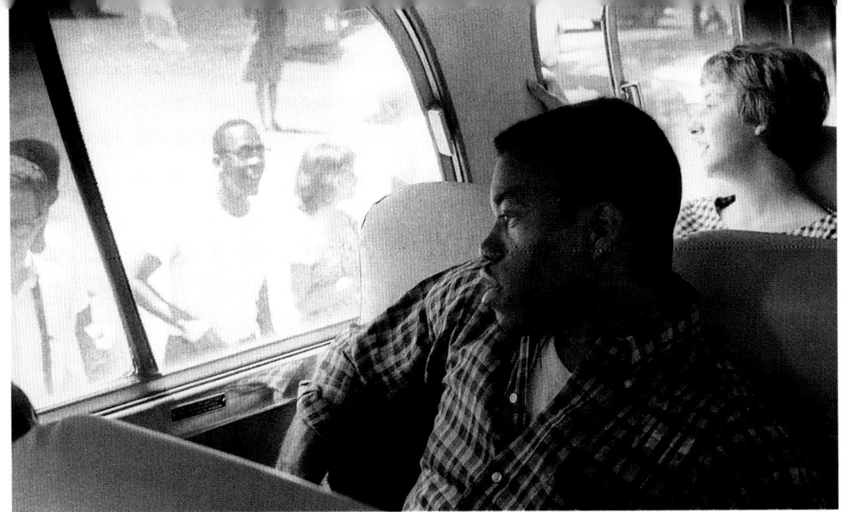

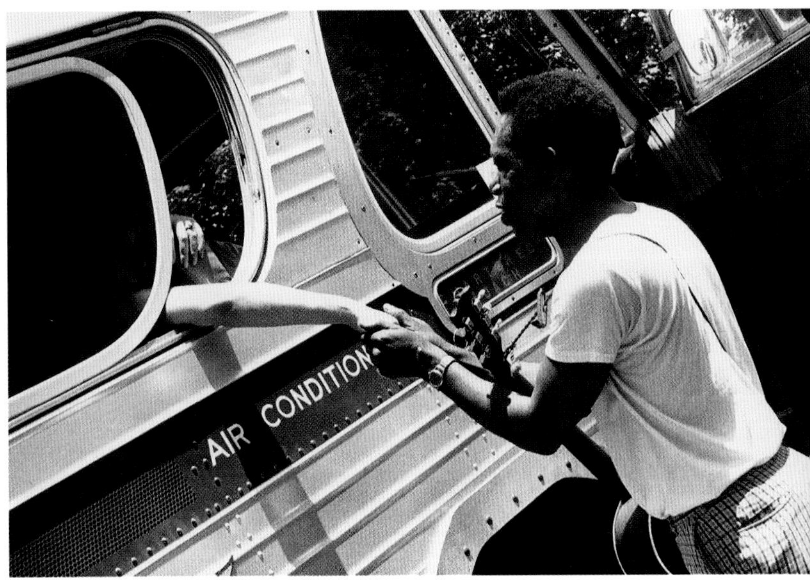

Movement anthem "We Shall Overcome." We went out the door, and with arms linked, marched down the tree-lined pathway redolent with the green scent of spring, singing "We shall not, we shall not be moved…" Mississippi Freedom Summer would continue on.

Bob Moses was the Snick director of operations in Mississippi. In 1961 Moses, a twenty-six-year-old native of Harlem with a degree in philosophy from Harvard, went into Mississippi to help the local community in the Delta town of Cleveland. Despite numerous beatings, jailings and shootings, he and other Snick workers had managed to establish several Freedom Schools. Sneaking in and out of plantations, often in the dead of night, they had even mounted an effective voter registration drive. Like his namesake, Moses had begun to lead some of the most lethal

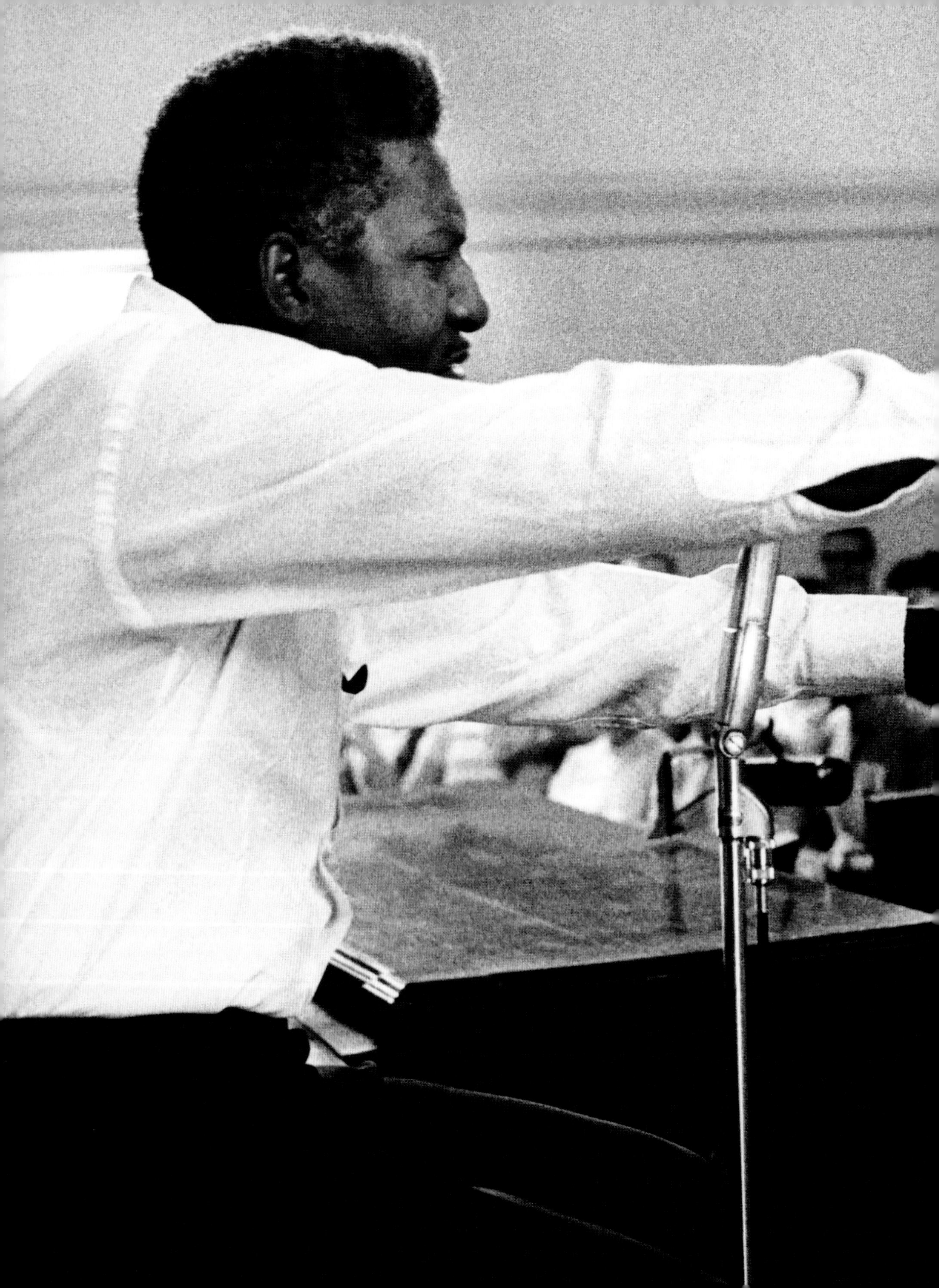

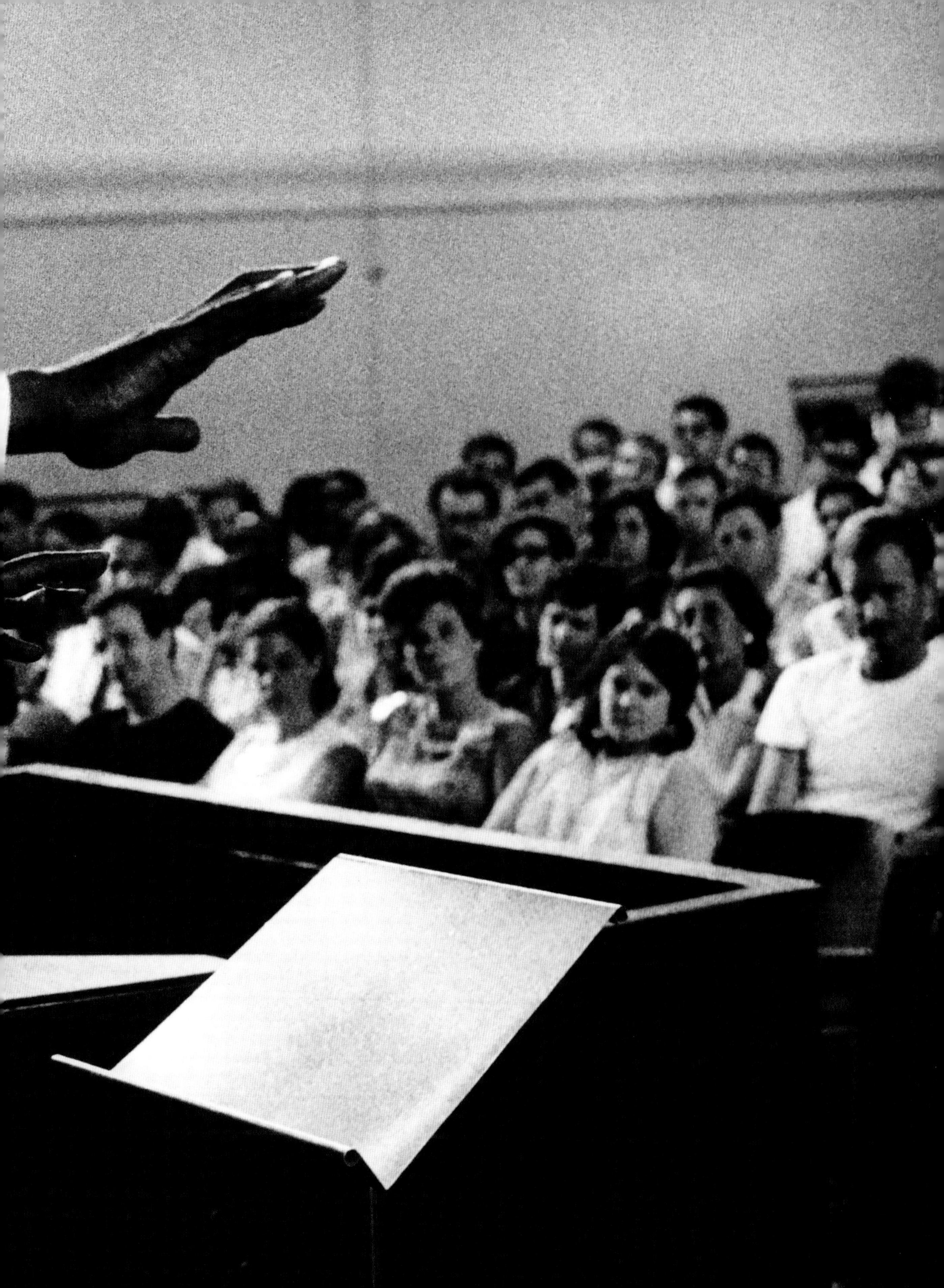

counties of the southern Black Belt out of the wilderness of segregation. Within the broad Civil Rights Movement, Snick had often been criticized for their youthful intemperance, but no one could deny their courage, and to these tough, battle-scarred veterans of Snick, Bob Moses was a god. Physically he was nondescript—average height with a slightly stocky build—but what distinguished Bob were his eyes: large, bright, ever curious, with a prodigious intelligence shining through his thick glasses. There was an undeniable spiritual presence to the man, and of all the remarkable people I met in the Movement, Bob Moses has left the most lasting impression.

I spent most of that summer in Atlanta sweltering in that claustrophobic darkroom, which was neither ventilated nor air-conditioned. In the heat of summer, my chemical solutions, which I painstakingly cooled to the appropriate sixty-eight degrees, would jump an alarming ten degrees before the end of the film run. At night, in the dimness of the safelight, I could hear rats scampering around my feet. The worst time I can remember was one hot afternoon when James Peacock, a native Mississippian, came in to cook up a pot of chitlins in the adjacent Freedom House. The smell of this Southern staple was like someone had dumped the contents of an outhouse into the darkroom. The vile smell lingered for days. To add to my misery, I felt estranged from all the new people coming in and out of the Snick office, and there were one or two I grew to positively loathe. The only real exception was Jeannine Herron, a lovely Quaker woman, who did her best to ease my darkest moods.

I leaped at every opportunity to get out of Atlanta. On one occasion, I went with Danny Lyon to southwest Georgia to cover the election campaign of C.B. King, a lawyer in Albany and a Civil Rights leader who was running for the 2nd district congressional seat. There was to be a rally for him in Americus, and on arrival we went straight to the courthouse to apply for press accreditation. After Danny filled out the application, he looked up and pointed to a poster hanging on the wall that showed a group of Black men playing poker. Underneath the table, the man on the left is shown passing an ace, sandwiched between his toes, to his accomplice. With a big smirk on his face, Danny said, "Hey Tom, look at that—ain't that just like them n******." I was shocked until I realized that I had just received my first lesson on how to survive as an undercover agent for the Movement. The lesson didn't take too well, for later, outside the courthouse, I turned my camera on a group of white men standing outside a fire hall. Threatening to shove the camera up "where the sun

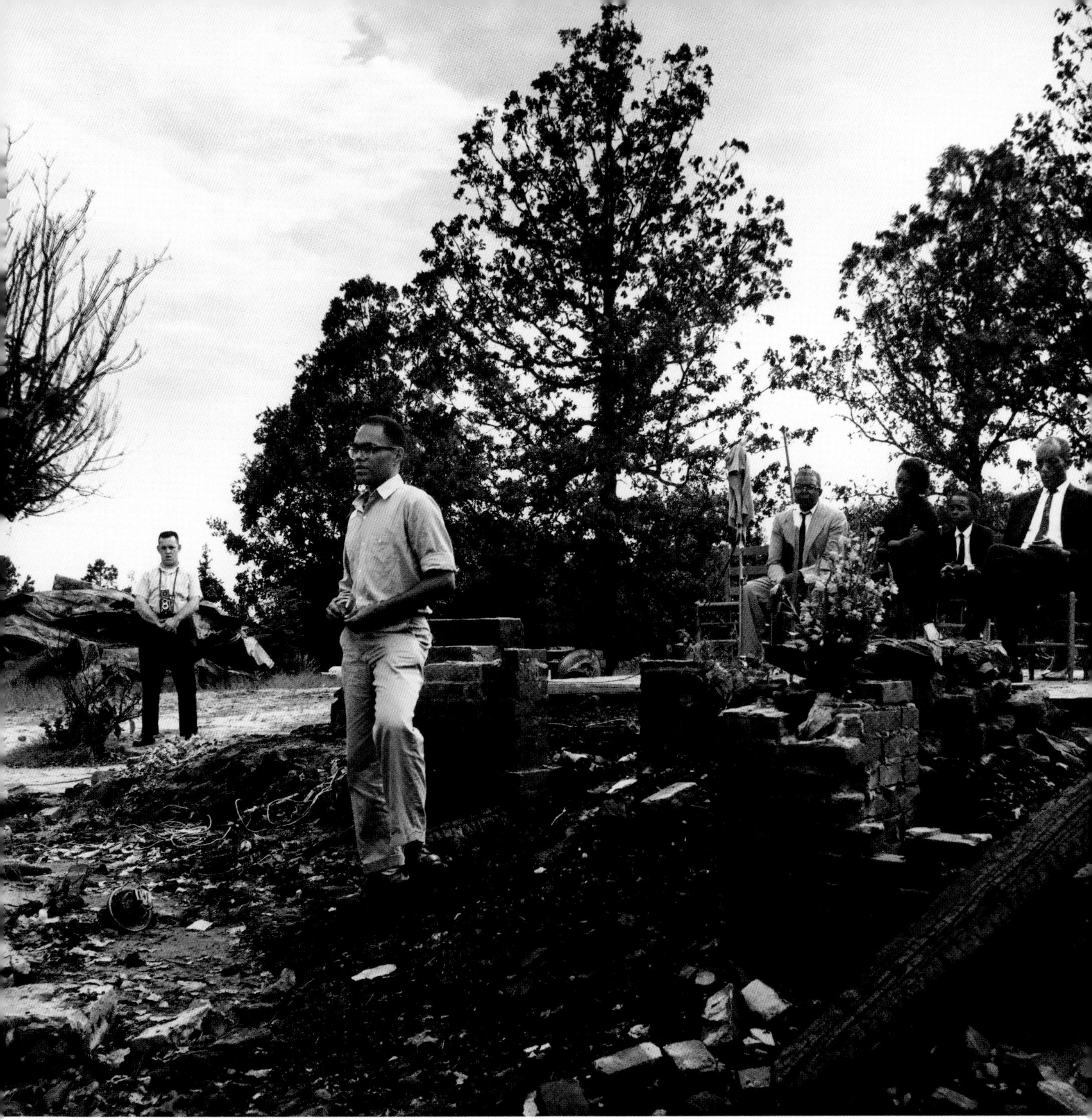

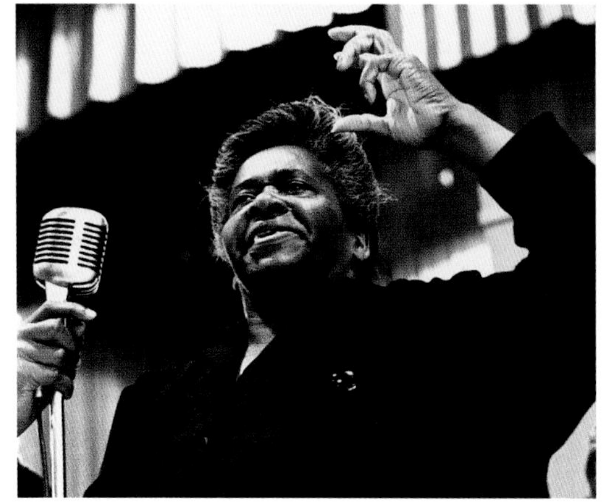

don't shine," they pushed me around, but I managed to escape without any real damage.

In early August, I managed to sneak away for my first real visit to Mississippi. I went first to Jackson to meet up with Fletcher, who was living in a rental house used as a base by Bob, Cliff Vaughs—an edgy volunteer from California—and other Snick photographers.

Unfortunately, Cliff was there when I arrived, and he took every opportunity to show that I was not wanted. We had never clashed, but it was evident he had a low opinion of me, probably because I was the antithesis of the super-cool freedom fighter, an image that he took great pains to cultivate. I always sensed that Cliff had a huge chip on his shoulder and a desperate need to prove himself. That attitude often provoked violence, which resulted in a needless waste of costly equipment and was, I felt, an abnegation of his responsibilities as a Movement photographer. Fortunately, Cliff left after a day, and I had a good time with Bob visiting the nearby projects. We caught a fish in the Mississippi River and kept it alive in our bathtub long enough to hold a mock trial. We found the fish guilty and ate it for supper along with some raw oysters, my first taste of this heavenly delicacy. I wanted to see the Delta, so I drove north, and once I had passed through a tunnel of green on a narrow dirt road overgrown with kudzu vine, an invasive plant imported from Japan, I got my first glimpse of the Black Belt. I fell immediately in love with the beauty of this land, with is fields of black, rich soil stretching endlessly into the horizon. I felt at home in the Delta, for its flat landscape was much like the land of my boyhood days. I passed the home of a sharecropper and stopped to take a picture. Peering through my wide-angle lens, the simple structure, with its time-worn wood, seemed not to be of human design but rather just another outgrowth of the fertile soil. I wondered when the human seeds had been planted to sprout the people of the Delta, their dark tonality blending seamlessly with these fields of cotton that had been worked since the days of slavery.

I continued on to the project in Ruleville, home of the indomitable Fannie Lou Hamer, and there I learned that the FBI had bulldozed an earthen dam southwest of Philadelphia (Mississippi) and uncovered the bodies of the missing Civil Rights workers. James Chaney, a local Mississippian and CORE field worker, had been badly beaten and shot repeatedly. Michael Schwerner, a Jew from Brooklyn and a veteran CORE field secretary, was killed with a single bullet, as was Andy Goodman, a new white volunteer from Queens College. These three were the first victims of Freedom Summer '64. I drove down to attend a memorial service for James Chaney held in the ruins of a bombed-out church outside of Philadelphia, and I can still picture Ben Chaney, James' younger brother who must have been about ten years old, standing amid the debris, dressed smartly in a dark suit and speaking passionately of the love for his big brother. He vowed to continue to fight for the cause that had taken his life. I can also picture Bob Moses sitting forlornly on a foundation stone until an old woman walked over to take his hand.

I had to get back to Atlanta; my work was piling up and I was anxious to see the images that I had taken. The next morning, I was preparing my first film run when Julian came down to ask me to look after an urgent matter. A support group in New York hadn't received their shipment of Snick promotional material that was needed for a big fundraising event scheduled for that same night. I put together a new package and drove it out to the express freight office at the Atlanta International Airport. As

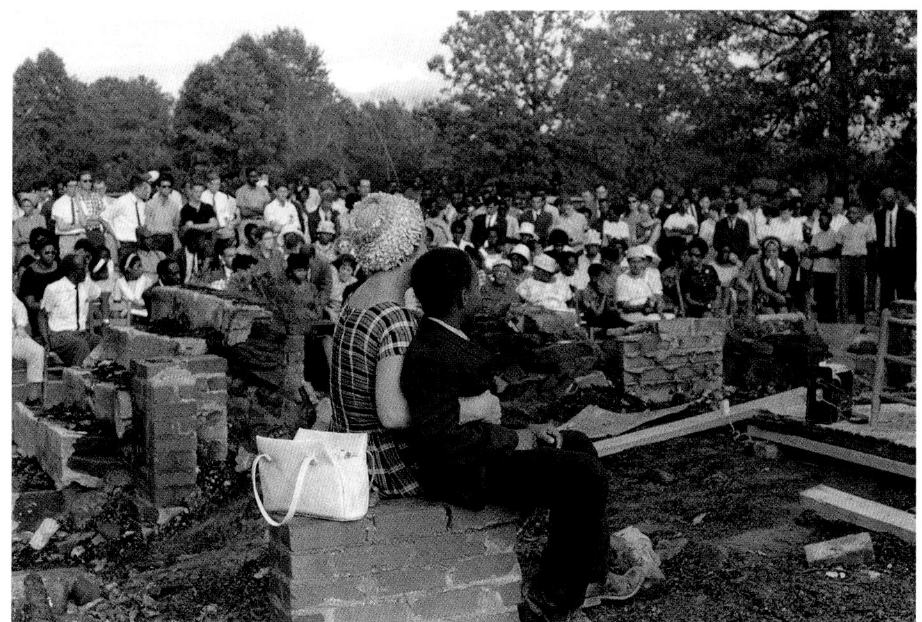

James Chaney's memorial service at the burned ruins of Mount Zion Methodist Church [with his brother Ben Chaney in the foreground], near Philadelphia, Mississippi, August 21, 1964

I was filling out the waybill, I explained to the kindly silver-haired clerk the urgency of my mission. "I think," he said, "our truck mighta already left to take a load out to the next flight to New York, which leaves in about a half an hour, but if I hurry, I might be able to catch up to it. You wait here and help yourself to some coffee, and there's iced tea in that cooler." I was perplexed because he must have known I was a Civil Rights worker, and his kindness was not only unusual but was also over and above the call of duty. When he returned to tell me he had made it and the package would be delivered by late afternoon, I thanked him profusely for his extra effort. "Well, you know," he said, "I guessed from the waybill that you're probably Japanese. I'm from Texas and my brother was part of the 'lost battalion' that was surrounded by the Germans. He told me he'd be dead if it weren't for those brave boys of the 442. Best damn soldiers he'd ever seen." I really didn't know what he was talking about, but I learned later that he was referring to the heroic rescue of the 1st Battalion, 141st Infantry, originally a unit of the Texas National Guard, which was surrounded by the German army in the Vosges Mountains of France in the fall of 1944. Two earlier rescue attempts had failed, but the third, conducted by the 442nd Regimental Combat Team, a special unit of Japanese Americans, broke through and saved the remaining 230 men of the "lost battalion." The 442 suffered over four hundred casualties, which was almost half its roster, and went on to become the most highly decorated unit in American military history.

I was finally able to work on my Mississippi film, and with the first batch of contact sheets, I saw the beginnings of my own photographic vision... It was the best work I had done. On one of the hottest days of the summer, I was sweltering in the darkroom when Fletcher slipped in to hand me a cooling drink laced with a shot of Southern Comfort. Like most Asians, I have a violent reaction to alcohol, and it only takes a small amount to send my heart racing and turn my body bright red; nausea and a splitting headache are sure to follow. I went outside to cool off on the front steps. Worth Long, whom I met during my visit to southwest Georgia, was just about to get into his car, but he stopped dead in his tracks when he saw my transformation from mellow yellow to fire-engine red and called up to the office for others to come see this amazing spectacle. As the small crowd gathered, Stokely Carmichael, the fiery advocate of Black Power, happened to amble by. I had been warned to be wary of Stokely and his constant baiting of white workers for any hint of "do gooder" paternalism, but I'd always liked Stokely for his passion and brassy energy. A ready audience was irresistible to

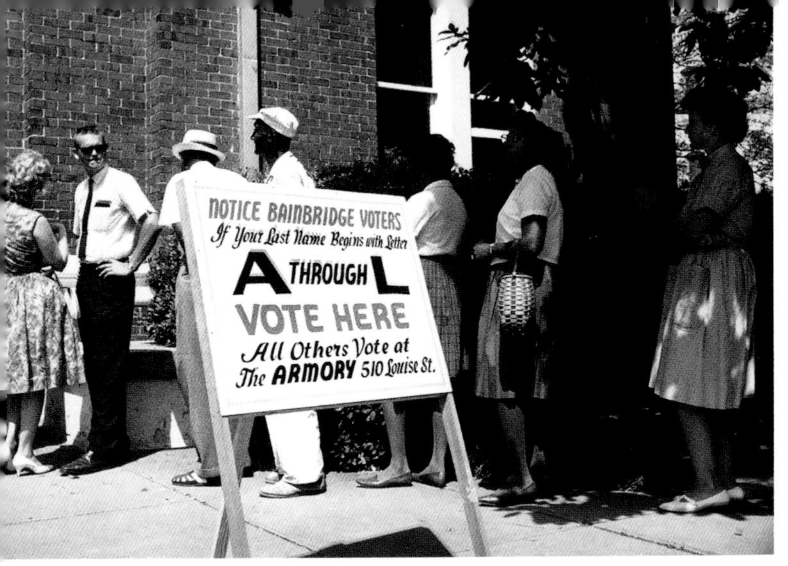

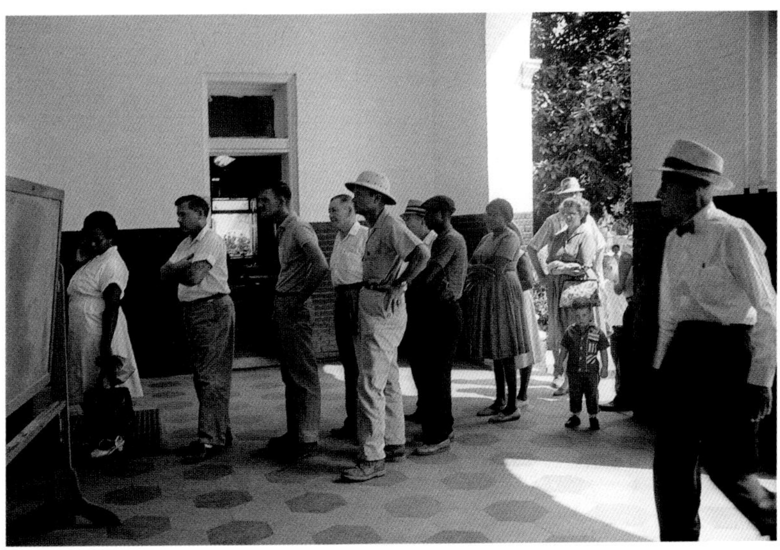

him, and true to form, he challenged me with, "Hey, white boy, how many poor n****** you saved today?" Emboldened by the bourbon and knowing that, with Stokely, the only good defence is a stout offence, I hit him with a dose of the "dozens": "Hey n*****, who the fuck you callin' white? Stokely, not only is you coloured, but you is colour-blind, and don't give me any of your bullshit about how you is descended from one of the seven great tribal chieftains of Africa, 'cause while your great, great, great-grandfather was chuckin' spears, mine in Japan was buildin' mighty cities and creatin' great works of art." Our audience was rolling with laughter, but I wasn't quite sure what to expect from Stokely. All he said was "Damn," and he gave me a high five and walked away, chuckling.

TOP
Voting, C.B. King's campaign for Congress, Americus, Georgia, September 10, 1964

BOTTOM
Voting at courthouse, C.B. King's campaign for Congress, Americus, Georgia, September 10, 1964

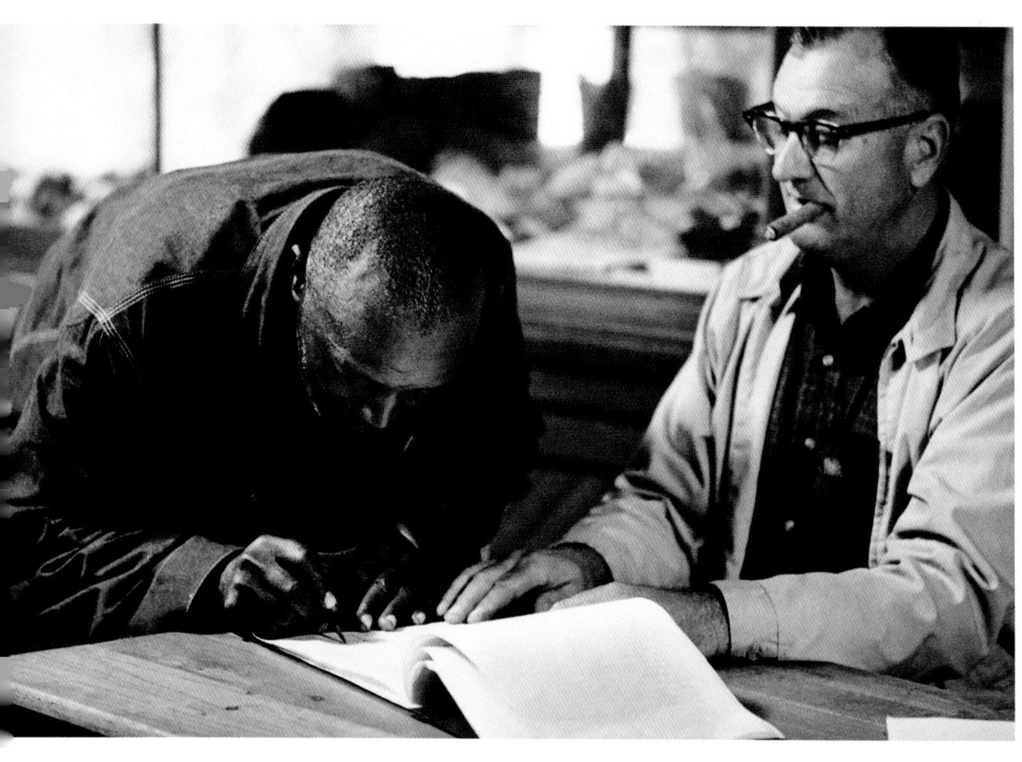

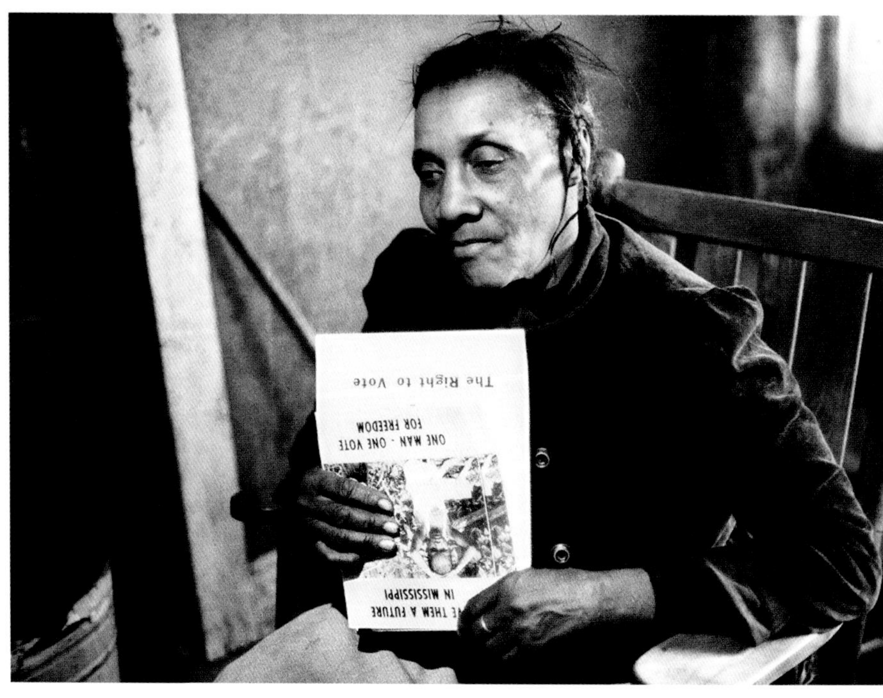
The Right to Vote
ONE MAN · ONE VOTE
FOR FREEDOM
...VE THEM A FUTURE
IN MISSISSIPPI

Being Asian in the Deep South had its distinct advantages. We were a racial anomaly in the Black and white world of the South, which allowed us to move freely between the two solitudes. We were a rarity in the Deep South and neither racial group knew quite what to do with us. Except for Brother Ed, I can't remember seeing another Asian face in all the time I was in the South, and as far as I could see, we were the only Asians in the Movement.

Given the Nikkei experience with racism in both the States and Canada, I had expected to see more Asian Americans in the Movement.

Freedom Summer '64 was drawing to a close, and many of the volunteers were preparing to return to their campuses; others would remain. The documentary photo project was also winding down. Most of the young field photographers had returned home. In the first week of September, I went into Mississippi to replace Cliff Vaughs, who had gone back to California after yet another beating at the hands of an angry mob. I drove with Worth Long into Neshoba County, and in the fading light of early evening, I remember passing nervously by the Philadelphia courthouse and the headquarters of the infamous Sheriff Lawrence Rainey, who was indicted but never convicted for his role in the murder of the three Civil Rights workers. His deputy, Cecil Price, along with six others, would eventually be convicted in a federal court and serve time for denying the civil rights of their dead victims. The Justice Department knew that, in a Mississippi court, it would be impossible to get a conviction for the murder of Civil Rights workers.

The undercurrent of violence was as much a part of Mississippi as its heat and humidity. In the back of my mind, I was aware of the very real possibility that I could be shot driving through the Delta in the dead of night, or that the Freedom House, church or home of a local Movement supporter that I happened to be in could be bombed or torched at any moment. In my most paranoid moments, I imagined being tailed by the local police or a Klansman, who would pull me over to demand why I, a supposed foreign journalist, was living in the local Freedom House. Fortunately, except for one incident when I and my local sharecropper guide were chased off a plantation outside of Ruleville by the shotgun-toting owner, I was never seriously threatened. For the most part, I never felt consciously afraid, for I knew that it would be impossible to function while living in constant fear.

I felt like a prisoner suddenly released from a sentence of hard labour, for I was now finally out of Atlanta and in the field. The following months

TOP
Man registering to vote
with white official with cigar,
Panola County, Mississippi,
c. fall 1964

BOTTOM
Woman with pamphlet at
a voter registration drive,
Panola County, Mississippi,
c. fall 1964

I spent roaming throughout the Delta to capture its haunting beauty were my happiest and most productive period in the South. Unfortunately, it was interrupted by a Snick retreat at Waveland, Mississippi, to review the summer programs and discuss the future of Snick. In early November, I drove down to this pleasant town in the southeast corner of the state on the Gulf of Mexico, but it turned out to be a brutal week, which, from my perspective, marked the beginning of the end of Snick and my own involvement with the Movement. At an earlier meeting in Atlanta, the first real cracks in our solidarity had appeared, and the Waveland retreat only served to exacerbate the growing dissent and disunity. Casey Hayden and Mary King, two long-time, white office workers, made an impassioned plea on behalf of the women in the Movement; the rampant male chauvinism in Snick, they argued, was as demeaning and damaging to women as white racism in the South was to Black Americans.

Stokely responded by saying he felt the only position for women in the Movement was "prone," but his half-hearted attempt at humour was met by only a few nervous giggles in the growing tension. The greater danger to Casey and Mary, and indeed to Snick itself, was a more central division that was tearing us apart. On one side of the divide were the advocates of Black Power, made up primarily of members from the North. With their impassioned and sophisticated rhetoric, leaders like Stokely Carmichael and Courtland Cox tended to overwhelm their mainly Southern opponents, who still clung to the belief that non-violence could eventually lead to the fulfillment of an all-inclusive, egalitarian America. Stokely, for whom non-violence was only a tactic, had argued in the past that Snick offices and Freedom Houses lay in an arsenal of guns to combat the increasing waves of violence. Unfortunately, John Lewis, the principal advocate of Gandhian non-violence, was still on tour in Africa. Since he was still highly respected and much loved by many in Snick, he might have been able to not only defend the Southern position but also to slow the rapid erosion of Snick. In his absence, the voices calling for a fundamental change in Snick and its leadership grew ever more strident.

Freedom Summer '64 had been an undeniable success, with greatly increased voter registration and the establishment of essential programs and services, but, ironically, its very success contributed to its dissolution. The volunteers who decided to remain in Mississippi had swelled the Snick staff to over two hundred, which was placing

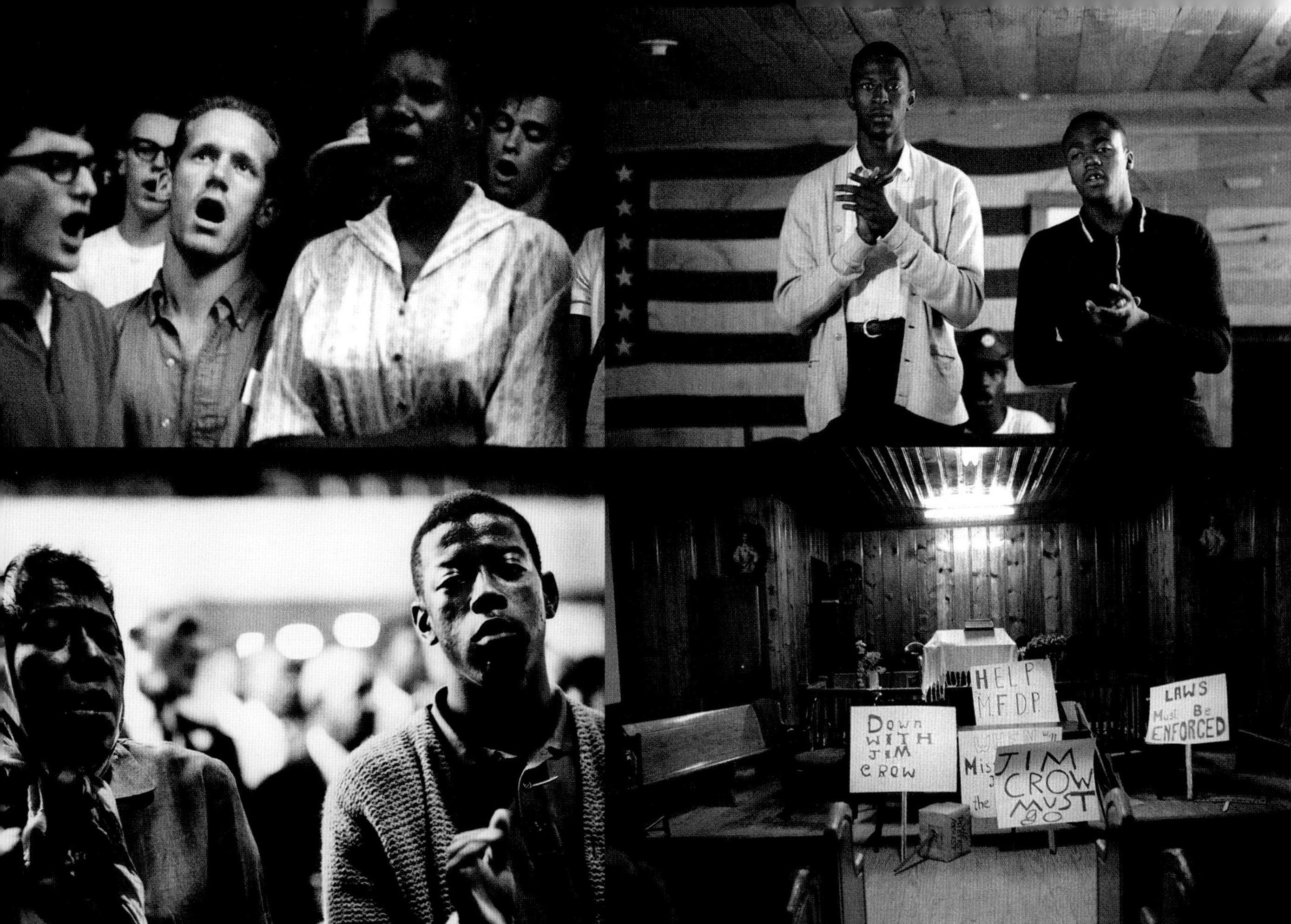

impossible demands on our limited resources. And since most of the attention had been focused on Mississippi, Snick workers in other states complained that they were being ignored and denied their fair share of Snick resources. The influx of so many new people into the Movement also heightened fears that Snick was being overtaken by white members. Undoubtedly, there had been the rare instance of a deliberate white seizure of leadership, but I suspect that any white ascendancy was the natural and inevitable result of placing white students—with their superior education, skill sets and confidence born of their privileged position in society—in a milieu of local Black members disadvantaged by their legacy of slavery and segregation. But the most destructive result of the summer was the appalling realization that, in 1964, America still placed so little value on the lives and suffering of its Black citizens. We were all aware that the intense media coverage of Mississippi was due largely to the presence there of so many children of prominent white

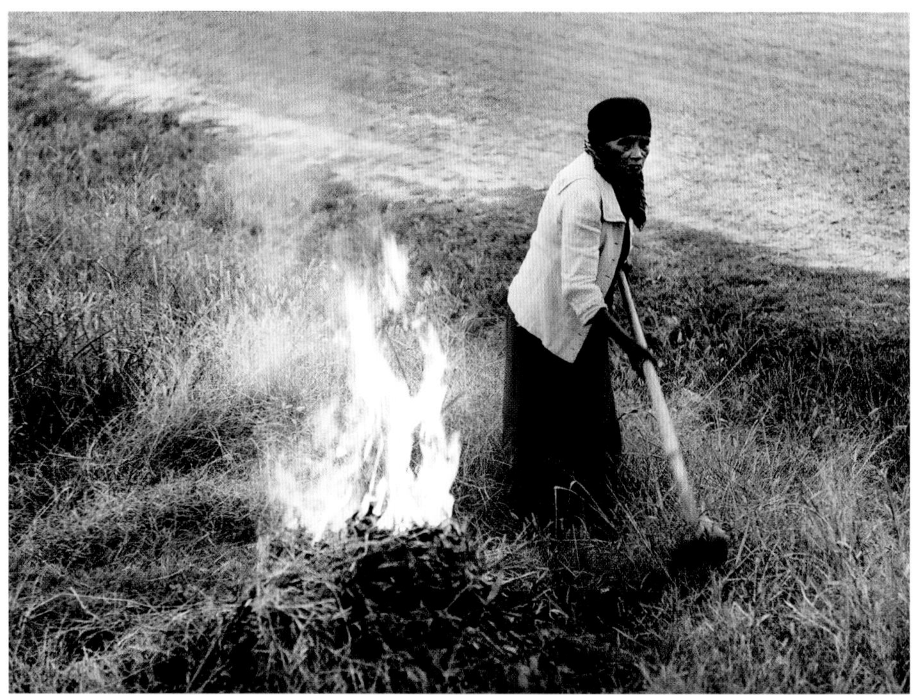

families. Had James Chaney been driving with two other local Black people, there would not have been the same national furor and intense manhunt for their murderers. In their search of the swamps and rivers of the Delta, the FBI had dug up other Black bodies long reported missing, and their deaths went largely unmarked into the pages of history. It was a bitter pill to swallow, which served only to further inflame the call for Black Power.

As a Nikkei, I was torn on the issue of Black Power, and for once my racial neutrality was of no help. On one hand, I could well understand the call for Black pride, and I personally took to heart that the first step toward any real change was to cast off the historically imposed slave mentality and replace it with a new, proud self-image, grounded in an affirmation of their African heritage and in pride for their historic courage that enabled them to survive centuries of slavery and segregation. On the other hand, I felt the leap from there to the Black Power political agenda—the establishment of a separate and independent Black state in America—was not only logically invalid but also illusory.

By mid-week in the retreat, the atmosphere had become so corrosive that a number of Snick veterans, mostly from the South, left embittered, disillusioned and fearful for the future of their organization. I left a few days later and continued my exploration of the Delta.

I had been in Mississippi for nearly three months. I was anxious to get back to Atlanta to see what I had managed to capture on film and to prepare for a much-anticipated visit home for the holidays. At the end of the first week of December, after stopping off in Indianola to take a picture of a burned cross in front of the Freedom School, I headed for Snick headquarters. I'd been driving all day, and it was past ten by the time I crossed the border into Georgia. Whenever I reach the point of exhaustion, I begin to hallucinate, so when I saw a huge, black boot coming down from the sky to crush the car in front of me, I knew I had to take a break before completing the final leg of my journey. I pulled into the next truck stop and walked into a small, pleasantly quaint restaurant clad in aged barn boards. The place was half filled with redneck truckers and gaunt farmers dressed in dirty coveralls, and as I took my seat at the counter, I could once again sense all eyes boring into my back. A busty, blonde waitress came over, and after I placed my order of coffee, the blue plate special and a piece of a luscious-looking pecan pie, I walked to the washroom in the back to wash up before dinner. Looking around, I was startled to see an alarming array of weaponry hanging on every available inch of wall space—rifles, shotguns, muskets, derringers, revolvers, automatics, machine guns, bombs, grenades, knives, swords, bayonets. The place was a veritable monument to the cruel destruction of human flesh. Back at the counter, I was halfway through my meal when the waitress turned up the volume on the counter radio, saying, "Don't y'all love this song?" When the baleful country music ballad ended, the DJ announced it was time for their daily feature and invited his audience to go back in time to relive another moment in "the history of our great nation." After a few seconds of the hiss and crackle of an old recording, the stentorian voice of Franklin Delano Roosevelt began to fill the room: "Yesterday, December 7, 1941—a day that will live in infamy—the United States of America was suddenly and deliberately attacked by naval and air forces of the Empire of Japan..." I gobbled up the rest of my meal, cancelled the pecan pie, slapped a bill on the counter, slowly crept out the door, ran to my car and tore off for Atlanta.

The following two weeks were an exciting period of discovery, with each day bringing more startling images shimmering into reality from their chemical bath. My images from the Delta revealed another leap in the growth of my vision. My ordeal in being chained to that infernal darkroom turned out to be one of those blessings in disguise, for at the end of the summer, with its miles of film and stacks of prints, I had managed to achieve a sense of what constitutes a great image, and I now had the technical skills to turn that awareness into a fine print. It was a quiet time, for Bob Fletcher and I were the only remaining summer photographers. At night, after hours in the darkroom, we would share late meals and long, meandering discussions about our summer and the possibilities for our future. Bob was also going home to Detroit, so before leaving, I invited him to drive up to Chatham to celebrate a traditional Japanese New Year.

As I wound my way north, I wondered whether I would ever return to the South. As it turned out, the decision would be taken from my hands, for a little over a year later, Snick would undergo its one radical revolution. The first to go was Forman, followed soon after by the ousting of John Lewis. Damaging rumours of an imminent takeover of Snick had been circulating for over a year, and with the change in leadership, word spread quickly that Snick was now in the hands of a militant Black Power group that would use any means, including violence, to realize their dream of a separate Black nation. The new regime under their chairman, Stokely Carmichael, would purge its white workers. I knew this racial cleansing would cause untold pain to so many veteran Snick members, both Black and white, who had worked, fought and bled together for their American dream. Snick's traditional base of support, especially in the Northern campuses, soon crumbled, while the other major Civil Rights organizations that had always been leery of these brash, young upstarts finally washed their hands of Snick. For all intents and purposes, that was the end of Snick as a major force in the Civil Rights Movement.

I drove through the night and passed through the tunnel into Windsor. Once I was on to the 401 to Chatham, I stopped the car, got out and knelt on the ground. It felt that good to be back. I didn't know then that I would continue to be swept along in the tidal wave of youthful energy and idealism that had begun in the Deep South and was now sweeping across the frozen Canadian landscape, but I could now meet these new challenges armed with a growing sense of self and the tools of a powerful new medium.

I feel so very fortunate and privileged that, at a critical juncture in my life, I arrived at such a luminous moment in history and became part of a movement that would transform the face of America and the world.

I will always be grateful to my brothers and sisters in the Movement for welcoming me into their midst: John Lewis for inviting me to visit Snick headquarters; Annie Pearl Avery for taking me under her wing; James Forman for putting me on the Snick payroll; Danny Lyon for introducing me to the magical world of photography; Bob Moses for being Bob Moses; Bob Fletcher, my soul brother in the Movement; Brother Ed, my erudite and honourable Nikkei ally; and so many others for the gift of their friendship.

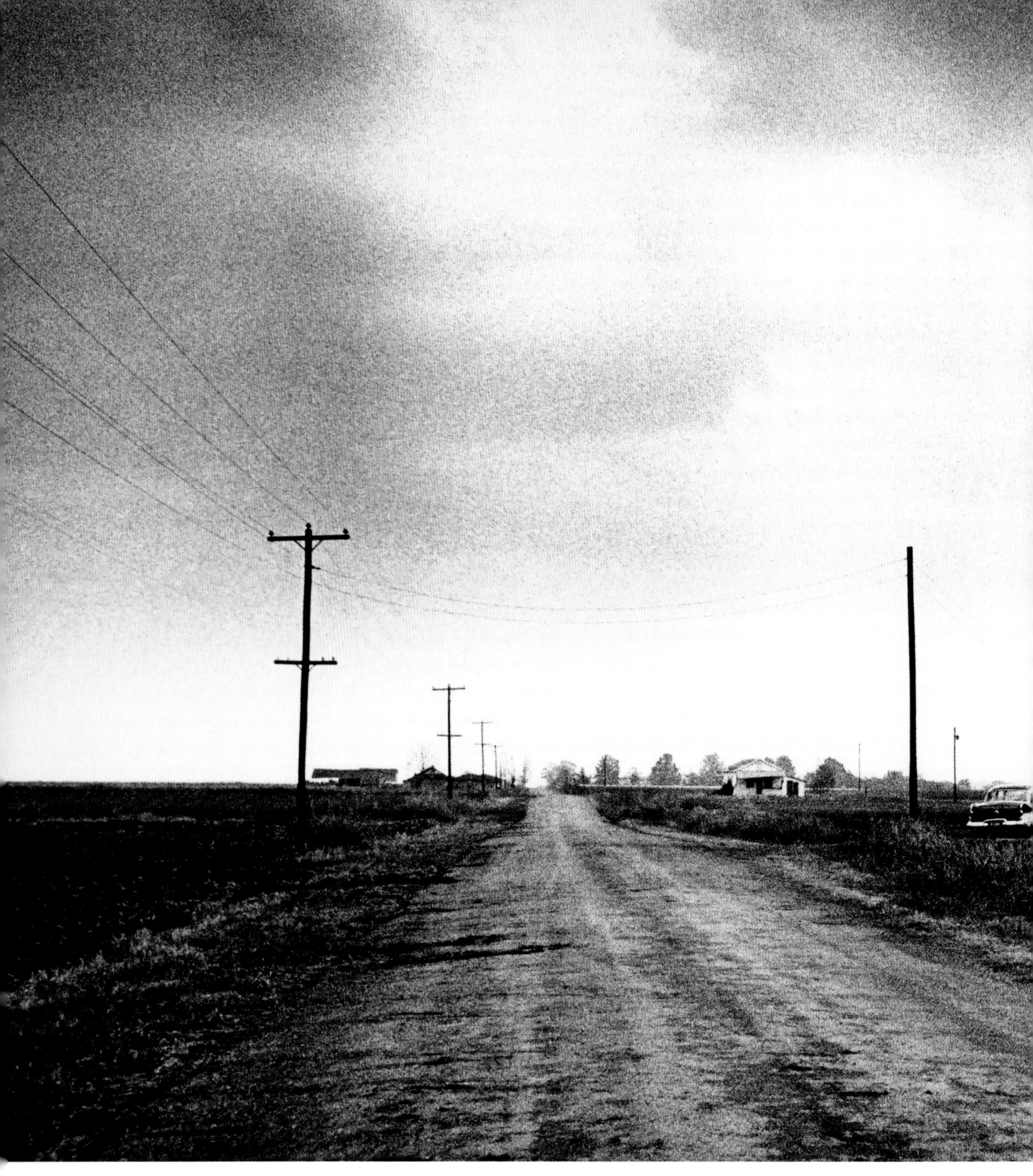

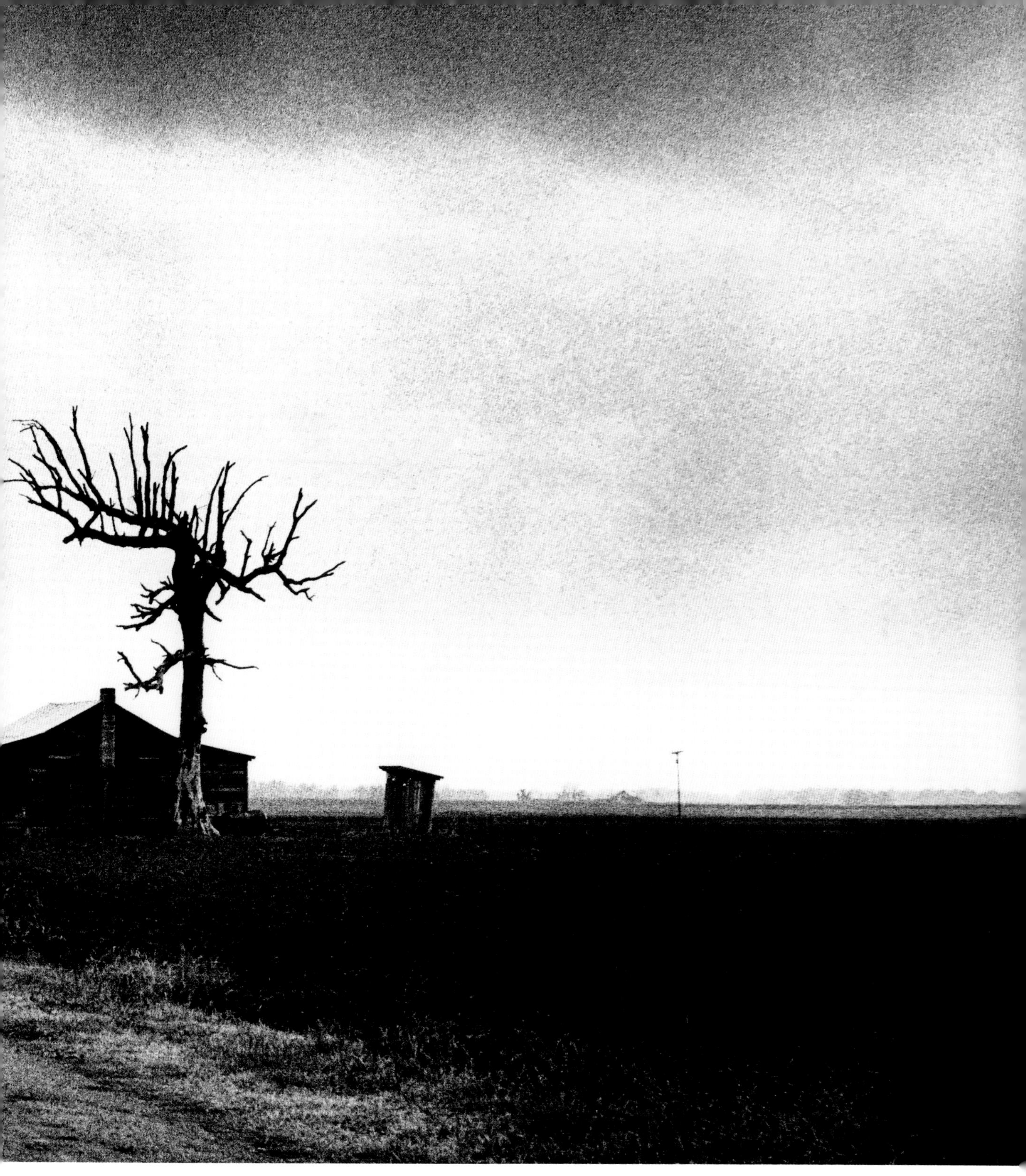

Mississippi Delta landscape, outside of Yazoo City or Ruleville, Mississippi, c. 1964

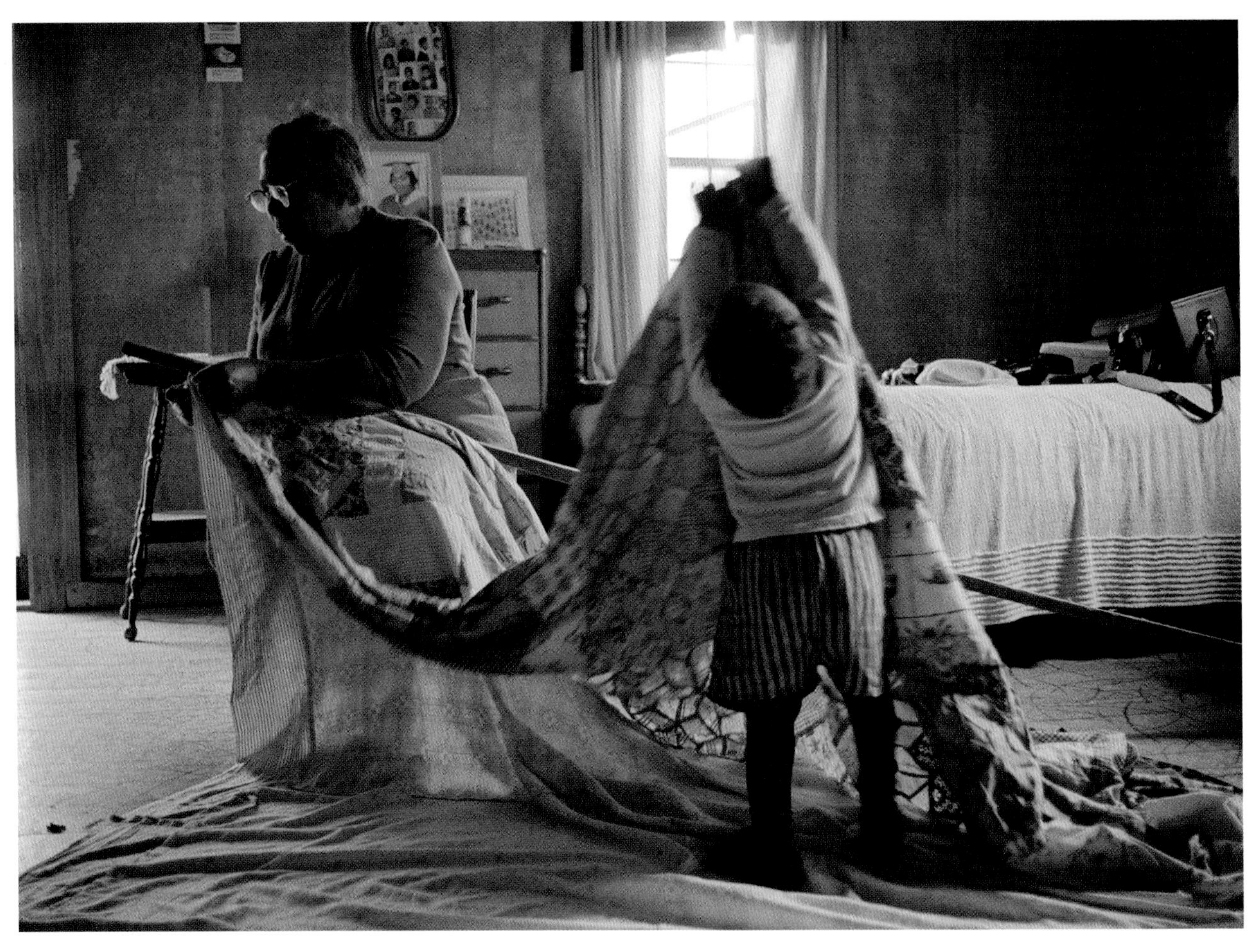

Sharecropper family at home quilting, Ruleville, Mississippi, December 1964

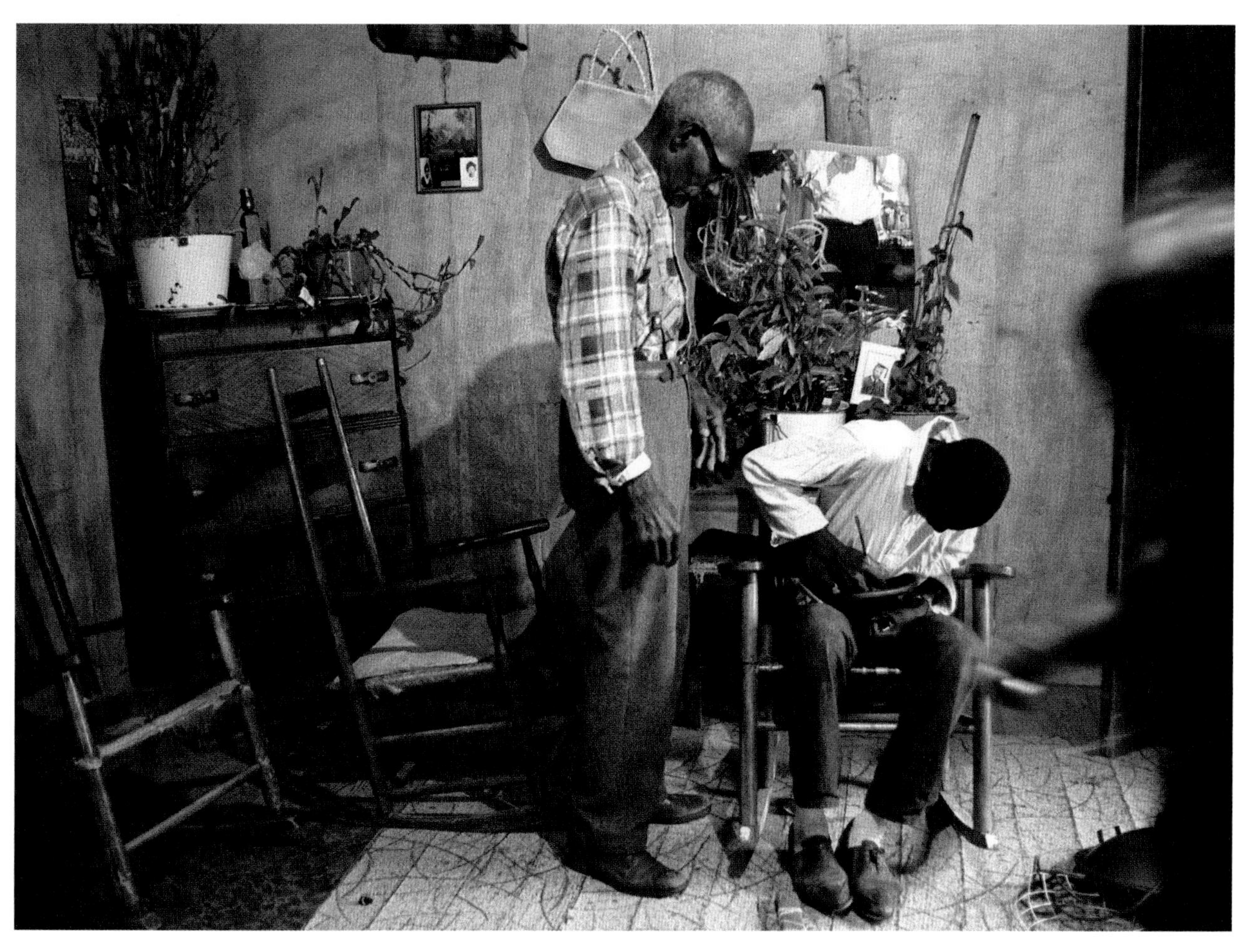

Sharecropper family at home, Ruleville, Mississippi, December 1964

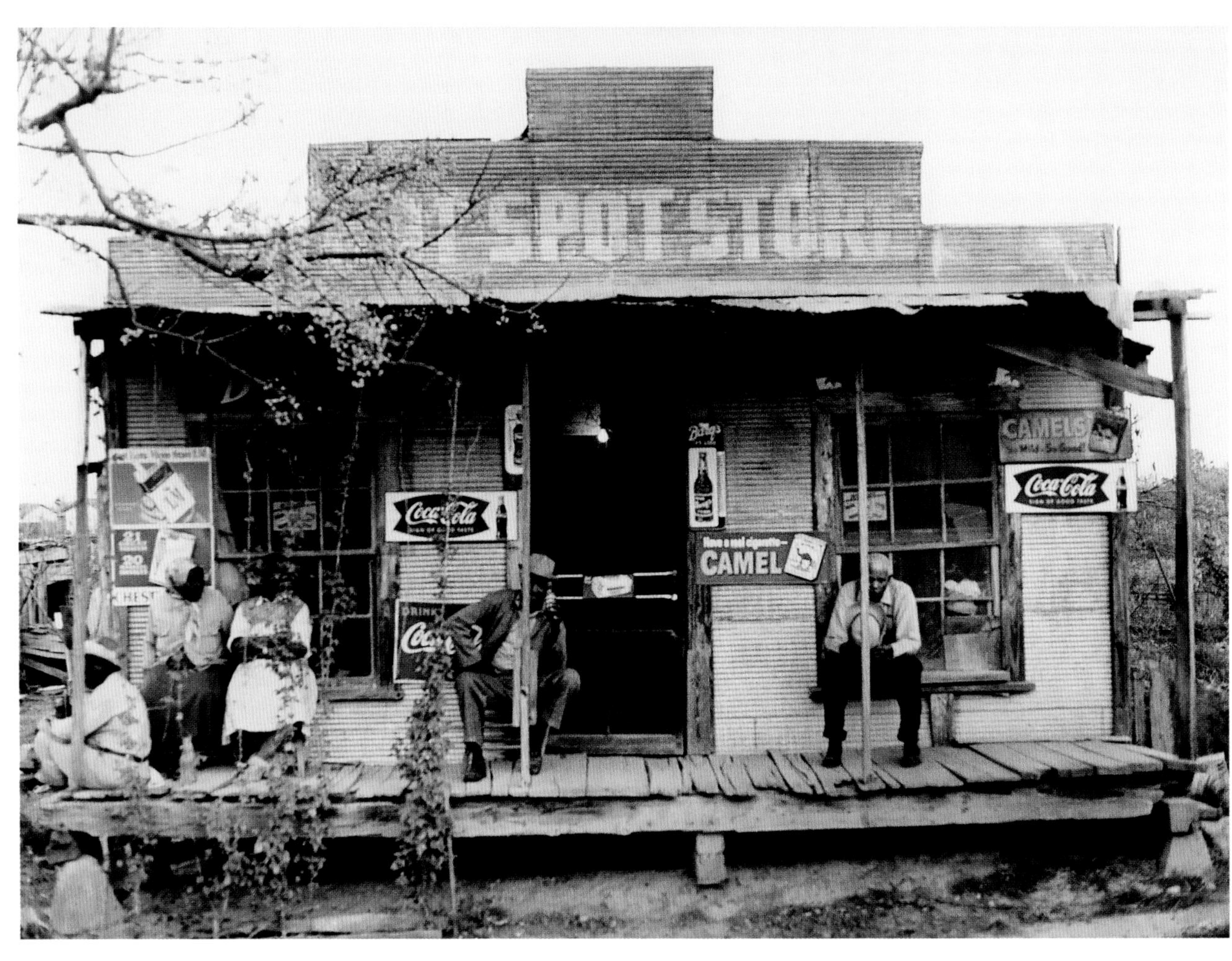

Sharecroppers during a voter registration drive, Mississippi, December 1964

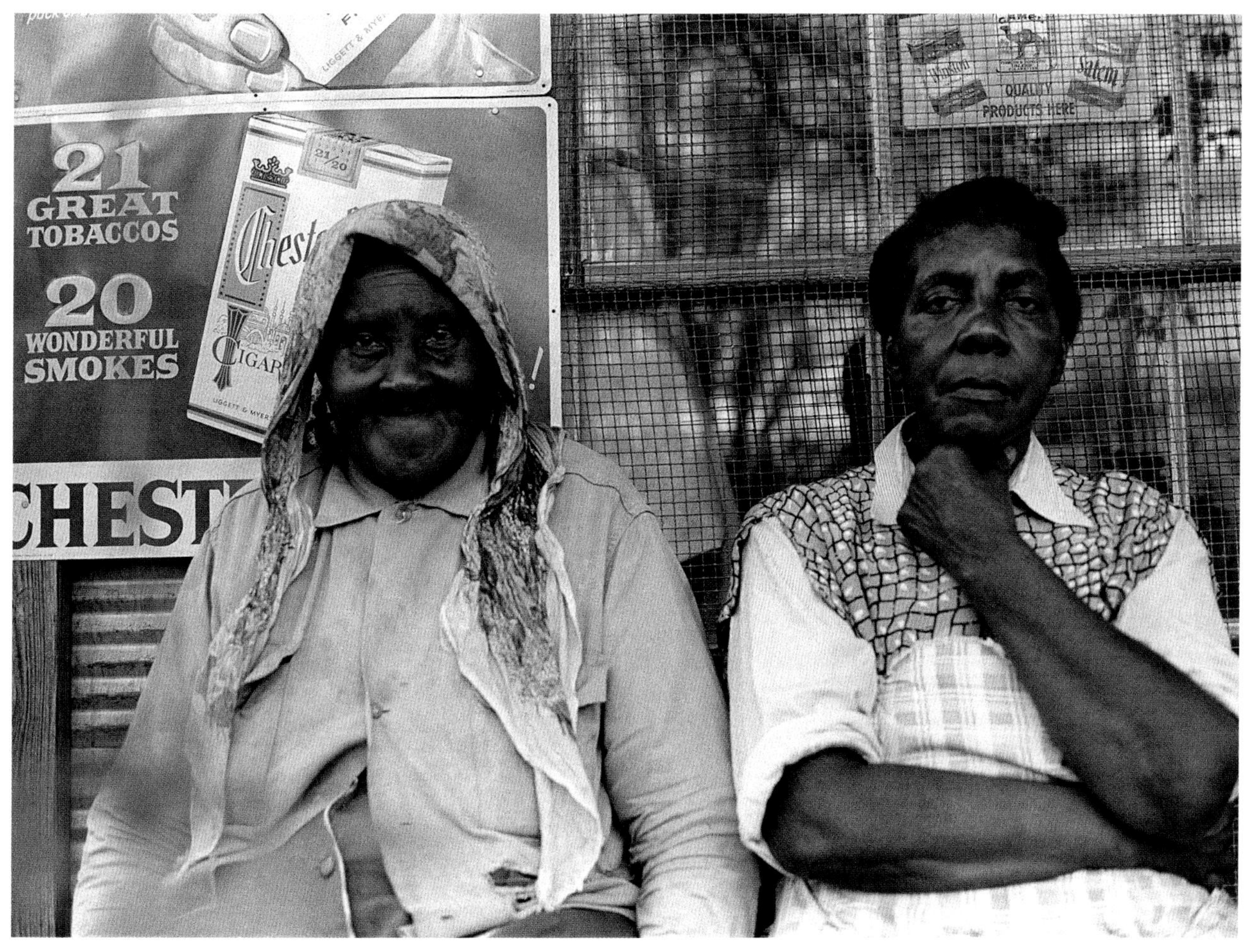

Sharecroppers, Mound Bayou, Mississippi, December 1964

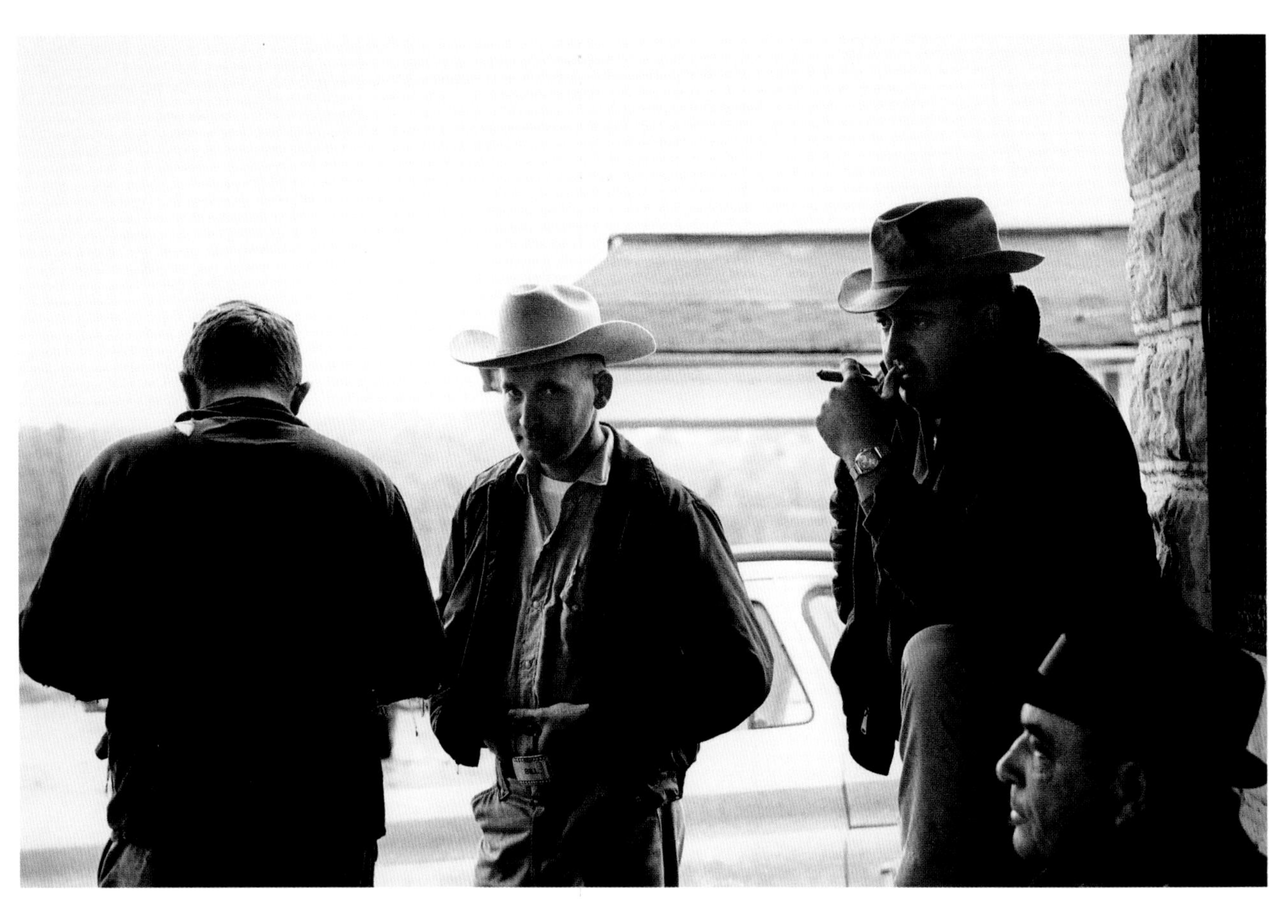

   White men intimidating sharecroppers registering to vote, Panola County, Mississippi, c. fall 1964

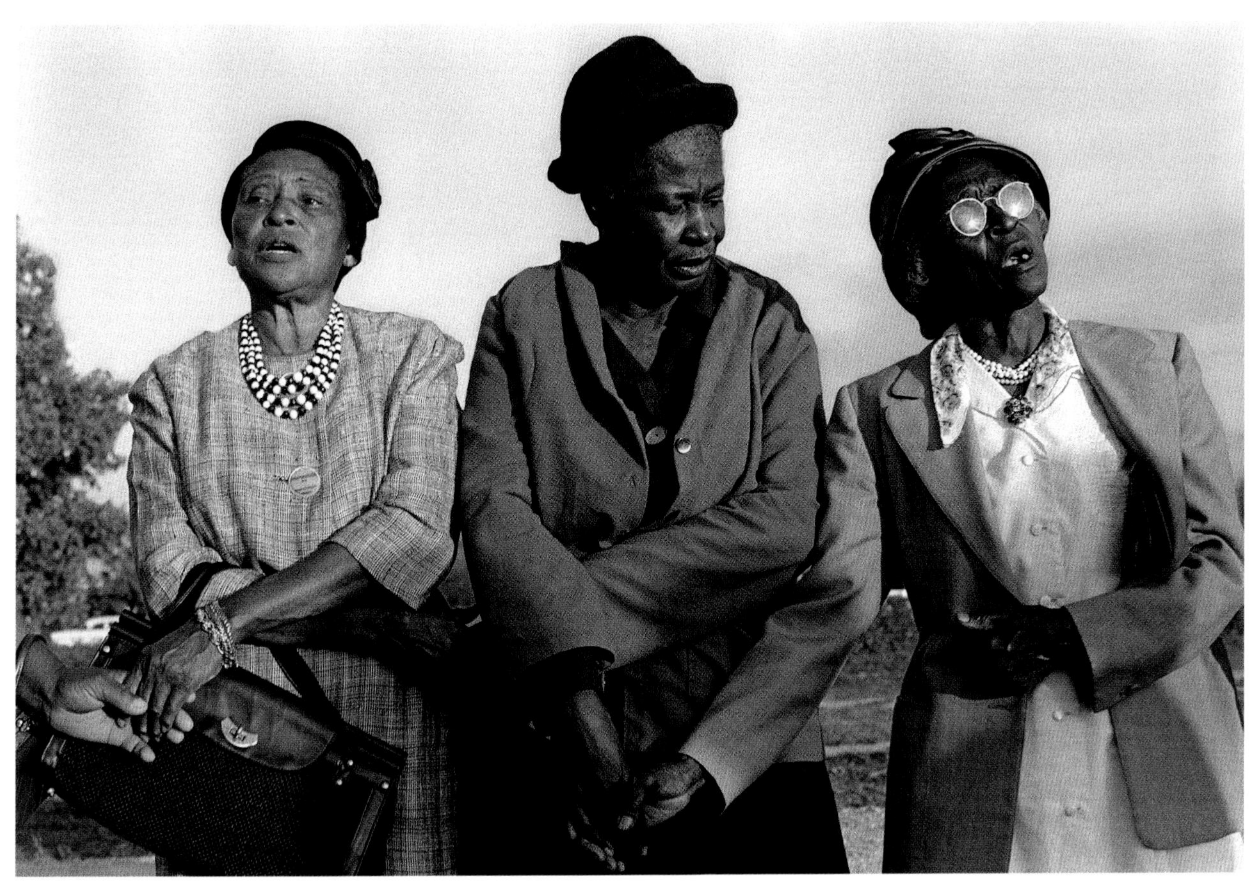

Women singing at a mass rally, Winstonville, Mississippi, December 1964

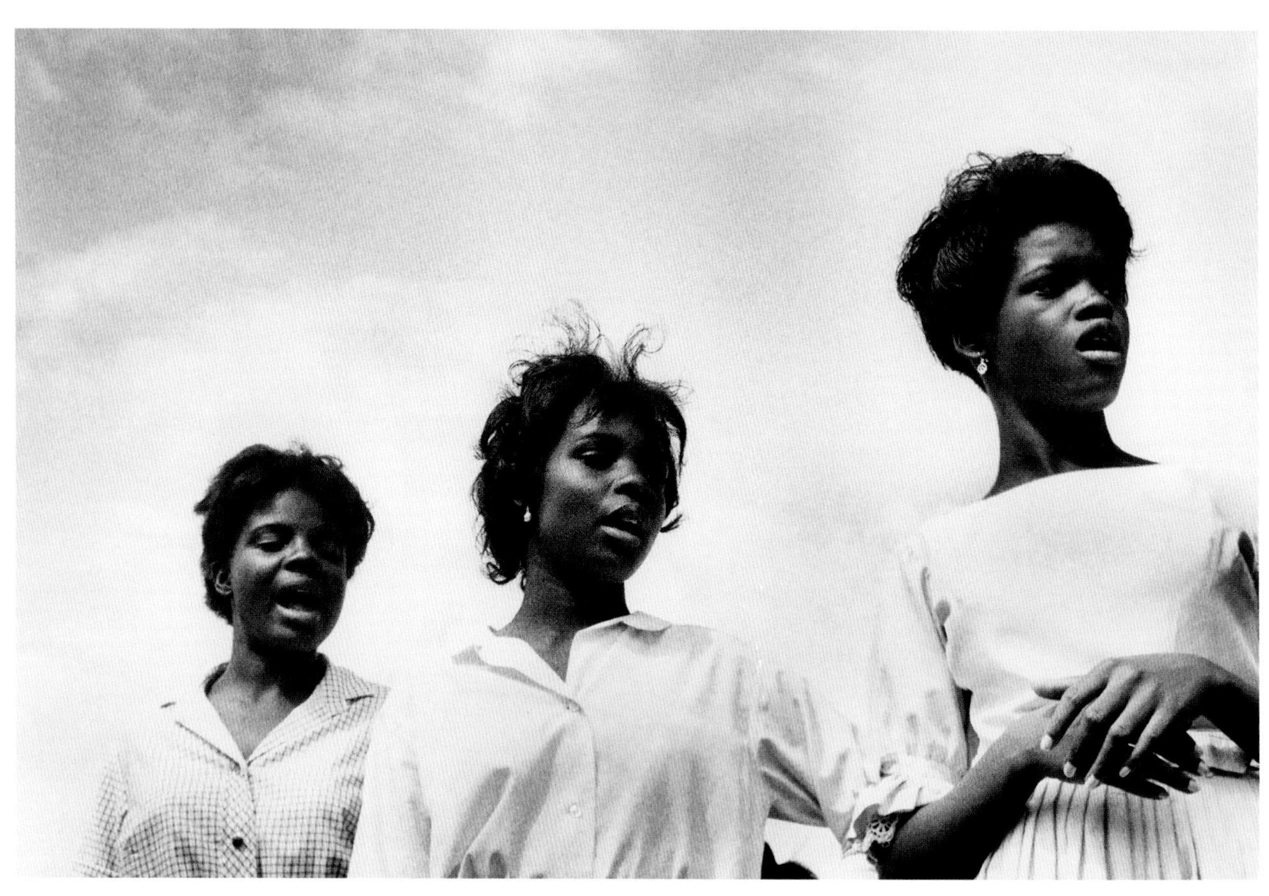

     Three singers at a barbecue for C.B. King's campaign for Congress, Americus, Georgia, July 27, 1964

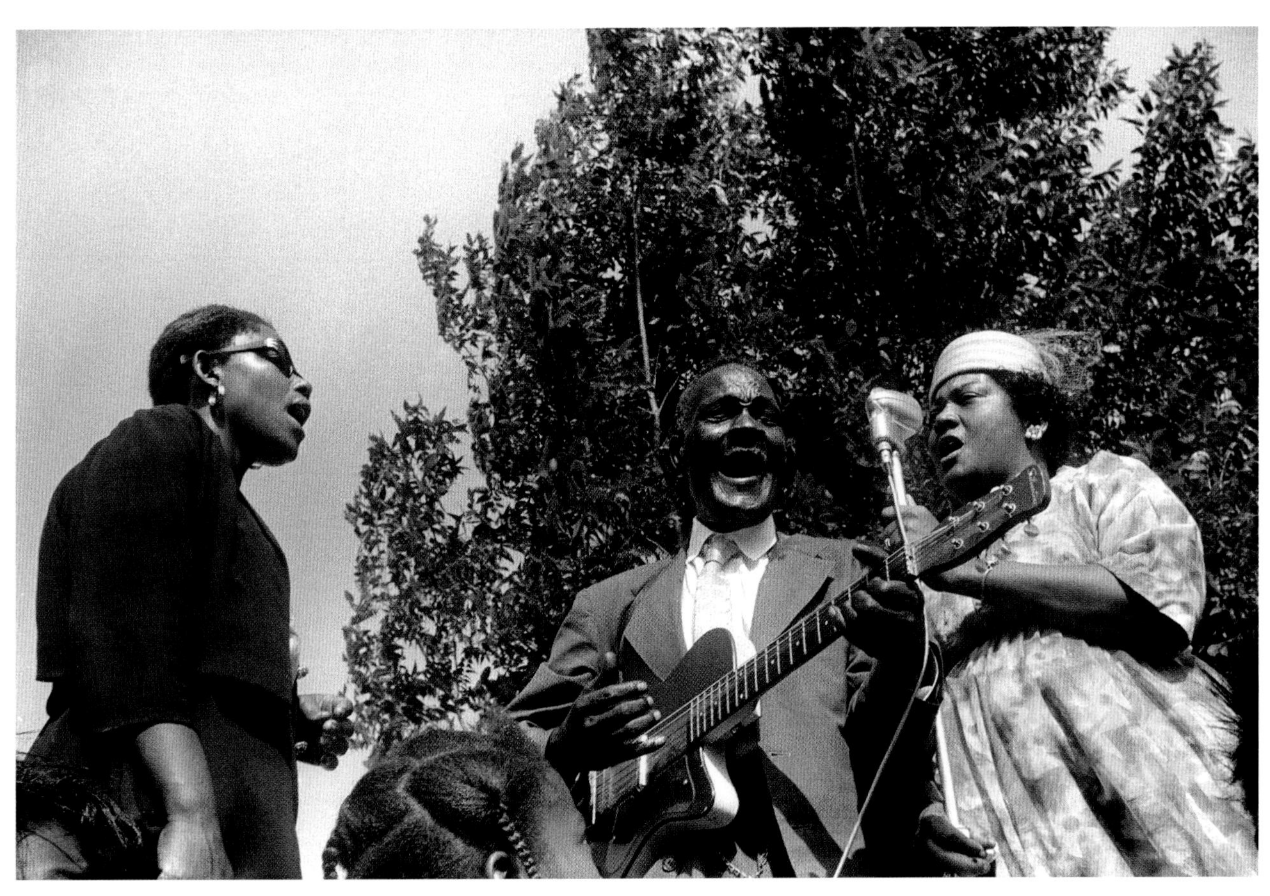

Barbecue for C.B. King's campaign for Congress, Americus, Georgia, July 27, 1964

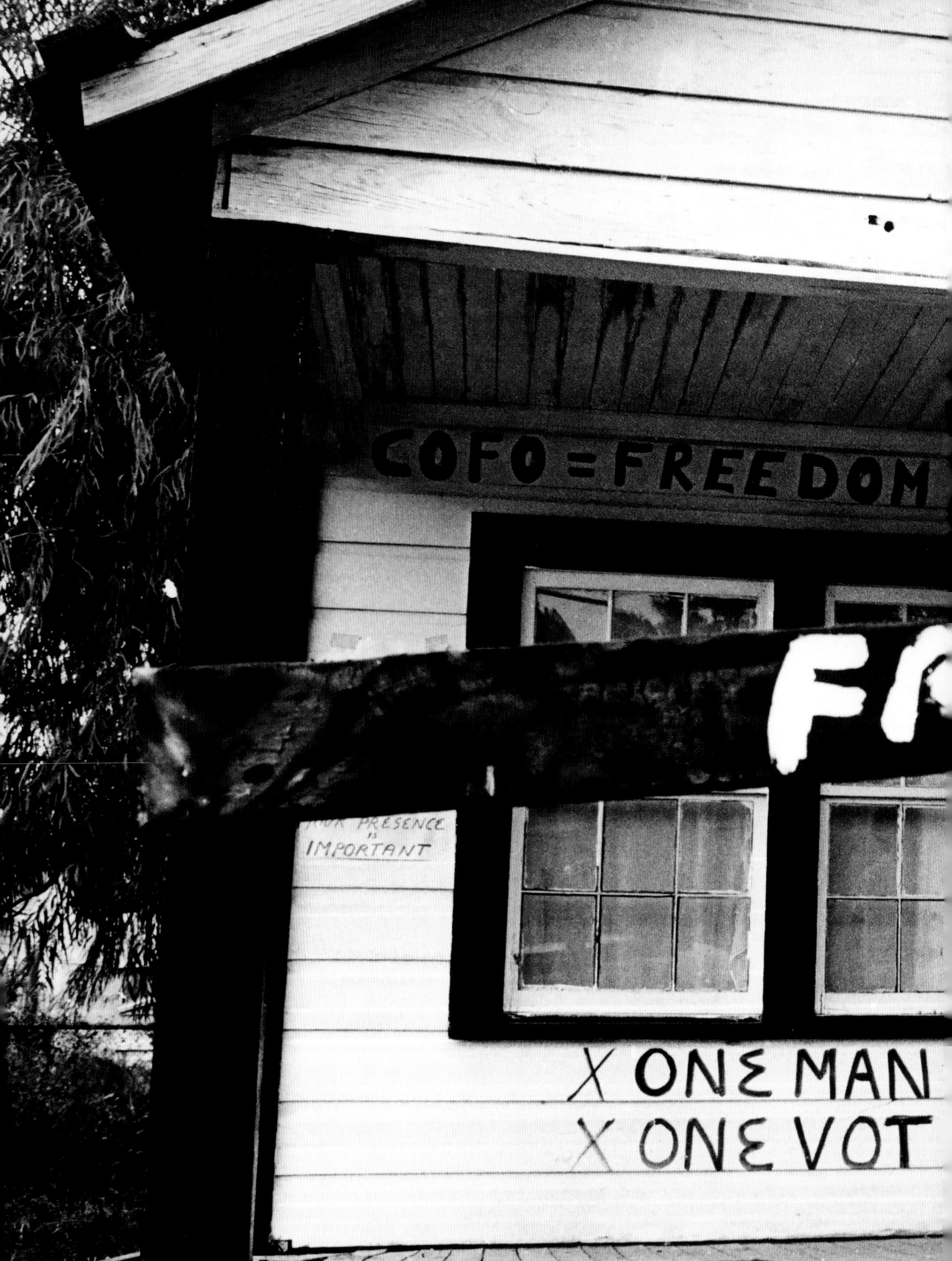

COFO = FREEDOM
YOUR PRESENCE IS IMPORTANT
FR
X ONE MAN
X ONE VOT

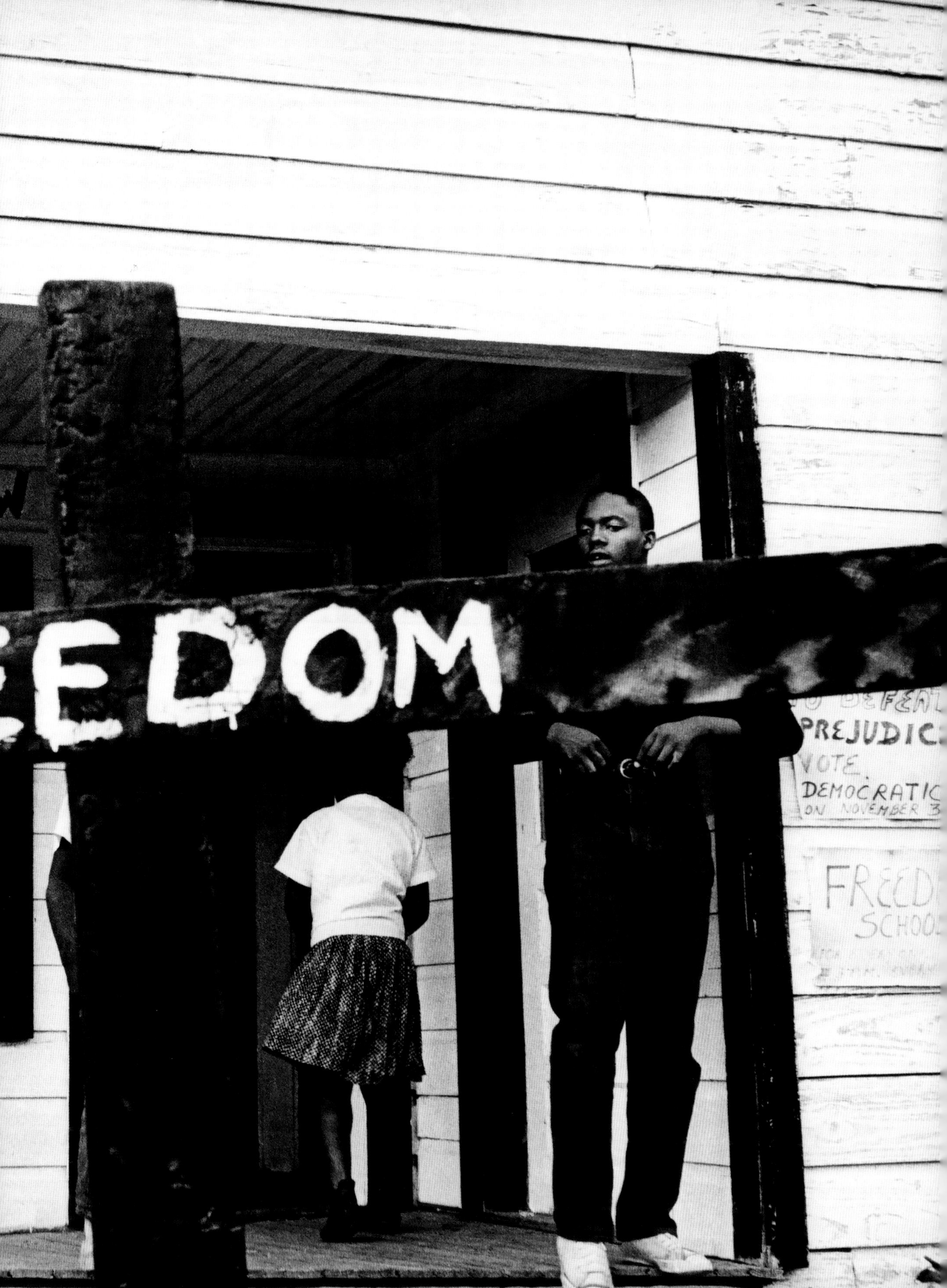
EEDOM
O DEFEAT
PREJUDIC
VOTE
DEMOCRATIC
ON NOVEMBER 3
FREED
SCHOOL

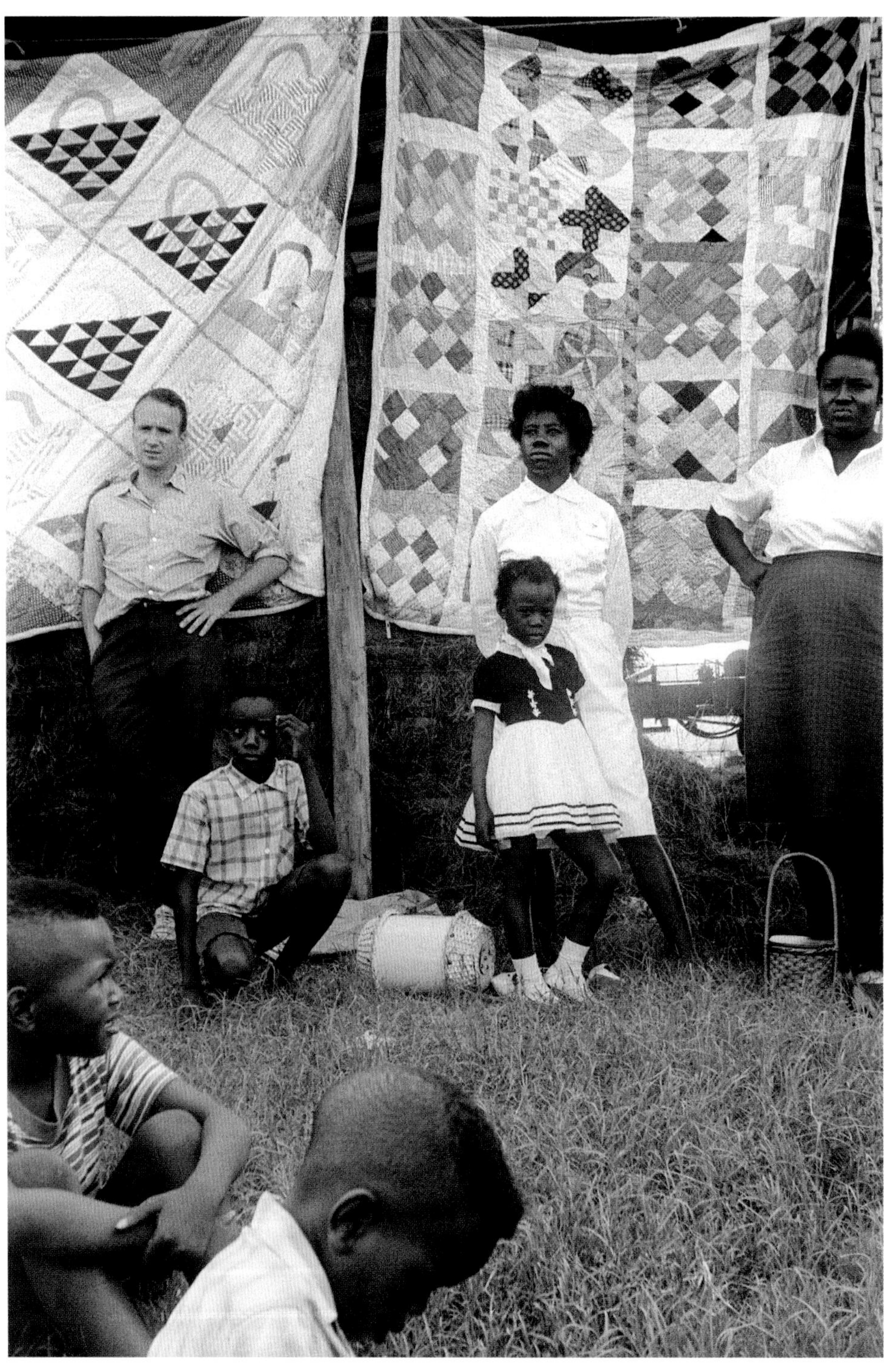

PREVIOUS SPREAD Burnt cross at Freedom School, Pascagoula, Mississippi, c. fall 1964
Barbecue for C.B. King's campaign for Congress, Americus, Georgia, July 27, 1964

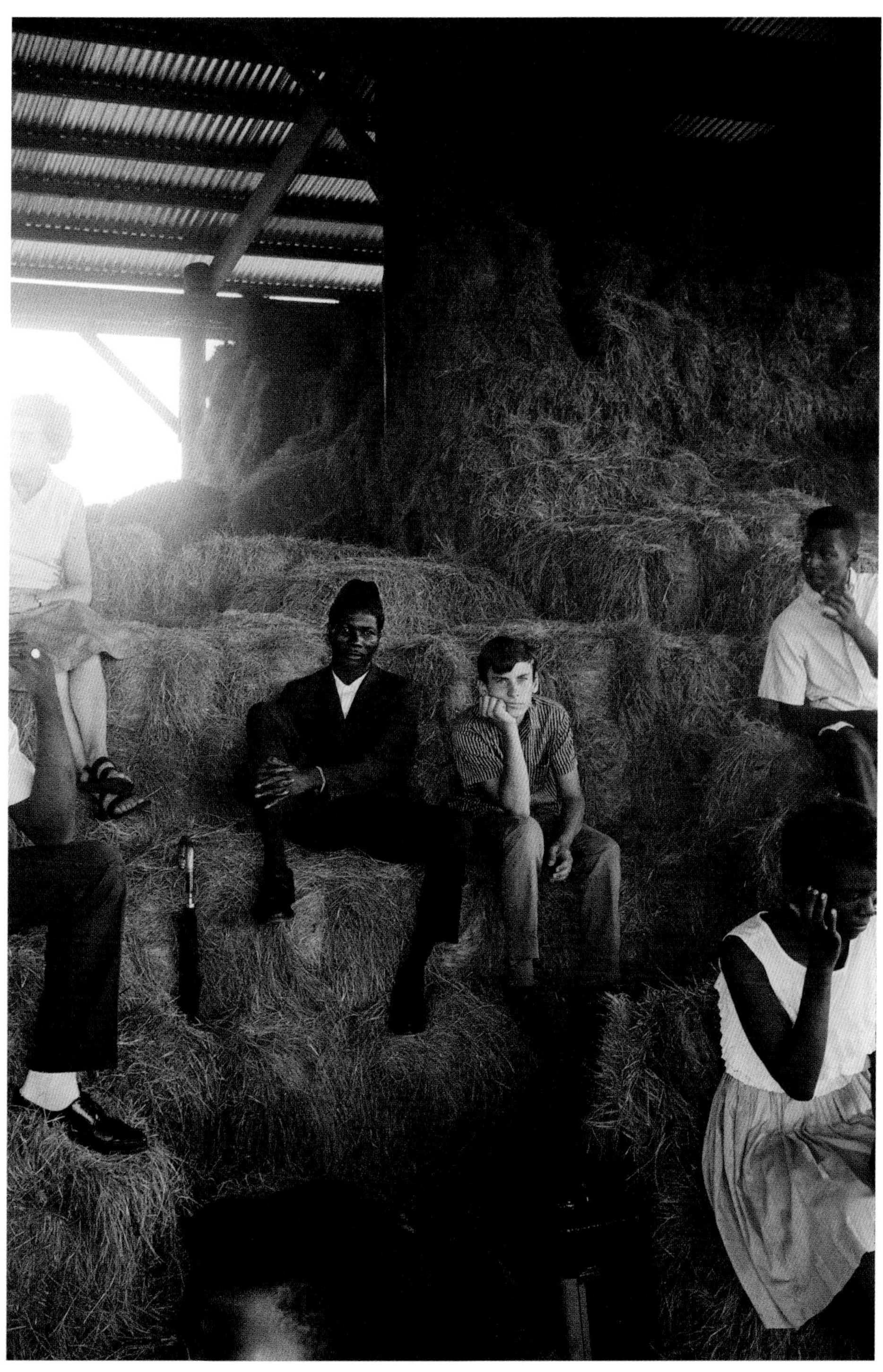

Barbecue for C.B. King's campaign for Congress, Americus, Georgia, July 27, 1964

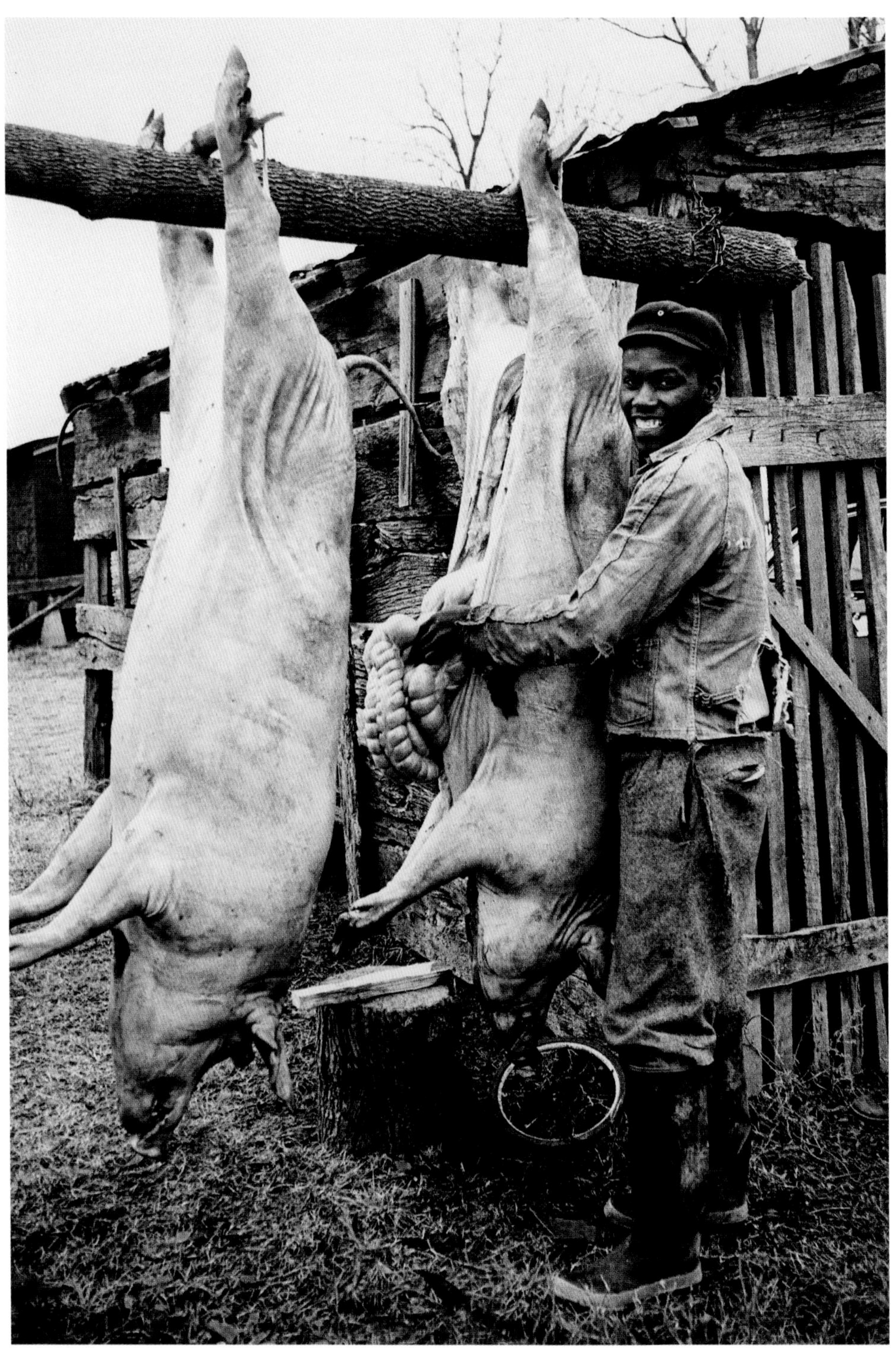

Pig slaughter, Panola County, Mississippi, c. fall 1964

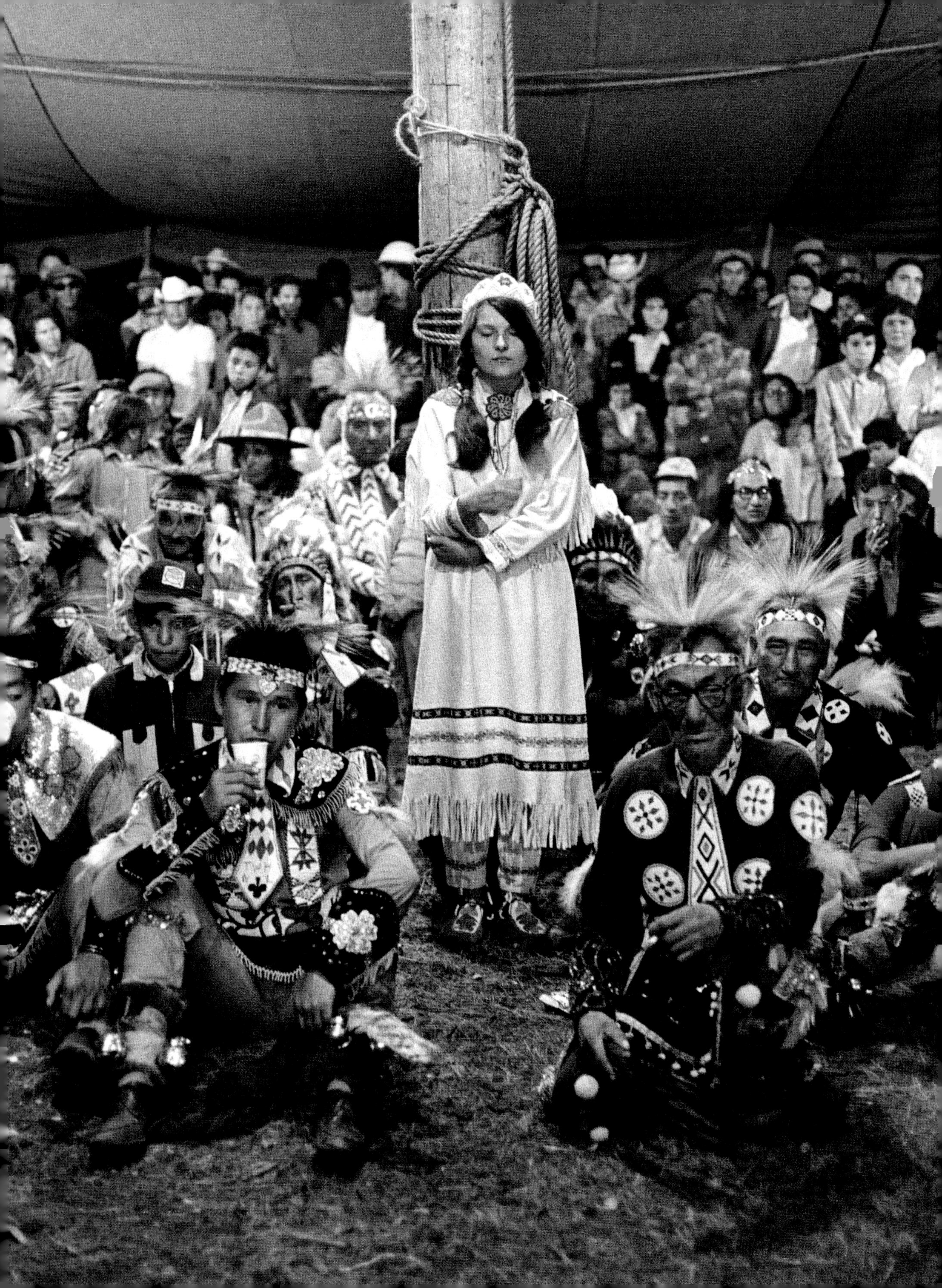

5

I HAD A JOYFUL holiday season at home, even though our traditional Shogatsu was only a pale imitation of the communal exuberance that I had known in my youth; it was falling victim, as so many other Nikkei traditions did, to our dwindling numbers—especially amongst the Issei—and our assimilation into the mainstream. Still, it was good to relive this ancient ritual with my mother and to see Matsuda-san and other old friends on that day. Bob Fletcher and his wife Marilyn did make it up for Shogatsu, albeit rather late after suffering a minor accident on Highway 401. It was their first encounter with Japanese food, and to the delight of my mother and myself, they happily demolished every dish placed before them.

I spent another week with my mother in Chatham, gradually decompressing from the stress of the Movement. The first few nights, my sleep was disturbed by dreams of violence as the tensions of the Southern Black Belt gradually began to leach from my system. During the icy cold days, I took long walks. After having spent time in the South, I began to see our old neighbourhood in a different light. When we first moved to Chatham, my parents never expressly forbade me from playing with the Black kids in our neighbourhood, but I knew they were not happy with my new friends. Undoubtedly, they shared some of the xenophobia of their homogeneous, insular homeland, but I suspect the larger reason is that they wanted to insulate us from the abject poverty and sense of

Sioux powwow,
Fort Qu'Appelle,
Saskatchewan,
August 1965

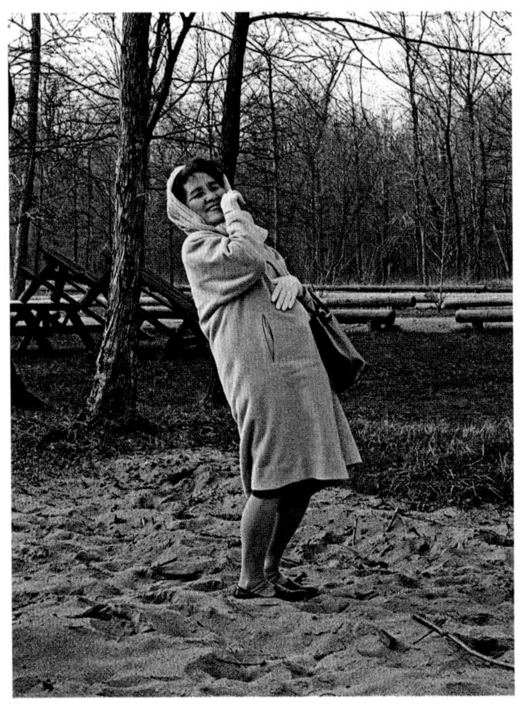

hopelessness in the Black community. In the early years, our neighbours were an odd Black couple: John, a tall, handsome man who was one of the original recyclers—their backyard was filled with all manner of scavenged junk—and his companion, a shuffling old woman who could have been either his wife, sister or mother. We were all afraid of catching some dreaded disease, for we often heard John hacking and coughing up rivers of contagion. Since their house had neither electricity nor plumbing, my father granted John permission to use our outdoor tap, and some nights, when I was out back, John, who was coal black, would suddenly materialize out of the darkness with bucket in hand and scare the daylights out of me.

Even though I should have known better as a fellow victim of racism, I somehow absorbed the common consensus that the plight of our Black neighbours was the result of some genetic deficiency or inherent lack of character. Working with my Black brothers and sisters in the Movement had been both instructive and humbling, for many of them were my obvious superiors in terms of both character and intellect. As I continued my walk, I wondered what had happened to my old childhood friends and considered how different our lives might have been had we inherited a different world. I had lost touch with all of them at the end of elementary school, which was the dividing point in our lives, for I, like most Nisei, went on to high school, while my Black friends either dropped out or enrolled in the technical school. Jake, one of my favourite playmates, lived a block away, and since they had TV long before we did, I was at his house almost daily. One day I walked in and caught Jake furtively playing his parents' secret cache of records. I was at first shocked and then captivated by the bluesy back beat and the outrageously suggestive lyrics: "My ding a ling, my ding a ling." It was my first inkling of a vibrant Black subculture, which, to my amazement, was strong enough to produce and market its own music. Jake and I, along with some of our other Black friends, joined the local boxing club, and with our righteous anger, we used to beat the hell out of the white kids. Jake and the others were much better fighters than I, but when we got into the ring, they carried me to the end of the bout. With his physical grace, charming wit and zest for life, Jake, to my mind, could have been another Stokely Carmichael. Across the street and a few houses down lived another good friend, the gentle and studious Paul. His family had a huge vegetable garden, and I used to go over to help Paul with his chores. Since he was just as much an avid reader as I was, we would share our most recent discoveries from the public library as we hoed or picked peas. I now saw in Paul many of the admirable qualities that drew me to such people as John Lewis or Bob Fletcher. In our final year of elementary school, our parent-teacher association sponsored a formal debate, pitting myself and Barbara, a tough Black girl from the neighbourhood, against Louise, the daughter of prominent doctor, and Arthur, the son of the local Ford dealer. It was a classic battle of white against coloured, the social elite against the dregs of society. Ruby Doris Smith, the feared head of the Atlanta Snick office, reminded me of Barbara, who was fiercely competitive and had a razor-sharp mind. However, the daunting whiteness of the occasion overwhelmed my partner, and we lost. The arguments of our opponents were limp at best, and had there been a more level playing field, we could have easily carried the day. As I wended my way home, I realized that the greatest sin of institutionalized racism is the waste of human treasure.

It was time to move on, but I wasn't sure where. Though I still felt committed to the Movement, I was no longer confident of my future with Snick, which was on the verge of imploding. In any event, I wasn't ready to go back to the South, for I needed time to recharge my batteries after the accumulated stress of the past year. I decided to go to Toronto, since, outside of the South, it was the only place I had contacts: two older brothers and a cousin, the SUPA people, and the film crew of *This Hour Has Seven Days*—the popular public affairs program on CBC that was setting new standards in television journalism. I met them when they came to Atlanta to film a segment on the Movement. After providing them with a grisly photo of a lynching of two Black men in Georgia around the turn of the century, they reciprocated by sending me press credentials, which I hoped would offer me another layer of protection in Mississippi. I needed to thank them personally.

The big city of Toronto had always been a mecca, and I can still remember my first trip there. My parents and I piled into my uncle's

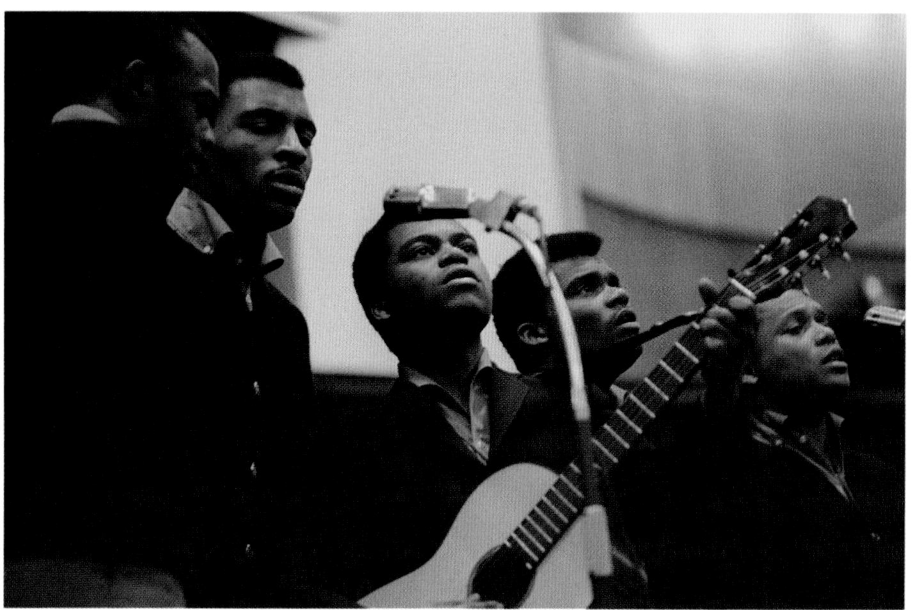

new car to begin the long drive on the two-lane highway to Toronto's grand Canadian National Exhibition, a glorified country fair. When we arrived, our reservations at the upscale York Hotel had mysteriously disappeared, and my oldest brother Sam had to scramble to find other accommodations. Despite this humiliating beginning, my cousin Jim and I had a magical time at the CNE, and I can still see the miles of headlights stretching before us on the drive home. When I was in my teens, a contingent of local supporters would travel to Toronto to cheer for our team in the annual Nisei softball tournament. The real attraction, however, was the big dance. In the hope of finding the girl of our dreams, we would shop carefully for new outfits; my boldest fashion statement was white pants matched with a charcoal-and-pink sport coat.

Initially I stayed with my brother Peter, who was struggling through his final year at the University of Toronto's School of Architecture. Eventually I was able to find a reasonably priced, furnished apartment on the third floor of a stately house in the Annex, the residential area surrounding the spacious U of T campus. It snowed on the first night, and I can remember staring out the window for hours, watching fat snowflakes dancing through the light of a streetlamp. It was such a delicious feeling to be cocooned in my own inviolate space after the hurly-burly of the Movement, when it seemed there was never a moment when I wasn't surrounded by others. As someone who has always needed quiet moments of solitude, I realized the lack of privacy there had played a

SNCC Freedom Singers concert at Convocation Hall, University of Toronto, Toronto, Ontario, March 1965

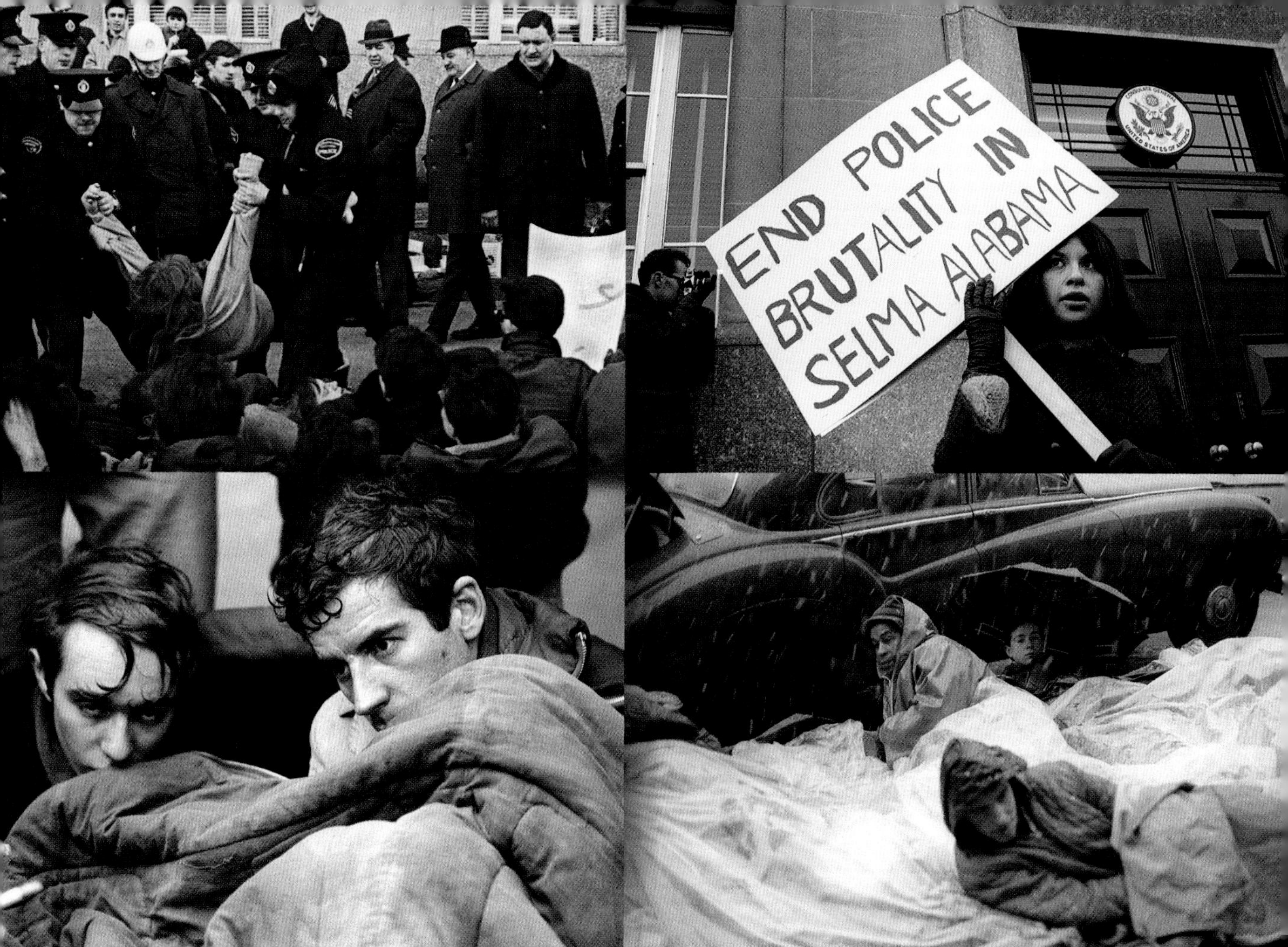

large part in my burnout. As I snuggled under a blanket, I wanted, for a while at least, to have nothing to do with political causes. But it was the 60s, and it was impossible to remain isolated for very long.

The U of T chapter of the Friends of Snick had organized a benefit concert with Harry Belafonte and the Snick Freedom Singers. I went to Convocation Hall to photograph the concert, and as I was shooting near the stage, Belafonte stooped down to shake my hand. At the end of their performance, Matthew Jones, the lead singer of the Freedom Singers, asked me, a "fellow freedom fighter who had been with them on the front lines of battle," to come on stage and join hands with them for the singing of "We Shall Overcome." In the eyes of the audience, I was the real deal, a heroic veteran of the Civil Rights Movement, and although I took full advantage of my status, a part of me felt like an impostor. Unlike the true heroes of the Movement, I had never been jailed, bitten by a police dog, shot at or beaten.

TOP RIGHT AND LEFT,
BOTTOM RIGHT
Student Union for
Peace Action (SUPA) sit-in
at the US Consulate
to protest brutality during
the Selma, Alabama, March,
Toronto, Ontario,
March 1965

BOTTOM LEFT
Student Union for
Peace Action (SUPA) sit-in
at Parliament Hill to
protest the Vietnam War,
Ottawa, Ontario,
March 1966

After the concert, I went down to the CBC studios and was welcomed by Beryl Fox, one of the creative forces behind the remarkable *Seven Days* program. After looking at some of my recent work, she said I had a good eye and thought I would benefit from meeting John Foster, the veteran cameraman of their production crew. John and his gracious wife Pam Hyatt Foster, a prominent Canadian actress, more or less adopted me, and I was a frequent visitor to their home. Beryl herself was a compelling figure, intense with a powerful and creative intellect, a handsome blonde woman with an intriguing hint of tragedy in her deep-blue eyes. She was very helpful with my re-entry into Canadian society and, suspecting that I was penniless, managed to offer me the occasional photographic assignment. I wanted to deepen our relationship, but she said that even though I had a unique vision and she expected great things from me, our relationship could go no further. It was a gentle letdown but a dismissal nonetheless, and I was deeply disappointed that I couldn't get to know this fascinating woman more intimately.

I was slowly integrating into Toronto society when Selma, Alabama, exploded onto the world scene. A march from Selma to Montgomery, Alabama, had been organized to protest the killing of Jimmie Lee Jackson. As the marchers attempted to cross the Edmund Pettus Bridge, they were attacked by state troopers wielding nightsticks. As I watched the newscast, I could see that John Lewis was once again at the head of the marchers. When the melee began, I was afraid he was one of the bloody bodies seen through the swirl of tear gas. I wanted to be there, but driving would take too long, and my Beetle was starting to show the effects of its hard use. I called Julian Bond in Atlanta to get an update and learned that, thankfully, John was all right. There was no way I could ask Snick to use its limited resources to fly me down to Selma, and I was almost broke. At the end of a harried and frustrating day, I hadn't solved my dilemma, so I drove over to John and Pam Foster's home, accepting their dinner invitation. When John saw my frenzied state, he gave me a shot of Scotch and one of his tranquilizers, which had the opposite of its intended effect. After dinner, I drove back downtown, but I was too hyper to turn in. For once, the thought of returning alone to my cozy apartment was unappealing, but there was nowhere else to go. Then I remembered an earlier call from one of the SUPA people asking me to attend a meeting at Hart House on the U of T campus to organize a Selma protest demonstration. When I walked in, a group of neatly dressed, middle-class white students were earnestly discussing whether,

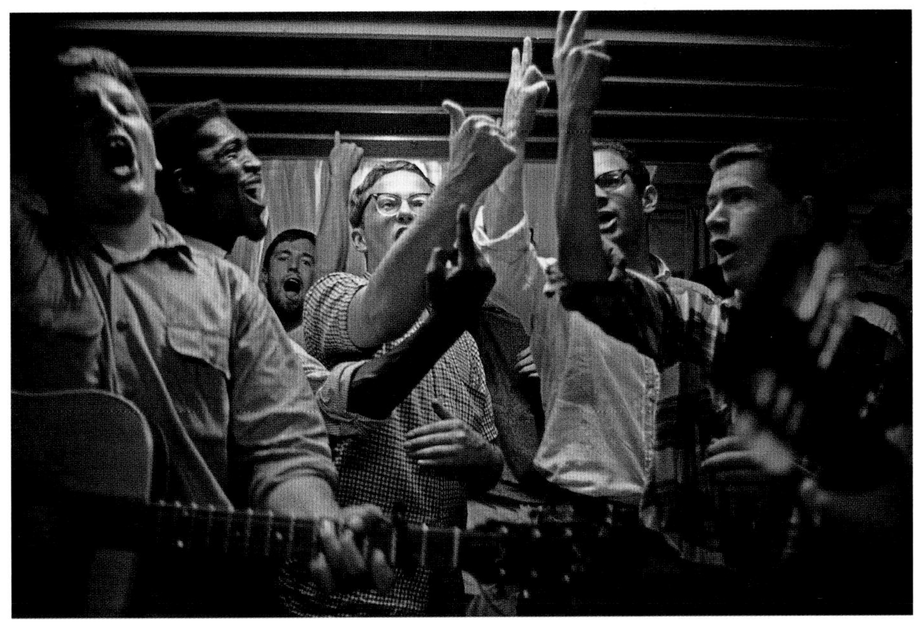

in addition to protesting the violence in Selma, they should also indicate their concerns about the Vietnam War and nuclear disarmament. Stoned on the earlier shot of Scotch and the tranquilizer, I leaped in with my best imitation of Stokely Carmichael's rabble-rousing rhetoric: "What I been hearin' is a bunch of bullshit. You all want to go down to the American Consulate to show you're worried about them poor n****** down in Selma, and also maybe somethin' otta be done about the war in Vietnam, nuclear disarmament, cruelty to dumb animals and whatever the hell else. It ain't about parading your white liberal concerns and educatin' the ignorant masses. The only purpose of demonstratin' is to raise shit, and the more shit, the better. So if you go down to the consulate, you got one and only one thing to say: This shit happenin' in Selma is wrong, it's got to stop, and you're going to lay down your body and not move 'til them marchers reach Montgomery."

When I finished, there was a shocked silence. These polite, earnest students had never heard such a polemic. The discussion gradually resumed, and in the end, they decided to stage a sit-in at the American Consulate. As I was leaving the meeting, Ken Drushka, a reporter for the *Globe and Mail* whom I'd met the previous year when he was the editor of the U of T *Varsity*, came up to me, and with eyes flashing and fingers stabbing the air, he said, "Incredible... If you had spoken like that when you first came here, we would have marched with you down to Mississippi."

Student Union for Peace Action (SUPA), Toronto, Ontario, March 1965

The next morning, I walked down University Avenue with about twelve warmly dressed students carrying placards, blankets and sleeping bags, and they did indeed lay their bodies down on the snow-covered sidewalk in front of the American Consulate. None of us in this staid and conservative city expected the explosion that followed. By six o'clock that evening, the number of demonstrators had quadrupled, and others waited in line to add their bodies to the sit-in. The demonstration was front-page news and the lead story in both the local and national electronic media. A hastily organized centre at a nearby church became a hive of activity, with donations of warm clothing, blankets, hot food and drinks arriving in a steady stream. The phone rang constantly with inquiries from reporters and concerned individuals and organizations wanting to know how they could help. During the day, I saw a wealthy matron, perhaps from the exclusive Forest Hill area, take off her full-length fur coat and drape it over the shivering body of a young demonstrator before continuing on her walk. Even the normally insular Chinese community became involved; a delivery van from Sai Woo in nearby Chinatown stopped in front of the demonstration to drop off buckets of chow mein, sweet-and-sour ribs and fried rice.

For myself, this unexpected development was a godsend, for I had reached the point where I didn't know where my next meal was coming from or how I would pay the next month's rent. Also, my cozy isolation was wearing a bit thin, and I was eager to get back into action. Suddenly all my wishes were granted: a twenty-four-hour source of food, plenty of new people to hang out with and beautiful young women eager to spend the night with a genuine freedom fighter.

As a result of the spectacular success of the Selma demonstration, the leaders of SUPA felt they were on the verge of a mighty revolution, and to tip the balance, they would organize the dispossessed across Canada. Their model was the "grass roots" projects that Snick and other organizations had so effectively waged in the Deep South. Their targets would be the urban poor, such as the Trefann Court community in Toronto; Indigenous reserve lands in Saskatchewan; and the Doukhobor communities in the interior of British Columbia. I was skeptical, for Canada is not the Deep South, and although there were serious issues in these target areas, these young, inexperienced, and at times naïve students would not be responding to the groundswell of discontent that had arisen in the "grass roots" communities of the South. In fact, they really would be "outside agitators." I was asked to join in this revolution by travelling across the country to photograph these projects. At that point, I had two choices. One was to return to the South, but all indications were that Snick was on the verge of collapse. Most of the people I had worked with and respected had either left or been ousted, so rejoining the Movement seemed no longer to be a viable option. I decided to accept SUPA's invitation, for it offered me the chance to not only continue my artistic development but also to explore, for the first time, the immensity of my own land. And who was I to say that these efforts couldn't lead to significant change?

I was becoming more and more a part of what the media labelled the "New Left," the coalition of political activists that arose on the heels of the Civil Rights and Anti-War Movements in the US. I felt strangely aloof from this community. Without the life-and-death dimensions of the South, I could not feel anywhere near the intense camaraderie that I had shared with my brothers and sisters in Snick, but more importantly, I was the only person of colour in this new group. I was still a stranger in a strange land and felt an instinctive need to be subversive and to exploit every advantage.

In preparation for the summer projects, SUPA had organized a series of seminars at its Spadina Avenue office. I happened to walk into the middle of one of these sessions led by Matt Cohen, a rather awkward-looking student from Ottawa. To maintain my tough activist persona, I was obnoxiously dismissive of all the intellectual theorizing. After the seminar, Matt came up to me and said quite politely that I was a total ass. It was the first time anyone had dared to call me out on my tired act, and with great relief, I could now begin to discard one mask and be more myself. Matt and I soon became fast friends, and over the coming decades, we would be each other's best friend and soulmate. Matt, who would go on to become one of this country's most distinguished authors, was an absolute genius—he and Bob Moses were two of the most brilliant minds that I've had the pleasure to encounter. Compared to his megawatt intellect, my brain had the output of a nightlight, but we had a great time playing off each other, for we shared the same absurd view of the world. Matt was a Jew and, like myself, had known the humiliation and pain of intolerance. Although we never talked openly of these experiences, I believe it was our shared sense of being outsiders that bound us together.

I was also developing a strong friendship with Ken Drushka. I was surprised to learn we were nearly the same age, for when we first met, he seemed to me to be the epitome of the haggard, world-weary,

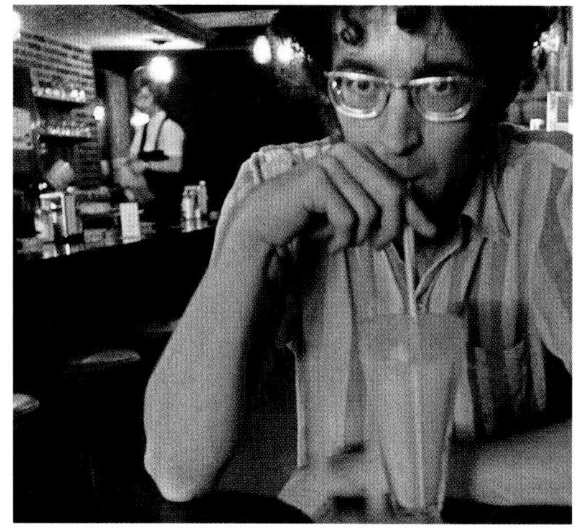

Matt Cohen,
Toronto, Ontario,
1973

"ink-stained wretch." But with his growing involvement with SUPA, he seemed to grow younger each day. In short order, he would quit his job with the *Globe and Mail* and leave his pricey home in the Annex to his wife and two children. At the end of the 60s, Ken, unlike the rest of us, made a clean break and, with his new love, literally rode on horseback into the western sunset. He would eventually settle in Vancouver, where he published numerous books and became a recognized authority on silviculture and the logging industry in British Columbia. Ken claimed that I was the one responsible for the radical change in his life, and I never knew whether that was a compliment or a curse.

Ken, Matt and I became inseparable: the Three Musketeers of the Movement, although in most instances we were more like the Three Stooges. Every now and then, Matt would present us with his newest five-year plan, which dealt in large part with how he would juggle his relationships with the many women in his life. With a gleeful grin, he would lead us through his labyrinth of unassailable logic and stunning insight until, ta-da, he would arrive at his brilliant conclusion. At that point, Ken and I would glance askance at each other, for we both realized his conclusion made absolutely no sense, and if acted upon, it would, as it so often did, lead to unmitigated disaster. Both of these friends, Ken and Matt, would play a critical role in my life's journey.

Summer was suddenly upon us, and I was busy attending to the final details of my photographic tour across Canada. The finances for the trip had been resolved when Clayton Ruby, a SUPA member who would become a celebrated trial lawyer, had arranged for me to be placed on the payroll of one of his father's business ventures, a sleazy sex-and-scandal tabloid. During my time with Snick, I once went on an expedition to New York to raise funds and equipment for our photo operations and was assisted by Harvey Zucker, a generous Movement benefactor, who ran a studio on Bleecker Street. Harvey offered to process my film and mail back contact sheets along with a technical critique after each leg of my journey. All the necessary arrangements had been made, and I was eager to get back on the road. Despite the thousands of miles on the odometer, my Beetle was still in fine working order.

My first stop was in the prairie province of Saskatchewan, where I joined up with Michelle and Greta, two students from the University of Regina who were part of the Student Neestow Partnership Project, working with Indigenous communities. I stayed with them in their one-room, flea-infested shack on the James Smith Reserve. The first day I walked onto the reserve with three Nikons hanging from my neck and shoulders, I sensed that something was strangely different. In the South, whenever I walked into even the most depressed plantation community or urban ghetto, I would be immediately surrounded by eager, laughing children begging me to take their picture. Here, on this reserve, I could only see the occasional small face peering warily from behind a window or open door. These fearful children were the end result of past government policies that amounted to nothing less than cultural genocide. In earlier times, the children of Indigenous people were forcibly removed from their homes and placed in the now infamous residential schools, where they were taught the white man's ways. In addition to being punished for such grave offences as speaking their own language, a large number of these children were also sexually abused. In more recent times, the Canadian government has formally apologized for its policies and made attempts to undo some of the damage inflicted on Indigenous people.

After travelling around the southern part of the province, seeing other reserves and participating in the occasional powwow, I travelled north to Green Lake, where Rob Wood, another SUPA volunteer, was living with a Métis couple. Once again, I was crammed into a small, airless shack in which most of the oxygen was depleted by the constantly used wood stove and the Coleman lamps with their harsh, glaring white light. After spending a week in this environment, surviving on a diet made up largely of white bread, potatoes and the occasional piece of canned or dried meat, my brain had turned to mush. One night, Rob took me to visit a social worker in nearby Prince Albert, and our gracious hostess brought out a tray of precious *mikan* (Japanese oranges) sent as a holiday treat by her mother. I couldn't stop eating the delicious fruit; my body demanded more. After my fourth or fifth orange, the dull film of lethargy and depression lifted, and I could think again and entertain prospects for a bright future.

The next morning, I couldn't stand the thought of reverting back to my zombie-like mental state, so I headed south to the Trans-Canada Highway, which would take me to British Columbia and the gentle community of Doukhobors who represent a fascinating chapter in Canadian

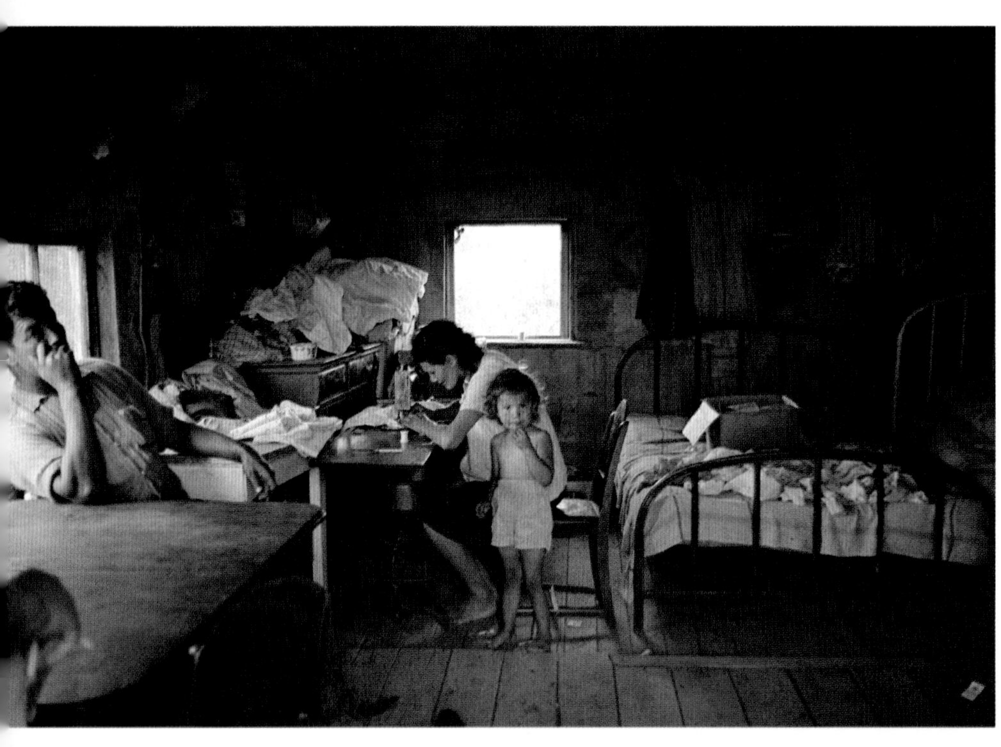

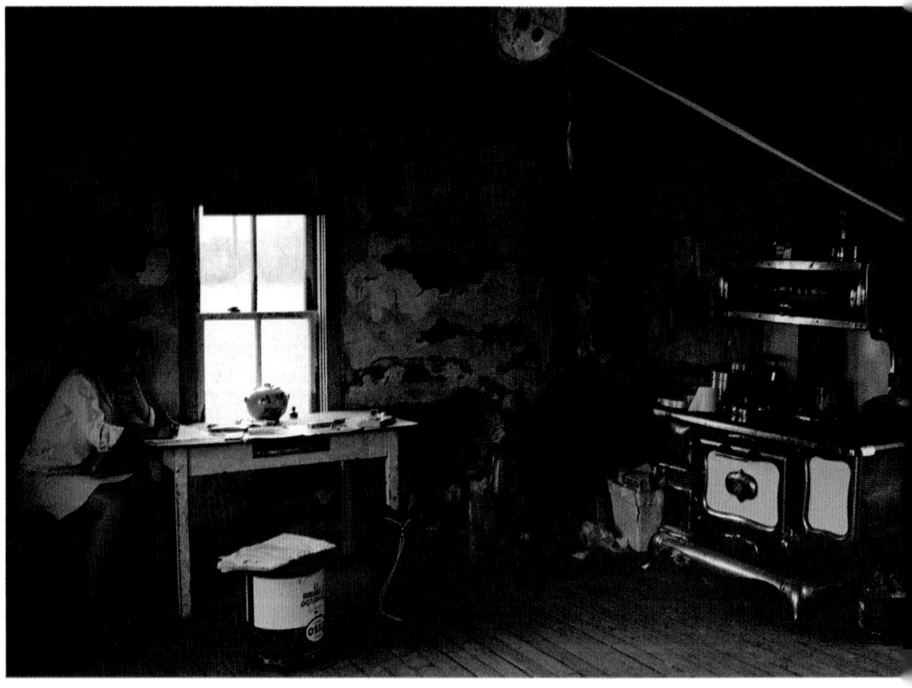

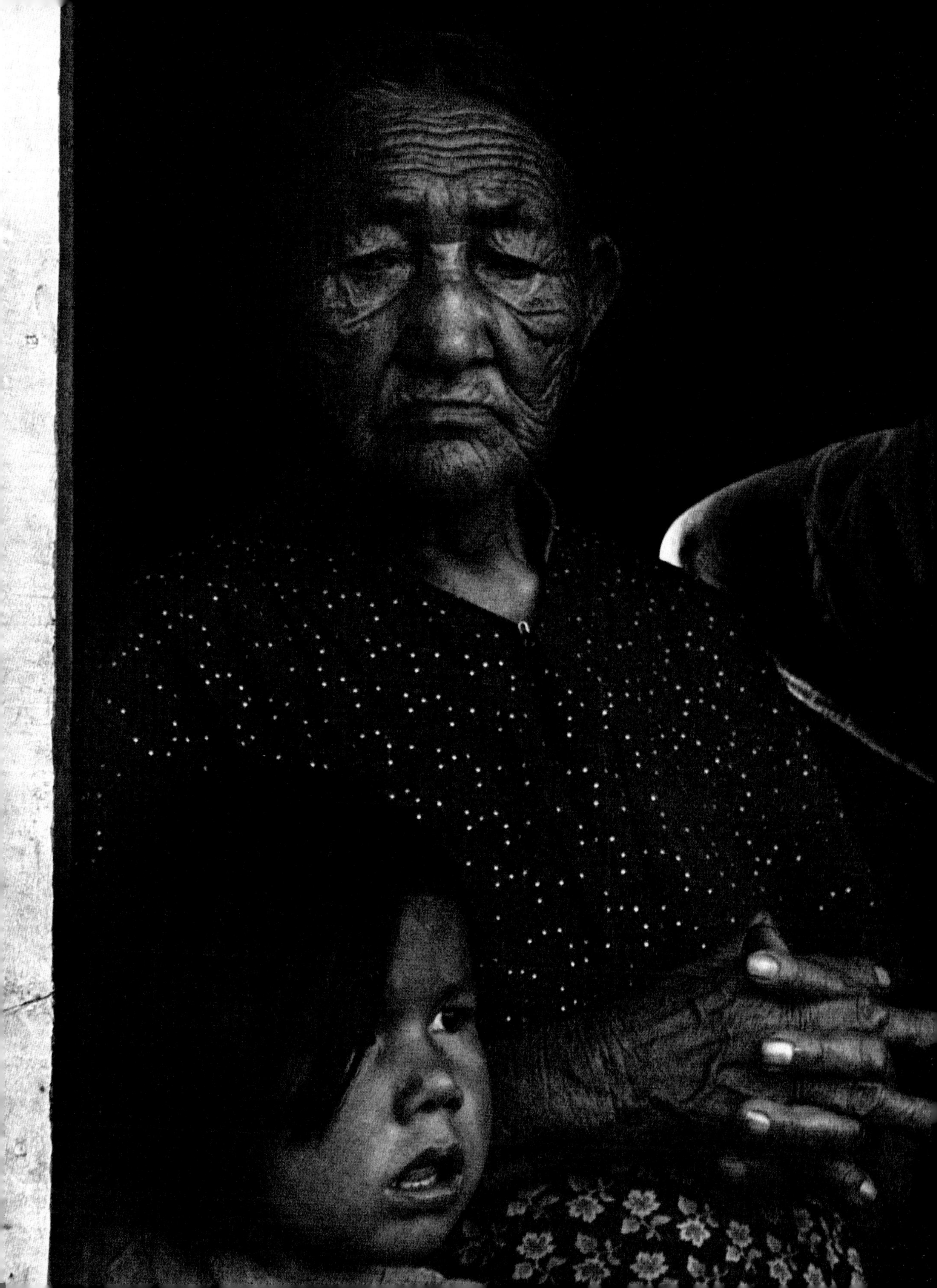

history. The Doukhobors are a pacifist religious sect, originally from Russia, where they were persecuted mercilessly by the Czarist regime around the turn of the century. When intellectuals like Tolstoy brought their desperate plight to the attention of the world, the Canadian government interceded by accepting them as immigrants and agreed to honour their requests to not serve in the armed forces, to own property only communally and to educate their children within their own schools. They first settled in Saskatchewan, but when the provincial government began to renege on the original agreement, their spiritual leader, Peter Verigin, went in search of a new home. He eventually arrived in the Slocan area of British Columbia, where he felt it was God's wish that this lush, green valley be their new promised land. The Doukhobors trekked across the Prairies and settled around the present-day village of Brilliant, where they began to clear the land for their orchards and fields of berries and vegetables. They were not only hard working and cohesive but also brilliant agronomists, so the community quickly prospered and became a major economic force in the area. During World War I, the Doukhobors, in lieu of military service, sent cases of canned fruit from their new factory to the Canadian Army fighting in Europe. According to Doukhobor legend, one soldier was curious about the distinct label on his can of peaches, and when he learned of the Doukhobors and their religious beliefs, he threw away his rifle and refused to kill another human being.

The Doukhobors soon ran into the same conflicts in British Columbia that they had experienced in Saskatchewan. As the BC government began to exert pressure on them to take individual title to land and send their children to Canadian schools, the community began to factionalize into three groups: the independents, who turned completely away from their community; the Orthodox, who still believed in the Doukhobor ways and tried their best to adhere to its precepts; and finally, the militant Sons of Freedom, who demanded strict adherence to their religious beliefs and would fight to maintain their purity. For most Canadians, the word Doukhobor conjures up visions of the Sons of Freedom, with their acts of arson and the spectacle of their protest marches in which massive Russian bodies—men and women—would parade naked down various urban streets to draw attention to the loss of their religious freedom. As it was explained to me, the incidents of arson were, for the most part, internal. The Freedomites would gather at a Doukhobor home and order everyone outside. "You have taken individual title to this land," they would say, "and your home is now an abomination in the eyes of

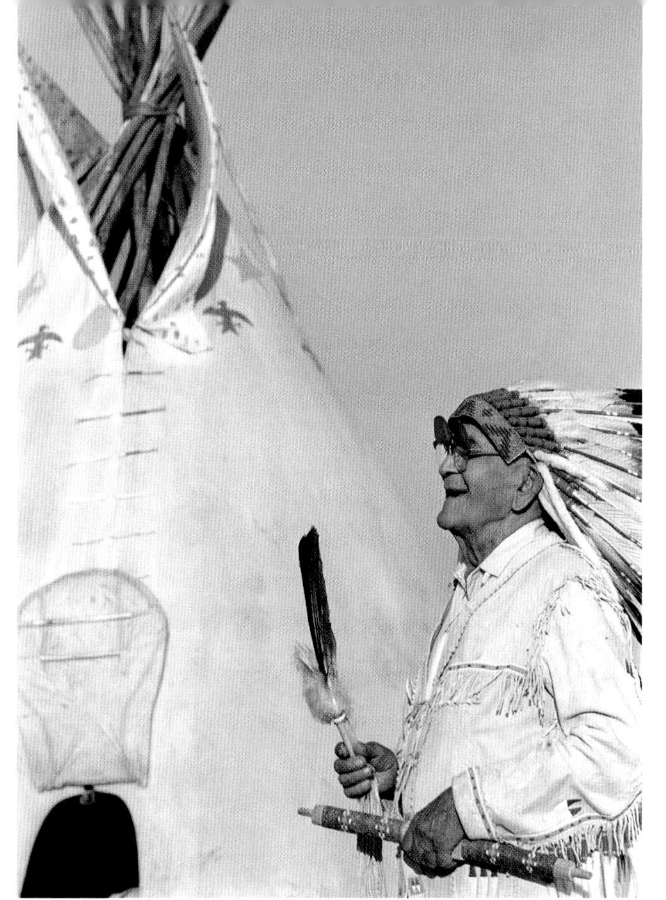

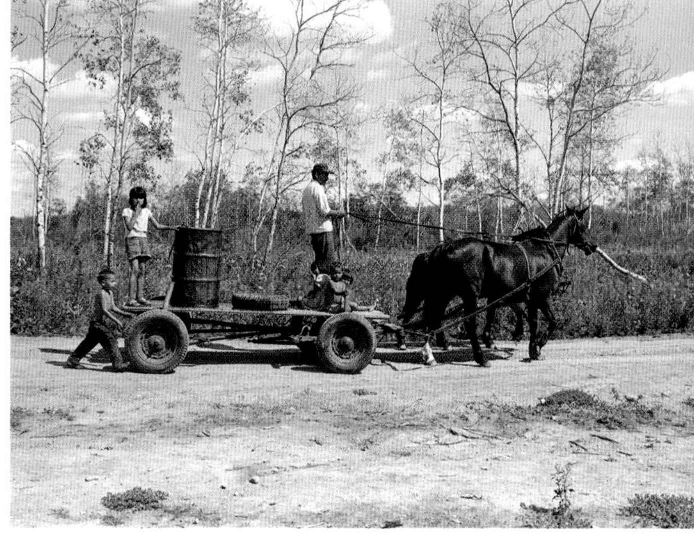

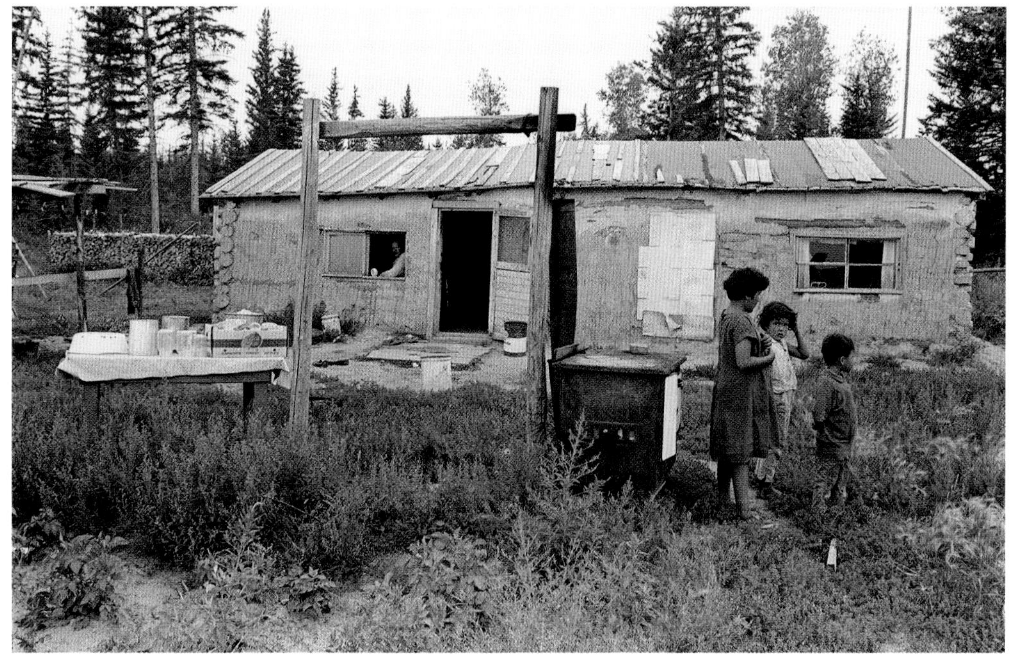

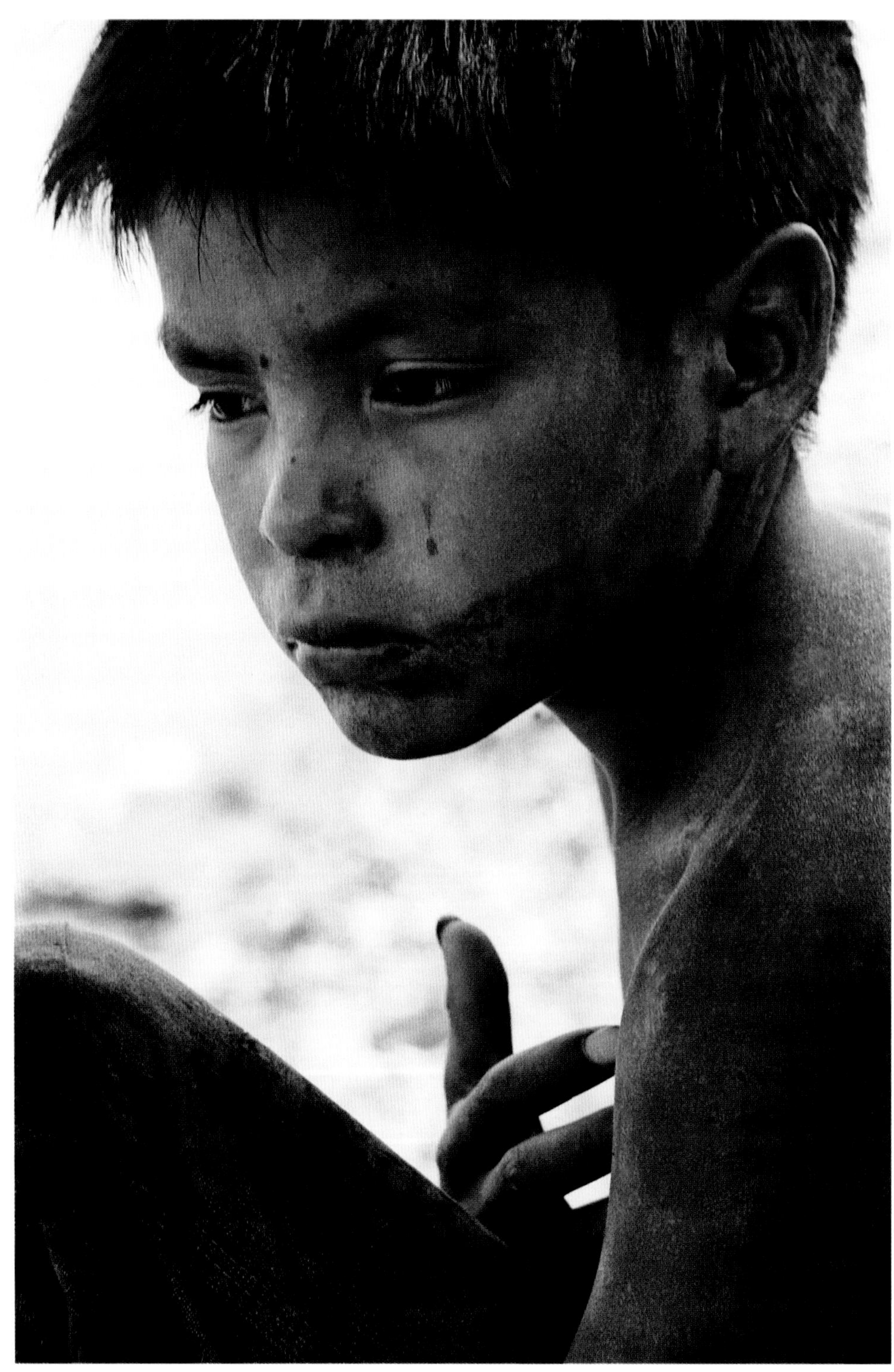

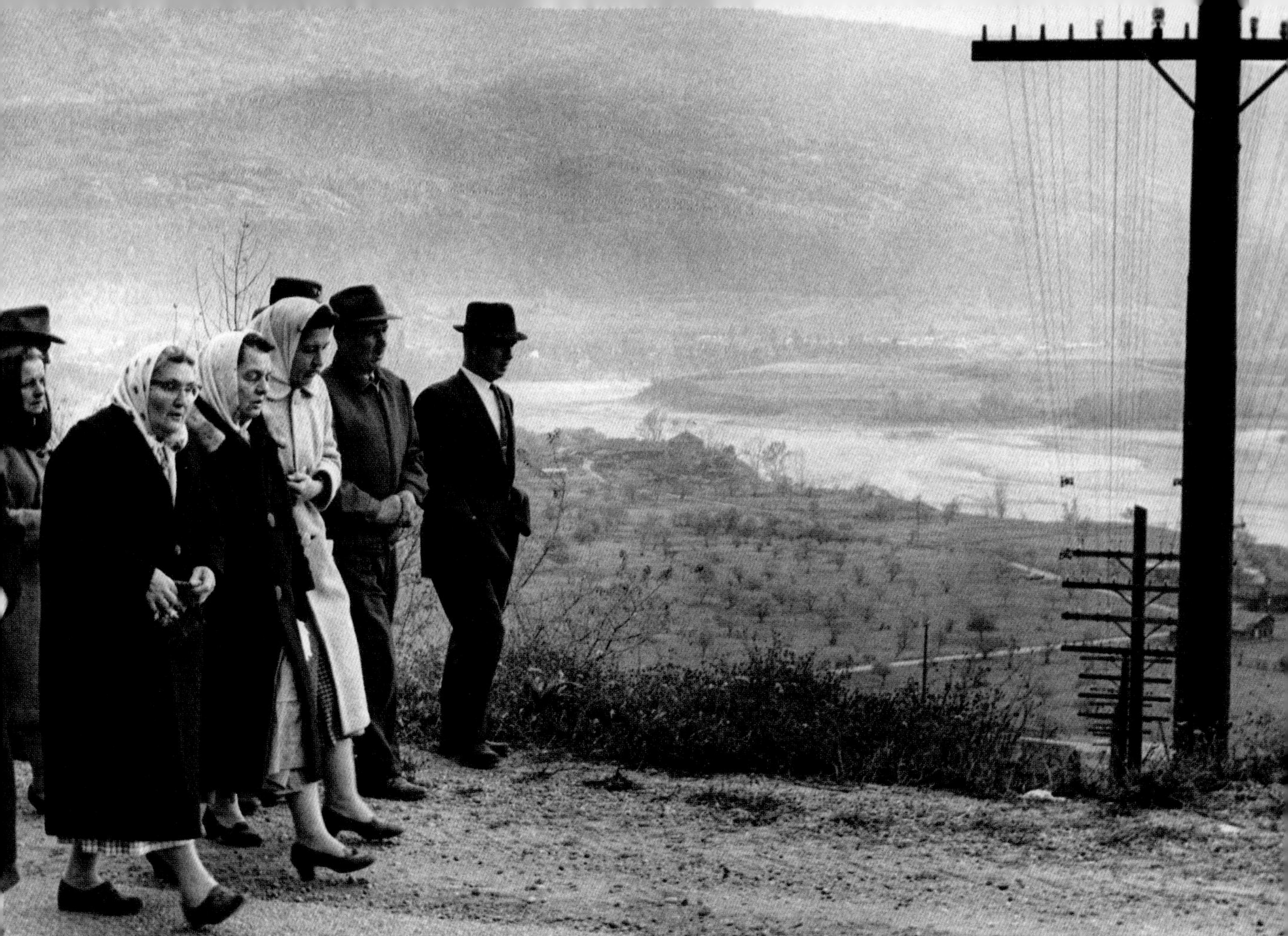

our God. We are very sorry, but it must be destroyed." Everyone wept as the torches were put to the house.

I was eager to meet this community, for we, the Nikkei, have an affinity with the Doukhobors. The camps that incarcerated us during World War II were later used to hold Doukhobor children who were taken away to attend regular schools. During the war years, the Doukhobors—who were the only outside people who would have anything to do with us—came by the camps to surreptitiously hand us produce from their orchards and gardens. It was early evening by the time I reached the Slocan Valley, and once I crossed the bridge to Brilliant, I went in search of the home of the Popoff family. Earlier, Peter Boothroyd, the SUPA project director, had said I would need help finding his rented house in the adjacent Doukhobor village of Ootischenia, and that the Popoffs could guide me there. The elderly Popoffs welcomed me into their neat, single-storey home, and Mary immediately began to set the table while

FACING
Boy at Sioux powwow,
Fort Qu'Appelle,
Saskatchewan,
August 1965

Peter "the Lordly" Verigin
annual memorial service,
Brilliant, British Columbia,
November 1965

143

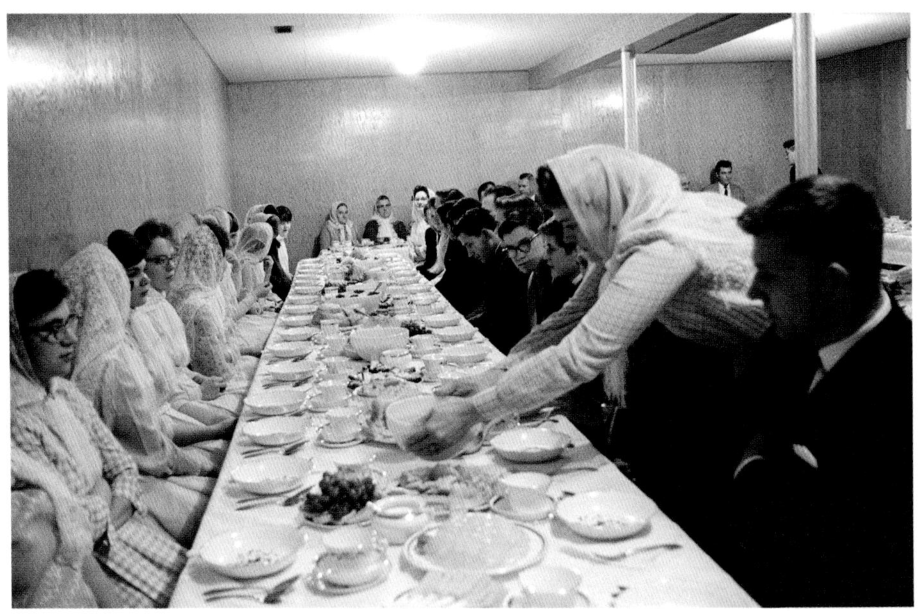

ordering her husband, Mike, to go outside and pick some vegetables. I refused their offer of dinner, not so much out of politeness but more from a dread of borscht, a staple of the Doukhobor diet. My only previous encounter with borscht was once in New York when Bob Fletcher and I stopped off at a deli for lunch. Bob ordered borscht, which turned out to be a disgusting bowl of blood-red liquid topped with dollops of sour cream, which reminded me of the scum floating on McGregor Creek. Anything that looked that awful had to be bad. The stout and genial Mary insisted I eat, and hustled off to her kitchen, returning with a big bowl of borscht, which turned out to be a slightly orange-coloured, creamy, buttery potage of fresh vegetables, perfectly seasoned with salt and dill. The taste was pure heaven and matched well with the home-baked bread, freshly churned butter and sweet garden vegetables. After I had a third helping of the delicious soup, Mike guided me in his car to Peter's home.

The next day, Peter took me on a tour of the Slocan Valley, which was still dotted here and there with traditional Doukhobor communal sites. These consisted of two large, wooden buildings flanking a central courtyard, at the end of which was a central bakehouse with a large, red-brick oven. After visiting with Doukhobor families, we drove over to South Slocan and wended our way down a narrow country lane to reach the secluded home of Helen and Peter Damaskov. As former members of the Sons of Freedom, this couple had spent a combined period of over three decades in Canadian prisons. But despite their advanced years and stormy history, they acted like two teenagers in love. Helen had just bought a blender, and she offered me a glass of her most recent discovery: a thick concoction of pureed grass from her front lawn. The taste was vile. Over the ensuing meal, which was much more palatable, we engaged our hosts in a lively debate over ideologies (they were staunch socialists) and the fate of revolutionary movements around the world. After dinner, they invited us to share the blistering heat of their rustic sauna. We finally left after making promises to return, which we were happy to do, for in this remote corner of the province, we had found two silver-haired allies who, despite their many tragedies and defeats, were still unbowed and so fully engaged in life.

Peter Boothroyd had to leave to finish university, but I decided to stay in the valley until it was time to go to a SUPA conference scheduled for early December in Edmonton, Alberta. Our nearest neighbours, Walter and Vera Kanigan, arranged for me to stay with a man named Joseph, who was living alone after his mother had passed away and his father had found work in Nelson. There was plenty of room in the house, and Joseph, who was about my age, turned out to be an easy companion. It was an ideal situation until one day when his drunken father returned for a visit. When the father reeled into the house, Joseph accused him of being a hopeless drunk who had sold his Doukhobor soul for a pint of rye whisky. With mounting fury, the father shouted back, "You are no good, Joseph, and no son of mine. I know you, Joseph, and you just wait: one day there will be a war, and they will come for you, and you are such a coward that you will go off and fight." This ugly confrontation offered a tragic glimpse into the deeply divided Doukhobor soul and its losing battle to preserve its integrity.

Every year, the entire Doukhobor community comes together to commemorate the death of their first great leader, Peter "the Lordly" Verigin. I took it upon myself to use this occasion to thank the community, on behalf of SUPA, for their support and hospitality. The night before the memorial service, I wrote a short speech and drove over to the Kanigans' to have it translated into Russian. Over the next hour, standing before Vera and Walter, I practiced twisting my tongue around the hard Slavic syllables… *Slava hospidu, dorogia druzia.* The next morning, I walked into the old community hall in Brilliant, now packed with worshippers. The centrepiece of the large room was a simple, round, wooden table covered with a white linen cloth on which were placed bread, salt and

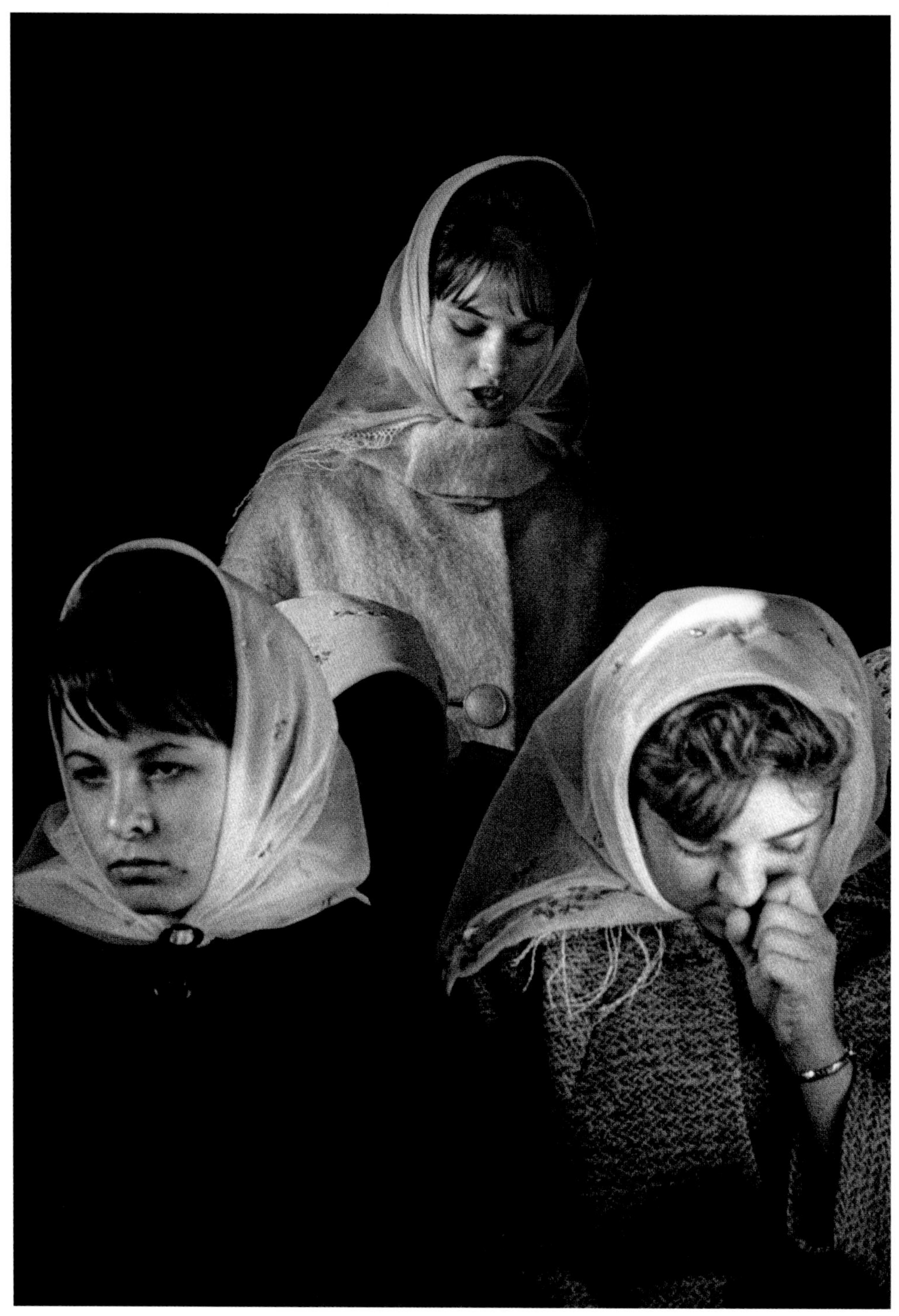

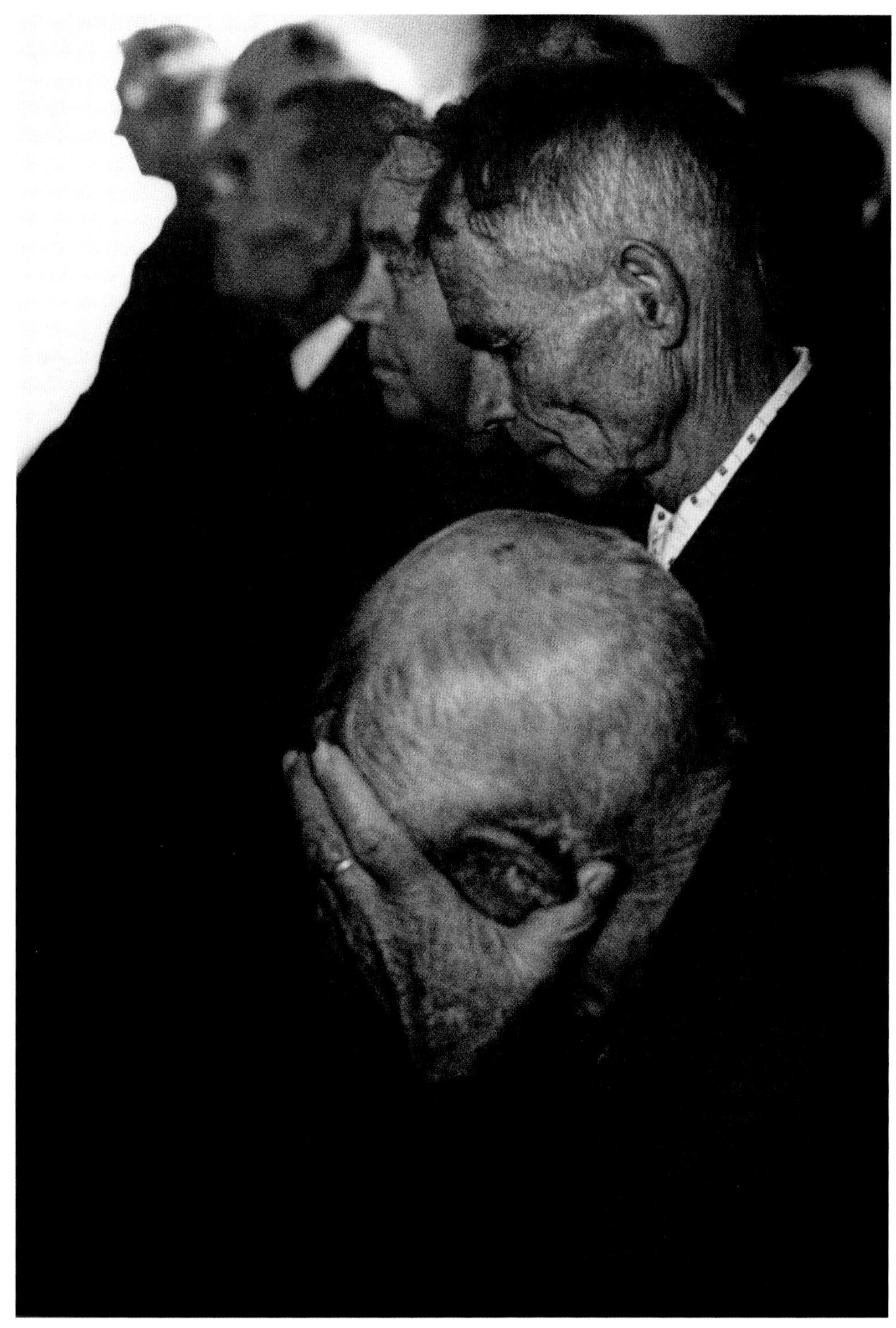

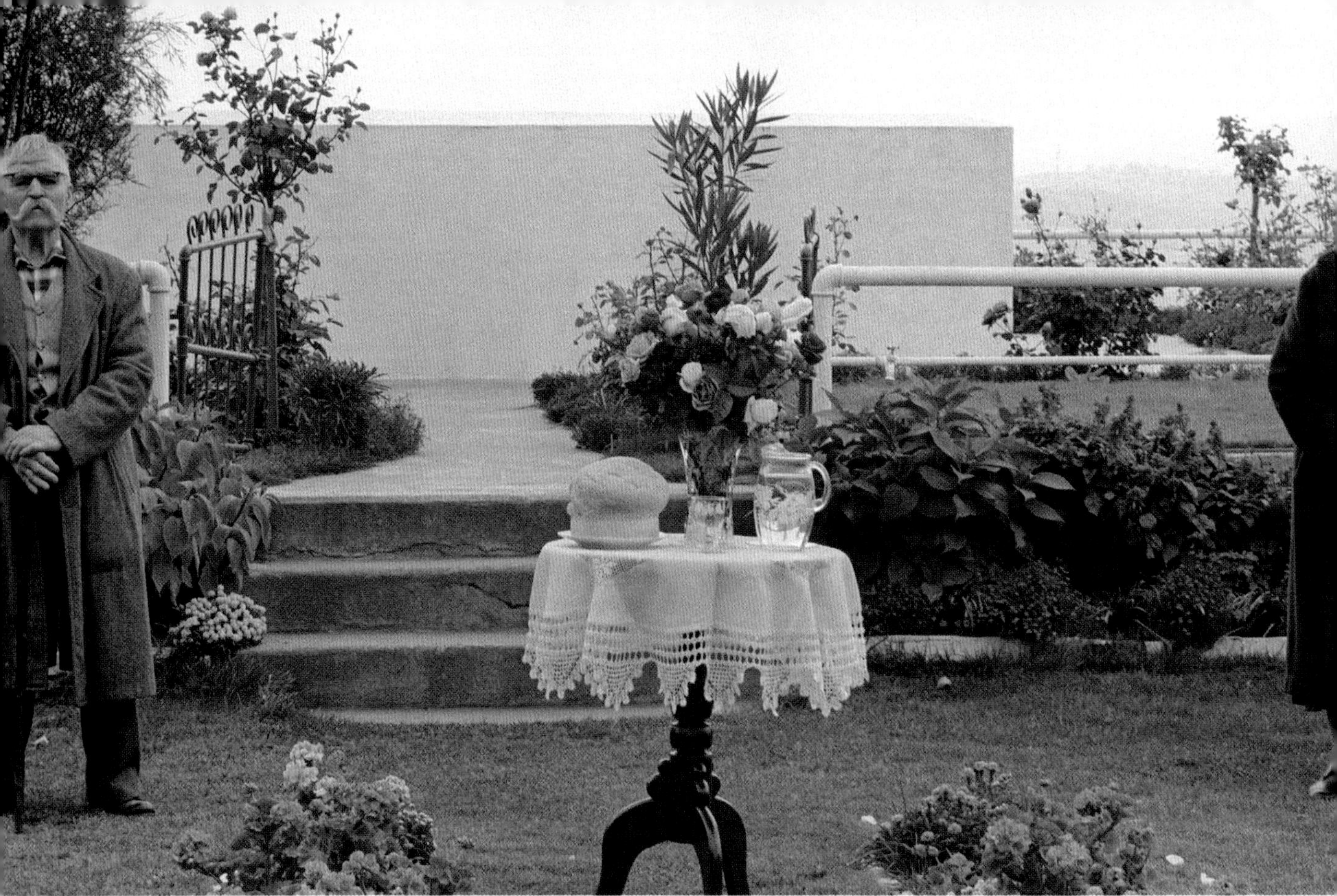

water: symbols of the purity of their way of life. After prayers and the hauntingly beautiful hymns sung by the choir, we all trekked outside to begin our slow march up the hill to the stately tomb of Peter Verigin. The ceremony concluded back at the community hall, and after further prayers, I stood up to give my speech, which, thankfully, I got through without any major slip-ups. The matriarch of the community, who was a direct descendant of the Verigin line, stood up after me and chastised the young for abandoning their culture and language when a perfect stranger could come into their midst and speak in perfectly fluent Russian. When the ceremony ended, she came up to me and began speaking in rapid fire Russian. I could only nod, for I couldn't understand a word she was saying.

My time in the Slocan Valley was coming to an end. To prepare for the long drive to Edmonton, I went to a garage in nearby Castlegar to have my ailing Beetle inspected. The mechanic's report wasn't good: one cylinder was almost totally shot and the other three were operating at about sixty percent. The consensus was that it would be insane to try to drive to Edmonton. However, I had neither the time nor the money for repairs, so I continued on to South Slocan to spend my last night with the Damaskovs. A final meal of borscht and an invigorating hour in their sauna would be good preparation for the coming ordeal. The next morning, I awoke to a world transformed by the season's first heavy snowfall. When I crept down the lane to the highway, I could only guess where the road lay in the near total whiteout. My first obstacle was the Kootenay Pass, with its daunting elevation of over five thousand, eight hundred feet. As I crept up toward the summit in second gear, huge semis would come whipping by and blind me with clouds of snow. I made it over the top and cruised down, but when I reached the next intersection and tried to make a left turn, my steering wheel wouldn't budge. Fearing the worst, I got out to inspect under the front bumpers and discovered that, in my ascent and descent of the Kootenay Pass, I had churned up enough to snow to totally encase the tires in a compacted mixture of snow and slush. With the pointed end of my tire iron, I spent the next hour freeing my tires from their frozen prison. The next hurdle was the Crowsnest Pass, but since it was of much lower elevation, I breezed through. When I reached the flatlands of the Prairies, I began to feel a bone-chilling coldness. A weather report on the radio announced that, with the wind chill factor, the temperature was hovering around forty degrees below zero. After a few miles, my windshield frosted over, and the only area cleared by the inept heater was a ten-inch quarter moon in the bottom left corner, forcing me to drive, for the next seven hours, scrunched down in my seat with my neck awkwardly cranked on my shoulder.

It was still bitterly cold by the time I reached Edmonton, and on the way to the conference, my car felt like a solid block of metal whenever I hit a bump in the road. I remember very little of that conference except for a general feeling of despair and dissolution, which was eerily similar to the mood at the last Snick staff meeting in Waverley, Mississippi. The summer project had yielded little, neither great insights nor grand strategies for the expected revolution. Despite my earlier skepticism, I too was devastated. On the last night of the conference, I found a quiet corner and wept openly, for I sensed that it was the end of the 60s and the end of the dream of a bright new millennium that had awakened the passions of an entire generation of North American youth.

After the conference, I still had the gruelling task of driving back to Toronto. Thankfully, Henry Tarvainen offered to go with me. Although I had managed to coax a bit more warmth from the heater, the Beetle was

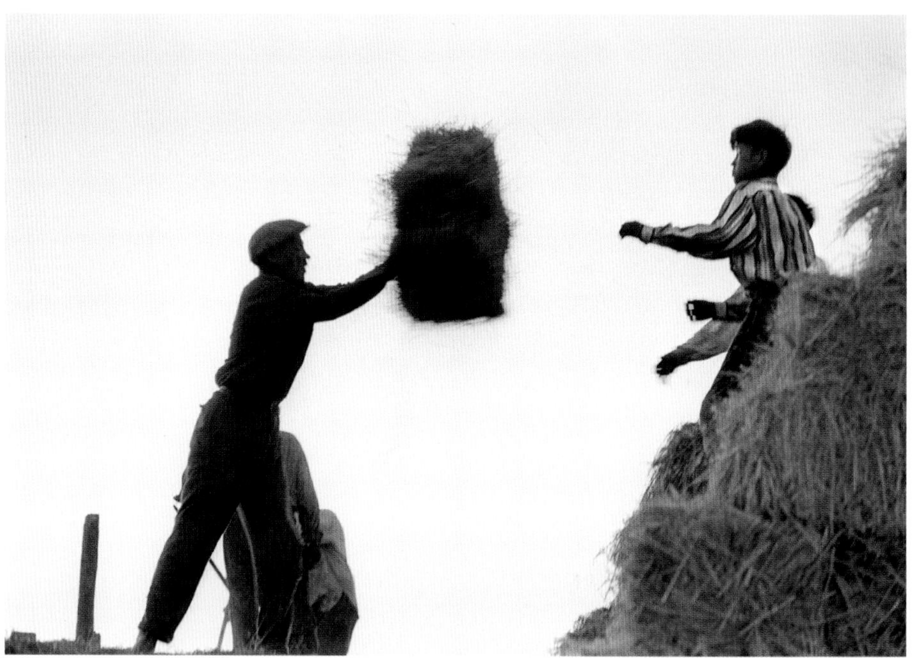

still very cold. We managed the long, non-stop drive by taking four-hour shifts with one of us driving while the other lay in the back, nestled in my down sleeping bag. We had just driven past Regina when the brakes failed, but, since it was the middle of the night, we had no choice but to carry on. When we reached the outskirts of Winnipeg in the early morning, I managed to coast into a large truck stop with a restaurant and two service bays. I walked over to the mechanic who, fortunately, had once owned a Volks and agreed to look at my brakes. Henry and I went into the restaurant for breakfast. Just as we were finishing our second cup of coffee, the mechanic came in and announced that he had found an easily reparable leak in the brake fluid line, and now my car was ready to go.

After another day and a half of hard driving, we finally caught sight of the bright lights of Toronto on the horizon. Exhausted and half frozen, we had made it home.

James Smith Reserve,
Saskatchewan,
August 1965

FACING
Cowessess Reserve,
Saskatchewan,
August 1965

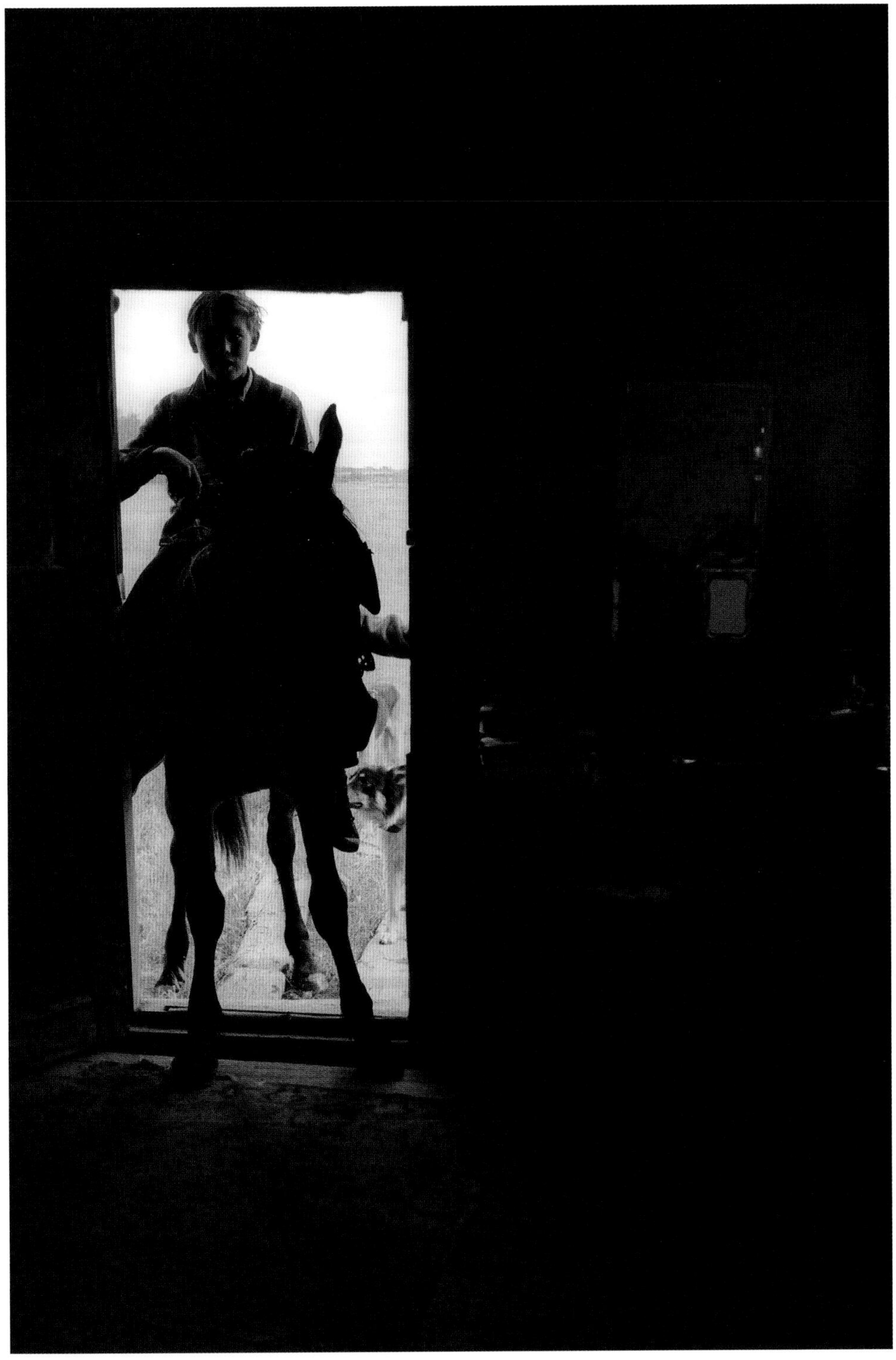

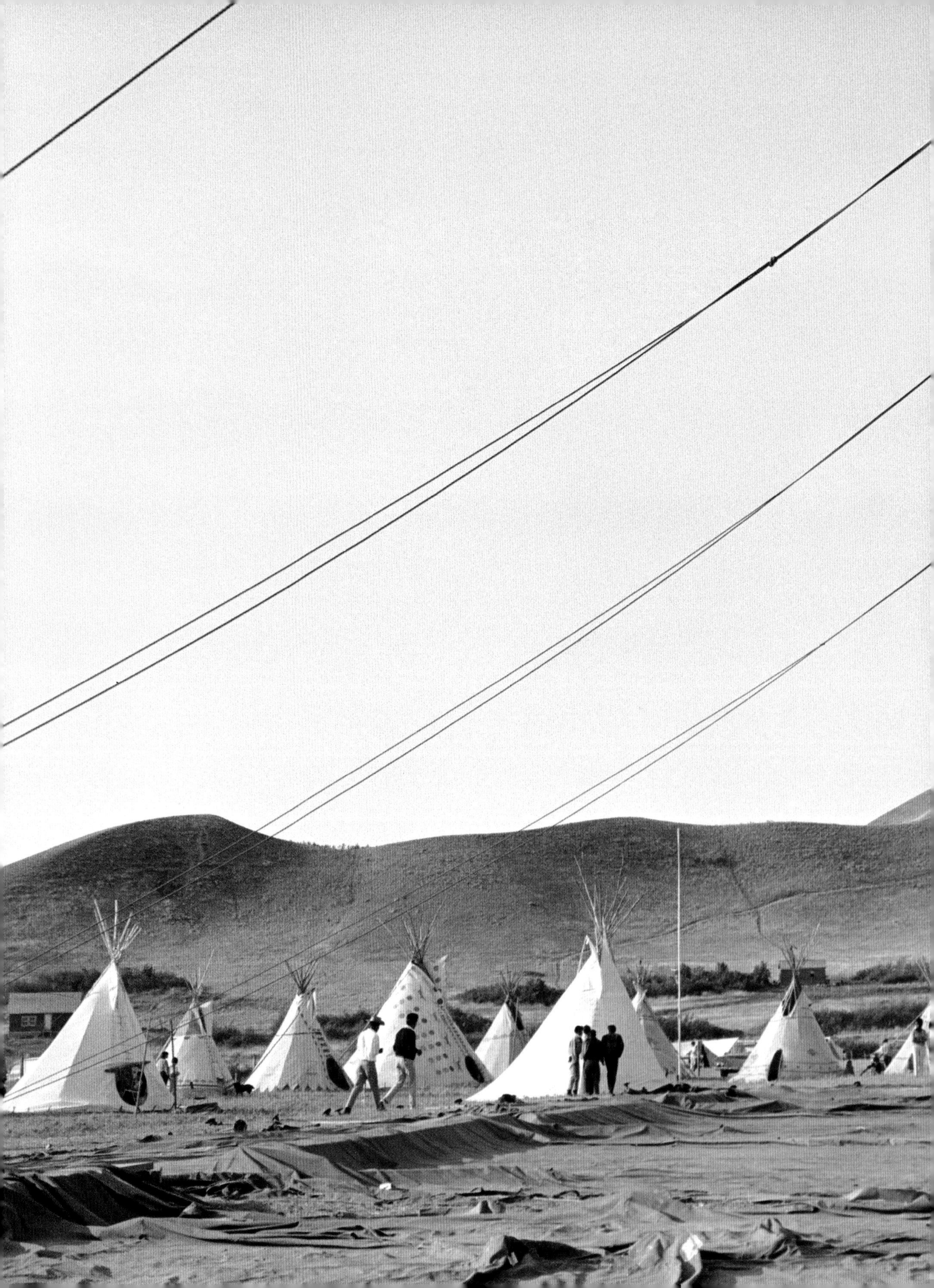

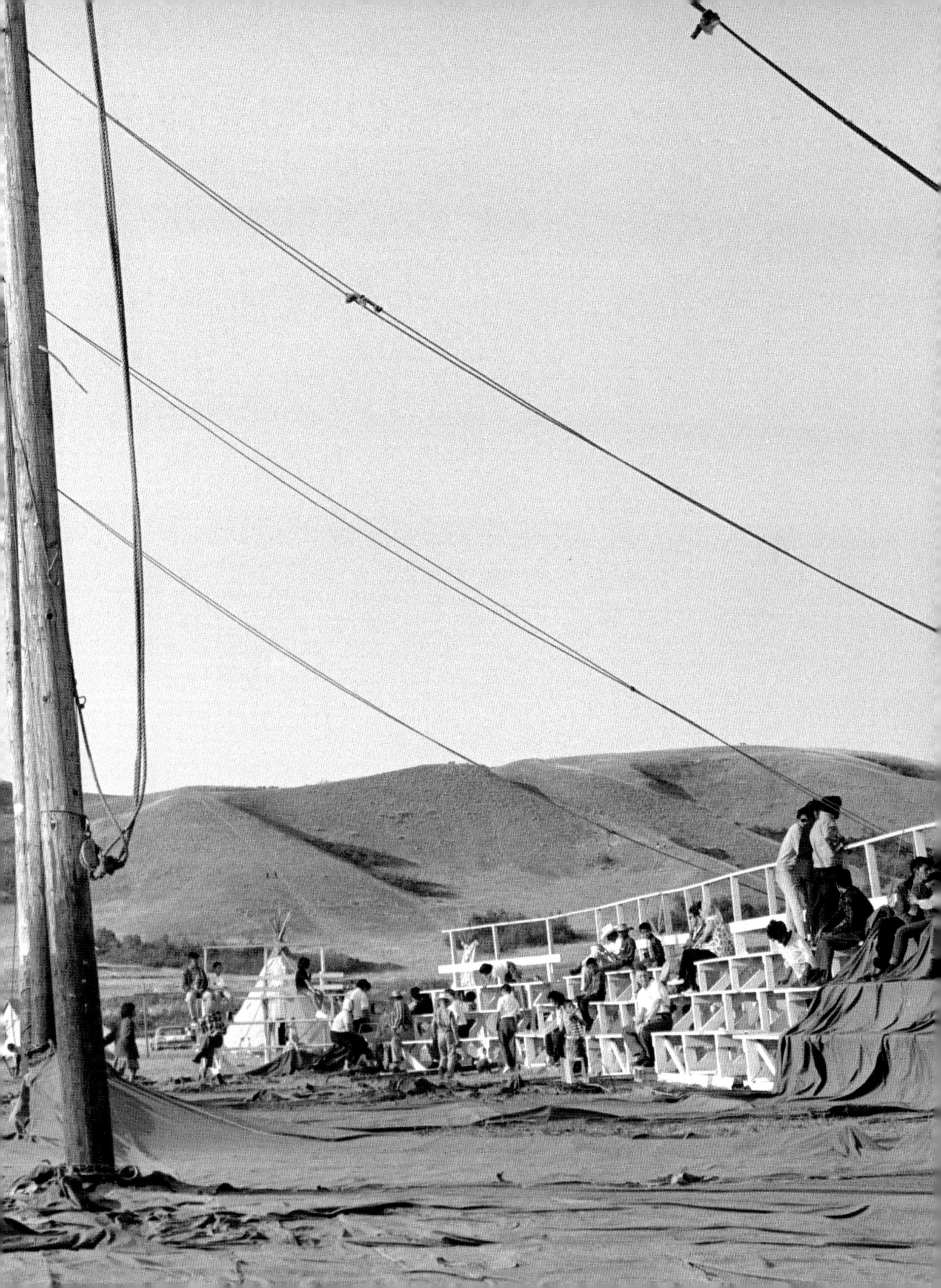

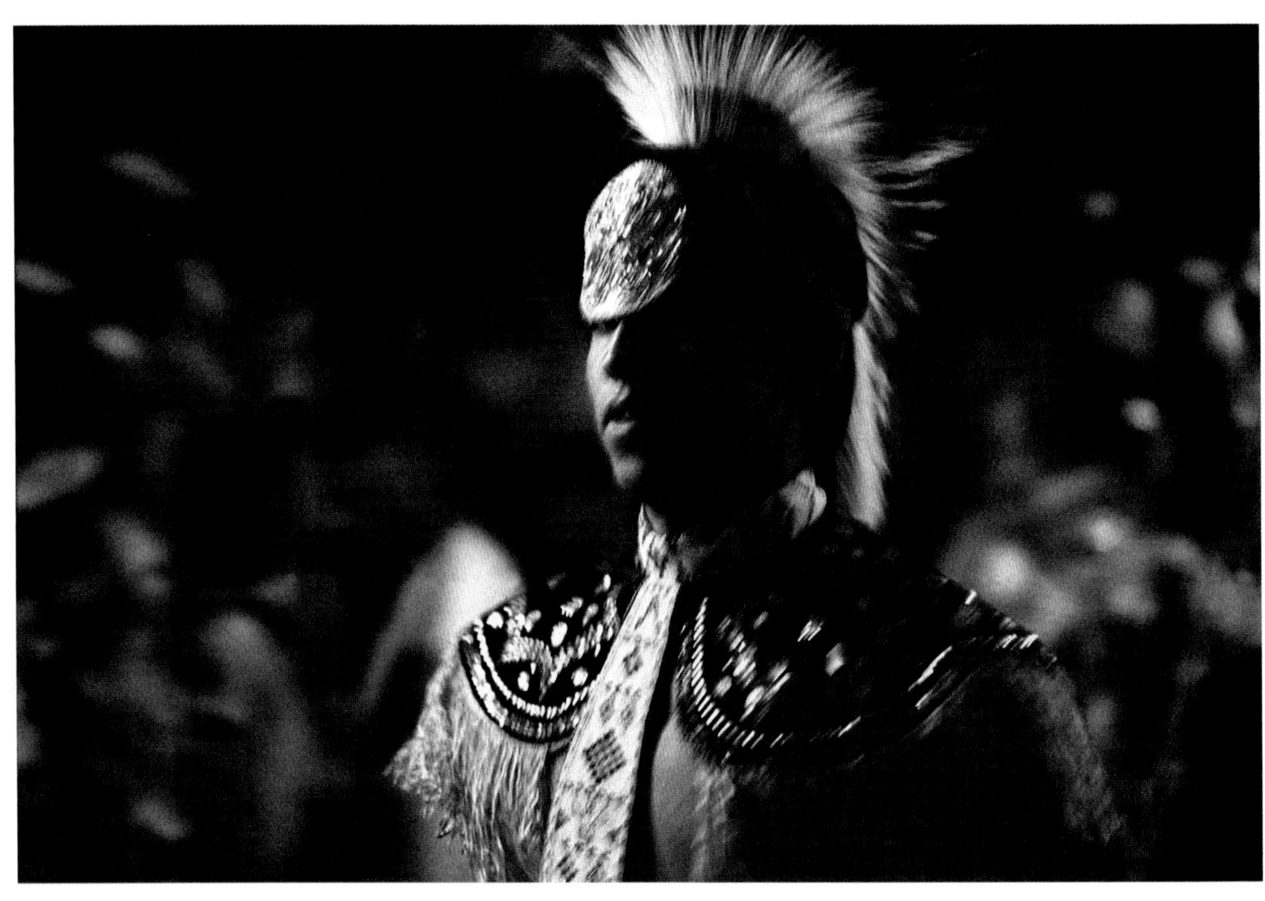

PREVIOUS SPREAD Sioux powwow, Fort Qu'Appelle, Saskatchewan, August 1965
Sioux powwow, Fort Qu'Appelle, Saskatchewan, August 1965

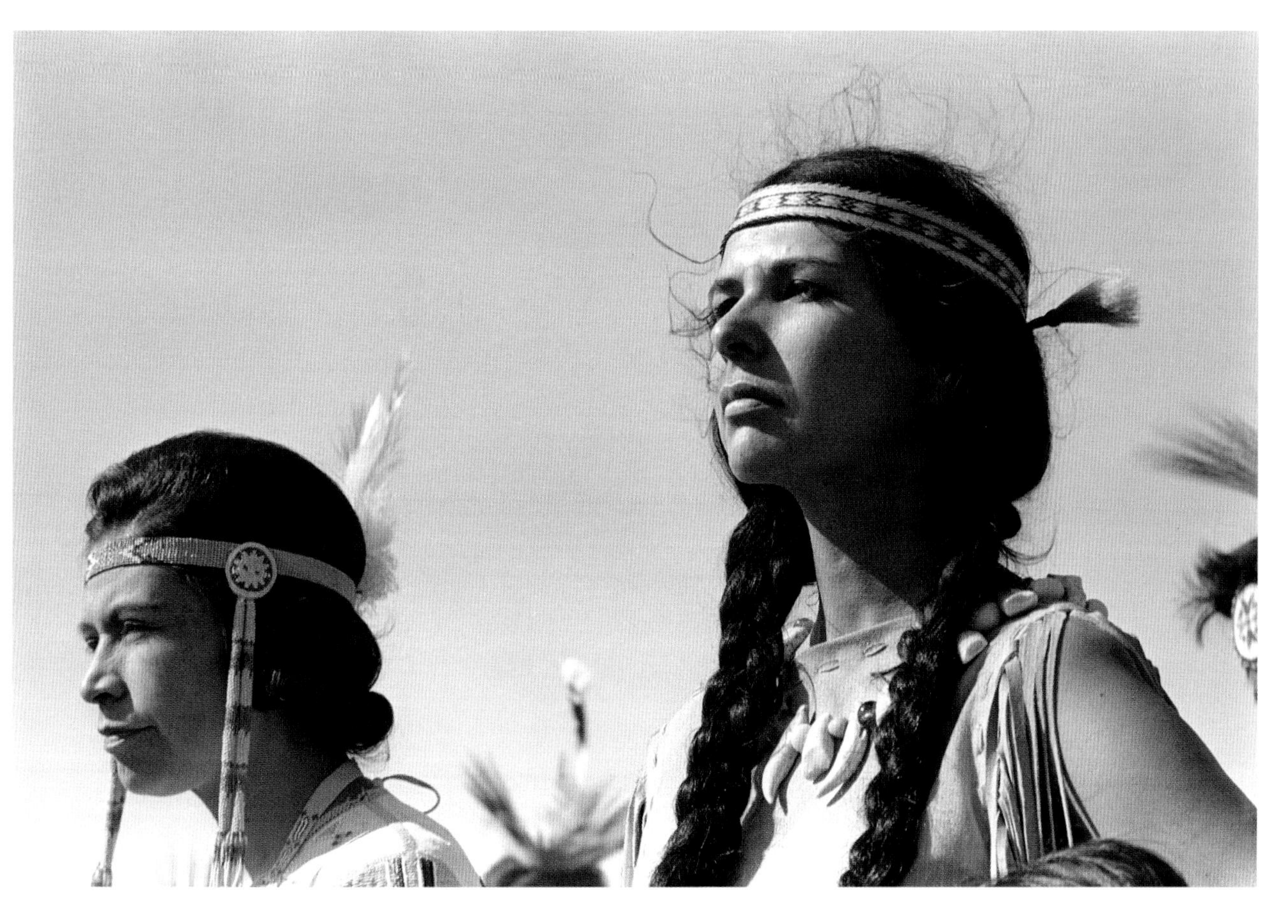

Alanis Obomsawin [on the right], Sioux powwow, Fort Qu'Appelle, Saskatchewan, August 1965

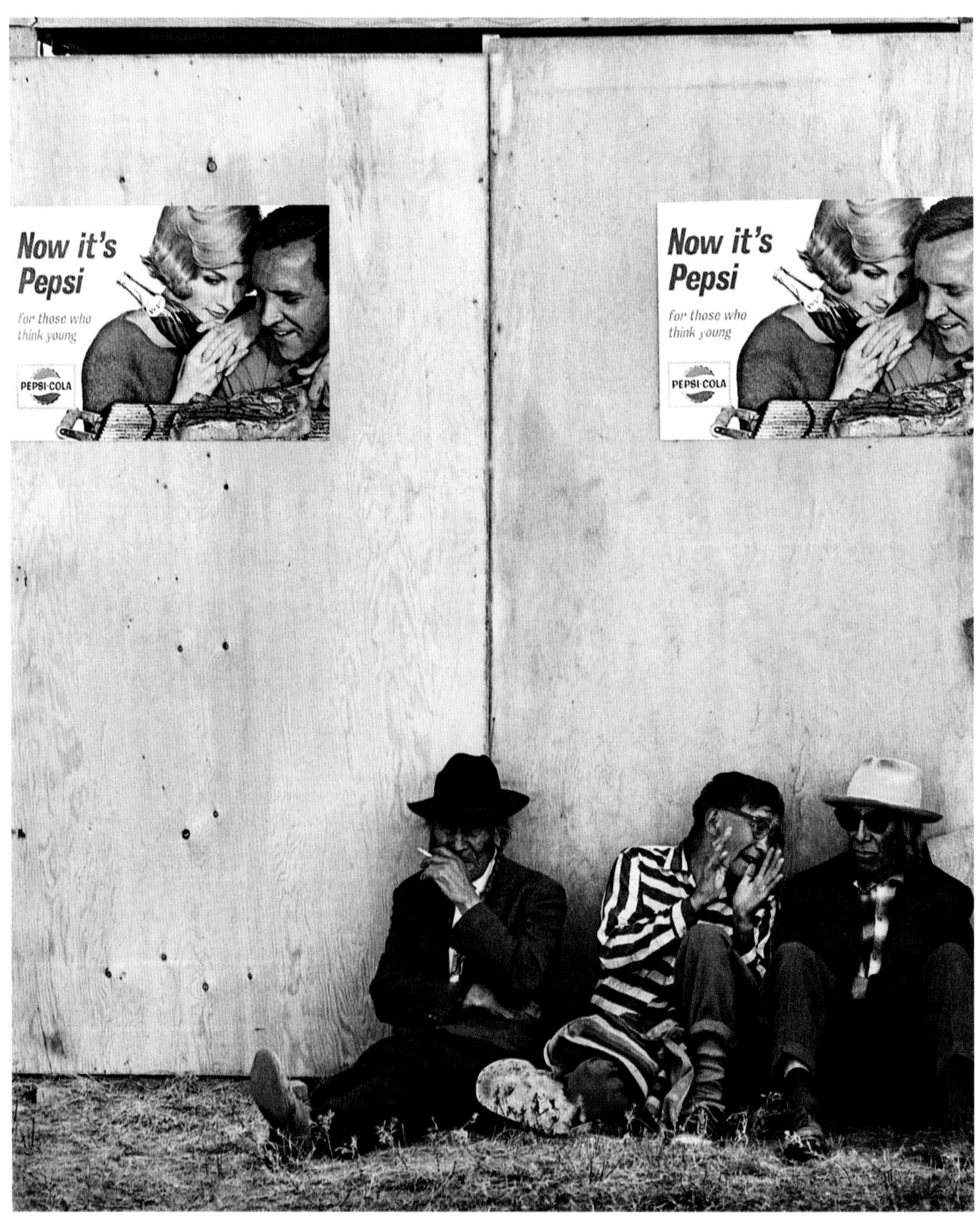

   Three men under a Pepsi sign at Sioux powwow, Fort Qu'Appelle, Saskatchewan, August 1965

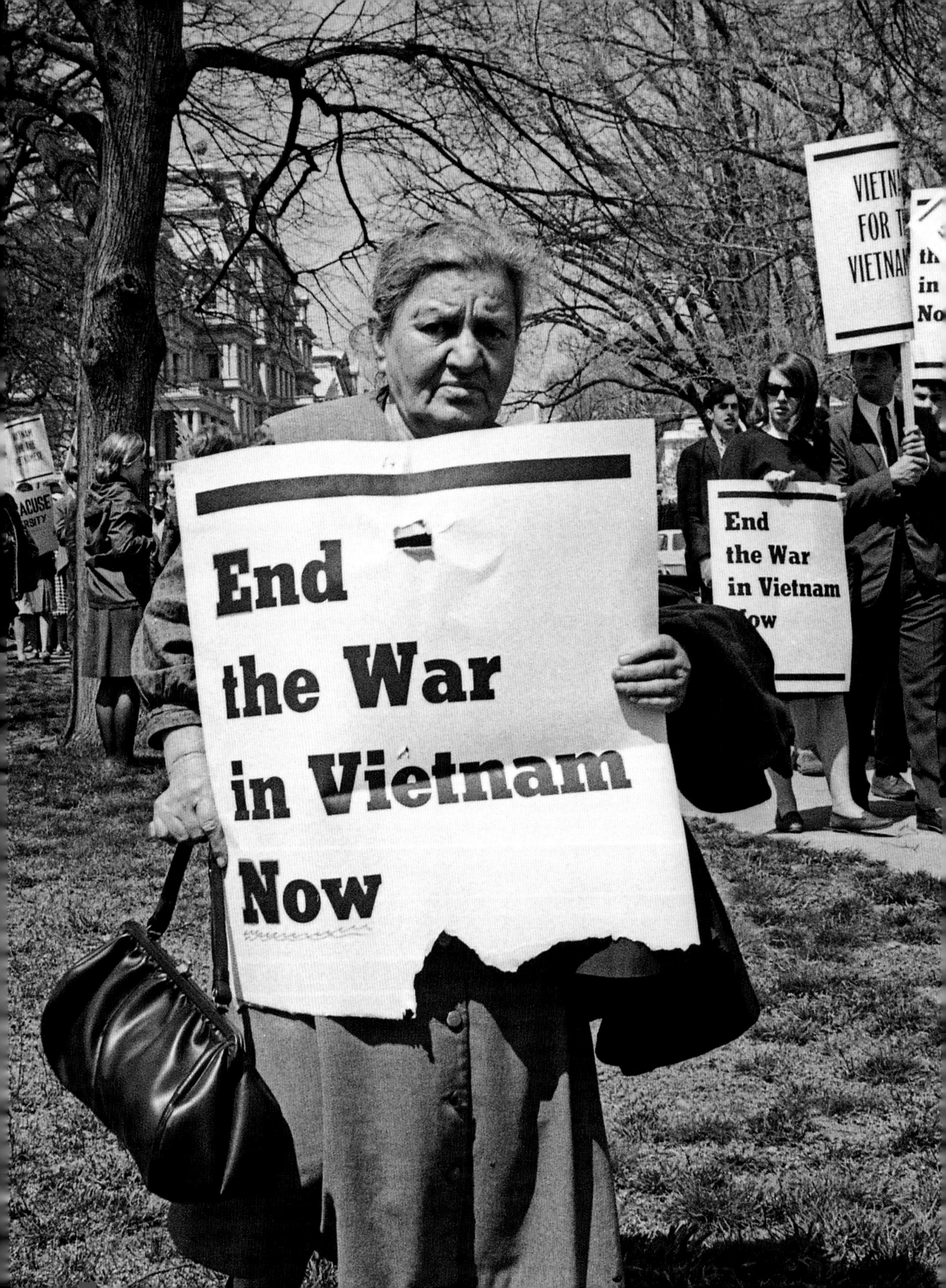
End
the War
in Vietnam
Now
End
the War
in Vietnam
Now
VIETNA
FOR T
VIETNAM
th
in
No

6

IT WAS TIME FOR me to work on all the film that I had accumulated over the past two years. Harvey Zucker had extended an open invitation to me to come work in his studio, so in late February, I drove down to New York. Halfway through my work, I got a call from Art Pape, one of the leaders of SUPA, asking if I would be willing to fly up to Ottawa to shoot a sit-in protest against the war in Vietnam. SUPA volunteers from across the country were already converging on the nation's capital. I was reluctant to leave my work, but the adventure of riding in a plane for the first time was irresistible. My maiden flight on a jet was more than I had hoped for. I couldn't believe that such a massive machine could accelerate so quickly, much less get off the ground. I was met at the Ottawa airport and taken directly to the school auditorium, where Staughton Lynd, a lawyer, political activist and former Yale professor, was scheduled to speak. As I entered the crowded hall, I happened to catch a glimpse of a petite and perky woman, and in that brief moment of eye contact, I sensed that a significant moment in my life had just occurred… *Some enchanted evening, you may see a stranger…*

The next morning, we all gathered at the church headquarters and headed off for Parliament Hill. The demonstration wasn't as massive as we'd hoped, but still, there was a respectable number of protestors. They plunked themselves down on the snow-covered walkway in front of the huge stone building that was the seat of our national government.

March on Washington to protest the Vietnam War, Washington, DC, April 17, 1965

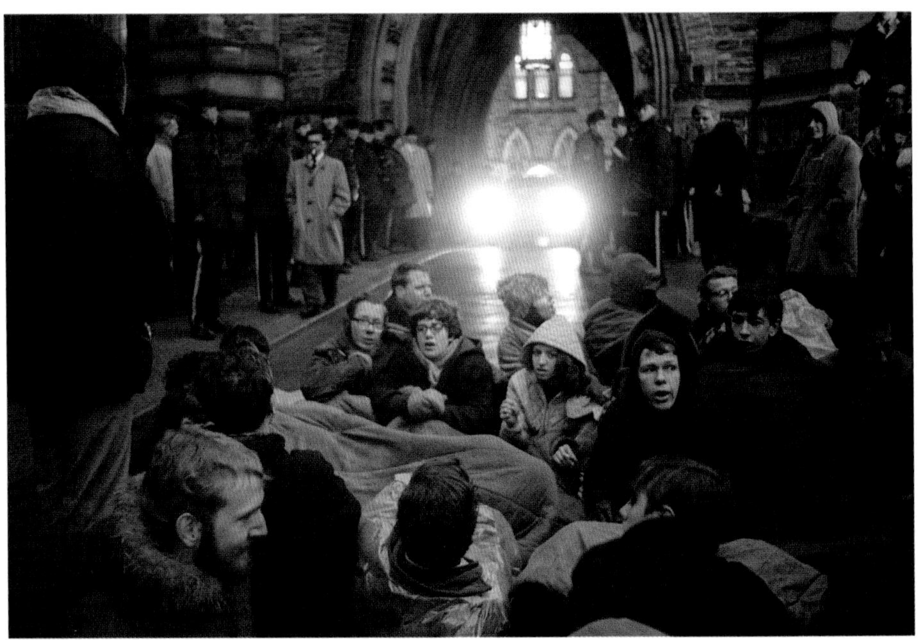

They were immediately surrounded by the parliament's Mounties and ordered to disperse. When nobody moved, the head Mountie called on the Ottawa police to bring up a paddy wagon. Apparently I wasn't very convincing as a photojournalist, for I was summarily thrown in with all the demonstrators. The experience was totally absurd, so on the ride to the city jail, I went on a rant about the indignity of my false arrest, which had everyone, including our police guards, rolling with laughter. I glanced over at Art Pape, who was positively beaming, for his lifelong dream of being imprisoned for his political beliefs was about to be realized. After a few hours sitting in jail, we were released and went back to the church headquarters.

When I entered the meeting hall, I was greeted with a cup of hot coffee in the hands of the attractive woman I had spotted the night before. She sat me down on a chair, introduced herself as Libby and, after stripping off my salt-encrusted boots and sodden socks, proceeded to massage my frozen feet. We spent the night together in a cozy nest under the pulpit of the church chapel.

I had some business to take care of in Toronto, so I accepted her invitation to ride with her to nearby Kingston, where she was living with her two young children after escaping from a bad marriage in the States. The next morning, I awoke in her bedroom and looked around for my

Student Union for
Peace Action (SUPA)
sit-in at Parliament
Hill to protest the
Vietnam War,
Ottawa, Ontario,
March 1966

clothes, which were freshly laundered and neatly hung on a chair. At the feet of the chair sat my leather boots, cleaned and polished to their original luster. Libby waltzed in, carrying a tray loaded with a cup of steaming coffee, a glass of freshly squeezed orange juice and a freshly baked scone slathered with butter and strawberry jam. At that point, it was game over. I was hooked.

After a couple of days in Toronto, I flew back to New York to finish up my work. After another week of concentrated effort, I left the city with three handsome portfolios: *The Black Belt South, The Native People of Saskatchewan*, and *Bread, Salt and Water: The Doukhobors of BC*. One day I received a phone call from Tom Hathaway, an American draft dodger and scion of the wealthy Boston family known for its eponymous dress shirts, asking if he could come over to look at my work. After the viewing, Tom, who was an active member of SUPA, offered to finance my nascent career. By some miracle, I was once again saved from having to do something drastic, like getting a real job.

I spent the next week scouring the want ads until I found a suitable location for my studio. A narrow, two-storey storefront building on Queen Street in Cabbagetown was ideal: modest rent, central location and ample space for my living and work needs. Armed with a couple of "how-to" books on plumbing and electrics, I went to work building a darkroom. Wishing to be as neat and precise as possible, I wired one end of an electrical cord to a plug, inserted it into a socket, tacked the cord along the wall and up the ceiling, and, at the exact point where the safelight would hang, cut the cord. I was jolted off the ladder, and my metal cutter now had a hole in it about the size of a subway token. After nearly being electrocuted, you would think I had learned my lesson, but I made the same mistake twice in one day. Once all the work was completed, I drove back down to New York, where Harvey and I went on a shopping spree, scouring the city for the best bargains on all the photo equipment and supplies I would need. Finally, a week after my twenty-sixth birthday, I opened my first studio. Many others would follow, but that one on Queen Street, like the memory of a first lover, would always be special.

For the first time, I had everything I needed, except for a photographic vision. I took my cameras on explorations into the more interesting areas of Toronto, but the streets, now silent after the clamour of the early 60s, offered no inspiration. The decade of dissent was being displaced by the banalities of flower power and the delusional indulgences of drug culture. Society was undergoing a shift of consciousness. The Civil

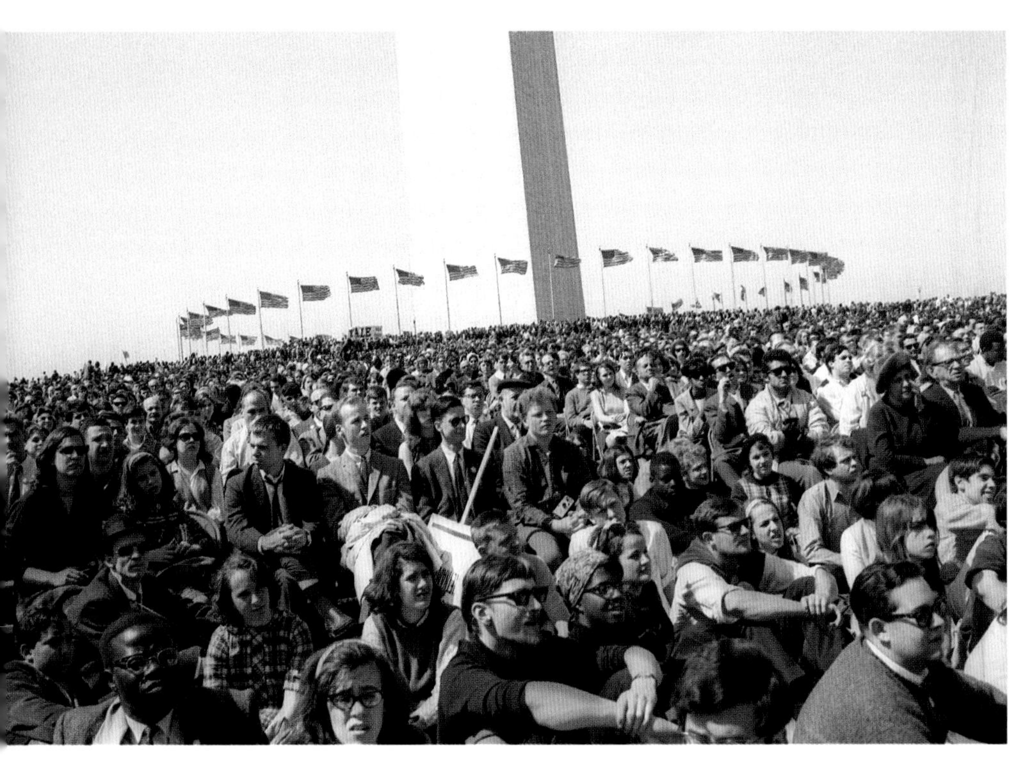

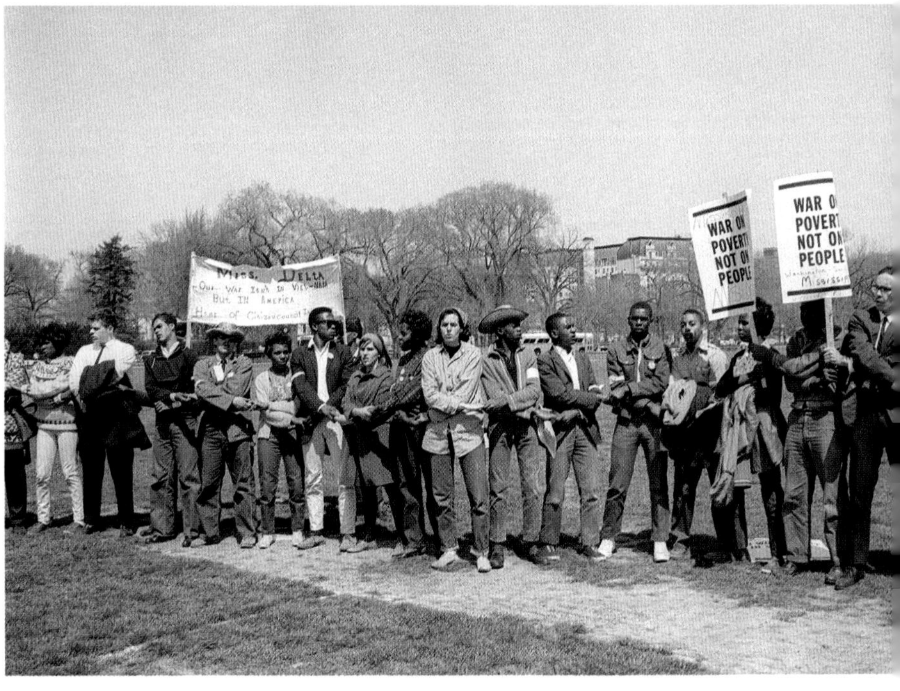
MISS. DELTA
OUR WAR ISN'T IN VIETNAM
BUT IN AMERICA
WAR ON
POVERTY
NOT ON
PEOPLE
WAR ON
POVERTY
NOT ON
PEOPLE

Rights Movement, the war in Vietnam, CIA-backed support of repressive regimes—all these issues chipped away at the image of America as a benign democracy and revealed instead a superpower bent on hegemonic domination. The old WASP culture was now in full retreat, and a new generation began to look to the ancient cultures of the East for new truths. The songs of protest were giving way to the psychedelic lyrics of the Beatles, who had found inspiration in Hindu mysticism and the ethereal music of Ravi Shankar. Timothy Leary was touting LSD as the gateway to some eternal truth, and Zen became the latest "in" thing. I was rather bemused by it all, for it seemed that almost overnight I had gone from "dirty Jap" to guru, and even though I realized that it was the just the flip side of the same racist coin, I welcomed this change of identity, for it opened up a whole new range of possibilities. I once met a Sansei woman who told me that, in high school, she could never get a date despite her good looks and sparkling personality. However, after John Lennon staged a love-in at a New York hotel with Yoko Ono, she had to fight off an army of suitors.

My life was still in limbo, and I was desperate for any new direction. So when Henry Tarvainen asked me to go with him on a tour of Cuba sponsored by the Canadian Union of Students, I jumped at the chance. All we had to do was get to the airport in Mexico City, and the Cuban government would look after the rest. In late July, we piled into his father's commercial vehicle, a Volkswagen van with "Tarvainen Cleaners" emblazoned on the side, and headed south. In Texas we ran into the tail end of a hurricane and nearly got blown off the highway. In Oklahoma it was so hot we had to close our windows, for having them open felt like being hit with a blast from a furnace. We finally arrived in Mexico City and went straight to the airport. While waiting for our flight, local operatives of the CIA went around taking our pictures. They weren't at all covert about it, and Henry and I took our place beside a swarthy peasant dressed in a colourful serape and a big sombrero. After having our picture taken, I wondered what would happen if I replied in kind, so, unpacking a camera, I boldly stepped in front of one of the agents and snapped off a few frames. Nothing happened for a while, and then I felt two hands on both my elbows, and I was suddenly floating through the room and up a flight of stairs before being dumped into a room where an obese Mexican man sat behind a desk with a .45 Colt prominently placed in full view. Sticking out his hand, he said, "Passport," and I handed the document over. The hand came out

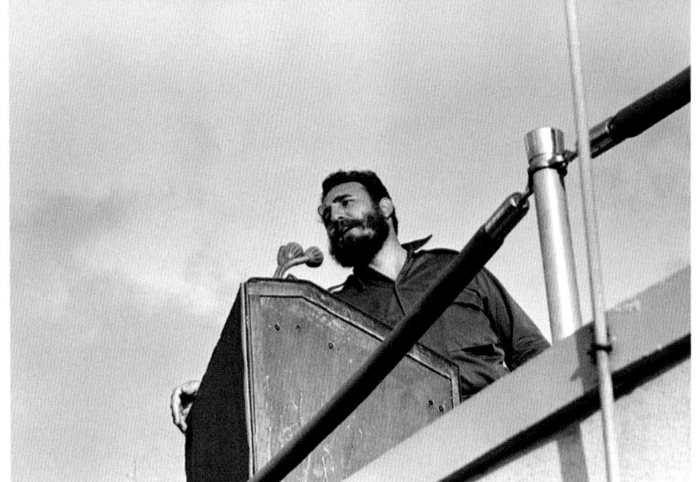

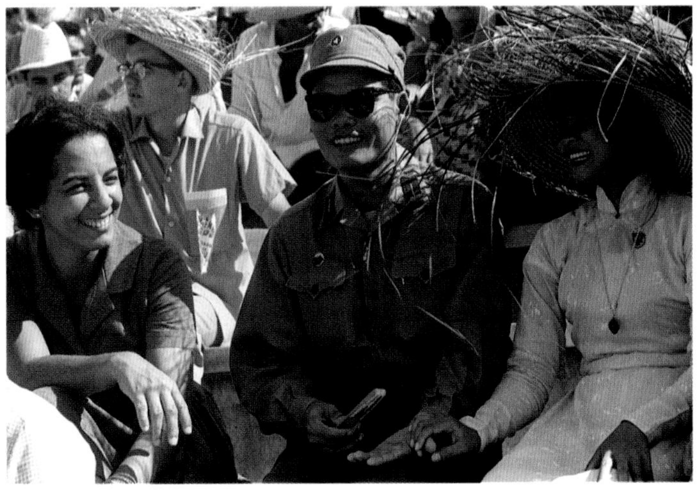

again, and he said, "Camera," but I said, "No, *señor*." I suggested as an alternative, "Film, *película*?" He nodded. I made a big show of rewinding the film and handed over a dummy roll that I had palmed, a trick I had learned as a Movement photographer. I wasn't really interested in the images, but I thought I should keep in practice. It was an incredibly stupid thing to do, for my trip to Cuba could have ended then, and I could still be languishing in a Mexican jail.

On arrival in Havana, we were met by our two guides, the skinny Jose and the stout Manuel, who would be with us throughout the tour. They drove us to the Habana Libre Hotel (formerly the Habana Hilton), and after checking into our luxurious suite, Henry and I went down to join the others for dinner. The cuisine was haute but surprisingly tasteless, for the American embargo had stopped the importation of essential spices. We were in time for the 26 de julio celebrations to mark the anniversary of the Cuban Revolution, so the next day, we were

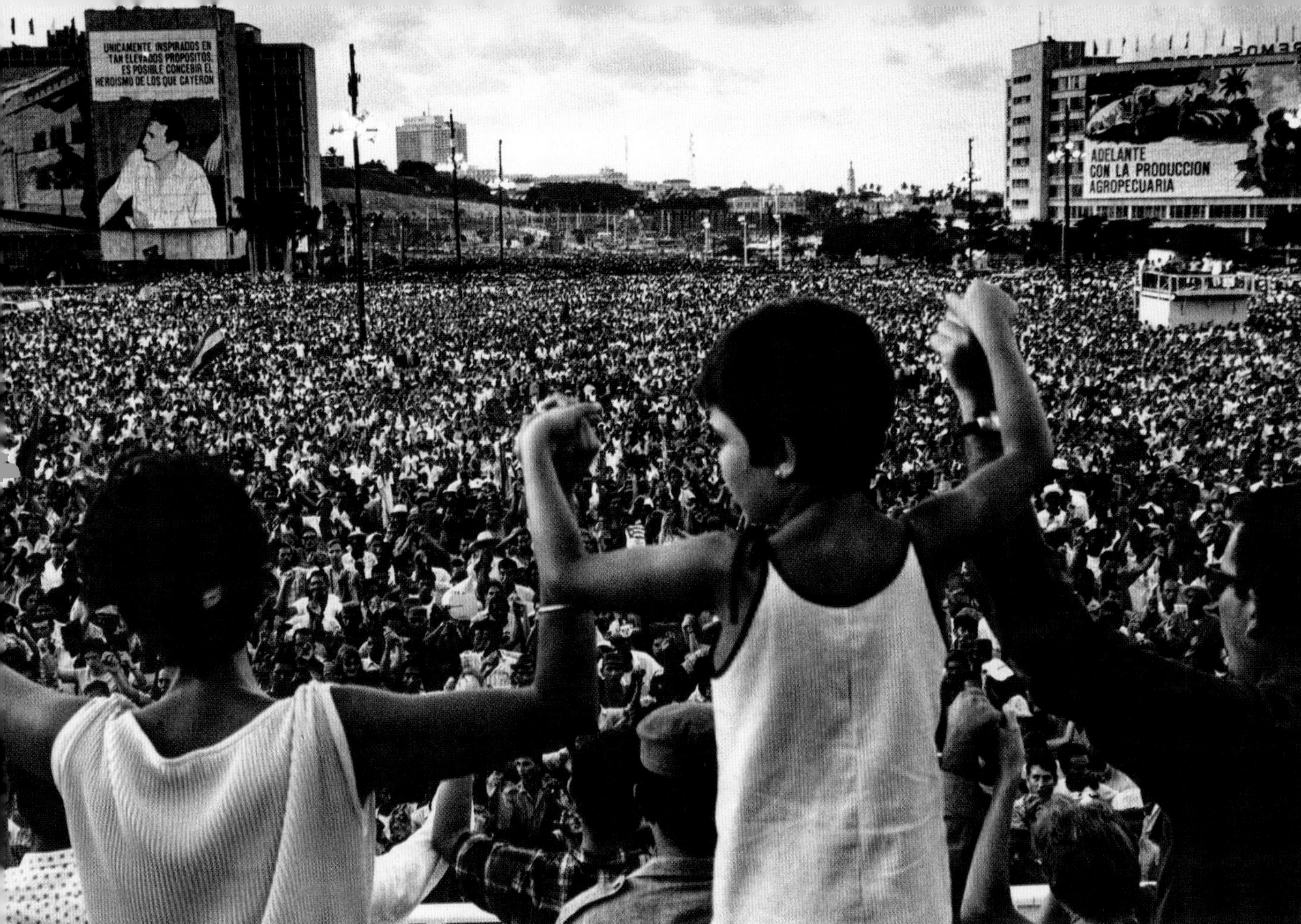

escorted to the Plaza de la Revolución, which was jam packed with a crowd of well over a hundred thousand people. Fidel Castro, who can roll his *r*'s like no one else, spoke for what seemed like hours, and yet the attention of the adoring crowd, standing on the bare concrete with the merciless sun beating down on them, never wavered. The only discordant note in the revolutionary fervour was the cases of Coca-Cola in their original mini bottles.

The next morning, we piled into a bus to begin our tour of the island. Cuba is a beautiful country, and the place I remember most is a resort area with thatch huts built on stilts over a peaceful lagoon. The huts were connected by walkways, but I thought it would be more fun to swim. Later at dinner, I raved about the beauty of the resort and my enjoyment of swimming to the other huts. Jose said, "*Señor* Tom, be careful, for there are crocodiles in the lagoon." I don't know whether he was pulling my leg, but I never took another swim there.

26 de julio celebration at Plaza de la Revolución, Havana, Cuba, July 26, 1966

I was getting tired of the strictures of the tour and being constantly surrounded by the same group of people. There was one Carleton University student, a total ass who was a constant embarrassment to us and an insult to our host, for he dismissed everything as a failure of Castro, the dictator, and his repressive regime. I wanted to wander off by myself to photograph and meet the Cuban people and get a sense of their daily lives. Our guides twice allowed me to escape the bus, and both times I was arrested for photographing a military installation, but the armed guards were friendly, and the matter was soon resolved after a phone call to the tourist bureau. What impressed me the most were the Cuban youth, glowing with health, spirits high, passionately engaged in their revolution.

After those two weeks, we arrived back in Havana to enjoy a few days of free time before flying back to Mexico. That night, Henry and I went on a walk and met two nurses, who took us on a tour of their city. They were delightful companions, and eventually we wound up at a rather seedy establishment. The ladies went in and plunked down some pesos in front of a man sitting behind a glass partition. Henry and I weren't sure what was happening, but we followed them up the stairs, and we paired off into separate rooms; I got the better of the deal, for my companion was a stunningly beautiful, cinnamon-coloured Cuban woman who explained that we were in a *posada*, which was Cuba's version of the Japanese love hotel. I don't know how Henry fared, but I had an unforgettable night of love in Havana. After our hour was up, we escorted our "dates" to their hospital. Overcoming the language barrier, my paramour and I arranged to meet the next night at these same gates. The next day, I could hardly wait for the appointed hour. When I arrived ten minutes early, my Latin lover was already waiting, but instead of the frilly dress of the day before, she was dressed in an army uniform with a rifle slung over her shoulder. Tearfully she explained that she could not go with me, for she had been unexpectedly called to guard duty. That was the first and only time I was stood up because of military necessity.

On our last night in Cuba, our guides called up to our rooms to ask if they could drop by to say their final goodbyes. They entered and handed us each a bottle of Bacardi rum and a box of Romeo y Julieta cigars. We chatted for a while, and then they segued into the real purpose of the visit. I had brought some of my Mississippi photos, and during the tour, I showed them to Jose, who pointed two fingers to his eyes, then to my photos, and finally to his heart. Jose said he had talked to Fidel about

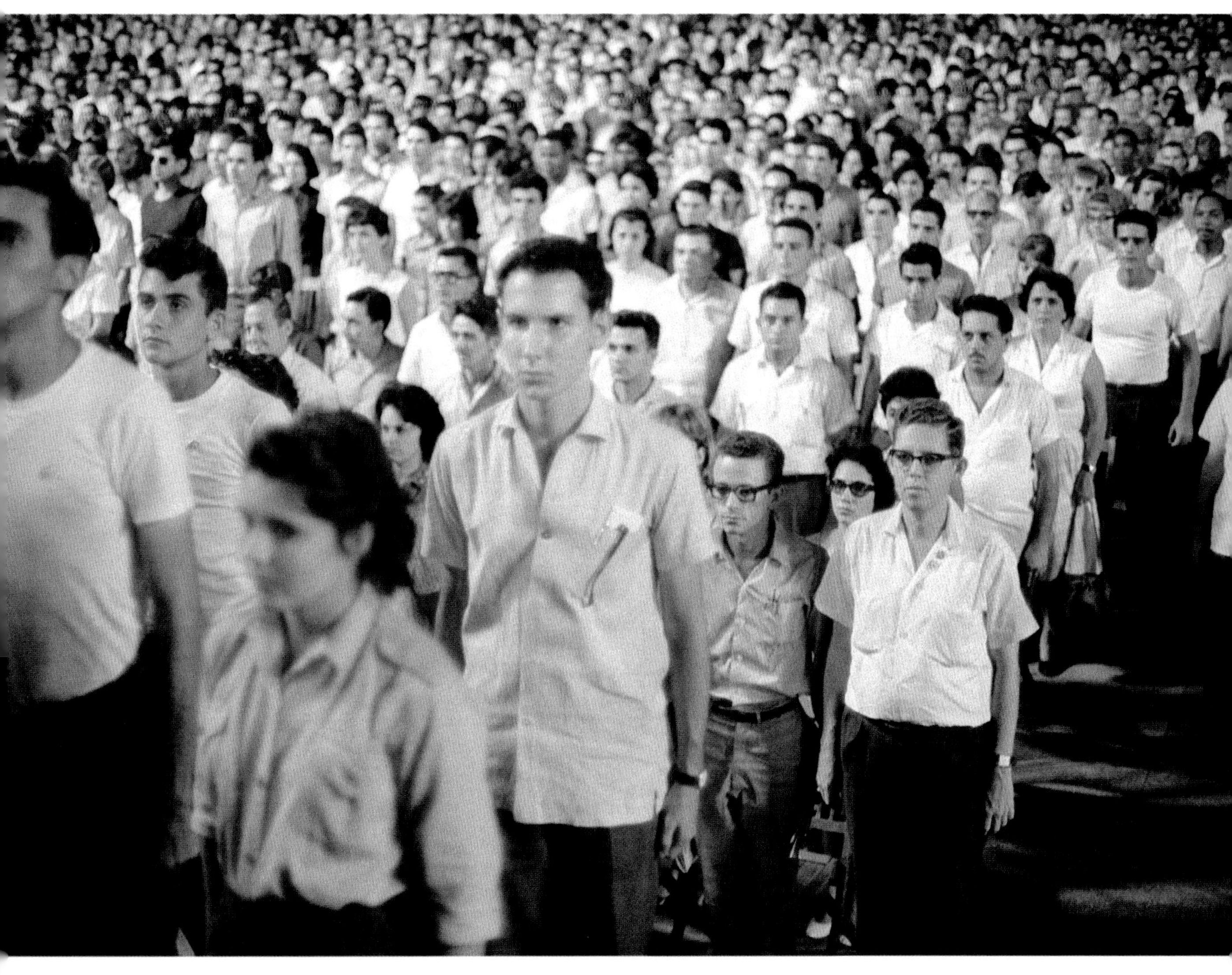

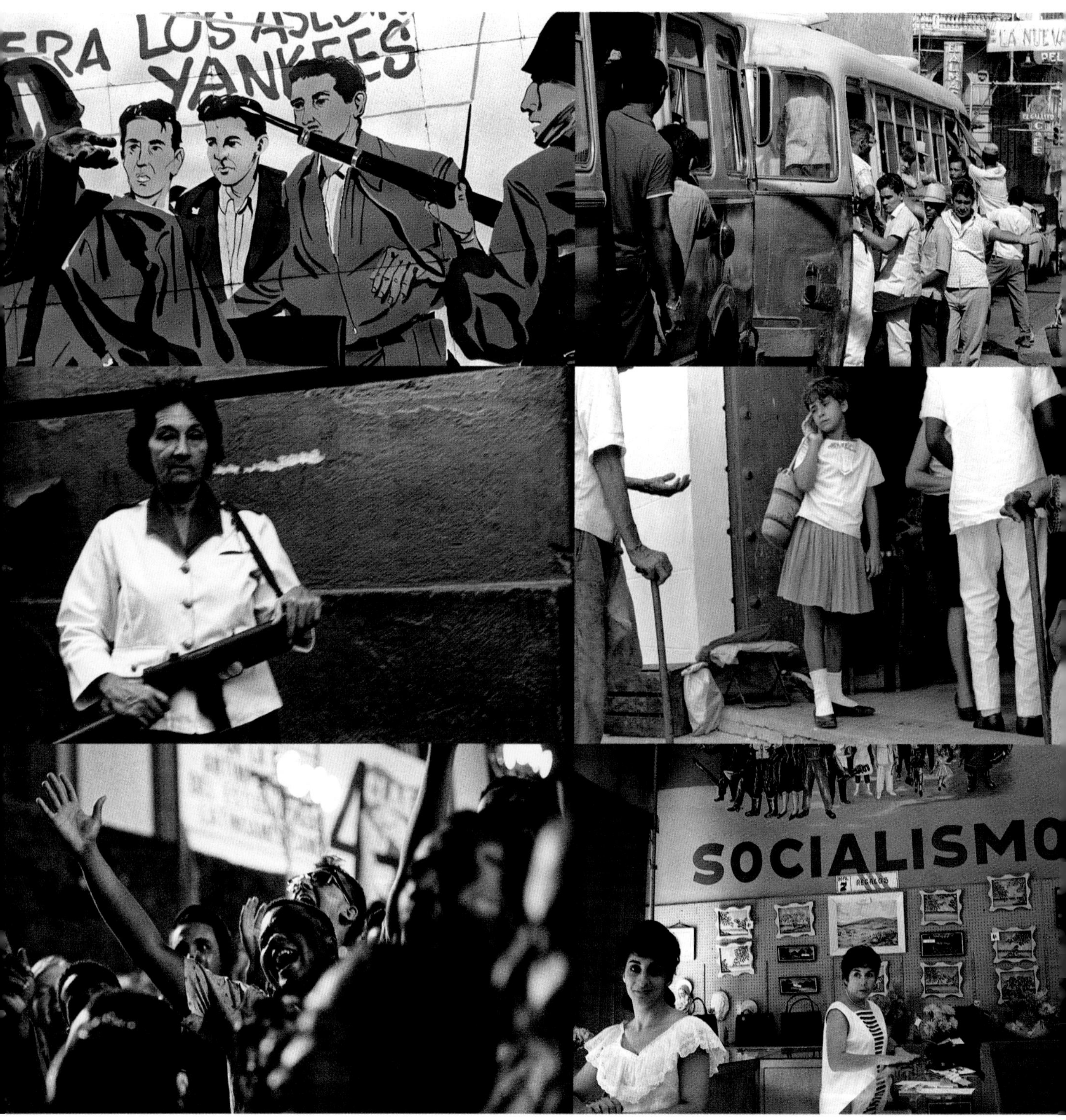
ERA LOS ASESIN
YANKEES
SOCIALISMO

my moving photographs, and that Fidel would like me to stay for however long to photograph their revolution. Picking up on the conversation, Manuel broke in with, "Fidel is also very interested in the project you mentioned." During the tour, Henry and I told them of a Students for a Democratic Society conference that we had attended in northern Michigan; one of the proposals discussed was to form a brigade of American activists to go to Vietnam to rebuild schools and hospitals destroyed by American bombs. "But of course no imperialist company would dare to bring you to Vietnam," continued Manuel. "Fidel will order one of our battleships to cruise down the St. Lawrence River to Montréal, where we will pick up you brave Americans and take you to Vietnam." Henry and I glanced at each other with the unspoken question, "Who are these guys?" We had assumed they were simple functionaries on the bottom rung of the Communist regime, but here they were, apparent buddies of Fidel and commandeering a damn battleship. We thanked our guides for their parting gifts and promised to be in touch.

The next morning, we went to the Havana airport. While we waited in the lounge, a big, intimidating man dressed in a suit came in and ordered the obnoxious Carleton student to stand aside. With arms swinging wildly, he went on a long rant about how the student was obviously a "running dog lackey of the imperialists" and that if he dared show his face in Cuba again, he would be arrested and shot as an American spy. Granted, the student had been a total ass, but this kangaroo court was a bit over the top, and I was glad to have turned down the request to stay.

When we arrived at the airport in Mexico City, a United Airlines flight had just landed. The planeload of American tourists was walking toward me, and as I looked at their pasty white, obese bodies and dull, listless eyes, I couldn't help comparing them with the vibrant youth of Cuba. I had no doubt which civilization would ultimately prevail.

When I arrived back in Toronto, Libby, who by then had moved to the city, had left several messages asking me to call the Company of Young Canadians (CYC) in Ottawa. I had heard of the CYC, which was modelled on VISTA, the domestic Peace Corps in the States, and dismissed it as just another government attempt to co-opt the New Left. I suspected that they wanted me not for my subtle mind and artistic genius but for my dubious ability to lend them credibility. The fact that the CYC needed me to legitimize their efforts reminded me of the old Woody Allen joke: I wouldn't want to join any club that would have me for a member. I

LEFT TO RIGHT,
TOP TO BOTTOM
Havana, Cuba,
August 1966;
Santiago de Cuba,
Cuba, August 1966;
Woman guarding
building, Havana,
Cuba, July 1966;
Regla, Havana,
Cuba, August 1966;
Closing of the fourth
Congress of Latin
American Students (CLAE),
Havana, Cuba,
August 1966;
Cuba, July 1966

returned their call and politely said that I wasn't interested in joining, but they were persistent. In the end, they made me an offer I couldn't refuse, for I knew that both my camera equipment and my car would soon require a major overhaul.

In the fall, I covered two training and orientation sessions for the CYC volunteers who would be manning summer projects similar to the ones that SUPA had attempted the previous year. Except for one or two projects, I had little hope for their success, since the CYC people were just as—if not more—inexperienced and naïve as their SUPA predecessors. After these sessions, I heard nothing more from the CYC, and yet every two weeks, a fat government cheque would slide through my mail slot. My parents would have been appalled at this transgression of the work ethic, so I offered to make a cross-country photographic tour of CYC projects. They refused my offer (which confirmed my original suspicion), but with mounting guilt, I persisted until they finally relented.

When summer arrived, Libby and I jumped into my new Peugeot compact station wagon and headed west. During the past holidays, I had been caught in a seasonal roadside safety check, and my Beetle failed every single test. It wasn't worth spending the money for the necessary repairs, so I drove the car to an auto wrecker's and sold it for scrap. Over thousands of miles and through countless adventures, my faithful chariot, no matter how aged and ailing, had never once failed me. I should have given it a proper burial. I should also have stayed home. By then I was truly bone-weary of social activism, and my ennui (been there, done that), coupled with the state of the projects, made for a desultory and unproductive tour.

We quickly reached the West Coast and rode the ferry to Vancouver Island, where I was to shoot a CYC project in Victoria. After completing the assignment, we decided to take a break and visit the legendary beauty of Long Beach. It seemed to take forever to traverse the island on a truly horrendous logging road, but the drive was well worth it. The national park, with its miles of sandy beach pounded by the waves of the Pacific Ocean, was breathtaking. When we looked back, we saw huge clouds of black smoke from a forest fire, which would cut us off from civilization for an entire week. Our time at Long Beach was the best part of the trip. We slept in the Peugeot and had no trouble surviving, for fellow campers would come by to share their bounty of periwinkles, clams and fish from the oceanic supermarket a few metres away. When the road finally cleared, we drove back

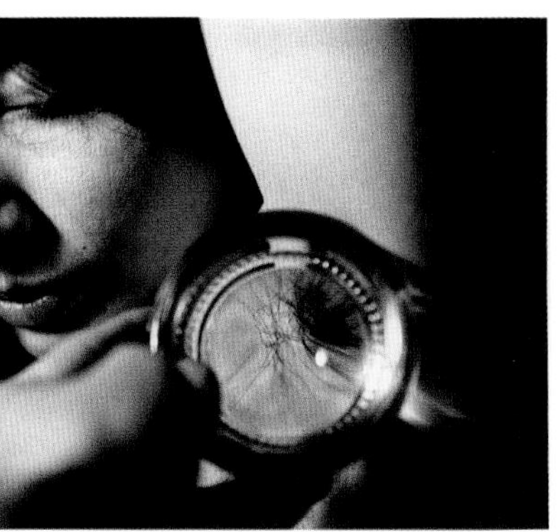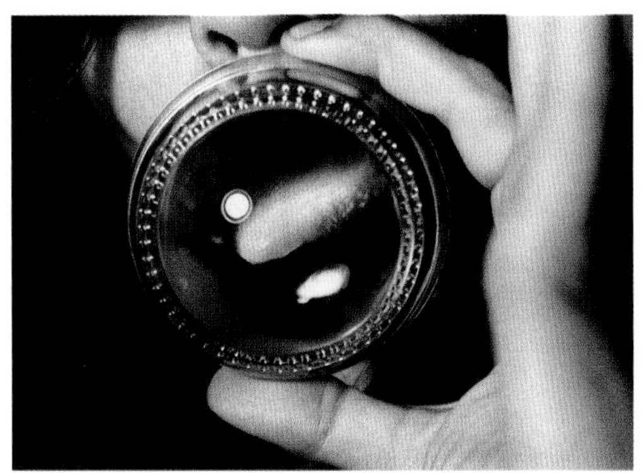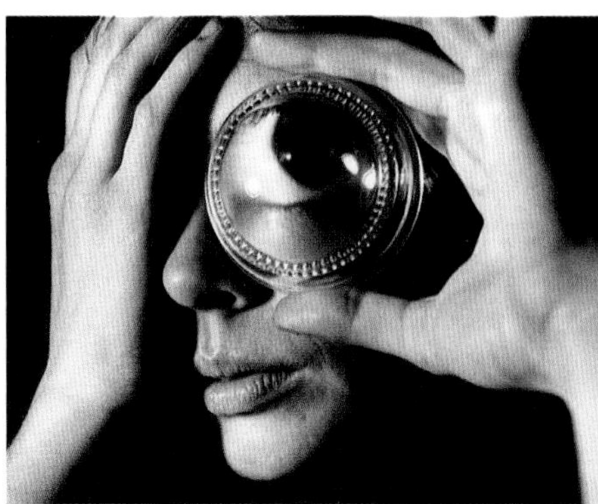

to Vancouver, where Libby caught a plane back to Toronto. We had decided to live together. She would make all the arrangements while I drove slowly back east.

By the time I arrived in Toronto, Libby had already managed to rent a large, three-storey house a few blocks north of my Queen Street studio. Not only had she cleared out my studio but had also, with the help of her brother Richard, built a new darkroom and workspace in the basement of the house. The main floor was rented to another couple; Libby, her two young children Gillian and Andrew, and I would occupy the second; and the third floor would also be rented out. My life had suddenly changed. I had gone from a freewheeling revolutionary artist to the head of a household complete with ersatz wife and kids. I freaked out and spent most of the first week in my favourite pool hall on Spadina Avenue, but gradually I calmed down and settled into my new life. I worked on the film from the summer, which, as expected, yielded very little. I felt that I had come to the end of the first phase of my life as a photographer and that I would never again take the same kind of pictures.

However, I still lacked an alternative vision.

I had always admired the brilliant American photographer Edward Weston, who I felt had striven to express the essence of human sexuality and sensuality. His nude studies, although beautiful, were only partially successful; it was in his disturbing photographs of such mundane objects as a green pepper or a seashell that he fully realized his vision. Though as a Movement photographer, I'd always been disdainful of the notion of art for art's sake, I decided to explore the classic genre of the nude. By this time, I had come to the painful realization that, in the shifting tides of history, revolutions come and go; but surely, the joy of looking at a naked woman could be something that lasts forever.

Kathy in studio
with loupe,
Toronto, Ontario,
September 1971

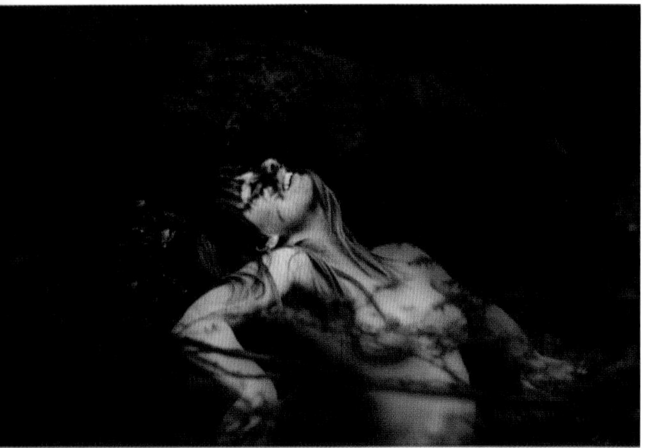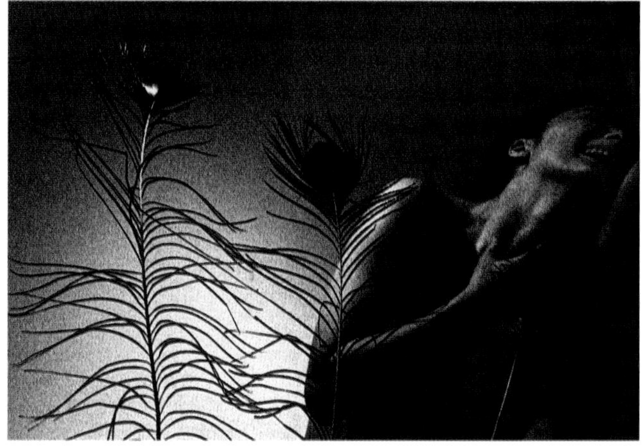

A few days later, I received a phone call from Carol, a bright, dark-haired beauty whom I had met earlier at a CYC training session. I mentioned that I was going in a new photographic direction and asked if she would be willing to participate as my model. She agreed, and we made arrangements to meet at my home the following day. The only workable space was my and Libby's bedroom, which was large and had plenty of light. So when Carol arrived, we went straight to the makeshift studio, where she began to take off her clothes. I had always thought she was attractive, but never in my wildest dreams could I have imagined the lush cornucopia of flesh that filled my lens. In my subsequent sessions with many other beautiful women, I was always surprised and delighted to discover that the drab covering of clothes can only give the barest hint of the treasures that lay beneath. I've always prided myself on my shooting compression—that is, to produce good images from any situation using the least amount of film. But at the end of the hour with Carol, I was shocked to see that I had used up a whole twenty-pack of Tri-X. After Carol left, I went immediately into the darkroom, and a few hours later, I eagerly gathered up the stack of contact sheets and went to my light table. The results were disappointing: one or two interesting images, but nothing of lasting value. The contact sheets, with frame after frame of specific body parts, revealed nothing more than my fetishes. Still, the experiment had been stimulating, and I was determined to carry on.

My next session was with our upstairs tenant, Linda, a short and saucy blonde woman from the Prairies who was working as a topless waitress. When she disrobed, I could see that she was well enough endowed to make a killing in her chosen profession. I was much calmer, but the results of the shoot, although better than the first, were still disappointing. I thought part of the problem could be that I had been shooting indoors, with all the restrictions that involves, and that I might do better shooting in the great outdoors. Libby, Linda and I drove to a farm owned by Libby's parents outside of Guelph. I felt much freer in this environment and began to recapture the excitement of tripping the shutter for what may be a great image. The session was interrupted when three hunters, armed to the teeth, came wandering by. The situation grew quite tense—an Asian rolling around in the meadow with two naked white women?—but after making a few rude comments, they moved on to hunt other prey. The results of this shoot were far more interesting, and although I wasn't totally satisfied, framing the figure within the natural landscape opened up a whole new range of possibilities for me. Unfortunately, the weather soon turned cold and wintry.

It was an insane winter. We lived in *interesting times*, which, in the context of the Chinese saying, is more a curse than a benediction. The societal norms of monogamy, marriage and the nuclear family were now seen as part and parcel of the bankrupt old order, while free love and a mindless "do your thing" philosophy became the ethical precepts of the new, hippy-dippy era. Although Libby and I should have known better, we were not immune to this moral maelstrom. Libby let it be known, in no uncertain terms, that I was still totally free. And Linda would be the test of this. The temper of the times may have had something to do with Libby's potentially destructive attitude, but I suspect that the greater reason was her fear, especially after witnessing my initial skittishness, that I would flee out the door and never return. The two of them entered into a conspiracy, and Linda, who was well aware of her sexual magnetism, teased and tempted me mercilessly, until one night I crept up the stairs to spend the night with her. The situation was too bizarre, and I could do little but toss and turn before coming back down the stairs and crawling sheepishly into bed with Libby.

And then one day, the phone rang. A former lover of Libby's, who had helped her escape from her marital prison, was in town for a few days. He was invited to join us for dinner. Now if I were your typical uptight, insecure male, alarm bells would be ringing, for he turned out to be a Black Adonis: tall, lean and handsome with gentle, contemplative eyes and a velvet voice that could melt butter. After dinner, I went into the darkroom to allow them time to catch up. Our guest had already left by the time I came back upstairs, and as Libby and I settled in for the night, I said, "Gee Lib, it's too bad the house is full, or else you could have spent the night with Blank." (I've erased his name from my memory bank.) "I mean, it's only fair since I had my night with Linda." Brave words, for I knew Gillian had friends over for a pyjama party, and Linda was entertaining a friend, and I'd be damned if I was going to check into a hotel. Just then, the capricious gods decided to have a bit of fun. Clop, clop, clop, came the sound of Linda's friend coming down the stairs, and once he was out the door, room suddenly opened up in the inn. The phone rang. It was Blank asking if he had left his keys at our house. After finding his keys, I asked Lib to tell Blank that I would bring them to him. It was showtime. Put your money where your mouth is—just slide it in beside your foot. As I was dressing, I told Libby that, when I got back, she should take Blank in hand while I went upstairs.

That night was one of the worst of my life. The anguish I felt went way beyond mere jealousy or any another flagellate emotion. After a sleepless night, I tiptoed down the stairs and, seeing the coast was clear, slipped into bed with Libby. I didn't ask what had transpired in our bed; I didn't want to know. After breakfast, Blank had a few hours before having to catch his flight, so we decided to have a game of chess. I've never played the game with such ruthless ferocity... Attack, attack, attack, kill, kill, kill. Blank went out the door, never to be heard from again.

Because of its unparalleled intensity, I felt there had to be a deeper meaning to the agony I felt that night, and after much thought, I came up with the following theory: as a species, we are unusual in the inordinate length of time it takes for our young to become fully independent, and over the centuries, we've learned that the best way to ensure their survival—and therefore that of our species—is through a stable home of two committed, monogamous parents. By allowing another man into our marital bed, I had threatened the security of our home, and the pain I suffered was just punishment for violating an ancient taboo still buried in my evolutionary memory. Of course, it could just as easily be said that I was reacting like your typical uptight, insecure male. The only certain truth that I gained from the experience is that there is no such thing as free love.

My relationship with Libby had barely survived the winter, and I had never been so happy to see the arrival of spring. We spent most of the warm months at our farm in the North Country near the town of Whitney, on the eastern entrance of Algonquin Park, which we had bought jointly with our friend Arden (Matt Cohen's first wife) and two other couples. On one of our excursions, I did a shoot with Libby in the large, weathered barn on our property, and finally, after months of failure, I managed to create images that were as strong and as distinctively mine as any of my earlier documentary work. I continued to build on this foundation in other sessions with Libby, Arden and Gillian. When I showed my *Miss Gilly* portfolio, the best of the farm series, to some friends, they half-jokingly said they were *worried* about me and cautioned against exhibiting the photos lest I be accused of paedophilic exploitation. I thought their reaction was absurd, for I knew that I had captured, with impeccable taste, the ineffable moment when a girl first awakens to the power of her approaching womanhood and that these images were, quite simply, beautiful. Case closed.

In the city, I was becoming more and more involved with Rochdale College, an ambitious project of the radical capitalist arm of the New Left (does that strike anyone as oxymoronic?). The plan was to build a twenty-two-storey concrete high-rise on Bloor Street, one of the most expensive properties in all the country, and to use its rental income to subsidize a free university. Instead of the customary faculty, Rochdale would invite a number of key individuals of various disciplines to act as "resource persons." Since Rochdale was to represent a radical new approach to education, these people would not have to do anything as mundane as teaching—they would simply exist in their rent-free apartments as a source of knowledge and inspiration for anyone interested. Over the coming fall and winter, I was commissioned to document the formation of Rochdale College and the various construction stages of the building itself.

That fall, I drove down to New York to visit with Bob and Marilyn Fletcher. I brought along some of my recent farm series, and after Bob looked through them, he shook his head in wonder and said, "Damn, Tom, there's so much love in those images." Love? I'd never thought of the photos in that light, but perhaps Bob was right—perhaps they were a desperate attempt to salvage something of permanence from the chaos of a dying relationship, to distill some perfect idealization of love that I was failing so miserably to achieve in real life. Perhaps love was at the root of all my work, whether it was the sense of wonder and oneness I felt with the wisdom in the face of an old woman beaming at me from her porch on a Mississippi plantation or the deep religiosity etched on the hoary face of a Doukhobor man sitting on a pew in the Brilliant hall.

At the end of our second year, Libby announced that she had had enough and would be moving to the Whitney farm to live with her two children and Arden. I wanted us to continue living together, but she was adamant, so at the end of the summer, we closed up our home. I decided to accept Rochdale's invitation to become one of their resource persons, and in the fall I moved into the largest of the apartments, a Zeus suite on the twenty-first floor. I was absolutely miserable. I missed Libby terribly and wondered what the hell I was doing living at the top of a sterile concrete box. Rochdale itself was a zoo, because opening a free university in the heart of Toronto was an open invitation to every strung-out kid and weirdo within a hundred-mile radius and beyond. I couldn't believe that a brand-new building could deteriorate so quickly. The first month, a Hells Angels–type biker gang took control, and after they played havoc with the building, the drug dealers took over. One night I woke up to discover a young addict going through my camera bag. I jumped up, grabbed a Nikon and shot off a few frames in case he escaped with some of my property. "Hey man, be cool," he said. "I'm just lookin' for a spike. What are you, a narc? And stop takin' my picture, it's a violation of my rights." I threw him out the door. It was lucky that I kept in good physical shape, for more often than not, the elevator was either broken or filled with such strange people that the best option was to trudge up twenty-one flights of stairs to my apartment. One day, while I was lethargically building my darkroom, Tom Sask, an old friend and snooker partner, came up to visit. After listening to my tale of woe, he said, holding out his hand, "Try this—it should straighten your head out." I swallowed the tiny blue pill, and after half an hour, my depression suddenly lifted like the sun breaking through the dark clouds. I happily went back to work and finished the darkroom in record time. I had discovered a wonder drug that would cure all my problems, so I went upstairs and got a prescription from a friendly doctor. The next day, I placed my vial of Ritalin on a shelf in my bathroom medicine cabinet. Each morning I stared at it, but I never took another pill.

Once the euphoria of the Ritalin evaporated, depression returned with a vengeance. My chief source of solace was Matt, who was sharing a smaller Aphrodite suite (also rent-free) with Stan Bevington, the head of Coach House Press. They were an odd couple, and I was fascinated and often amused to witness the intricate mental gamesmanship of these two unique minds. I went up to visit one night, and since Matt looked more befuddled than usual, I asked what was happening. "Stan just gave

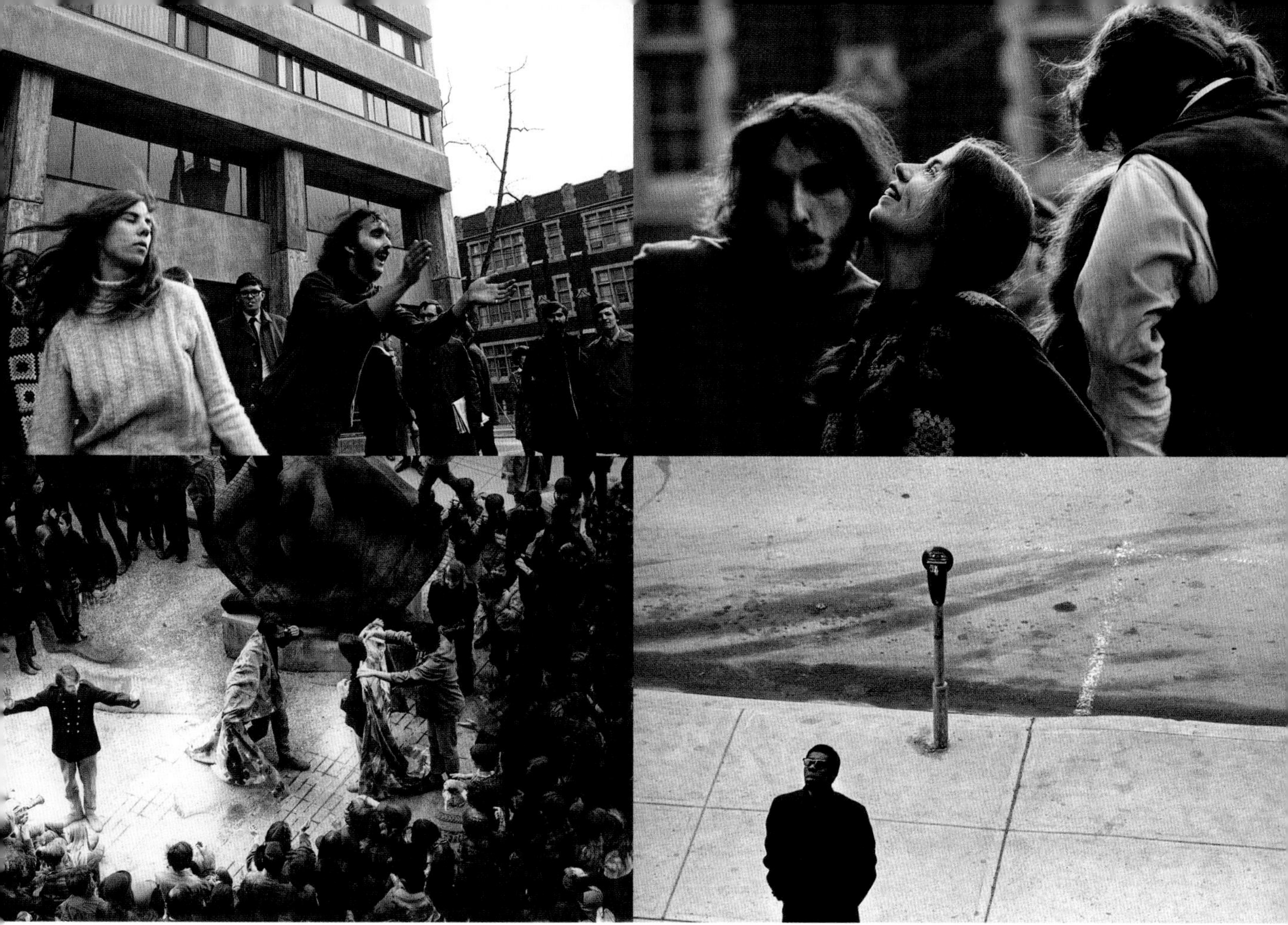

me a hit of this new drug," he said. "I don't know what it is or what it's supposed to do, but if you want, there's an extra tab." I was lonely, bored and depressed enough to swallow the pill, and when I felt the universe starting to shift, I said to Matt, "I feel an acid trip coming on, so I'm going downstairs to cool out in my studio." Once I got into my apartment, I felt an irresistible need to cocoon, so I locked the door, closed all the drapes, shut off all the lights, and buried myself totally under my down comforter. Instead of experiencing the expected psychedelic pyrotechnics of LSD, I proceeded to undertake a thorough mental housecleaning, carefully analyzing and resolving each issue that had been bothering me: Libby, my art, Rochdale, the meaning of life. I don't know how much time elapsed before Matt came down to check on me. I sat him down and, for the next hour, talked non-stop of all that I had just gone through. For once, Matt was speechless. The next morning, I re-entered the world of the living with fiery energy and renewed optimism.

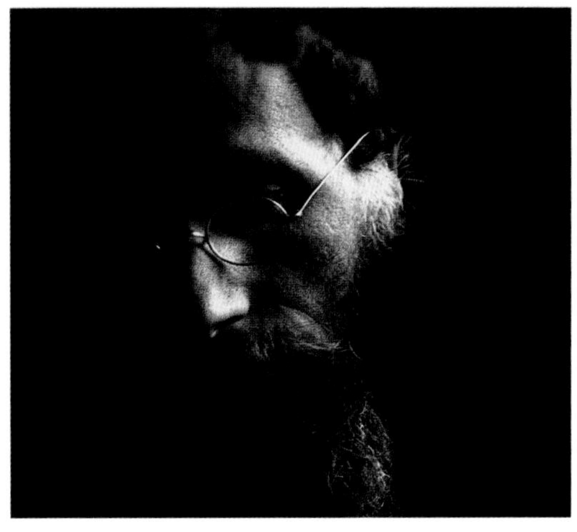

I began to build a new life totally independent of Libby. Rochdale was still much too chaotic for my taste, but I found a new home at Coach House Press. My first encounter with the press was a year earlier, when I was invited to a meeting at their first location on Bathurst Street. Since the point of the meeting was to plan a brochure and curriculum calendar for Rochdale, I brought along a box of my photos of Rochdale as well as some of my recent nude studies. When I entered, I was introduced to Stan Bevington, who was sitting at the head of the long, wooden table. With his tall, lean build, granny glasses and bushy red beard, I thought he looked like an overgrown gnome. We all took our places and dumped whatever we had brought on the table. After quickly scanning through the mounds of disparate material, he sat back down, took out a sketch pad and proceeded to lay out where each item would fit on each page of the brochure. I was awestruck by this tour de force of design—how could anyone absorb and organize such a massive amount of material in such a short period of time? A week later, a stunning four-colour brochure came rolling off the press.

After a steady stream of innovative and brilliantly designed books, Coach House Press had deservedly earned a reputation as *the* small artisanal publisher in the country. The press, then relocated to the alley directly behind Rochdale, was a charming mixture of old and new, with modern presses standing beside wooden cabinets filled with type for the letterpress and an ancient lead linotype machine clattering throughout the day. It was a stimulating environment, for Coach House had become a gathering place for young artists and writers from all over North America. Over the next few months, I would spend most of my time at the press working with Stan on the design of my first book, *Signs of Life*, which would be the first major production on their brand-new, impressively huge Heidelberg offset press. The publication of *Signs of Life*, like the other books that would follow, brought closure to a major phase of my life.

With Libby gone and our relationship in shambles, I began to seek the company of other women. One day I went to deliver some prints to

Stan Bevington, Coach House Press seminar, Toronto, Ontario, September 1968

the offices of *ArtsCanada* magazine, and as I was leaving, my eye was drawn to a long mane of glossy black hair cascading down the back of a woman sitting at a desk. I had to see who this luxuriant growth belonged to, so I went in to ask directions to the office of the editor whom I'd just seen. When she turned around, I was not disappointed, for I was greeted by the smiling face of a beautiful Asian woman. Her name was Nobuko, and she was a Sansei from a small town in California who had recently come to the city. Eventually I worked up the nerve to ask her for a date. After our first dinner together, we became constant companions.

Nobuko was everything that I could have wished for: warm, generous and fun-loving with a bright intelligence to add to her great beauty. She was the first Asian woman that I had become seriously involved with, and unlike my other relationships, there was an ease and familiarity and an unspoken sense of trust. I once asked Nobuko whether she had ever been involved with a white man. Never, she replied, for she felt it was hard enough for any two people to come together without having to struggle through the complexities of race. Besides, she had sensed that, in the white men she had known, the attraction they felt for her was not for her intrinsic worth but rather due to some fantasy of the demure and submissive Asian woman, an exotic species that their fragile egos could easily dominate. It was an intriguing perspective and one that I would later hear from many other Asian women, but there was an even more thought-provoking element of our relationship. Despite my growing fondness for Nobuko, I felt no sexual attraction to her, and this embarrassing and deeply puzzling failure forced me to seriously examine my life.

Since returning from the South, I couldn't help but notice a curious phenomenon: I was actually attractive to women. It seemed that women were more than eager to jump into my bed. When I began my nude studies, I targeted the most interesting and beautiful women in my social circle, and to my surprise and delight, they all readily agreed. One or two even volunteered their services. Surely the noble pursuit of art was not their sole motivation.

Despite the empirical evidence, I was still insufficiently free of my past to fully accept that I was *so beautiful*, as one woman put it. I always looked for any hint of irony or hidden motives. In the South, I had seen that, although some interracial relationships were founded on mutual affection and respect, others were blatantly exploitive. For some white women, bedding a Black man was either a way to prove their liberal

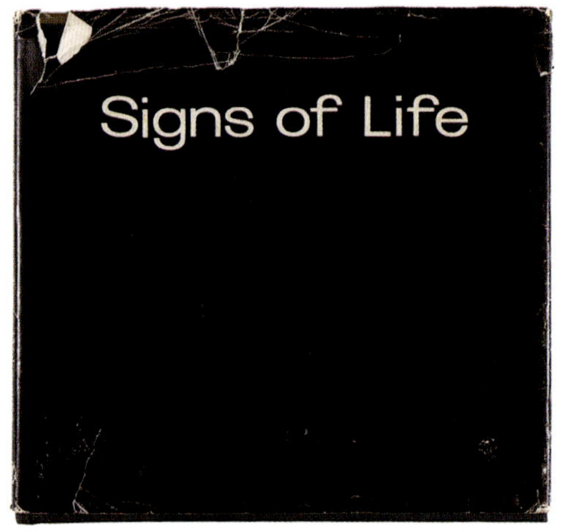

Book cover of *Signs of Life* (1969) published by Coach House Press

purity or else a means to assuage their guilt. The Black studs in the Movement would, in turn, prey upon these women to add more notches to their bedposts. Was I re-enacting this sick dance? How many of the women I had slept with saw me as an exotic Asian morsel to be sampled in order to fuel their rebellion? And what about myself? I knew that my formative years as an Enemy Alien had eaten away at my very core and left my sense of manhood in tatters. It had been hammered into my soul that, in the immutable order of the universe, white women were far beyond my reach, and even if I dared to break this barrier, I would be reviled, for was I not a loathsome aberration? Were my many sexual conquests nothing more than compulsive acts of defiance to prove, over and over again, that I was an equal, that I was a man? Was this compulsion the cause of my dilemma with Nobuko? Did I need the stimulus of forbidden white flesh to trigger a response? I believe that each of us seek love both to find someone to love us and to find in ourselves the capacity to love another. I was fairly certain that rutting around like a bull moose in heat was no way to satisfy this universal human need. These were troubling thoughts, but perhaps I was once again overthinking things, and my sexual activity was simply the normal behaviour of a healthy young man liberated from years of repression… But then again, who's to say that the idle flight of the nightbird is not a desperate search for food?

My time at Rochdale was coming to an end. The college was under serious financial strain, for the chaos and physical deterioration had continued unimpeded, which made renting the units difficult. I had managed to keep my rent-free status for over a year, but just before the holidays, I was called before the Rochdale council and ordered to pay rent or else leave. After one of my periodic rhetorical flourishes, I managed to win a three-month reprieve.

Fortunately, I was able to make an arrangement with the U of T housing authority to rent one of their properties, a two-storey coach house behind a stately manor a few blocks north of Rochdale. After the renovations were completed in the early spring, I moved in to build my fourth and final studio in the east. Nestled in the midst of several large maples, my coach house in the warm months was a cool and cozy retreat, but it was brutal in the winter. The electric heaters were insufficient to properly heat the poorly insulated building.

One fine spring day shortly after I moved in, Joan appeared at my door. As a former model and aspiring photographer, she had been directed my way by our mutual friend Beryl Fox. Like Libby, she had escaped a violent marriage with a sexual deviant, and I grew to admire her courage and resourcefulness in overcoming the damage of that brutal relationship. We became friends and eventually lovers. Our relationship was one that I would cherish over the coming decades.

Despite my deepening relationships with other women, I still felt bonded to Libby, though the growing destructiveness of our relationship made the bond feel more like a chain. Over the winter, I had made very few trips to the farm. I was perfectly happy with my new life, and driving all the way to Whitney in the winter was a major ordeal. However, in the summer, I made more frequent trips to the farm to get away from the oppressive heat in the city and to add to my growing portfolio of nudes. Libby spent part of the summer in the Maritimes visiting her father and developed a love of the East Coast. She put a down payment on an old house near the ferry terminal in the tiny province of Prince Edward Island. She had had enough of the hardscrabble life on the farm. We decided that, the following summer, we would go together to her new home in Prince Edward Island.

I had got interested in motorcycles after I jumped on the back of Stan's 175 Honda Street Scrambler, and when he decided on an upgrade —Stan was always a speed demon—I bought his Honda. I loved that bike—light, agile, yet powerful enough to zip me around city traffic. In the early spring, I optimistically decided to drive it up to the farm, but when I got off the 401 and headed north, the weather turned cold and nasty. By the time I arrived at the farm, I was drenched, totally covered in mud and so numb from the cold that I had to be helped off the bike. I knew we would need a bigger bike for our upcoming trip to Prince Edward Island, so I traded it in for a new 350 Honda. One day I rode my new bike over to the home of my brother Peter and his wife Ethel to visit with my mother, who had come up from Chatham to help with the arrival of their new baby. As I walked in, she asked what I was holding in my hand, and when I replied that it was a helmet that I need for my new motorcycle, she said, "*Baka*"—idiot—"why are you always getting into these dangerous situations and worrying your mother to death?" After

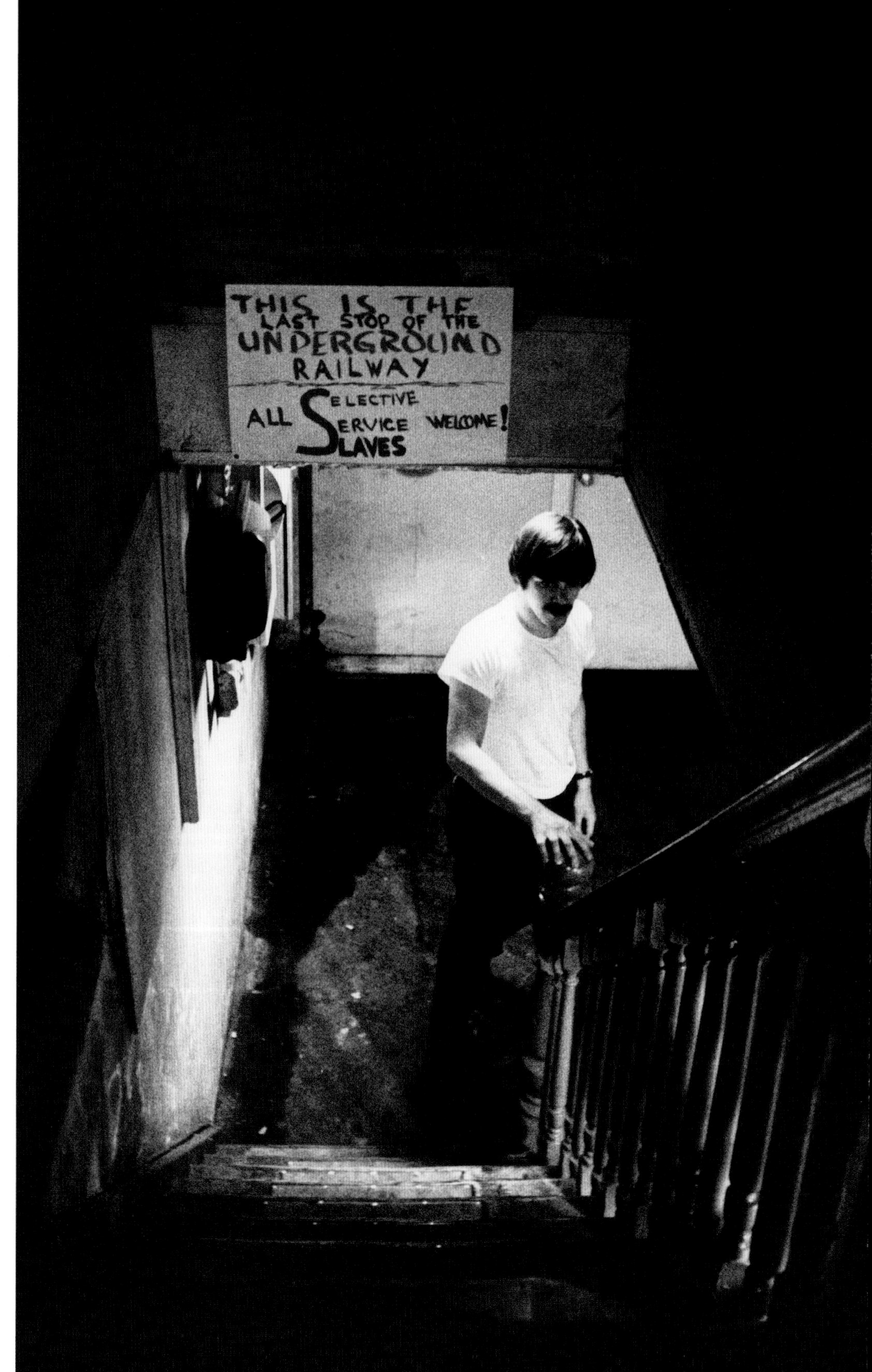
THIS IS THE
LAST STOP OF THE
UNDERGROUND
RAILWAY
ALL Selective
Service WELCOME!
Slaves

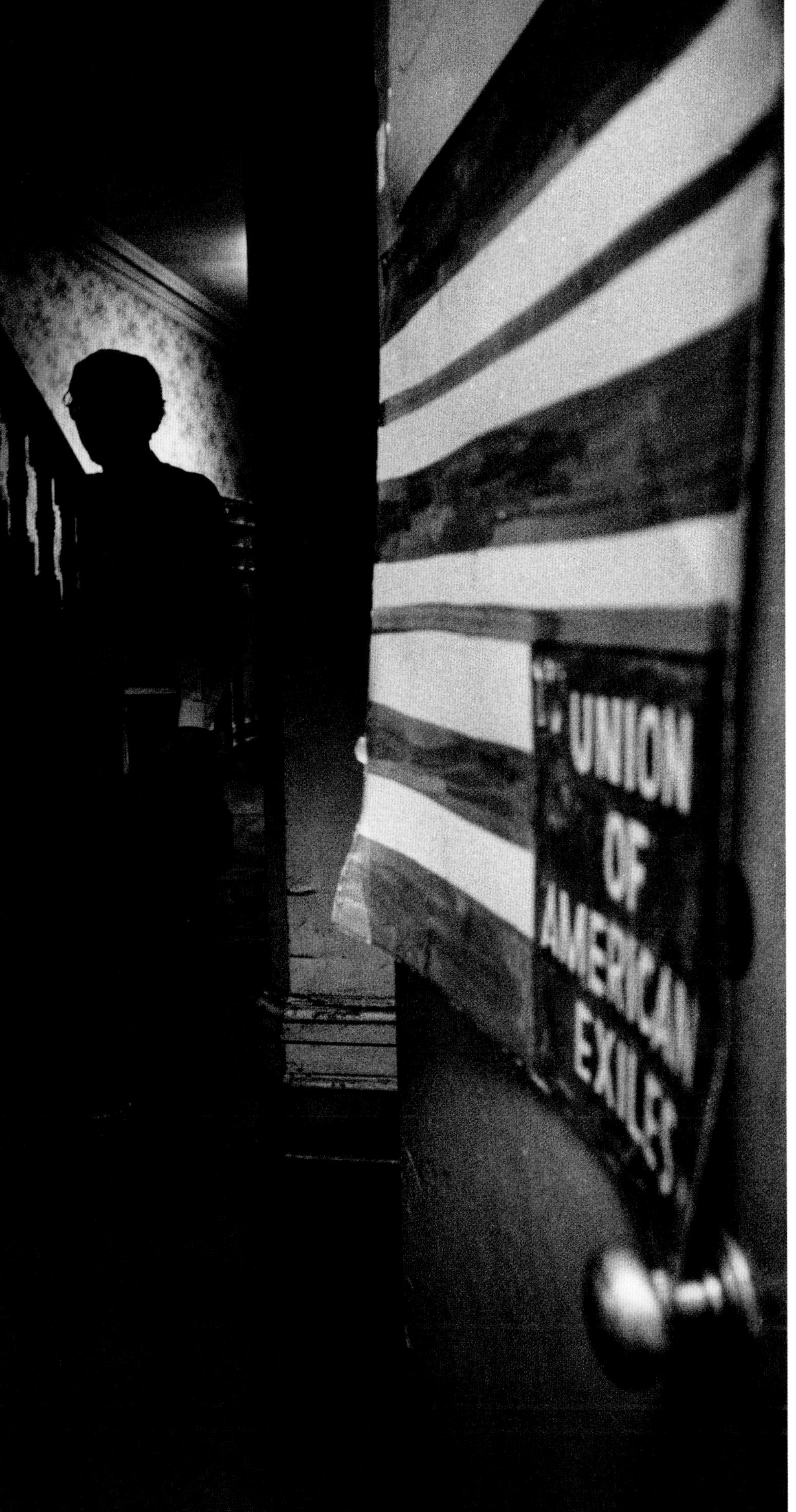
UNION
OF
AMERICAN
EXILES

lunch, she came outside to say goodbye, and I could see her eyeing the Honda suspiciously, but I also detected a growing glint of interest in her eyes. I offered to take her for a ride. "*Baka*," she replied, "I would never go near such a dangerous vehicle. But I've never been on a motorcycle, so I guess it wouldn't hurt just to sit on it." I have no idea how my mother, a very short and very stout woman, managed to hoist herself unto the back seat. I told her to hang on, for we were just going to coast down to the end of the driveway. When I hit the street, I flipped the ignition key, popped the clutch and snapped the throttle. By the time we reached the first intersection, I had the Honda cranked up over fifty miles per hour, and after careening around the corner, we circled the block at breakneck speed. Back at the house, I helped her off the bike. She was a bit wobbly, but the glint had grown to a positive glow of excitement, and after that day, she would coyly ask if I still had my motorcycle.

When summer arrived, Libby returned to the city. We crammed all our gear into two makeshift saddlebags and headed for the East Coast. We had only gone as far as Kingston before black smoke began pouring out of the overtaxed engine. We managed to limp into the city and were fortunate to find a Honda dealer to make the necessary repairs, but the bike was never the same. In our travel through New Brunswick, every now and then, we caught sight of a handsome young couple riding a big black BMW. We met them on the ferry to Prince Edward Island and invited them to visit. On the second day of their visit, the women baked bread and picked tiny wild strawberries to make jam, while we men dug up clams and bought six lobsters from fishermen returning to port. When all was ready, we hauled this bounty to the beach, where we built a huge fire to boil the large kettle of water, melt the pound of butter in an empty tin can and steam the clams in their bed of seaweed. We all got stoned, and in the light of a blazing bonfire, we gorged on a true bacchanalian feast.

The weather in the Maritimes is totally unpredictable, and it's not unusual for a dramatic change from sunshine to storm and back again to occur all in the space of a few short hours. Once, Libby and I were making love in our sunlit bedroom when, all of a sudden, black storm clouds rolled in and a clap of thunder shook the house and rattled our bed. I looked over at Libby and said, "My dear, did the earth move for you too?" The sun returned in the afternoon, so we drove across the island to the sand dunes on the north shore, where we managed to elude the occasional dune buggy zooming by long enough to shoot a decent series of Libby naked in the sand. I felt eager to get into my darkroom to see if these images of the human form melding with the sinuous curves of the sand would be as new and exciting as I had hoped.

The next day, I packed up my bike and headed back to Toronto. Libby would follow in a few weeks' time. That summer in Prince Edward Island would be our last period of unadulterated happiness.

Once back in my coach house studio, I immediately went to work processing the film from the dunes, but in my eagerness, I accidentally mixed the wrong developer and was horrified to see the rolls of blackened negatives. Fortunately, I was able to recover them by gently bathing each strip in a reducing bath, a process that took hours. When I finally had a set of dry contact sheets, I was relieved to see that the mix-up was a happy accident, as the increased contrast and enlarged grain only heightened the textural feel of gritty sand. The images themselves were stunning, and I could see that I was building a substantial body of work. They might someday become a book or exhibition that I would title *The Great Canadian Nude: A Mari Usque Ad Mare* ("from sea to sea," Canada's national motto). I now had a great series of images from the Atlantic coast, and to complete the concept, all I would need was a series from the Pacific shore.

Libby returned at the end of the summer and rented the bottom floor of a house on the east side of the city, four subway stops from my studio. Of the many homes she had created in the time I had known her, that one was the worst. The upstairs tenants were two big, Black Jamaican men, and one night I went out to the hallway and politely asked them to be a little less noisy as our children were asleep. The larger of the drunken two—who was obviously not a vegetarian—pulled out a knife and threatened to cut out and eat my liver, *mon*! I hated that house, so I spent more of my time at my coach house, where I continued to see the women that I had grown to know in Libby's absence. I knew I didn't have a leg to stand on, but I was still devastated when she began to have relations with some of my friends and acquaintances. We had reached the cruel endgame of the relationship, where two people know each other's most vulnerable points, and despite full awareness, couldn't stop reacting when the other pushed the right button. I felt like one of Pavlov's dogs. We were both immensely relieved when summer came and she went back to Prince Edward Island.

I withstood it for as long as I could, but in midsummer, I gave in to a need as desperate as that of a crack cocaine addict. I jumped in my car and drove non-stop to the island. When I arrived in the late evening, Libby was surprised and not too happy to see me. After the exhausting drive, I slept in very late the next morning, and when I finally stumbled down the stairs, Libby was standing in the front room with Lloyd, a rough local who lived up the road in an old motorhome with his wife and kids. They had their arms around each other's waists, and Lloyd somewhat sheepishly said he hoped that I didn't mind his "making friends" with Libby. It was the same old, same old, so I grabbed a bottle of gin, went down to the beach, and drank myself into a stupor. The next morning, I jumped in the car and drove non-stop back to Toronto.

On the way home, I realized my only salvation would be to put as much time and space as possible between myself and Libby. I was going to Japan. Earlier, my application to the Canada Council for the Arts for a second major award had been denied, but in its place, they were willing to provide a short-term grant anytime within the year. As soon as I got back to my studio, I called the Canada Council office in Ottawa and asked them to send me the grant money along with enough funds to cover a return ticket to Tokyo.

The idea of a pilgrimage to my ancestral homeland had been per-colating in my mind for quite some time. Searching for one's roots had become almost a national pastime. I had been aware that a number of my Snick friends had gone on extended tours of Africa. On one hand, I felt that Black Americans were too far removed by time and generations to have any meaningful connection to the continent where their fore-fathers were snatched by slave traders, but on the other hand, people like John Lewis, Bob Moses and Stokely Carmichael, people whom I highly respected, had gone to Africa, so perhaps I was missing something. As a Nisei, only one generation removed from Japan, I surely stood a much better chance at mining new truths and insights from the ancestral land.

I also wanted to learn how to play the shakuhachi (bamboo flute). One day I happened to turn on the tiny black and white TV in my coach house when the CBC was presenting a special concert presentation of East-West fusion music led by Seiji Ozawa, the handsome conductor of the Toronto Symphony Orchestra who had brought over a number of classical musicians from Japan. Ten of them, dressed in elegant *haori* and *hakama*, were now on stage. Each male musician held a strange instrument, a deceptively simple piece of bamboo about a foot long, cut at the slightly curved root end. They began to play, and I was blown away. I'd never heard anything like it, the sound so profound, so ethereal, so deeply moving. I had to know more. My past experiences with musical instruments were limited and largely disappointing. In my university years, I tried playing a ukelele and later graduated to a guitar, but I never got beyond the feeling of awkwardly trying to manipulate an external object. One day at our Cabbagetown home, Tom Sask came over with my birthday present, a beautiful, wooden tenor recorder. Given my sorry musical past, I was indifferent to this gift. But one evening I was stoned and listening to a Joni Mitchell record, and I picked up the recorder lying beside me. After a few half-hearted toots, something magical happened. Suddenly I became one with the recorder and with the music playing on the stereo, and I effortlessly began to play with and around the melody line. When the music ended, I was dumbfounded—for the first time in my life, I had experienced the essence of music. I believe that each of us is best suited to one instrumental category, be it keyboard, percussion, strings or wind. Obviously, wind was mine, and I hoped the shakuhachi would be my instrument.

Finally, I wanted to meet my sister Fumiko, who was born in Japan and never reunited with her family in Canada. Fumiko is the major tragedy in our family history. When my father called for my mother and her family to join him in Canada, my parents faced an agonizing dilemma. One of my uncles and his wife were childless and wanted Fumiko to raise as their own. To compound matters, my paternal grandmother, an ailing widow, wanted the child to be her companion and caretaker in her declining years. For my mother and father, abandoning their firstborn was unthinkable, but so too was defying the ancient edict of *oyakoko* (filial piety). In the end, the family circle could never be completely broken, and my mother sailed for Canada, leaving her firstborn child behind. My mother regretted that decision to her dying day.

What worried me most about the upcoming trip was meeting Fumiko, for how could I hope to bridge the abyss of age, culture and language that separated us when I lacked the rudimentary tool of verbal communication? I went to consult with my brother Peter, who, five years earlier, had interrupted his architectural studies for a sabbatical year in Japan. Fortunately, my brother met Fumiko at a high point in her life. She and her husband had recently moved to Osaka, and their future looked promising. Their new business was prospering, and they were enjoying their new life free from the confines of the isolated village in Kyushu and the dominance of her family clan. Peter told me not to worry, for our sister was a kind, lighthearted soul and they had a great

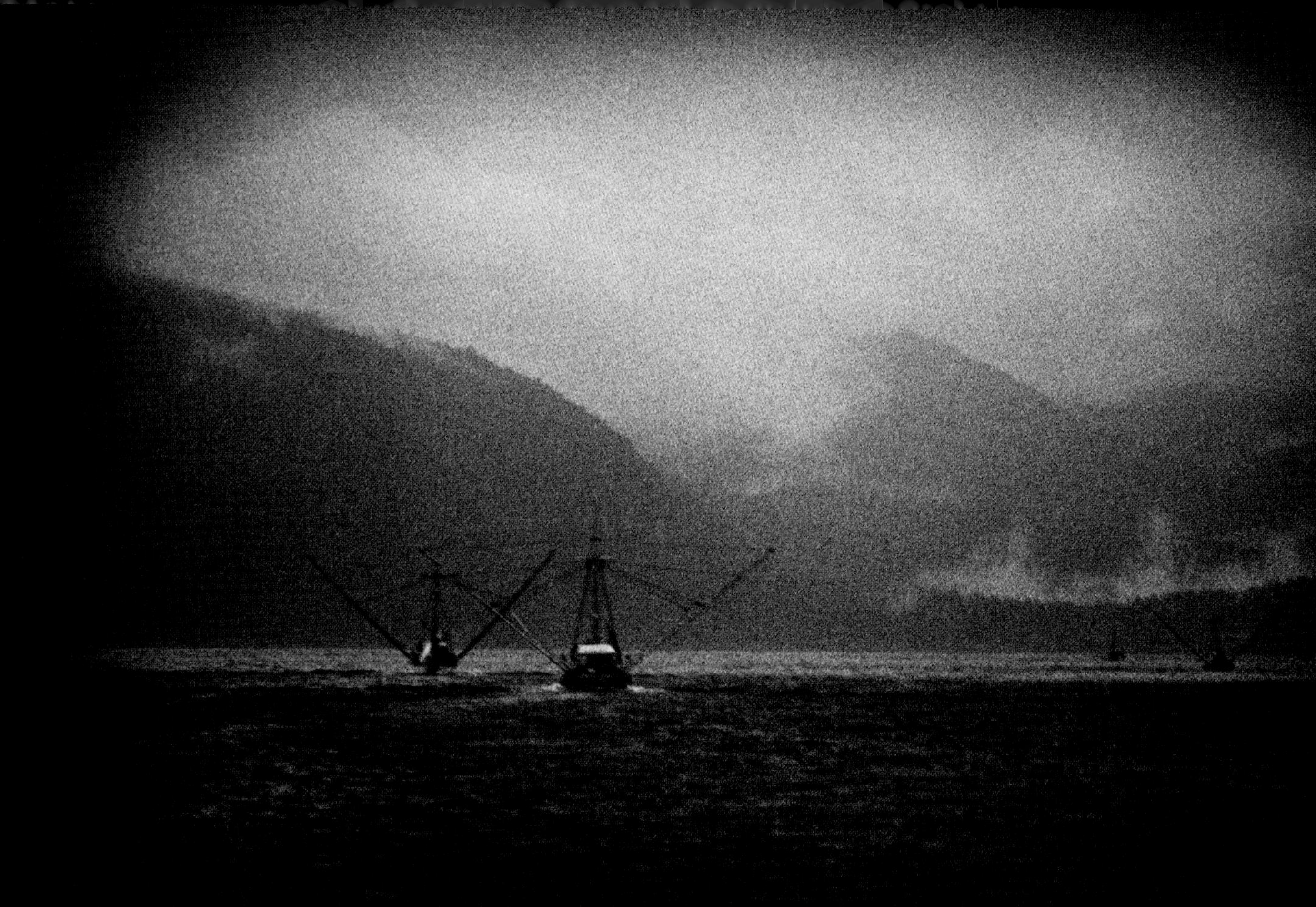

time together, joking and laughing. I was only slightly reassured, for how was I to make with the jokes when I couldn't speak the language?

Preparations for the trip seemed to take forever, but after my overdue passport arrived, I was finally ready to leave. Thankfully, I wouldn't have to go in cold, for Shin, a brash immigrant and student of photography whom I'd met during my tenure at Rochdale, had arranged for me to be looked after by his friends, the Nishibayashi family of Tokyo. At the end of September, I boarded my flight to Japan. On the long flight across the Pacific, I sensed that I was once again crossing a bridge that would change my life forever. Looking back, I wish I could say that at the major crossroads of my life's journey, I forged ahead with clear eyes and noble purpose, but the sad reality is that, in each instance, I was fleeing one disastrous love affair or another.

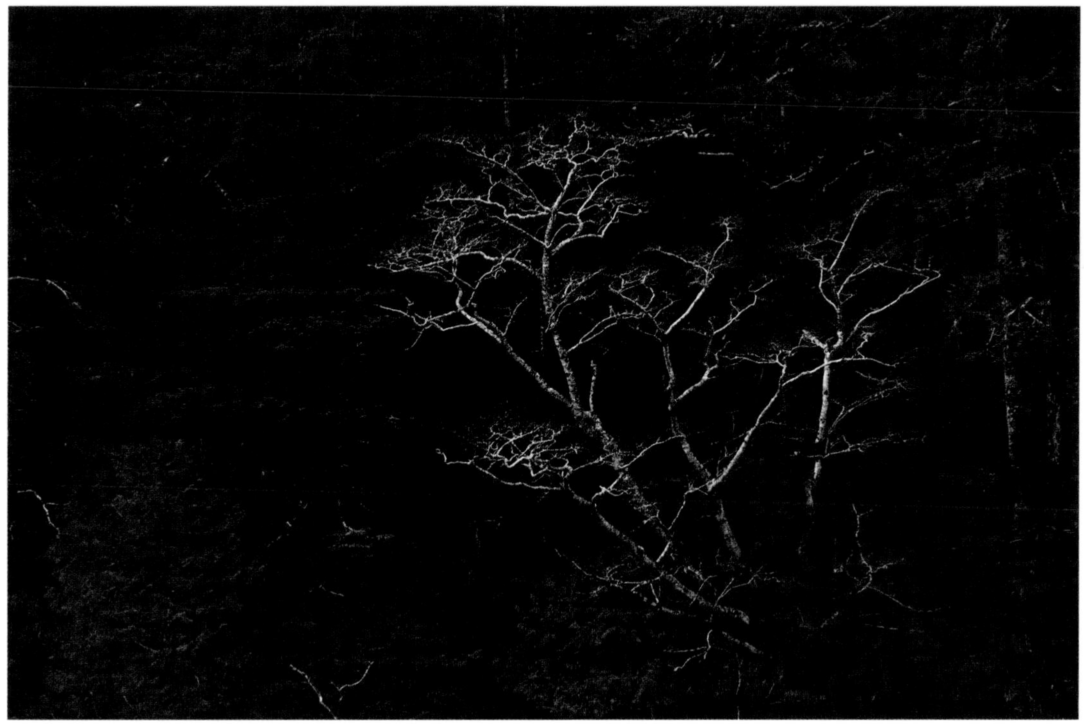

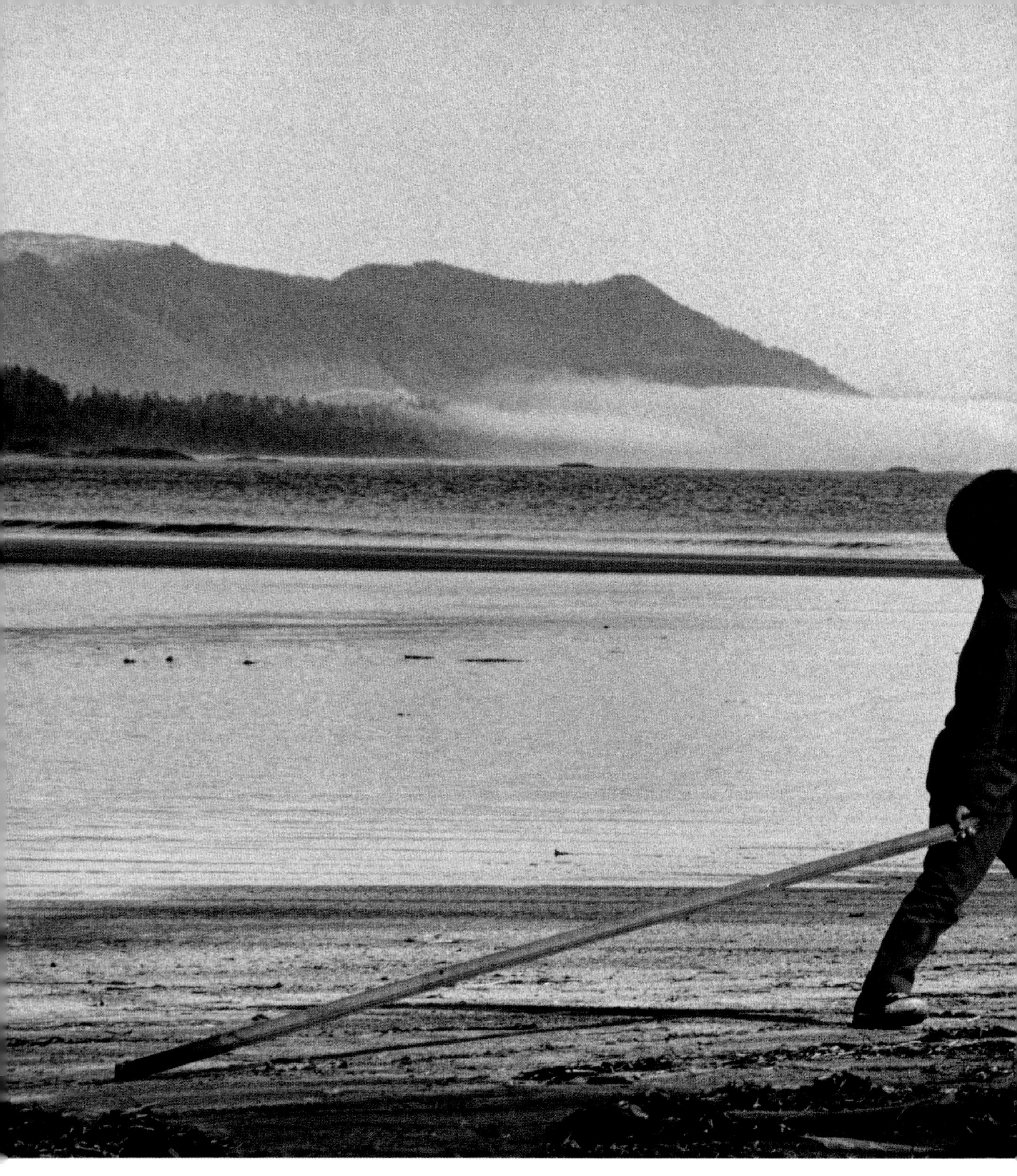

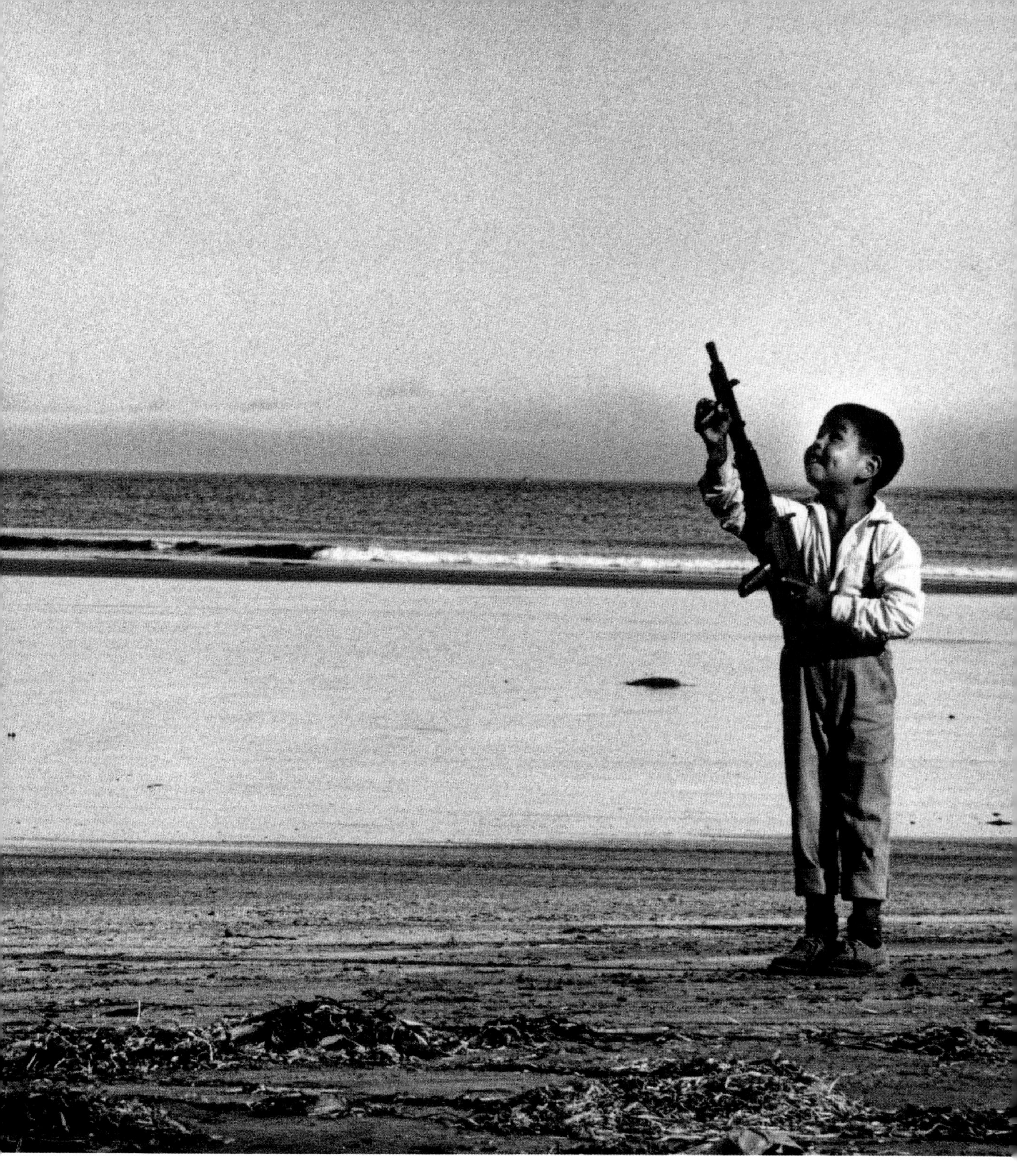

Children playing at Long Beach, Tofino, British Columbia, August 8, 1967

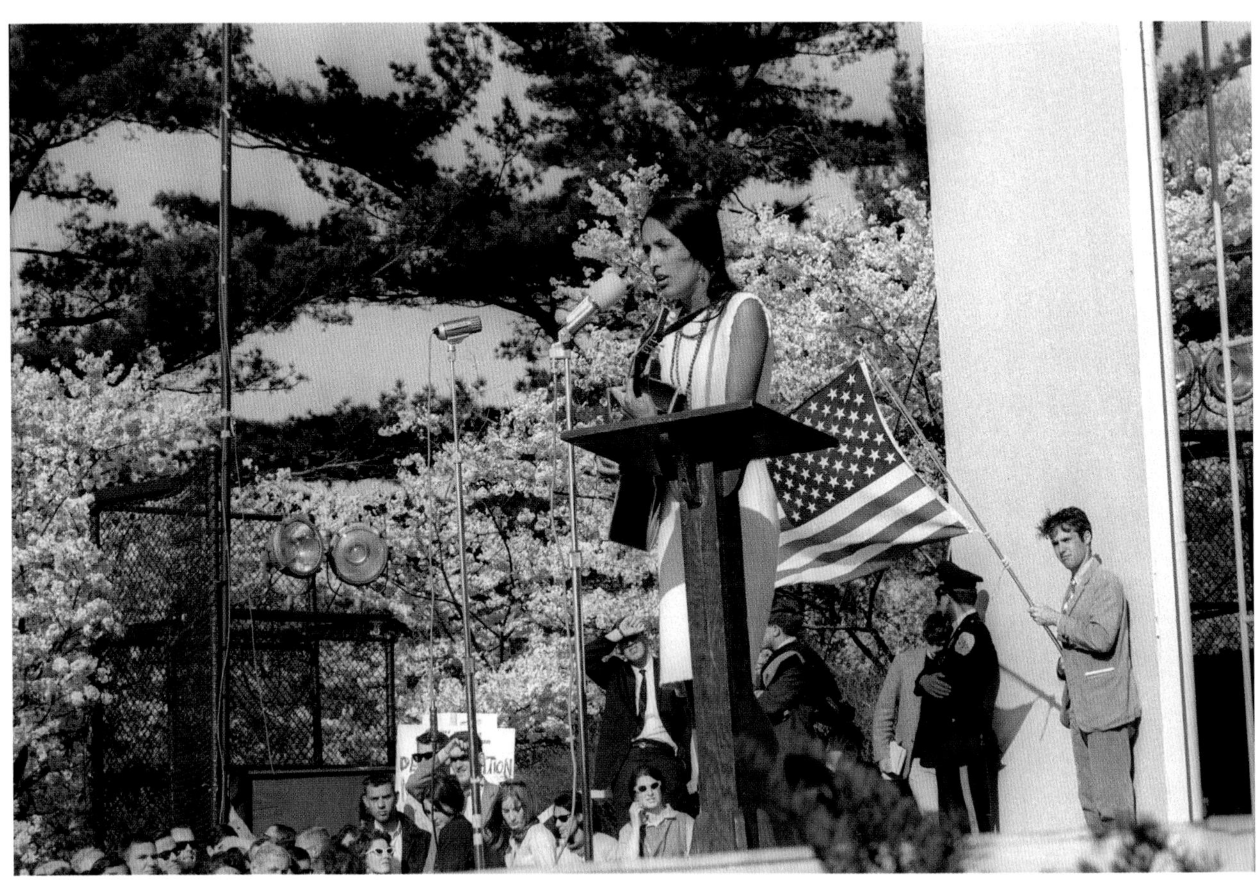

  Joan Baez, March on Washington to protest the Vietnam War, Washington, DC, April 17, 1965

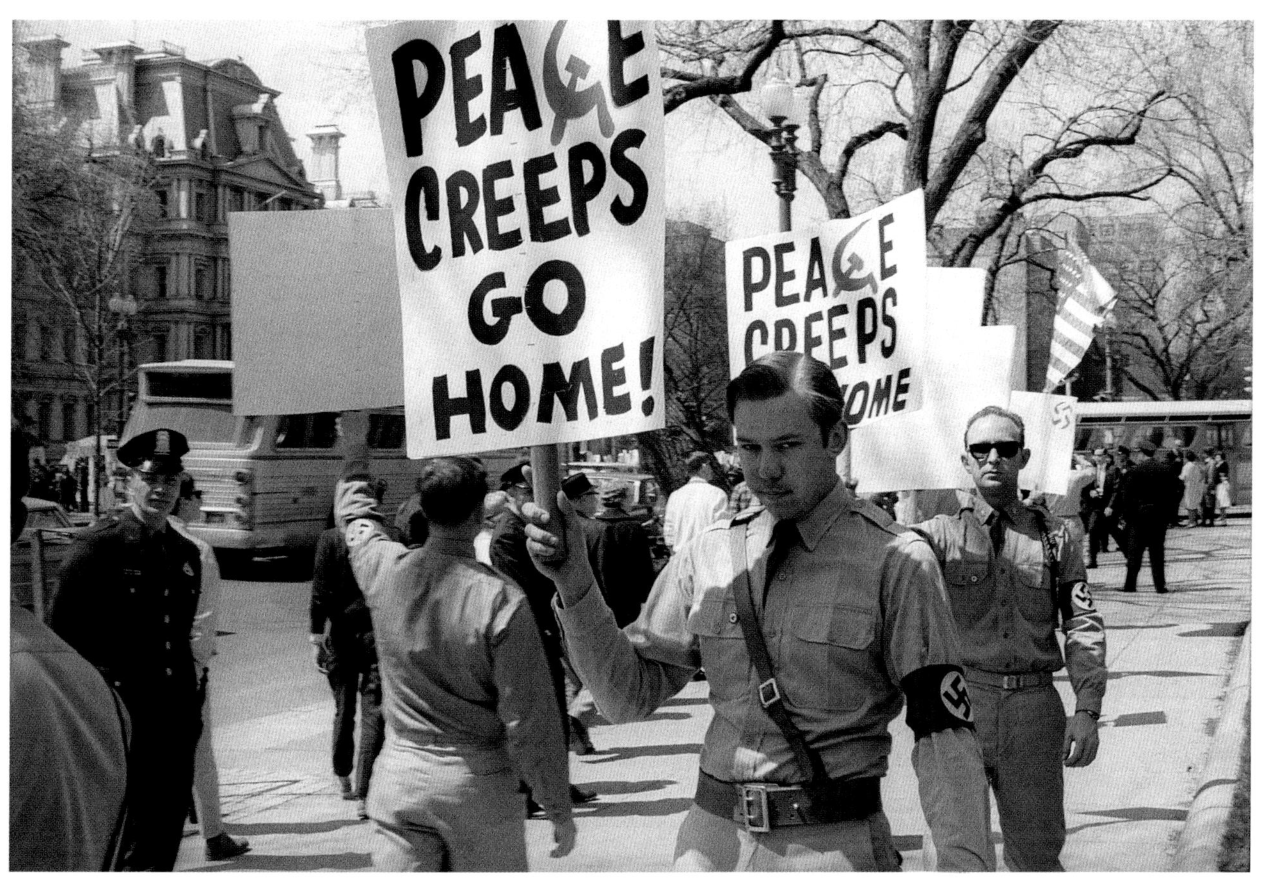

March on Washington to protest the Vietnam War, Washington, DC, April 17, 1965

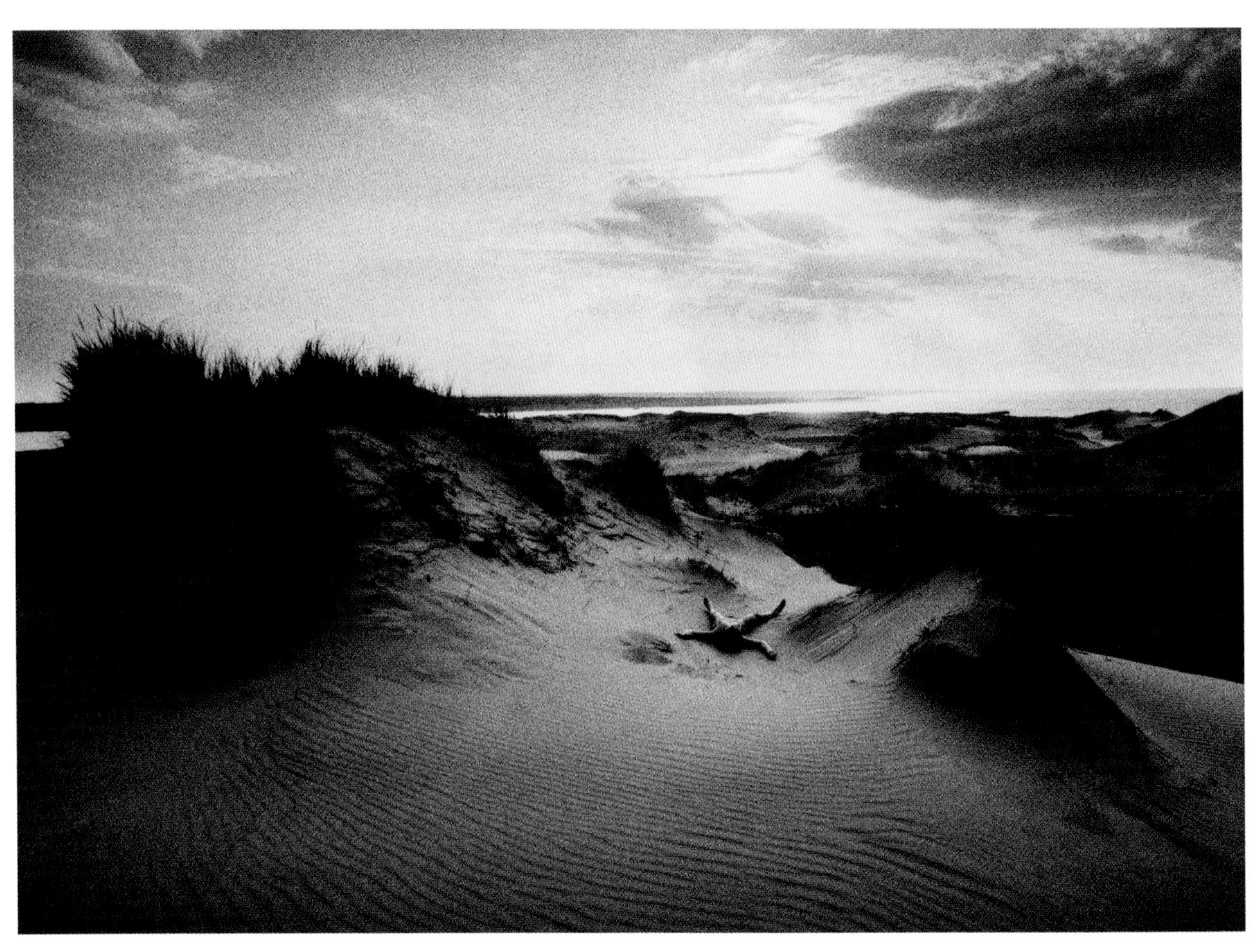

Nude Study, Libby, sand dunes, north shore, Prince Edward Island, August 1970

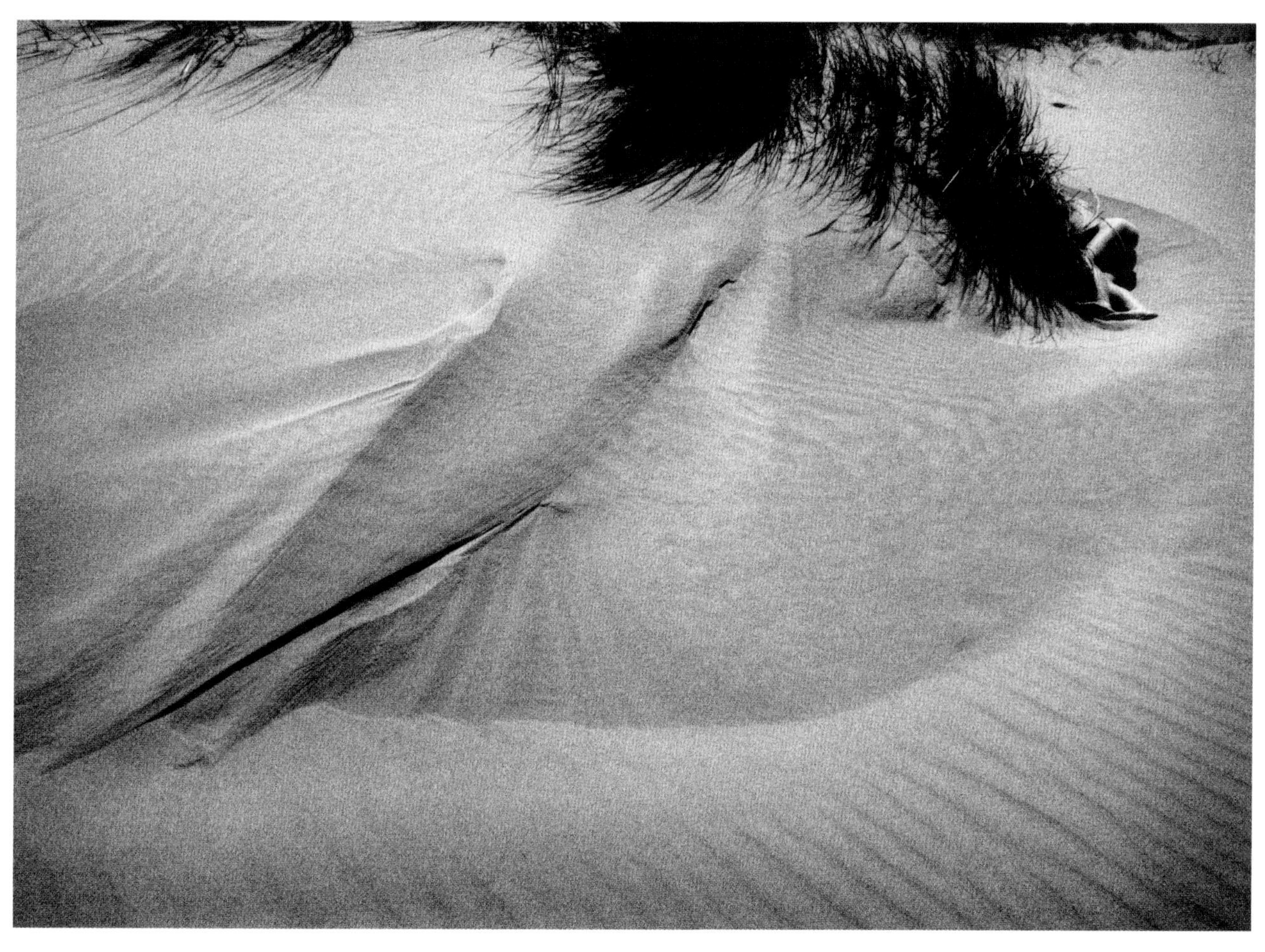

Nude Study, Libby, sand dunes, north shore, Prince Edward Island, August 1970

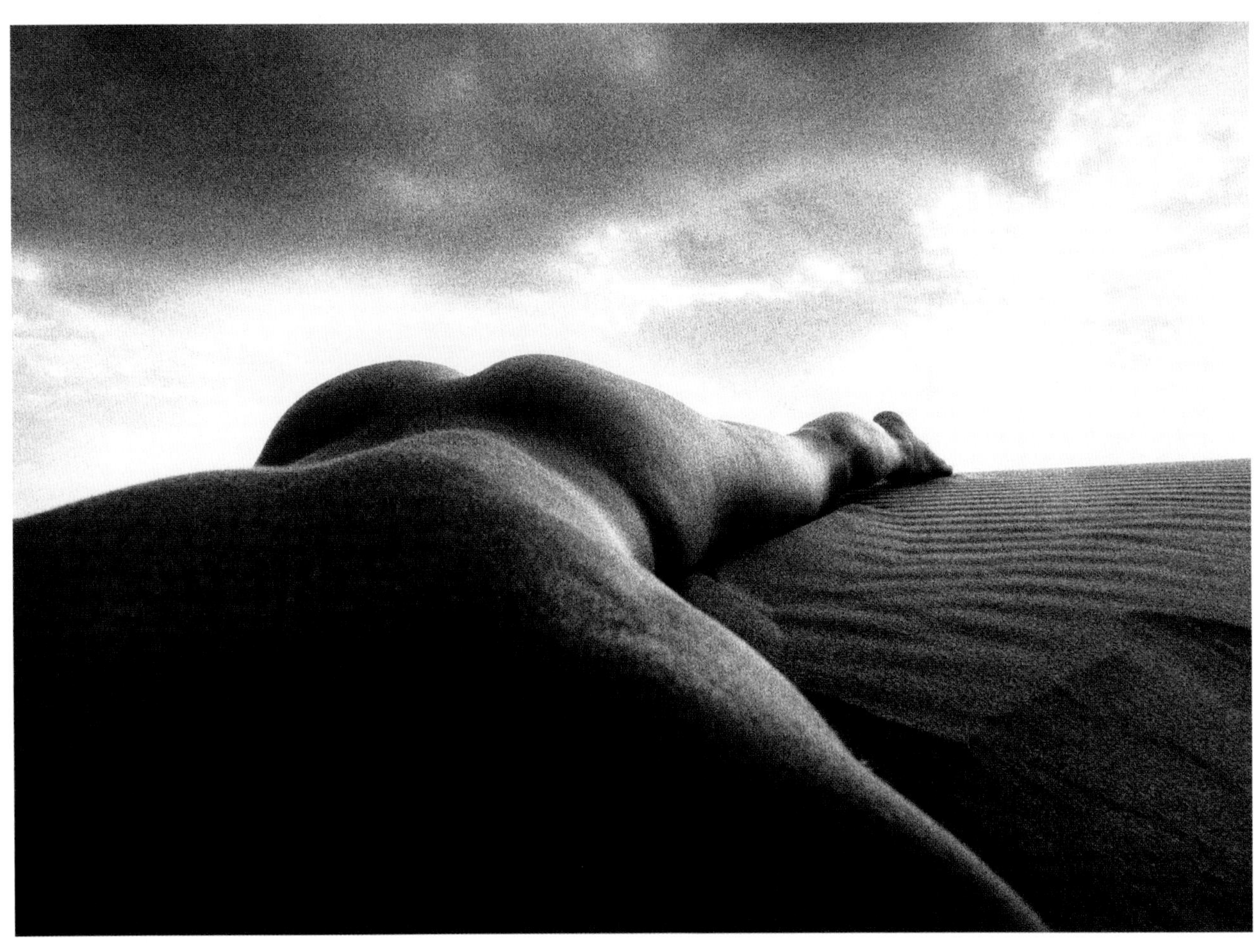

Nude Study, Libby, sand dunes, north shore, Prince Edward Island, August 1970

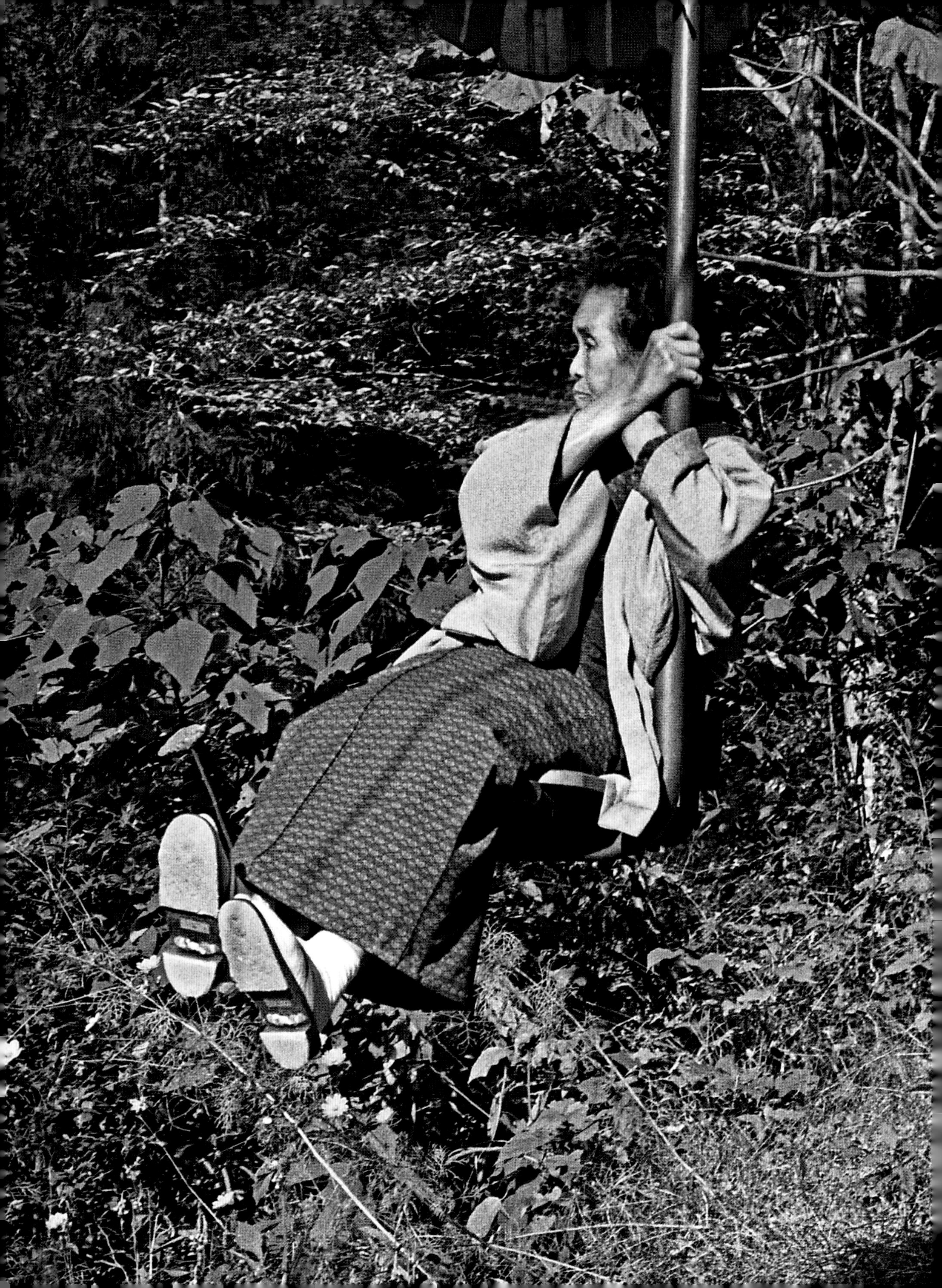

7

AFTER OUR PLANE LANDED at Tokyo's Haneda airport, we went into the warm and humid Tokyo night to board a bus that would carry us to the terminal. Like most North Americans, I held a stereotypical image of the Japanese as a polite, restrained people living in a well-ordered society, but when I cleared customs and entered the terminal concourse, I was met by a scene that can best be described as a three-ring circus. Black-haired tots whizzed by, their screams and laughter adding to the cacophony of an impromptu band marching up and down the concourse with their drums and plastic flutes. A fellow traveller entering behind me was greeted by a line of revellers carrying a long banner emblazoned with words of welcome and shouting *"Banzai!"* and *"Irasshai!"* They tossed him around like a beach ball before hoisting him up on their shoulders. It suddenly dawned on me that all the people in this densely crowded terminal looked, more or less, like myself. I was no longer a visible minority; this awareness was comforting and, at the same time, somewhat disquieting. I needed to be rescued from this madhouse and called the Nishibayashi home. A man answered, and after a failure to communicate, he handed the phone over to his son, who said that he and his brother would soon come by to pick me up. After a half an hour, I was approached by two young and handsome men. Shin was wearing bright red overalls, while Yo, his older brother, was clad in more conservative attire, except for a Davy Crockett coonskin cap complete with a long, bushy tail.

Mountain lift,
Nakatsu,
Oita, Japan,
November 1969

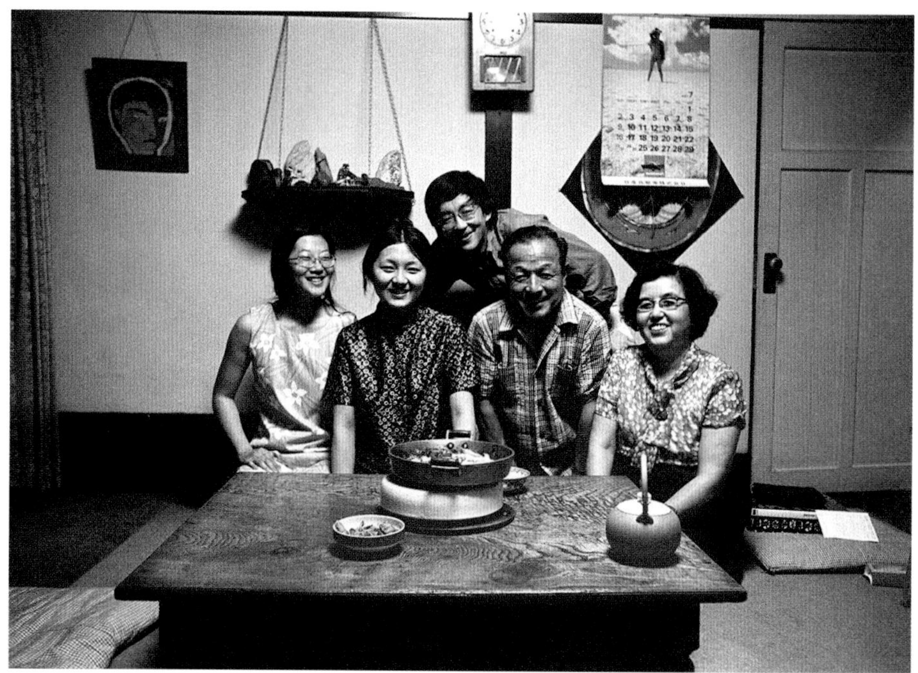

We piled into the family station wagon, a Datsun Bluebird. (Unlike North Americans, with their love of speed, brute force and deadly beasts, the Japanese name their consumer goods after more gentle forms of flora and fauna. The most popular brands of cigarettes are Peace and Hope.) We drove into the neon-lit urban jungle of Tokyo. Once we entered the pleasant residential ward of Ogikubo, the streets narrowed alarmingly, but Shin deftly avoided the oncoming traffic by a mere inch or two and brought us safely to their home, a traditional wooden house located behind a drab, two-storey apartment building. I entered a kitchen filled with beautiful, handmade kites. The father, a short, stout and jovial man, sat at a long wooden table, working on a tiny kite no bigger than a book of matches. Across from him sat his wife, a kindly looking woman whom I liked immediately, and who would become my confidant and mentor over the next few months. Despite the strains of language, I felt perfectly at ease and welcomed in this warm family setting. Mrs. Nishibayashi said I must be tired after my long trip, and suggested I take a bath and retire for the night. Yo showed me the *ofuro*, the family bath, and led me to his room, where I would sleep on the top of a set of metal bunk beds, recently vacated by Jun, the oldest son, who was now living with his uncle in Osaka.

I knew enough to wash and thoroughly rinse myself before entering the tub, but when I dipped an exploratory toe into the water, I almost screamed in pain. Like most older men, Mr. Nishibayashi, who was usually the first one to bathe, liked his water at a temperature that I couldn't believe any human could survive. After tempering the water, I soaked long enough in the square plastic tub for the weariness to dissipate from my bones. Wishing to be a proper guest, I emptied the tub and carefully wiped off every surface. When Mr. N. walked in to discover his nightly comfort had vanished, he must have wondered what he and his family had got themselves into.

I spent the next two weeks with the Nishibayashis getting over a cold and acclimatizing myself to Japan. During my second night in Tokyo, I was awakened by tremors shaking our bed. At first I thought Yo might be masturbating, but if so, he was having one hell of a fantasy, for the tremors grew until the whole house was shaking. I peeked down to Yo, and since he was snoring away peacefully, I went back to sleep. The next morning, Mr. N. informed me rather nonchalantly that it was just another earthquake. I was to experience four more over the coming months; one, which struck while I was in a pachinko parlour, was of sufficient magnitude to send a hail of steel ball bearings raining down on our heads while the rows of pachinko machines undulated like the hips of a hula dancer.

Yo and Shin took me with them to learn how to navigate the city by using its labyrinthian and amazingly efficient subway system. Fortunately for me, an illiterate Nisei, the signage used in all transportation systems throughout Japan has an added component in romaji English. At other times, Mr. N., who operated a business supplying ceramic tiles to the building trades, took me on his round of deliveries and, invariably, would find an open field in which to fly a kite. One night he took all of us to his favourite German beer garden in Ginza, where he stood up and sang "Bésame Mucho" in a surprisingly rich and powerful baritone. In the evenings, I retired to our bedroom to spend hours studying my collection of *How to Learn Japanese in Ten Easy Lessons* books, and slowly I began to recapture a language that I hadn't spoken since I was a small child. Living with the Nishibayashis was a tremendous help, for they updated the little Japanese that I did know, which, of course, came from my parents, who were of the old Meiji era. My utterances would often be met by either restrained laughter or blanks looks of incomprehension, like the time I said I was going to Shinjuku to see a Japanese *gento*

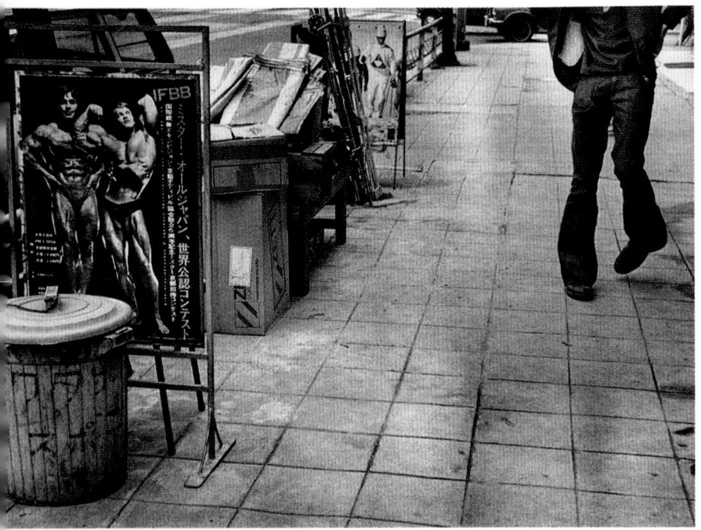
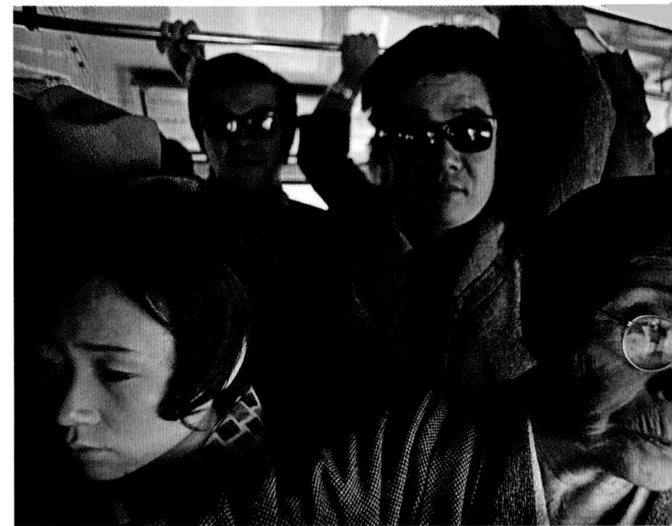

(movie); they had no idea what I had said until Yo looked the word up in a dictionary, which defined *gento* as form of lantern-picture show popular around the turn of the century. Since I wanted to develop as much proficiency as possible before facing the daunting task of meeting my sister, I thought the best way to accelerate the learning process would be to travel alone for two weeks throughout the northern end of the main island of Honshu.

Mr. N. offered to call Fumiko to let her know my schedule. I asked him to convey a little white lie, which was that I was on a government grant and my schedule demanded a photographic tour of Tohoku before the coming of the heavy snows of winter. After hanging up, Mr. N. reported that my sister was offended that I had broken proper protocol by not visiting her first (an omen of things to come) and that I must bring with me twenty presents for our relatives. On the advice of my brother, I had bought presents for my sister and her husband along with two bottles of Johnnie Walker for my two uncles, which I was told would be sufficient, but the added burden of twenty more gifts would not only be cumbersome to carry but would also put a big dent in my limited budget. Besides, I had no idea what to buy. I jokingly asked the Nishibayashis if it would be all right if I bought a big bag of *senbei* (Japanese rice crackers) and gave one piece to each of my relatives. Mr. N. said not to worry, and that he would take care of everything. The next day he returned from a trip to the local *depato* (department store), with twenty serving trays

202

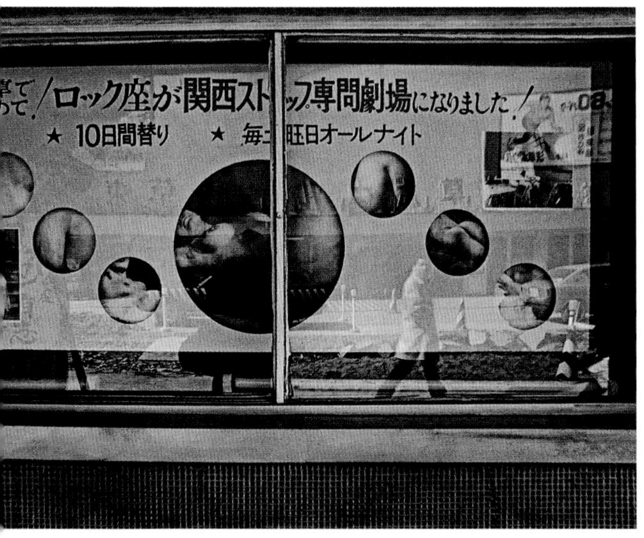

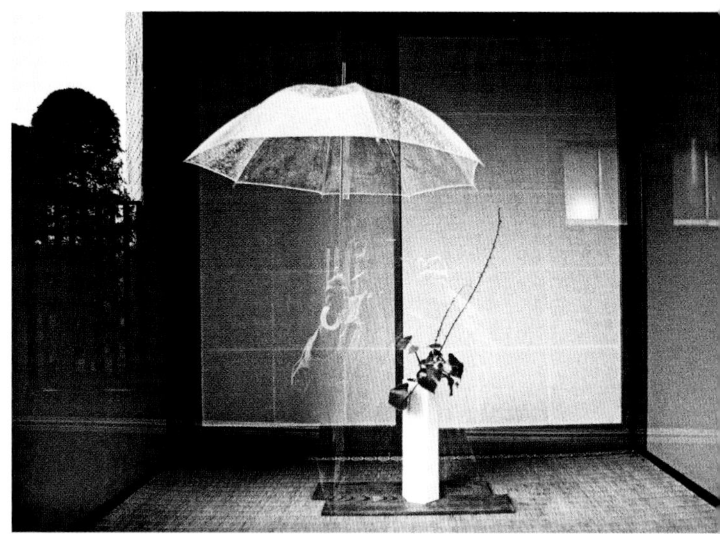

made of cheap tin garishly painted with floral patterns and scenes of the English countryside. I thought they were tacky, but Mr. N. assured me that countryfolk appreciate anything imported from the West and packaged them up for shipping to Shiida. I was now ready to begin my solo journey.

The Nishibayashis accompanied me to the cavernous main railway station at Ueno, and since I was about to be thrust upon his unsuspecting countrymen, Yo pulled me aside to tell me that the correct way to say "I don't know" is "*shiranai*" and not, as I had been saying, "*shirinai*," which literally means "I don't have a rear end." I boarded the northbound express with the faint hope of not making a further ass of myself. After a couple of hours, I transferred to a local milk run that would take me to the village nearest to my intended target, Osorezan (Terror Mountain), a sacred site where flocks of visitors come every year to have Osorezan's legendary mediums, who looked like the witches in *Macbeth*, put them in touch with the spirits of their departed loved ones.

The train I entered was half filled, and at each of the many stops, our numbers dwindled until there was only myself and an old farmer couple. At the next stop, which was not my target village, the couple got out, and when the train refused to move after the customary interval, I went outside, where I discovered, to my horror, that there were no more train tracks. Fortunately, the train master told me I was fairly close to Osorezan and phoned to make a reservation for me at a nearby inn. The

LEFT
Soft porn
movie poster,
Tokyo, Japan,
1969–70

RIGHT
Tokyo, Japan,
1969–70

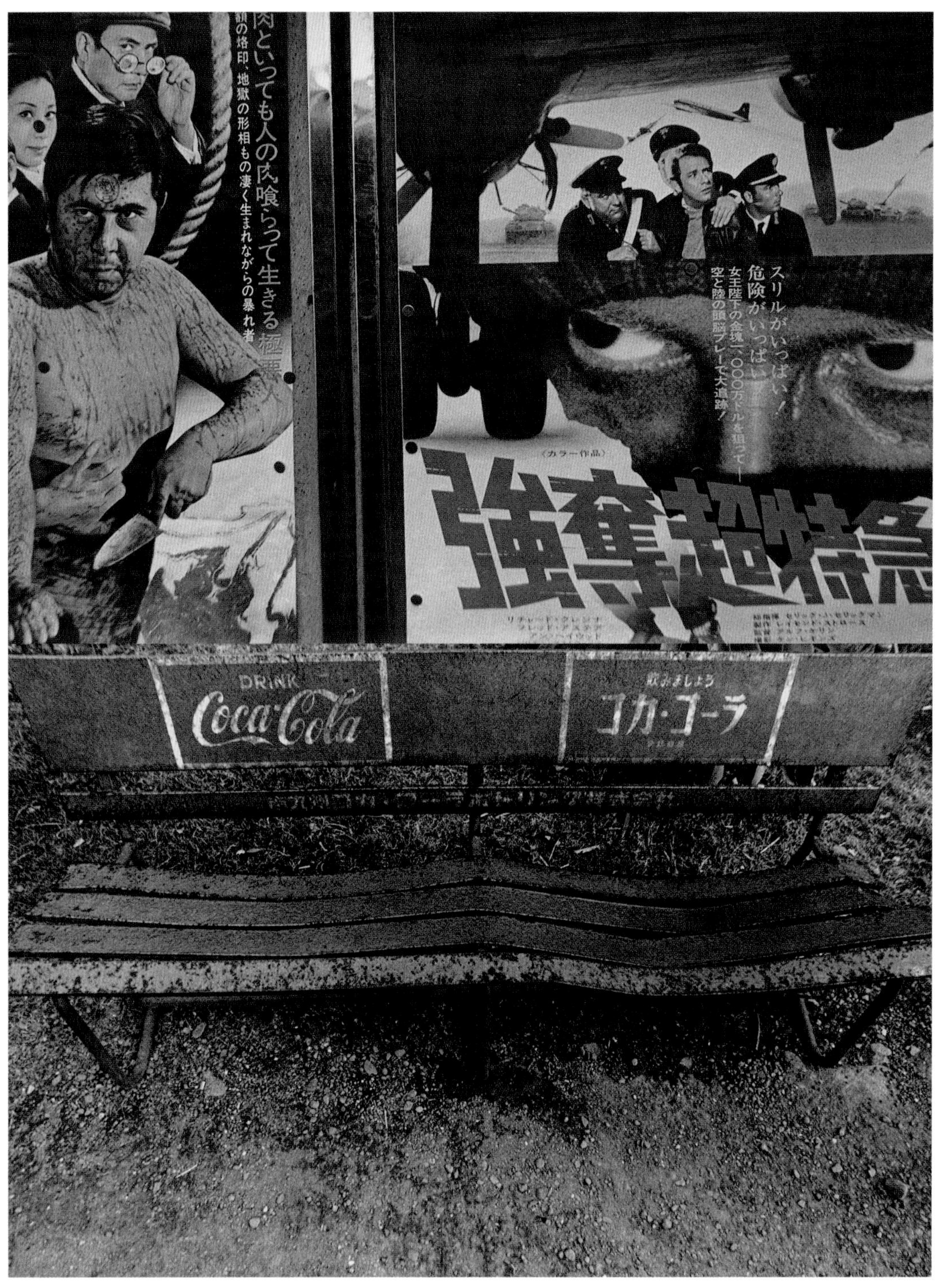
肉といっても人の肉喰らって生きる極悪人
額の烙印、地獄の形相もの凄く生まれながらの暴れ者
（カラー作品）
スリルがいっぱい！
危険がいっぱい！
女王陛下の金塊一〇〇〇万ドルを狙って
空と陸の頭脳プレーで大追跡！
強奪超特急
DRINK
Coca-Cola
飲みましょう
コカ・コーラ

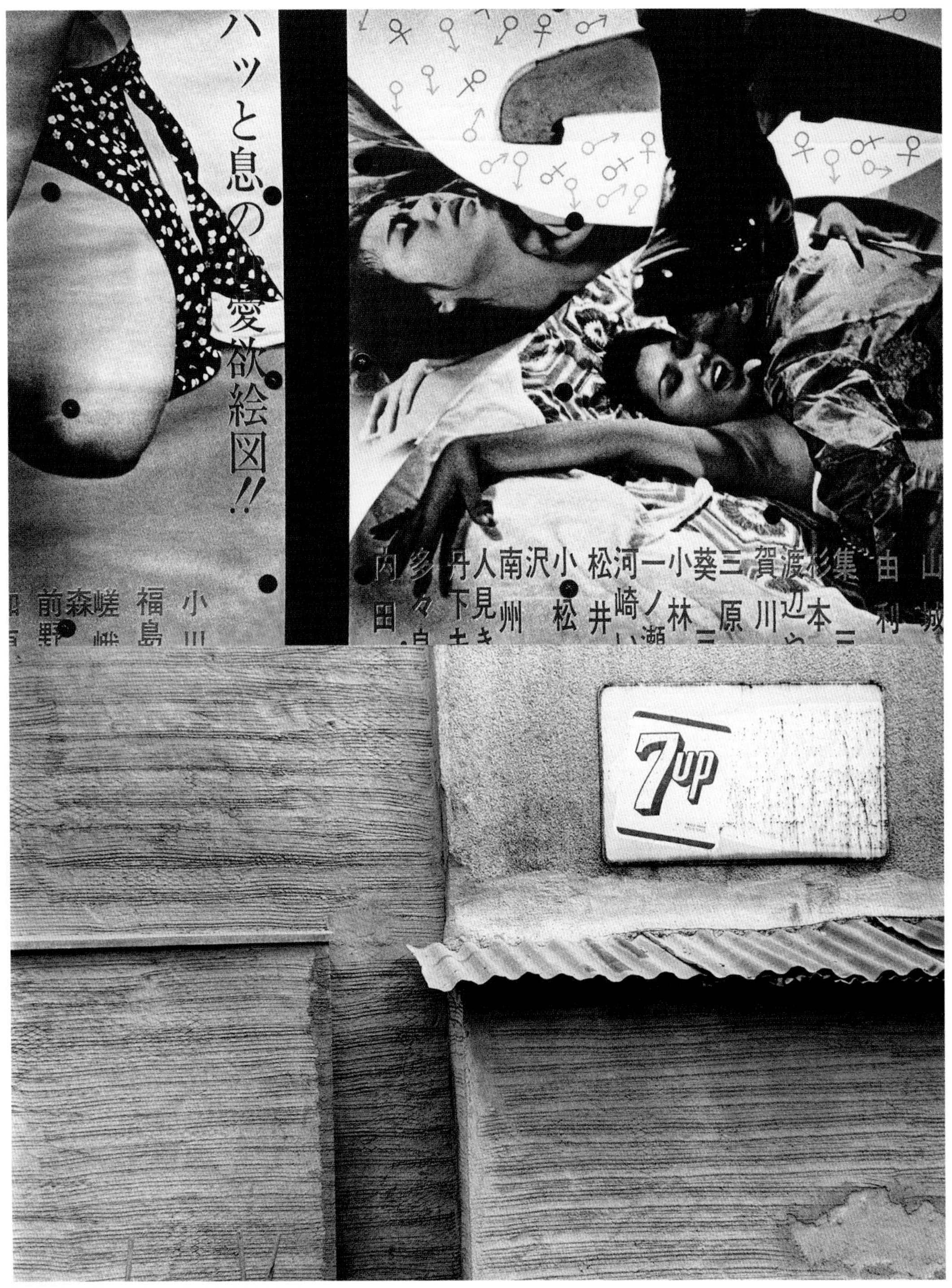
ハッと息の
愛欲絵図!!
肉多丹人南沢小　松河一小葵三賀渡杉集　由山
田々下見州　松井崎ノ林　原川辺本　利城
前森嵯福　小川
野　島
7up

next day, I took a bus to Osorezan and hiked up to the lava beds, where I stayed for the afternoon with nary a glimpse of the mediums. I spent another two days exploring the area, and each afternoon I returned to the mountain, but it must have been the off-season for the witches, which was too bad, for I thought the eerie moonscape of encrusted lava beds, along with the wizened mediums, would make for a great photo op. Besides, I was hoping to come away with my grandmother's udon recipe.

So far I had been disappointed to find that the calendar image of Japan in all its natural glory had been overwhelmed by a polluted, over-crowded agricultural and industrial wasteland. I thought I might find the idealized image if I were to travel to the most remote area of the island, and after checking my map, I targeted Kodomari, the last village on the northeast tip of Honshu. This time I made it to my destination without mishap, and I checked into a lovely *ryokan*, a Japanese inn, overlooking the strait that divided Honshu from the northern island of Hokkaido. The next morning, I strolled down to the waterfront, and when I peered over the concrete seawall, I was greeted by the sight of a mass of discarded black gumboots totally covering the surface of the water. The blonde head of a doll bobbed amongst the debris.

I found the most troublesome aspect of travelling in Japan to be food. Accommodations were not a problem, for I would approach either the station master or someone at the tourist bureau in the larger centres to find me the cheapest place to stay for the night. My preference was for a ryokan, which provides both a standard Japanese breakfast and a glorious *kaiseki* dinner featuring several exquisite dishes, all made from local ingredients. However, these Japanese inns were a luxury that I could ill afford, so most of the time I ate noodles sold from a cart outside the train station or else found one of the many small food stalls, which sold only a few simple items. Every now and then, I would crave a real dinner. Many restaurants in Japan have a glass case in front in which enticing wax replicas of their dishes are displayed. Entering one of these places, I would have to suffer the indignity of dragging a waitress out-side so I could point to the dish I wanted. Despite these problems, I ate well and never once had a bad meal. The Japanese restaurant industry is highly competitive, and the people themselves are renowned for their highly refined palettes.

After two weeks on the road, I was growing bored and weary of playing the tourist. My sojourn in a country where almost no one travels alone was a lonely experience, especially at the various local points of

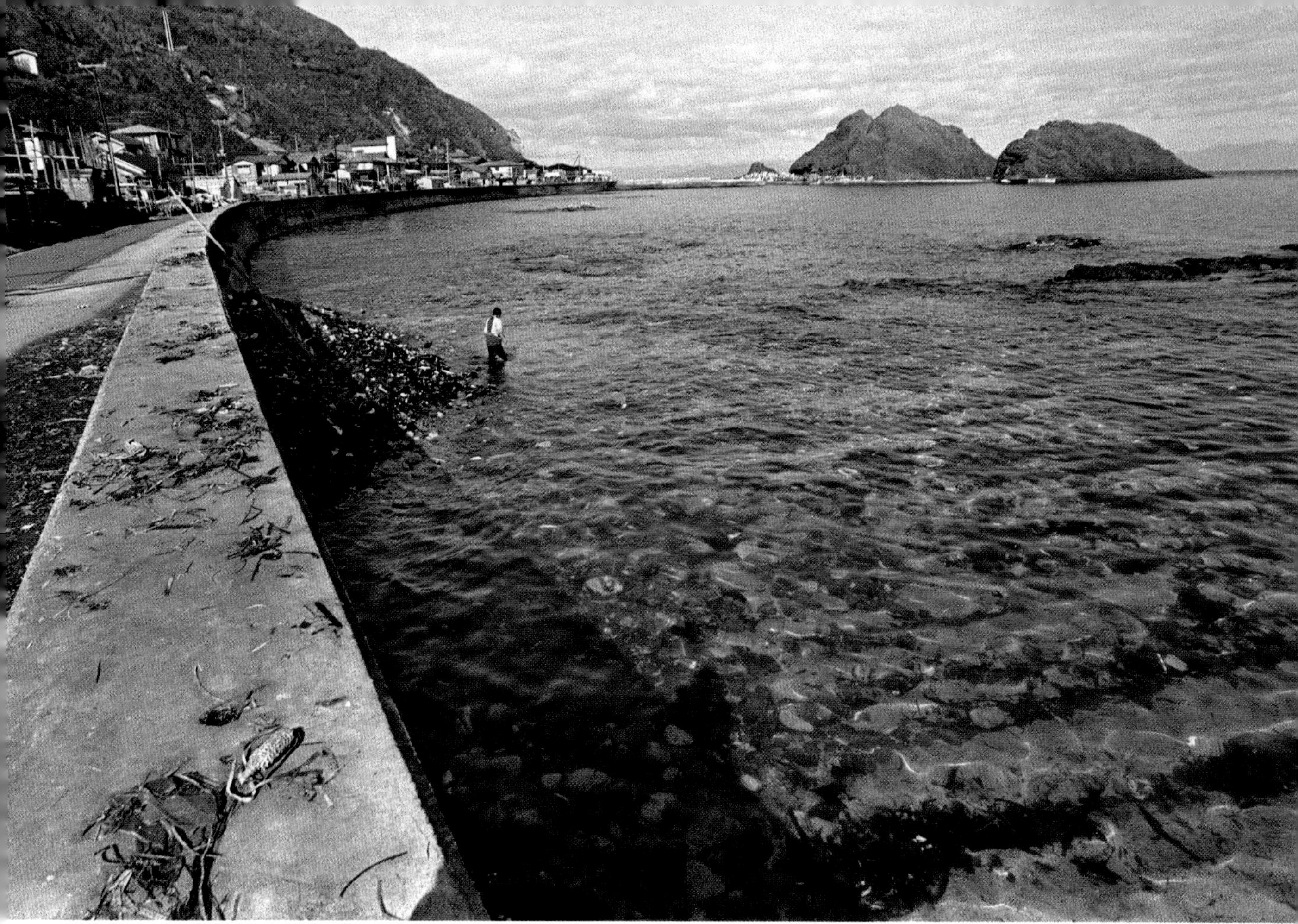

interest, where I would follow in the wake of a class of joyful students or a busload of tourists merrily following their flag-waving guide. I decided to return to Tokyo after a final overnight stay in the city of Sendai. On my arrival, I went straight to the tourism bureau, and after I rejected the list of pricey hotels, the worried clerk told me that the cheapest establishment would be most unsuitable for a foreign guest. I said I would be fine and took a taxi to my night's lodging, which turned out to be a foreboding building of grey concrete with absolutely no welcoming signage. When I entered the dreary lobby lit only by one naked light-bulb, I noticed several rough-looking men dressed in tattered and dirty work clothes standing idly by. I went to the front desk, where an older woman, who looked like a brothel madam, eyed me suspiciously but allowed me to check in. I went to grab my luggage and discovered that my camera bag had disappeared. My first thought was that one of the suspicious-looking men had walked off with it. I was in a state of panic

Kodomari,
Aomori, Japan,
October 1969

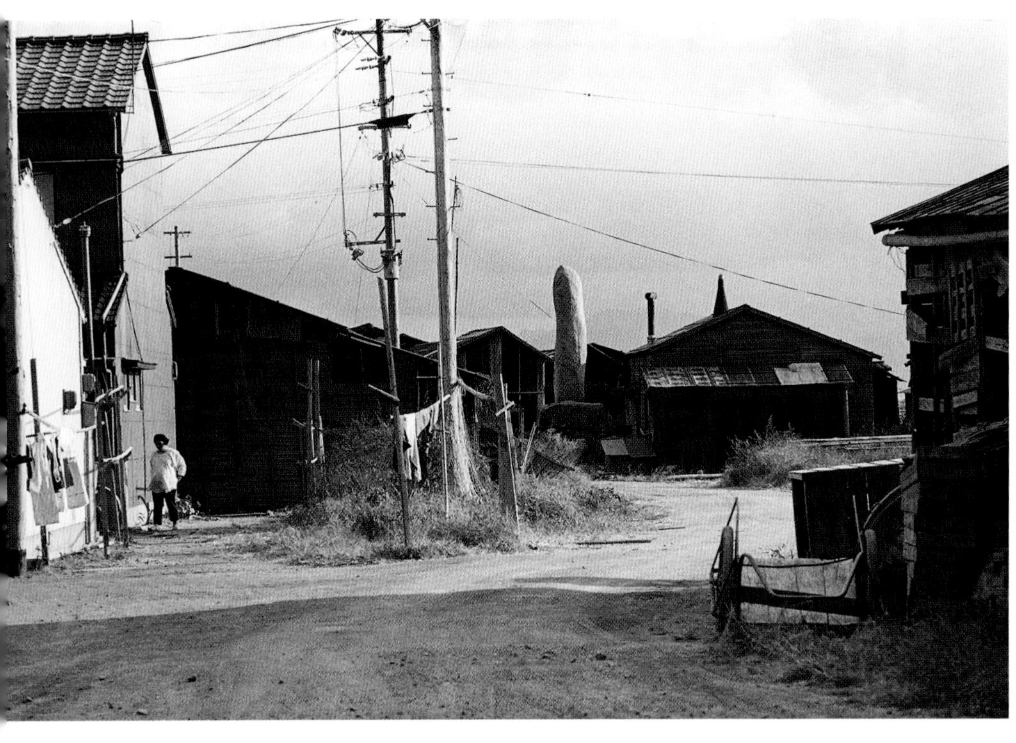

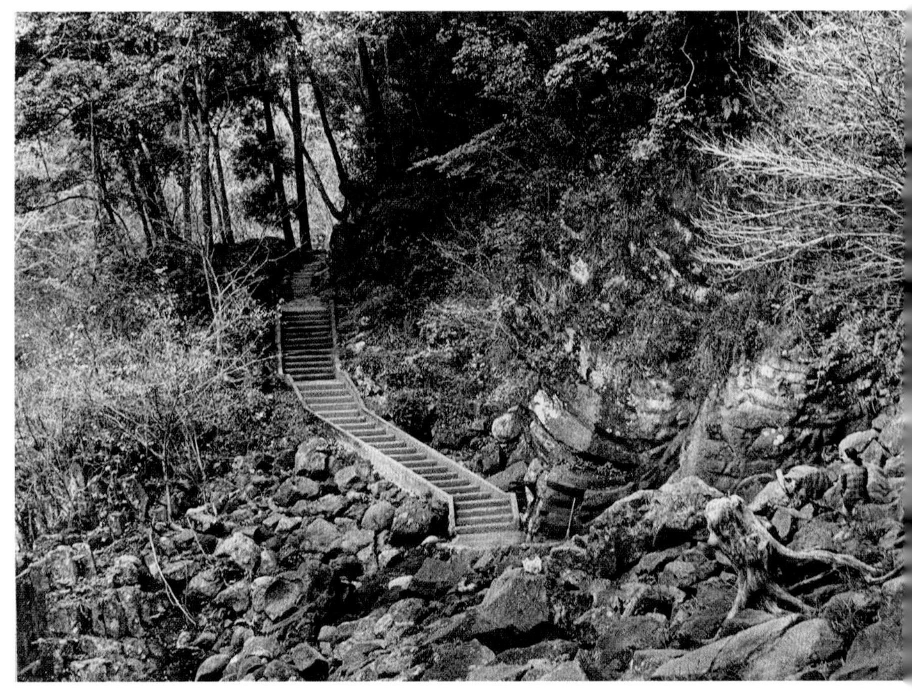

and making quite a scene when the phone rang—it was the lady from the tourist bureau calling to say I had left a bag at the station and she would have it delivered immediately. I needn't have worried, for on the whole, the Japanese are scrupulously honest, and their country has rightfully earned its reputation as one of the safest tourist destinations in the world.

I soon made my way back to Ogikubo, and it was such a relief to be back in the warm embrace of the Nishibayashi family. After a week of rest and recovery, I headed out again on the first leg of my long journey to meet my sister. The Nishibayashis and I piled into the Bluebird and drove to their family estate in Yokaichi, and after an overnight stay in their palatial, rustic home, I boarded the shinkansen (bullet train) bound for Osaka, where I was to board the overnight ferry that would carry me through the inland sea to Beppu. It was early evening by the time I entered the ferry's third-class compartment, a large room containing a raised sleeping platform with stacks of bedding on tatami mats. I plunked down beside a large family and brought out my language books. As I was memorizing the flowery phrases of greeting that I would shower upon my sister, I kept getting curious glances from the grandmother sitting nearby. I said, "*konban wa*"—good evening—and was invited to join their party. Soon others came over to meet this odd rarity, a lone foreign traveller sharing their space on the lowliest deck. The gathering turned into a lively all-night party, and by the time the ferry docked the next morning, I had consumed mounds of Japanese junk food, drunk more than was good for me and entertained two offers of marriage.

After disembarking, a white-haired gentleman stooped over a cane hobbled over and introduced himself as Matsumoto-san. I was shocked to learn that such an old man could be my sister's husband. After a lunch of ramen, we boarded a local train going north, and after many stops, we got off at the small station at Shiida. We walked through the fishing village, crossed a small wooden bridge, and after a pleasant stroll through a park with an ancient Shinto shrine guarded by two fierce stone lions, we arrived at a large, weather-beaten ryokan. When we entered, Fumiko appeared from a back room to greet me. The flowery phrases had flown out of my head, and I could only stare at this rather tall, rail-thin woman with a stern expression on her face, a total stranger who just happened to be my sister. The awkward silence continued until Matsumoto-san poked me in the side and urged me to say something. After a short, perfunctory conversation, she sat me down at a low table,

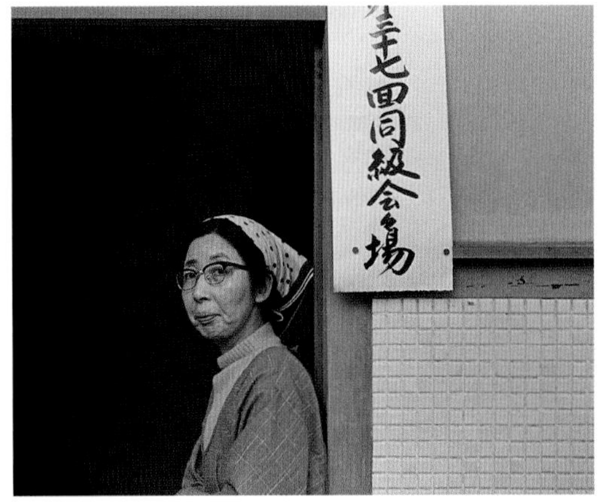

Fumiko at a ryokan,
Shiida, Fukuoka, Japan,
November 1969

brought me a Coca-Cola, and turned on the TV, on which John Wayne was wooing Maureen O'Hara in perfectly correct Japanese. After several hours sitting by myself, Fumiko reappeared to summon me to dinner. The atmosphere was strained as we tried to overcome the barriers of language, age and culture. When I addressed her as *Fumiko-san,* I was sternly rebuked and ordered to always use the honorific term for older sister: *onee-san.* Growing more and more confused and disheartened, I was relieved when the dinner finally ended. Fumiko led me to my room and showed me where I was to take my nightly bath. After changing into the *yukata* laid out on my bed, I entered the ofuro, a vast room with three large pools of steaming water and an end wall of floor-to-ceiling glass that revealed a picturesque scene of gnarled pines and the white peaks of ocean waves. As I lay basking in the ofuro, the *shoji* screen door slid open, and in walked my sister and her husband, who then joined me in the pool. I was struck by the irony of the situation, for here we were with our naked bodies sharing the intimacy of a bath while our hearts and minds were so very far apart.

The next morning, I went into the front room where all the gifts that I had brought were piled on the floor. I was rather offended to see my sister's gift amongst the pile, for I had spent hours shopping for just the right present: a lovely pendant crafted by an Indigenous Canadian artisan. To my Western way of thinking, gift giving is a spontaneous expression of gratitude or affection, but in Japan it is an automatic social ritual with its own complex set of rules. After the gifts were sorted through and divided, Fumiko bundled them up in a *furoshiki* cloth and ordered me to follow her outside. She strapped the bundle to the rear carrier of her bicycle, and the two of us walked to the village. Our first stop was a corner fish store, where Fumiko introduced me to its manager, who I believe was my cousin. I asked if he could show me a fugu. I had read about the puffer fish in one of my travel guides: the liver of this creature is so deadly that sushi chefs have to have a special licence to serve the prized delicacy, but despite these precautions, a number of deaths by fugu poisoning are recorded each year. After examining (but not touching) the fish, Fumiko led me to the side of the building and up a flight of stairs to an office, where we were greeted by an older man who I believe was my uncle. After bowing, Fumiko handed me one of the gifts, which I in turn handed over to our host. The rest of the afternoon was spent in a whirlwind tour to all my other relatives, and at each stop, they would ask me into their homes, but Fumiko adamantly refused—she never seemed to do anything with serene grace. I was disappointed, for I wanted to know who these people were and what limb they occupied on our family tree.

I was exhausted by the time we arrived back at the ryokan. That evening, when I was called to dinner, I was delighted to learn that my cousin the fishmonger had brought over a beautiful Imari plate with paper thin slices of fugu sashimi artfully arranged in the form of a Japanese crane. I eagerly bit into my first slice of this delicacy only to discover that the texture was rubbery and the taste bland; I could only surmise that at the heart of the Japanese love affair with fugu was the rather dubious thrill of playing Russian roulette with a fish.

I stayed another five days in Shiida, taking long walks through the village, the nearby cemetery with its moss-covered stone markers bearing the names of my ancestors, and the surrounding rice fields, where I would while away the hours by chatting with inquisitive farmers. Before leaving, I explained to Fumiko that my work schedule necessitated a photographic tour of Kyushu, but that I would stop off in Shiida for a short visit before returning to Tokyo. She accompanied me to the train station, wished me a safe trip and ordered me to return with another twenty presents. I didn't want this burden to be hanging over my head, so I got off at the next station and went shopping at a large *depato*. I had no idea what to buy, but finally settled on a lacquered box filled with colourful mini sculptures made of sugar, which I thought were pretty and not too expensive. I bought twenty of them and asked the clerk to ship them to my sister in Shiida.

I enjoyed Kyushu, which was tropical, less densely populated and had a greater feeling of open, unsullied space. For part of my circumnavigation of the island, I was accompanied by Bernice, a Chinese Canadian friend from the old Rochdale days, so all in all, this tour was much more pleasant than my first journey around Tohoku. The one memory that stands out from that two-week tour is a visit to the Nagasaki Atomic Bomb Museum. I am still haunted by the horrific images of human forms etched forever into concrete walls by the force of the blast.

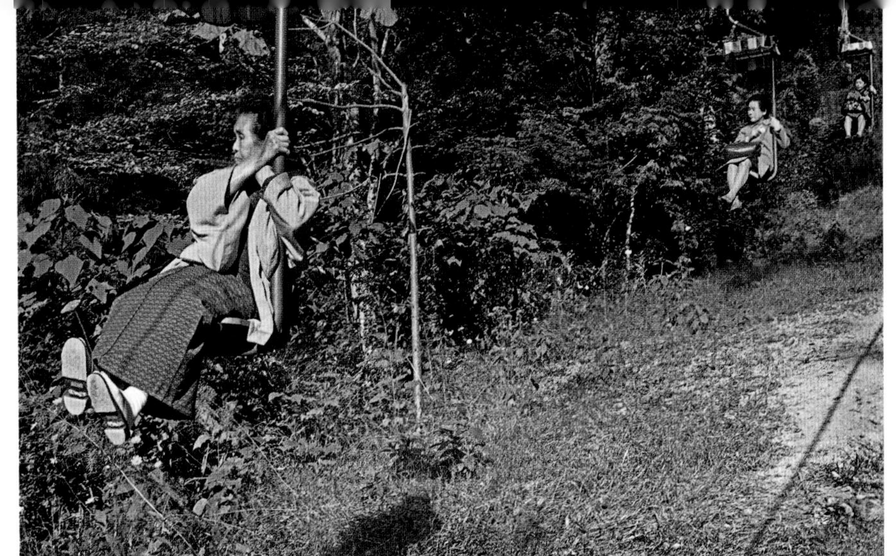

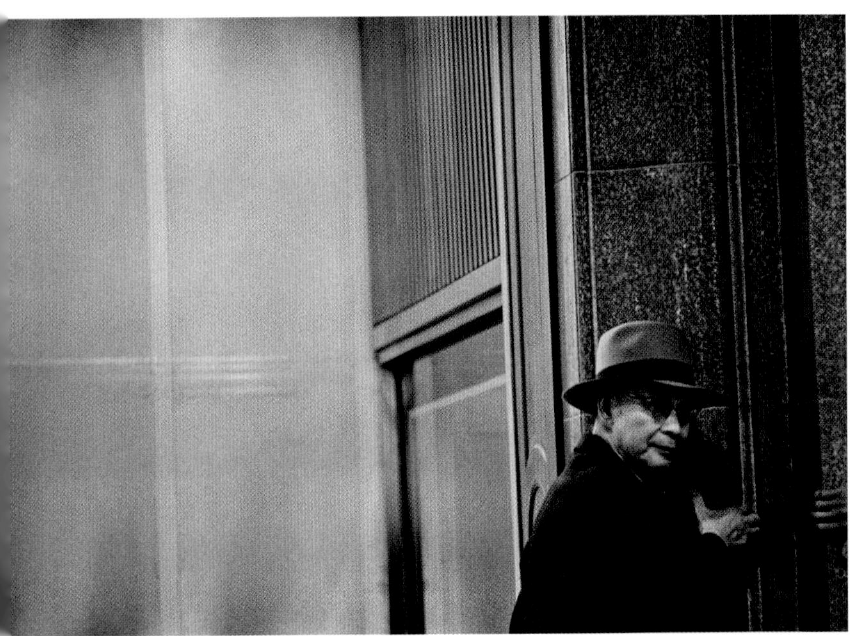

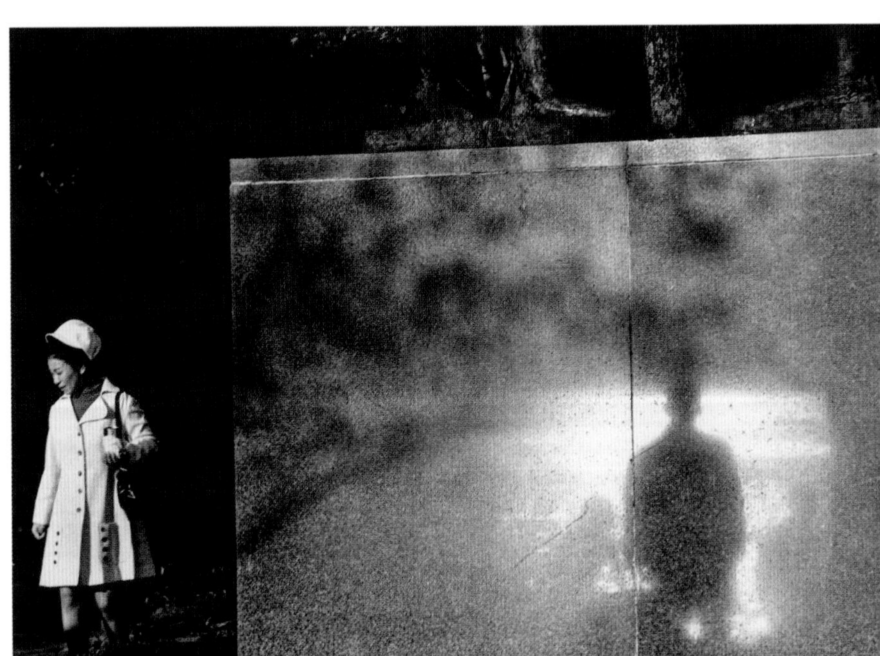

As promised, I arrived back in Shiida, and by the next morning, Fumiko was once again packing up the gifts that I had bought, complaining all the while that the lacquered boxes were totally inappropriate—I should have chosen a unique, local product from a point far away from Shiida. What's more, she was much too busy, and I would have to deliver the gifts by myself. I was shocked, for how could I possibly locate all the different houses that I had visited just once in such a short period of time? "*Shikata ga nai*"—it can't be helped, she said, as she shooed me out the door. My first stop was the memorable fish store, but my cousin wasn't around. I vaguely remembered climbing a set of stairs at the side of the building. When I reached the second-storey office, I was greeted by an older man who looked vaguely familiar. I bowed and handed him a present, which he rather reluctantly accepted. Back on the street, I was fortunate to run into my aunt—my mother's younger sister who had returned with her parents to Japan after the war—who kindly led me by the hand to all my other relatives. I was quite proud to have accomplished this seemingly impossible mission, but when I entered the ryokan, my sister shouted "*Baka!*" She had just been informed that the first person to receive a lacquered box was the janitor of the fish store. The situation was so absurd I couldn't help breaking into laughter, and when I peeked over at Fumiko, I saw she was desperately trying to maintain her stern composure.

On my last night in Shiida, my relatives hosted a farewell party for me at the home of my oldest uncle, a rather severe-looking kendo sensei. Before dinner was served, a quarrel broke out between my uncle—red-faced with anger—and my tearful sister. I couldn't understand what was behind this confrontation, which continued to escalate until another relative murmured that it was unseemly to argue in front of our honoured guest. The only person I could connect with was my grandmother—the same woman who had begged for Fumiko to stay in Japan—and since she was not only aged but also slightly deaf and somewhat senile in a delightful way, she was almost as isolated from the family circle as I.

The next morning, Fumiko accompanied me to the train station, and on our way through the village, we met a woman with a baby strapped to her back. She must have been a relative, for she tried to hand me a *sembetsu*, the traditional gift of money for a visiting relative to help with the cost of travel and gifts, but Fumiko rudely thrust the envelope back at the woman. Before continuing on, Fumiko asked to hold the infant, and as she oohed and aahed over the smiling child, the coldness of her face melted into a joyful, almost beatific smile. At the moment of our parting, I finally got a glimpse of the person that my brother had met five years earlier. The intervening years had not been kind to Matsumoto-san. A lengthy illness had forced them to abandon their business and return to the ancestral village where they would have to rely on the charity of their family, who found them menial work as caretakers of an inn. However, the greatest tragedy in my sister's life was her inability to bear children. Upon boarding the train, I felt neither anger nor resentment toward my sister, only a deep sadness that our meeting had not been joyful. As the train sped toward Tokyo, I realized my entry into her life must have reawakened painful memories of her earlier abandonment and that, to her eyes, I was the lucky sibling, a prosperous brother from Canada who could easily shoulder any burden. I wished that good fortune would return to her life and that, someday, my sister could even be reunited with her immediate family.

With my obligations now complete, I was able to discover and explore the many fascinating areas of Tokyo—which, to me, had the same frenetic energy and excitement as New York—now my second favourite city. Despite my aversion to further travel, I was able to see more of Japan on several outings with the Nishibayashis. Prior to coming to Japan, I had published a portfolio of nudes in *Camera Mainichi*, the nation's leading photo magazine, and so Shin, who was studying photography at a technical college, invited his class to the house to meet me. They invited me to join them on an overnight retreat to a seaside resort near Hayama. I gladly accepted, and on the night of our arrival, they plied me with glass after glass of sake, which I knew I shouldn't drink but could hardly refuse. Finally, I lurched down the hall to the bathroom where I got violently sick, and on the way back, passed out in an empty room, forcing Shin and his friends to spend several frantic hours searching for their wayward guest. With the arrival of winter, I went on a ski weekend to Karuizawa with Yo and Shin and their girlfriends. I'd only skied once in my life, and the brothers thought it might be fun to abandon me at the very top of the mountain. The slope was packed with skiers, and I had to wait for an opening before daring to glide across—not down—the slope. The only way I knew how to stop was to fall down. I would struggle to my feet and wait for the next break in the action. After what seemed an eternity, I reached the bottom, exhausted, thoroughly wet and with my feet aching from the ill-fitting rented boots. I was not amused. These less-than-happy outings were more than offset by a

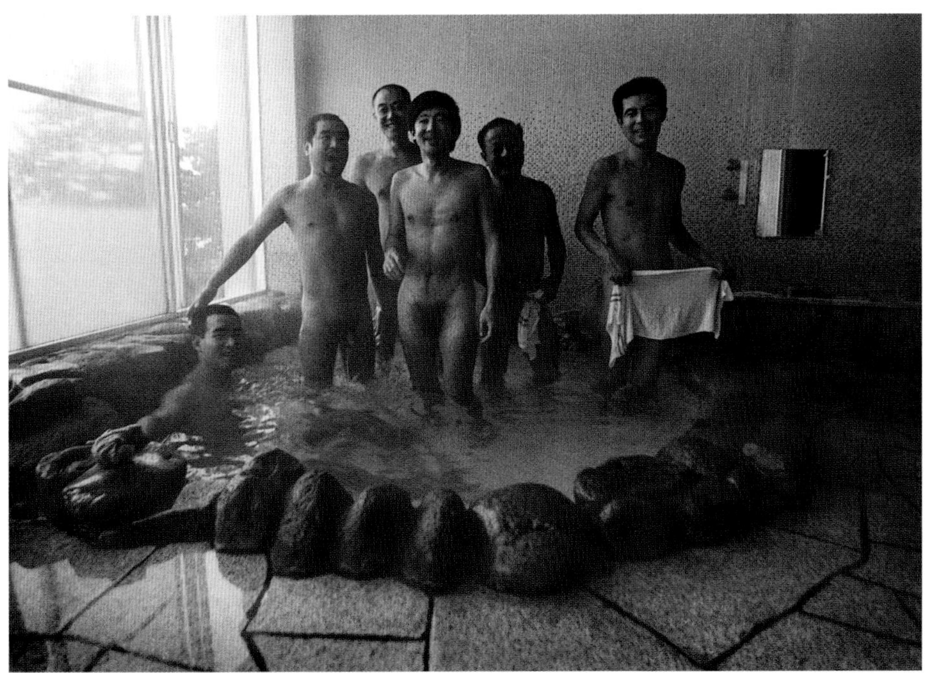

second visit to the seacoast, this time to the beautiful Izu Hanto, in the company of Mr. N. and the fellow members of his swim club. We stayed at an *onsen*, a spa fed by the mineral-rich waters of natural hot springs, and when I ventured outside in the open air, I discovered the ultimate pleasure for a weary traveller: the *rotemburo*, a pool of steaming water carved into a rock face with such grace that it flowed seamlessly into a stand of graceful bamboo.

I had been in Japan a little over two months when I began to think about returning to Canada. I had a sense that my romance with Japan was somehow incomplete and that there was much more to learn and discover, but I could come up with no legitimate reason to stay. A compelling reason appeared one evening as I was leaving the Ogikubo subway station. I was walking among a crowd of shoppers and workers rushing home for dinner when a taxi driver coming from behind beeped his horn, and when we all scurried to the edge of the road, I felt a painful elbow in my side followed by an "oops," and an apologetic "*Gomen nasai.*" After a few paces I realized that "oops" is not part of the Japanese lexicon, and when I turned around, I saw two young women ambling along, chatting merrily away in English. We stopped and introduced ourselves: Julie was a Sansei from Vancouver and an English

Tamio, Mr. Nishibayashi and friends in an ofuro bath at a hotel, Izu, Shizuoka, Japan, October 1969

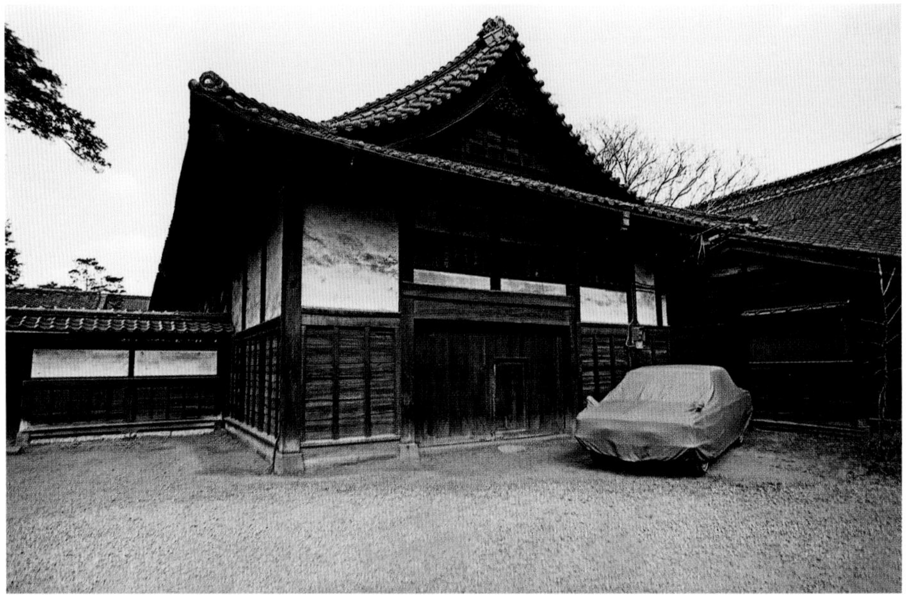

Covered auto at a temple, Tokyo, Japan, 1969–70

teacher; Rita was a scholar from Taiwan, studying Eastern religions at the international Waseda University. They were sharing an apartment a mere half block away from the Nishibayashis. We exchanged phone numbers and agreed to meet the next day for lunch. On the way home, my antenna was tingling, and Japan had suddenly become a whole lot more interesting.

I was drawn to the more ebullient Rita. Although she was the daughter of a wealthy Taiwanese industrialist, her English was perfect after years of study in the States. She was a delightful and, at times, maddening companion. One minute she would be a petulant child, demanding I join in her infantile games, and in the next minute, she would turn into the Wise Woman of the East, enlightening me with the mysteries of Tao and the transcendental power of qi taught to her by the master of her aikido martial arts class. I was totally fascinated by this woman-child. Shortly after we met, Rita left for Taiwan to spend the holidays with her family, but she promised to call as soon as she returned.

I spent the week before Christmas working in Shin's darkroom that he had built in the garage behind the house. On Christmas morning, I presented my family in Japan with a beautifully lacquered album complete with a music box and filled with images of the many joyous moments that we had shared. I was looking forward to the New Year, which had been such a glorious celebration in my childhood, energizing and uniting not only everyone in my family but also our entire community. Surely, now that I was in the motherland, Shogatsu would be even more spectacular. I was crushed when Mrs. N., on New Year's Eve, ordered a *jubako*, a tier of three nestled boxes filled with *osechi ryori*, from a local restaurant and plunked it down on the kitchen table the next morning. Only one or two of Mr. N.'s business associates stopped by that day. I went with Yo, Shin and their girlfriends to a temple, and that was the end of Shogatsu. Where was the week of feverish preparation, the pounding of mochi, the midnight ritual of soba, the steady stream of visitors? Obviously, Japan had undergone a radical transformation, and I realized that although we, the Nikkei in Canada, are a throwback to an earlier time; we are also keepers of the cultural flame.

When Rita returned from Taiwan, we became lovers. Whenever the coast was clear, I would rush over, make mad love in the afternoon until Julie returned and then go home to enjoy a quiet family dinner, hoping that I was not too ruffled and rank from my exertions. My enchantment with Rita and a growing sense that my real purpose in coming to Japan was now unfolding were enough to convince me to renew my visa. I asked Rita if any apartments in their building were available and what they would cost. The rental system in Japan, with its "key money" amounting to a deposit of several months' rent, was clearly beyond my means, and so too was the cost of installing a phone, which required a similarly large deposit. I talked with the Nishibayashis about my desire to stay for a few months more and said that if they were kind enough to let me continue living with them, it was only fair that I pay for my room and board. They refused outright, said that I had become part of their family and would be welcome to stay as long as I wished. Although I had tried to be a good guest, as outgoing and helpful as possible, I still worried that I was abusing their hospitality. But I couldn't see another way to stay in Japan.

Rita was also taking lessons on playing the koto (a classical Japanese instrument resembling a zither), and through her teacher, I managed to find a shakuhachi sensei. When I announced the exciting news to the Nishibayashis, Yo made inquiries amongst his friends and came back with an instruction book and an old, discarded shakuhachi with a quarter-inch crack running down half its length that he repaired with his glue gun. We all tried to play the instrument, and I felt rather smug that I, a foreigner, was the only one who could produce a note. The instruction booklet was indispensable, for it not only diagrammed the fingering for

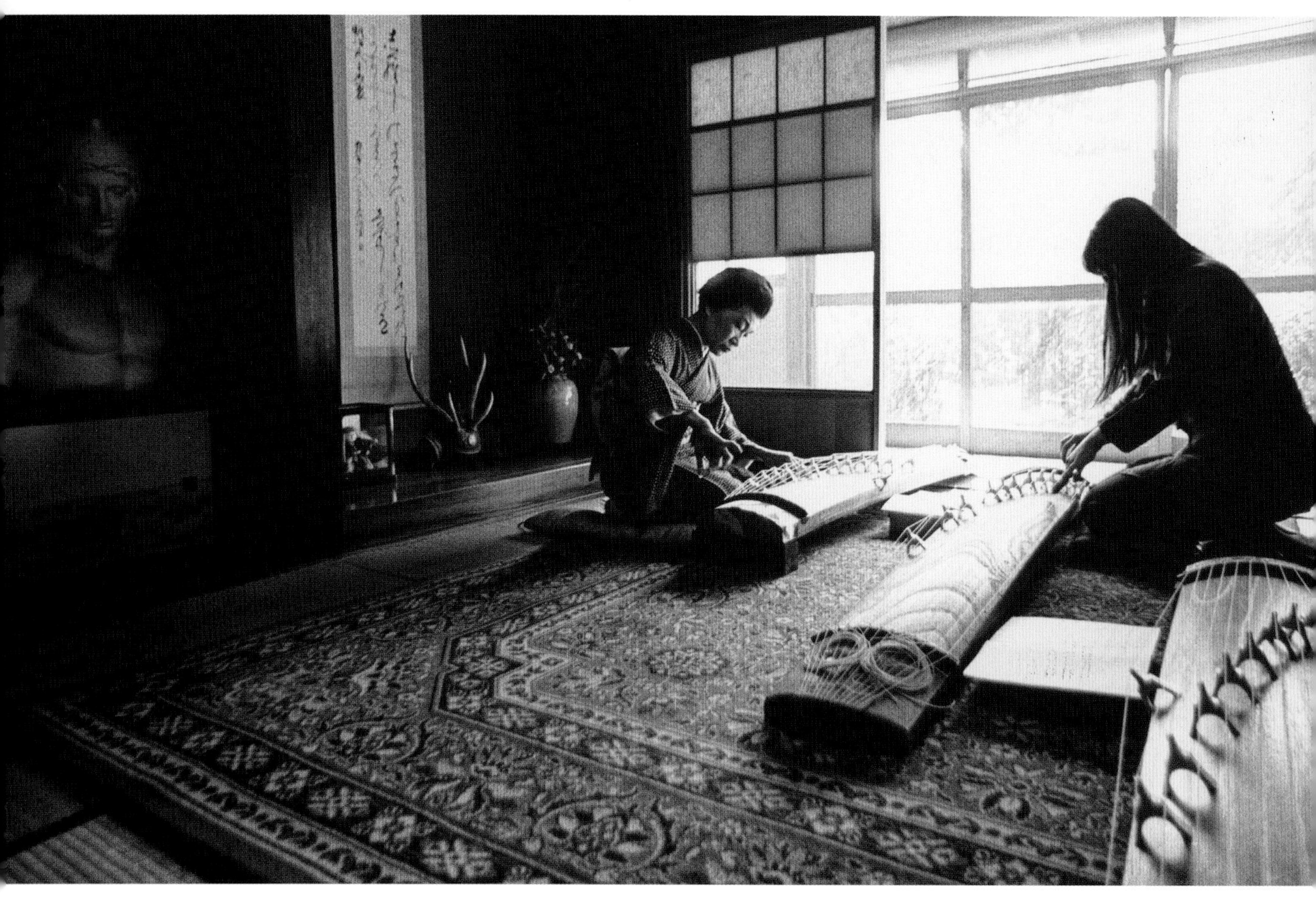

each note but also contained a collection of simple folk and children's songs written in Japanese tablature. I was as prepared as I could be when I rode the subway to the adjacent ward, where my first lesson was to take place on the second floor of a photographic studio. When I entered, I was dismayed to see two other students sitting in the same room and prayed that I would be the last one to receive a lesson. Unfortunately, when the current lesson ended, the teacher beckoned me to sit. With shakuhachi and book in hand, I took my place at one end of a low, wooden table across from the master, a distinguished, white-haired gentleman with a kindly demeanour (thankfully). The formal way of sitting is *seiza*, that is, kneeling with your legs folded back, feet together, toes touching the tatami mat, the weight of your body resting on your legs. I bowed to the master, who asked to see my instrument, and I rather ashamedly handed it over. After blowing a few notes, he pulled out a penknife from the sleeve of his kimono and proceeded to gouge around two of the holes. After blowing a few more notes, he was satisfied with the pitch and handed the flute back. Next, he leafed through my book to a page in the song section. "I will play 'Hotaru no Hikari' once," he said, "and then we will play together." I was delighted to hear the strains of "Auld Lang Syne" filling the room. We played together for what seemed an eternity but was actually only the allotted time of half an hour. When he signalled the end of the lesson, I tried to get up to make room for the next student, but I had lost all feeling in my legs. My brain kept sending the desperate message to my legs, which stubbornly refused to obey. I was becoming more and more embarrassed before my rather perplexed teacher and finally had to flop down and crawl ingloriously to the other bemused students. I had to stay for the next lesson as my legs were still dead weights, and when circulation finally began to return, I felt a sensation that the word "excruciating" couldn't begin to describe. When the lesson ended, I silently hobbled out the door.

Over the next few months, my days were filled with the shakuhachi, the occasional photographic foray, pachinko—I had become addicted to this Japanese version of a pinball machine—and, of course, Rita. One day I was waiting in Rita's apartment when she stormed in, slammed the door and threw her books on the floor. One of her classmates, a white exchange student from Boston, had molested her on the subway ride home from Waseda, and Rita was in a rage. "I can't stand Americans. Their bloated white bodies make my skin crawl, and they stink like rotten meat. They're animals, and all they're interested in is sex..." As I listened to her rant, I suddenly realized that what I was hearing was a reversal of all the racial stereotypes that I had heard so often in my childhood. The moment was an epiphany that crumbled the walls of white supremacy and reduced John Wayne, the unattainable icon of my youth, to a barbaric Pillsbury Doughboy with bad body odour. How could I have been blind for so long to the simple truth that racial stereotypes are nothing more than arbitrary constructs to justify one society's injustice, and that "dirty Jap" is not a true reflection of some immutable natural order? Recalling all the samurai epics that Rita and I had enjoyed at our favourite movie house in Shibuya, I realized also that each society creates its own ideal of beauty and manly nobility. One nation's Enemy Alien is another nation's heroic warrior, and from an Asian perspective, there was little doubt that Toshiro Mifune could beat the crap out of John Wayne.

My time in Japan was drawing to a close. With the coming of spring, the weather grew hot and humid, making life in the congested, polluted concrete jungle of Tokyo even more oppressive. Much of the magic of Japan had disappeared with Rita, who had returned to the States to continue her studies. I felt a growing need to escape this narrow, claustrophobic island nation with its endless procession of people all stamped from the same physical mould. In my longing for the epic scale and cleansing beauty of the Canadian landscape and the rich diversity of its people, I realized that, for better or worse, my sense of self had been forged in the crucible of my native land.

On my final day in Japan, Mrs. Nishibayashi asked me to accompany her to the commercial area surrounding the subway station. We entered a tiny shop filled with handicrafts from all parts of Japan, and after much deliberation, she chose a beautiful blue vase. Of all the people in her family, she said, she would miss me the most, and the vase was to serve as a reminder of the many afternoons we had spent by ourselves drinking tea and bridging the gap between our very different lives. The gift was not necessary, for I could never forget this gentle, wise woman who had revealed what was most worthy in the culture and character of Japan.

The next morning, the family accompanied me to the airport, and when my flight was announced, I bowed to Yo and Shin, who had become like brothers to me; Mr. Nishibayashi, the childlike master of the kite who presented me with a parting gift of his creations; and finally to Mrs. Nishibayashi, both of us struggling to repress tears of sorrow. With a final wave, I walked to the boarding gate. There were no words to adequately express my gratitude and love for this warm and generous family.

On the long flight home, I reviewed all that I had mined from my ancestral land. I had entered Japan with the childhood memory of an enemy nation of fanatics dominated by a treacherous and rapacious military, but what I found instead were the passionate and industrious Japanese people who had built, from the ashes of war, the modern economic miracle of Japan. I was proud to be connected, in some small way, to this both ancient and modern culture that was winning the admiration of the world. And yet I knew that I could never be Japanese, for the complexities of its culture and language were beyond my abilities to master; nor did I want to be Japanese, for I knew my Western individualism would inevitably prove to be anathema in this highly structured,

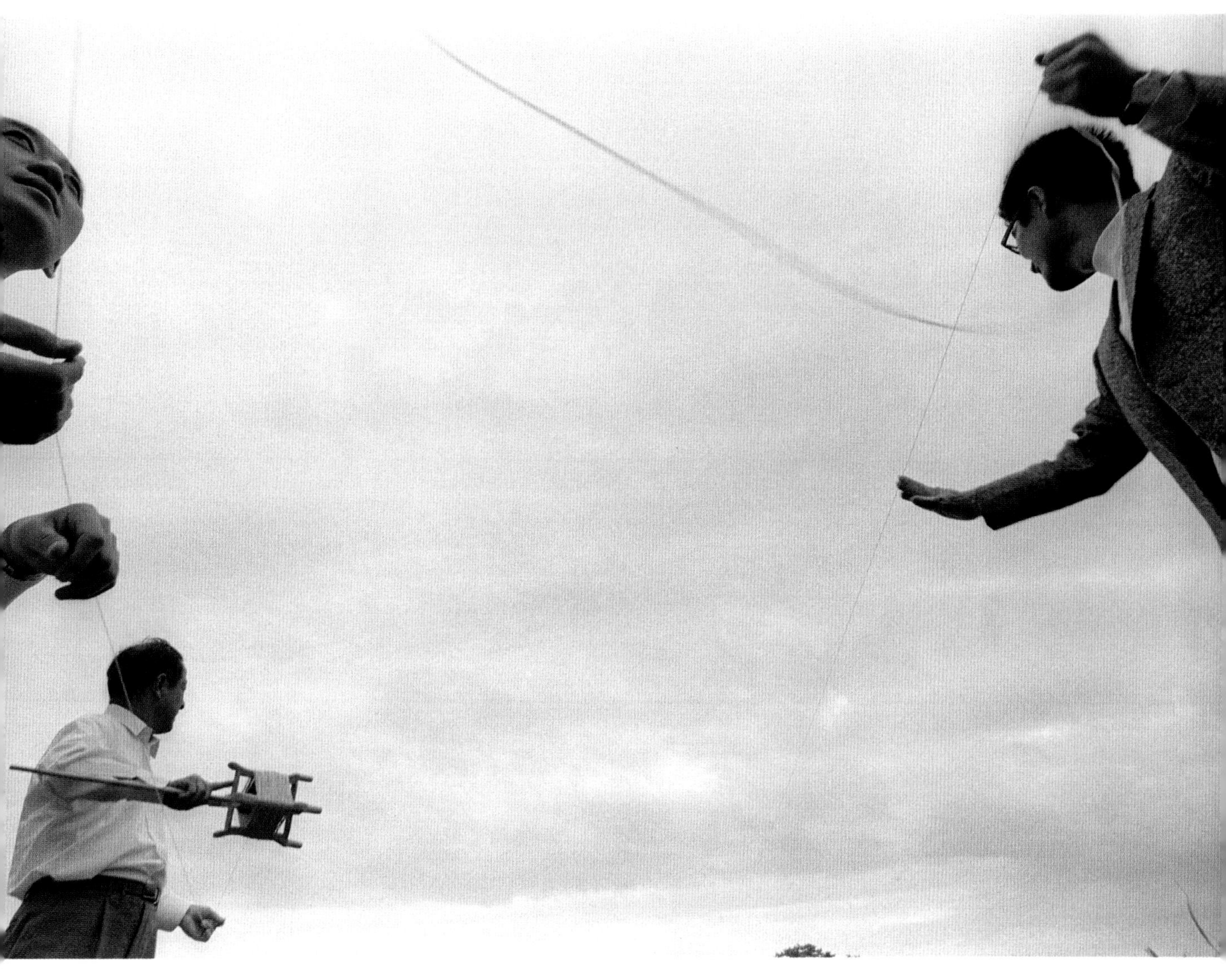

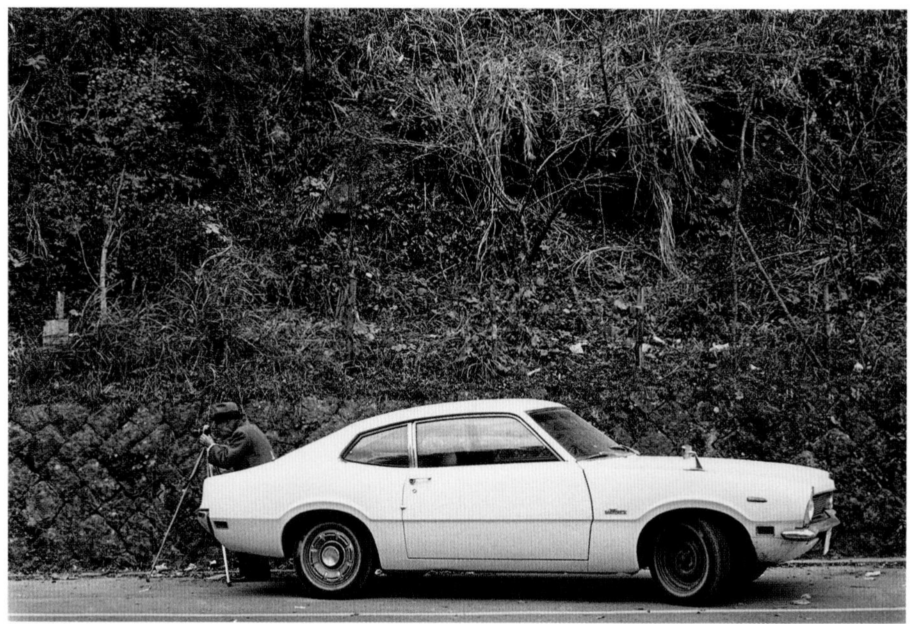

hierarchical society—I wouldn't last a day as a Tokyo salaryman. I had met Fumiko, and although we had failed to bond, I nonetheless felt fortunate to have had the opportunity to finally meet my sister. I had begun my lifelong love affair with the shakuhachi, and thanks to Rita, who allowed me to take over teaching her private English classes, I managed to buy a beautiful shakuhachi from one of the few remaining artisans who still make the ancient instrument. And from Rita, the crown jewel of my journey to Japan, I gained the freedom to cast away the worn-out cloak of Enemy Alien, which no longer had the power to define who I was or what I could be. Japan was the bridge that brought me home.

Photographer,
Nakatsu, Kyushu, Japan,
November 1969

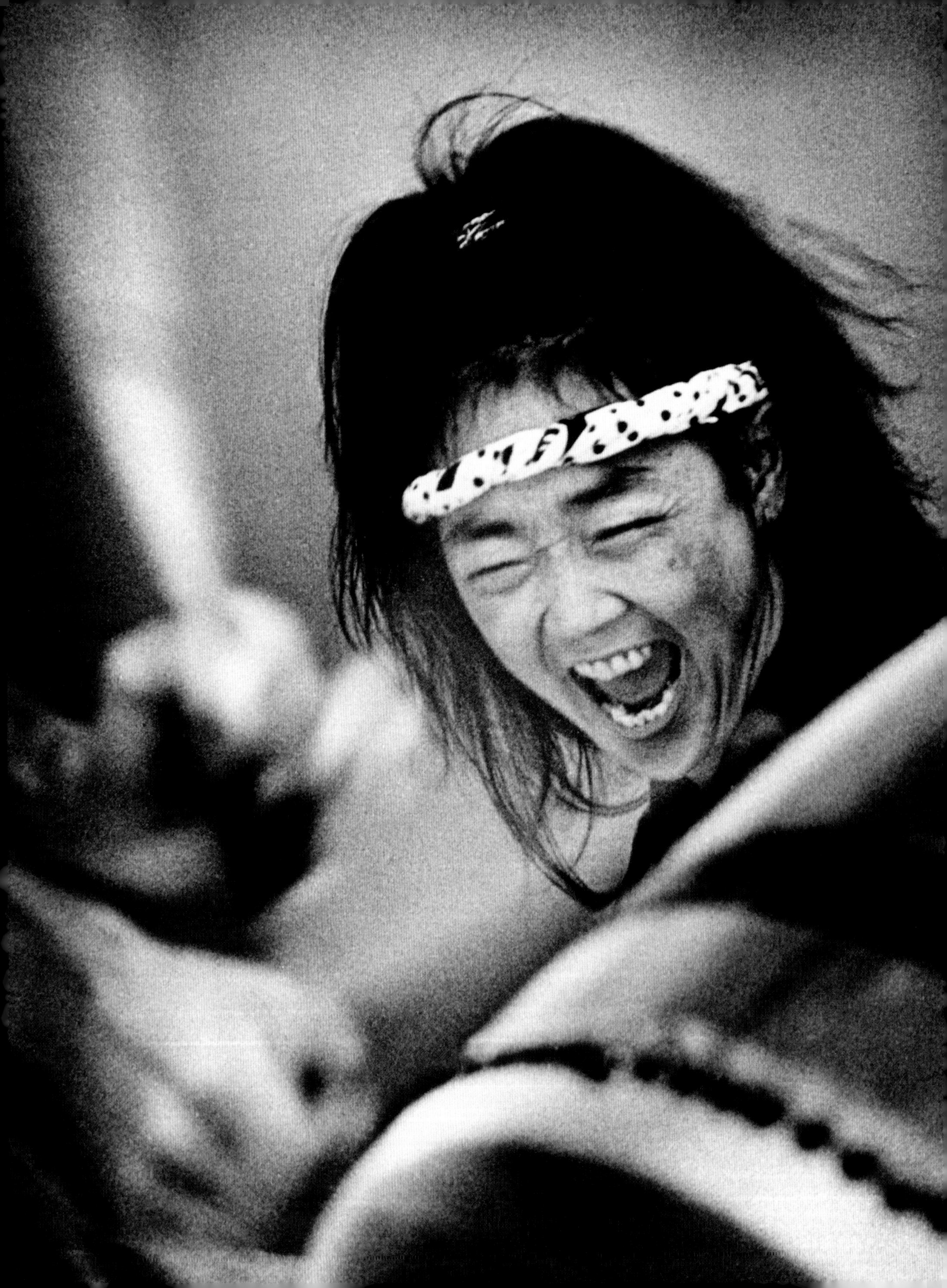

8

OUR PLANE LANDED IN Vancouver, where I planned to stay for a few days before catching the connecting flight to Toronto. On the bus ride into town, I couldn't help staring at the profusion of humanity—white, brown, Black, yellow—that I hadn't seen in over half a year. I stayed with Pat, an old friend from the SUPA days—the same woman who rode with Ken Drushka at the end of the 60s. When Ken came to visit, I told him all about my trip to Japan and how, at the end, the heat and humidity of congested Tokyo led to my escapist fantasies of a crystal-clear lake set in a virgin rainforest. "I have the perfect place for you," he said.

The next day, Ken and I took the ferry to Vancouver Island and drove up to Campbell River, where we boarded a float plane bound for West Thurlow Island, which was once heavily logged but was now uninhabited except for Ken, his new wife Laura and a few of their friends. When the pilot reached a long, silvery lake in the middle of the island, he cut back on the power and plunged down. In the sudden silence, I thought the engine had died and we were all going to die, but at the last minute, the pilot levelled the plane, skimmed the surface, and came in for a graceful landing beside a primitive dock of cedar logs. The island was all that I had hoped for.

Nestled under the branches of a huge old cedar was Ken's home: two large geodesic domes made from cedar struts joined to rounds cut from sewer pipes, covered with translucent plastic; in the clearing behind

Linda Uyehara Hoffman of Katari Taiko at the Vancouver Folk Music Festival, Vancouver, British Columbia, July 16–18, 1982

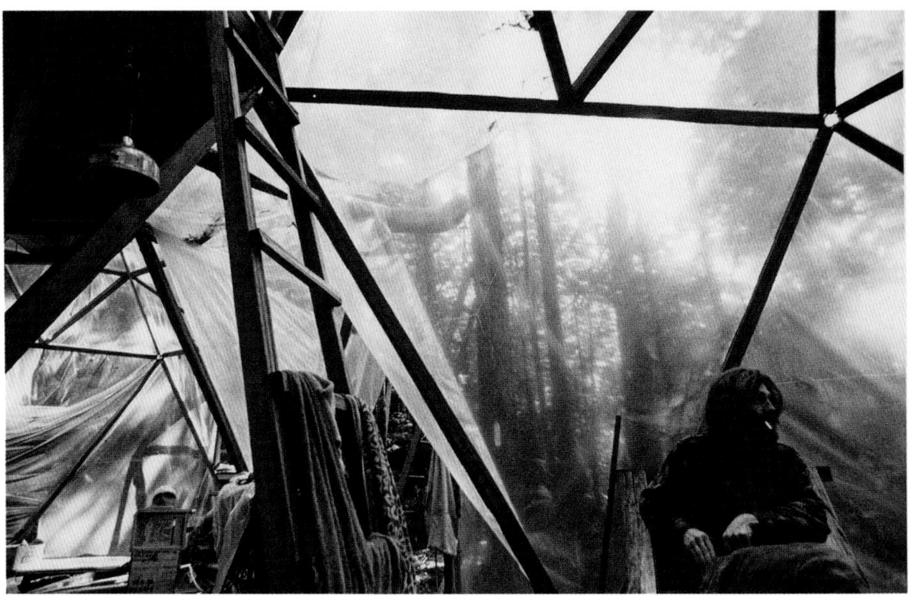

the main house was a smaller guest dome. I spent the next few days swimming, fishing for trout and taking long walks in the rainforest. In the evenings, I sat by the lake playing my new shakuhachi, and every now and then, wolves howled in concert. The magical island of Thurlow was a magnet that kept drawing me back to the West Coast.

I drove to Toronto with Arden and her new husband Al Mattes, who had also been visiting Ken, and except for an overnight stay in Winnipeg, we drove non-stop to Ontario. Instead of going straight to the city, we decided to visit Matt Cohen and his wife Susie at their farm on the outskirts of Kingston. After such a long absence, it was good to see my dear friend Matt. He had just quit smoking cigarettes, and to ease the pain of withdrawal, he was smoking dope almost incessantly, which made him even more delightfully insane. The next afternoon, I climbed up to the hayloft in their barn, and while I sat on a bale playing my flute, a blonde head suddenly popped up in the opening to the loft. It was Libby. At that exact moment, calm turned to chaos, as we were furiously attacked by a swarm of bees. I took it as a sign from the gods, and when order had been restored, I realized that the strategy of time and distance had worked, and the chains that had bound me to this woman, who had been such a major force in my life, were finally broken.

I had sublet my coach house studio to Joan and her cat, which had recently had a litter of four kittens, so when I arrived there, I was welcomed by a host of fleas. I spent my first night back in Toronto picking fleas off my body and drowning them in a glass of water, which was half filled by the time morning arrived. Despite this inauspicious beginning, I had a productive summer and fall working on my Japan material. But the winter turned brutally cold, and with each passing month huddled beneath my duvet, the grip of cabin fever tightened. I felt my life was in limbo, for my disenchantment with Toronto was reaching a crisis point, but I could see no means of escape. I found that the status quo, no matter how barren, represented an almost insurmountable barrier. About the only visitor I had over the winter was Matt, who thought it was a sign of my impending madness that his were the only tracks he ever saw in the snow leading to my door. I replied that if I survived the winter, I was heading straight for Thurlow Island. We agreed to go together.

I did survive, and in the summer, Matt and I piled into my Peugeot and headed west. When we arrived on Thurlow, Ken was overjoyed to see us, and blathered incessantly, for he had suffered a worse case of cabin fever than me, cooped up in his snowbound dome with Laura and his two boisterous children from his marriage to Pat.

One of the problems of living on Thurlow was the lack of available protein, and no one had been recently successful in shooting a deer. One night I borrowed Ken's beautiful antique Winchester 30-30 and walked up the hill behind his house. Halfway up the rise, I stopped at an outcropping of rocks, and when I shone my flashlight down to the valley below, three pairs of eyes, as bright as stars, gleamed in the darkness. Resting the Winchester on a rock, I took careful aim between one set of eyes and pulled the trigger. In the ensuing roar, the lights of the eyes blinked out like someone had thrown a switch. I scrambled down to the clearing, and after a few minutes' search, found a good-sized doe with its lower jaw shattered by my bullet. After cutting the throat to bleed out the animal, I scrambled back to the logging road and raced to Ken and Laura, who hurriedly dressed and accompanied me back to the kill site. Ken was an excellent teacher, and after handing me his buck-skinning knife, he led me through the intricate process of field dressing the deer. The first and most important step, Ken explained, was cutting away the powerful scent glands on the legs, for they could easily taint the meat, giving it an unpleasant gamey taste. After carefully wiping the blade, I cut around the anus and, with my finger under the blade, carefully continued the cut along the belly and up to the neck, which allowed me

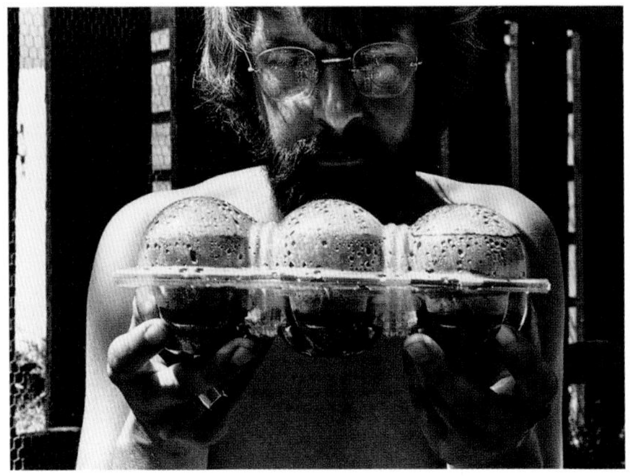

to empty the contents of the deer's inner cavity. After I cut away the neck and hooves to lighten the load, Ken heaved the carcass onto his shoulders for the long trek back to his dome. I looked back at the pile of offal on the ground and couldn't believe that such an enormous stomach—grey, fetid, steaming with the last wisps of life vanishing into the night air—could have come from such a small animal.

Back at the home site, Laura fired up two Coleman lanterns, and after Ken and I tied a rope to the forelegs of the deer and suspended it from the sturdy bough of a giant cedar, I proceeded to skin the carcass. When the work was done, I looked upon the deer in the harsh, white light of the lanterns and realized that, in the blink of an eye, I had taken the life of a beautiful wild animal and turned it into a piece of meat. This re-enactment of the ancient ritual of the omnivore had awakened a profound archetypal memory, which created a level of excitement and, at the same time, a sense of calm in me that I had never known before. Like our tribal forefathers in the distant past, I wanted to pay homage to the deer and to the gods that brought us together. In my photographic mind's eye flashed an image of a nude woman with a long mane of black hair embracing the naked carcass in a graceful S-curve. I vowed to return to this island to create not only that image but an entire series of a woman enacting the same deeply moving ritual that I had just undertaken. This series would be my final statement on the nude. I had found my artistic purpose in life.

In the fall, I found myself back in Toronto to face an even worse winter. My isolation was nearly complete, for Matt was spending the year living in the South of France. I wondered if I would ever get out of this damn city and find the energy to create a new life for myself. As the cruel winter wore on, I sank lower into despair, but when I reached rock bottom, I realized that to continue to live and grow, I had absolutely no choice but to act, to change, to move. My resolve was fortified one day when the mailman delivered a small package from Vancouver. I eagerly tore away the packaging to find a small, curiously shaped stone and a note from Greg MacDonald, one of Ken's friends that I had met on

Greg MacDonald
with bubble planters
at home, Vancouver,
British Columbia,
July 1974

FACING
West Thurlow Island,
British Columbia,
July–August, 1973

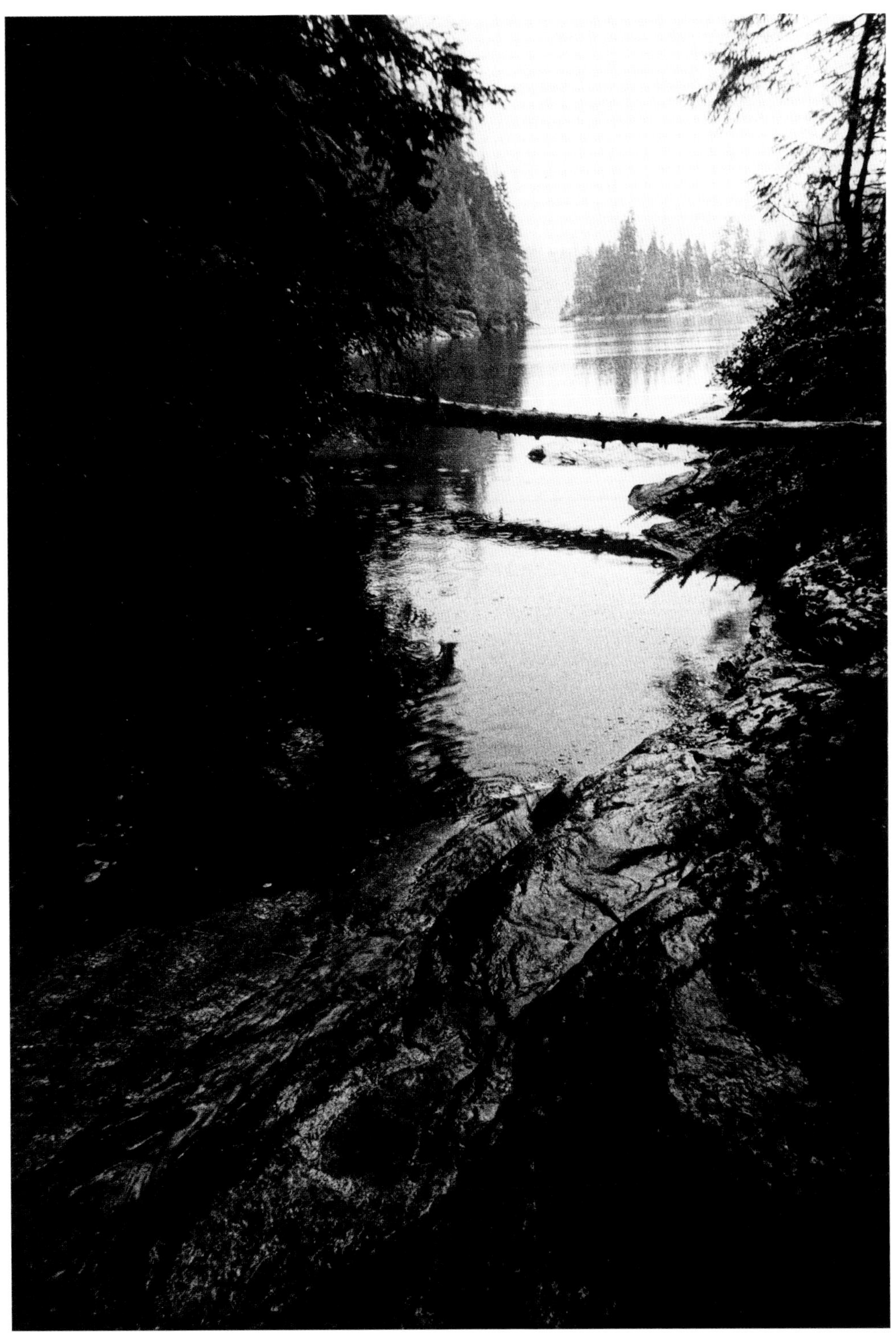

Thurlow Island. Greg wrote that the stone was from Helliwell Park on Hornby Island, and that if I were to accept this gift, it was incumbent upon me to return the stone to its rightful place lest I offend the spirits that guarded the magical park. I was rather surprised at all this mystical mumbo jumbo, for Greg had always struck me as a supreme rationalist. But then again, I was in no position to tempt fate.

In the spring, I traded my Peugeot in for a used Econoline van that I spent a month converting into a camper. Since I expected to do a lot of shooting over the summer, I packed up my darkroom and loaded it into the completed van. My first stop was beside one of the many small lakes that dot Northern Ontario. After a long swim, I cooked a hot meal in my improvised kitchen and broke down the bench into a comfortable bed. Compared to sleeping in the back of the Peugeot, or even worse, in the back seat of the Beetle, my camper was as luxurious as a five-star hotel.

When I arrived in Vancouver, I drove straight to the home of Greg and his lovely wife, Mary Ann. Their friend Leslie, a voluptuous Irish lass, was visiting, and since she was a frequent visitor to Hornby Island, we agreed to go there together so I could complete my mission of returning the stone to Helliwell Park. The next morning, we took the ferry to Vancouver Island and, after a short drive, took two smaller ferries to arrive at Hornby. At Helliwell Park, we climbed down a steep cliff of eroded limestone, studded here and there with sensual arbutus trees, their peeling bark revealing bulbous nodes like ripe breasts, and at the bottom I saw a profusion of rocks and boulders of such dramatic and unusual shapes that the shoreline looked more like a sculpture garden than a natural formation. Helliwell was indeed quite magical.

After I completed a successful test shoot with Leslie, we returned to Vancouver. I thought I was well on my way to success, for I now had a willing and vivacious model, but at the end of the first week of living together in her apartment, Leslie announced that her boyfriend, whom I did not know existed, was back in town. Though I probably could have convinced Leslie to come with me to Thurlow, I didn't want to come between her and her long-time lover, and I didn't want to endanger the summer shoot with such bad karma.

I had little choice but to seek help from Greg, who—I was to discover later—had a rather perverse sense of humour. With a wry smile, he suggested I call Pat, another of his friends, and the next evening I went to meet this newest candidate at her apartment in Strathcona on the outskirts of Chinatown. Pat turned out to be a willowy blonde, attractive enough but with a somewhat stiff and mannered air. Over dinner at a nearby noodle house, I explained the deer sequence to her, and she agreed to be my model. I had my doubts, but it wasn't like I had an infinite number of choices.

After a few days spent gathering supplies, I stored my darkroom equipment in her apartment and we travelled to Thurlow Island. After a few days, it was obvious that our arrangement wasn't going to work. Ken called on his radio for a float plane to pick Pat up, and the last thing she said before boarding was, "You know, Tom, if you've seen one tree, you've seen them all."

I was at a total loss as to how to save the shoot. The summer was wearing on, and I couldn't afford to keep travelling back to Vancouver. As a relative newcomer to the West Coast, the only contact I had was Greg, but after the disaster with Pat, I could no longer rely on his judgment. In desperation, I used Ken's radio to call Leslie, who was angry that I hadn't done more to persuade her to come to Thurlow and was totally offended that I had chosen Pat instead, a woman whom she loathed. In the background, Ken and Laura were chuckling away, for this intimate conversation filled with colourful descriptions of my less-than-sterling character could be heard by anyone within a fifty-mile radius. When Leslie hung up, my summer was in ruins.

I had little choice but to remain on the island to make the best of a frustrating situation, for going back to Toronto in abject defeat was not an option. Ken had managed to secure funding for a project to restore the salmon-spawning beds in the island streams that had been damaged by logging. When he offered me one of the positions on the project, I gratefully accepted, for being paid to live on this island paradise was a godsend. Given more time, I might still be able to complete the deer sequence.

The work on the spawning beds was to begin in the fall, so near the end of the summer, I went back to Vancouver with two other project members to buy all the supplies we would need for the coming months. It was raining when we loaded up my van and drove to Vancouver Island, where we were to meet up with Andy Dewman, a fellow project member and the owner of the *Dovre*, a small double-ender fishing boat. At the government docks in Campbell River, we loaded our supplies into the *Dovre* and chugged off in the pouring rain for Campeau, a sheltered cove on East Thurlow Island. There was no dock at Campeau, so we had to offload onto a skiff bouncing on the choppy waters. One of my cardboard boxes, weakened by the incessant rain, disintegrated and sent a load of precious food to the bottom of the sea. When we finally got all our supplies on shore, we loaded them onto the back of the crummy, an ancient flatbed truck, and drove to the shores of Simmons Lake. Offloading our cargo was a hazardous affair; by then, most of the cardboard boxes had been reduced to pulp. I walked around the end of the lake to my campsite on the opposite shore and, after stripping off my sodden clothes, crawled under a plastic sheet and crept into my sleeping bag. I was exhausted, but when the storm winds intensified, I became afraid that I hadn't securely fastened the tarp covering my supplies. So I got up, put on my wet and icy clothes, and walked back toward the truck. After retying the tarp, I was so tired that I decided to take a shortcut by walking along the mountain of logs jammed at the end of the lake. The logs were slippery with the rain, and halfway across, I plunged into the frigid water. When I was finally able to crawl back into my sleeping bag, I thought to myself, Well, Ken, here's another fine mess you've got us into.

Fortunately, the next day broke warm and sunny, and it stayed that way for the following month, which gave me time to put my house in order. I chose as my site a nine-by-twelve-foot, two-tiered wooden platform abandoned by a former homesteader. However, I was not enthralled by the rigid geometry of Ken's geodesic domes and wanted a more organic design for my home. The platform was nestled in a grove of alders, so I climbed up three strategically located trees, tied ropes to the tops and, with Ken's help, arched them over the platform. Then I taped together two long, ten-foot-wide pieces of plastic cut from my hundred-foot roll and suspended it from the bent alders using strings attached to eight-inch cedar rounds; a glob of cooked rice between the plastic and the rounds would prevent any leaks. With strings attached to smaller rounds, I pulled out the plastic at various points until I had created the comforting shape of a soft, plastic breast. After wrapping the ends of the plastic around a series of logs at the base of the platform, cutting an entranceway, and installing an airtight heater, my home was complete.

One night, I came home after visiting with Ken and Laura and discovered that the howling winds had ripped apart over half of the shelter's taped seam. The next morning, I retaped the seam, and after much thought, came to the conclusion that I hadn't allowed enough slack for the plastic. After unfurling a few turns of the plastic wrapped

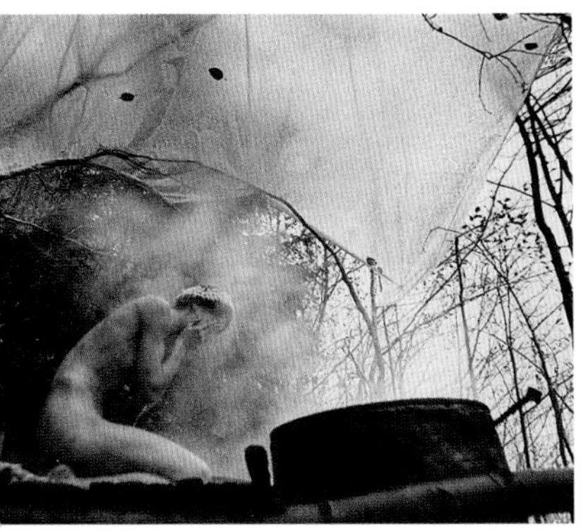

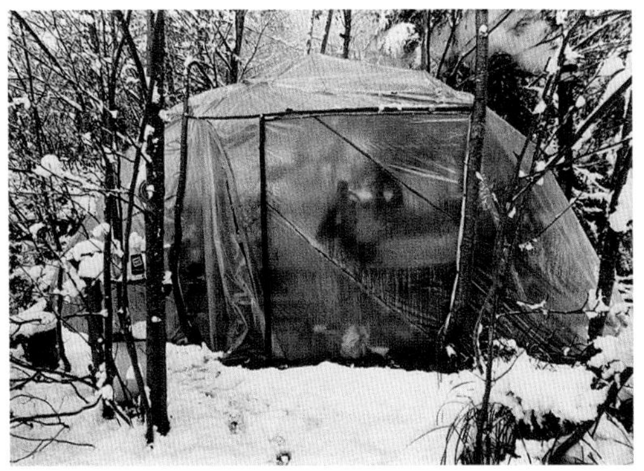

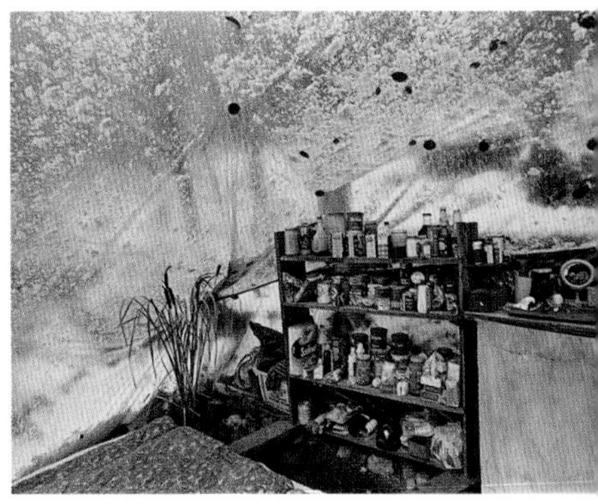

around the bottom logs, I had no further problems. My plastic bubble proved impervious to the coming rains and fierce winds that came roaring down the lake valley. Life was good. On the nights of a bright moon, I would lie in bed and watch the shifting patterns of wind-stirred leaves through the translucent screen of my plastic home. Andy and Brian Lewis, from across the lake, had come by with their chainsaws and chopped up a huge, thirty-foot fir log so that I would have enough wood for the winter. I even built an ofuro by welding a fire grate and drain to the bottom of a forty-five-gallon fuel drum that I salvaged from an abandoned logging camp. It would take a whole day to heat the ofuro, filled with countless buckets from the nearby lake, but in the winter months, it was pure bliss—not only for myself but for all the others on the island. I was even getting used to cooking in this new environment. On our shopping expedition, I had been advised to lay in a stock of dried food, which I had never cooked with before. When my fresh produce was running out, I threw the remaining limp vegetables and stew meat into a pot along with handfuls of peas, beans and lentils. A few hours later, I heard the sizzle of a grey mass of legumes pouring from the top of the bubbling pot like molten lava onto the airtight, and since I was loath to throw away food, I had to eat this gruel for an entire week. But I was enjoying my largely vegetarian diet, supplemented now and then with a welcome piece of fresh tuna left by Andy on my doorstep. One afternoon, after a morning spent chopping firewood, I was walking along the beach when I suddenly felt my body shift onto a higher plane that I had never experienced before, and haven't since.

One day in early September, it started to rain. In the weeks that followed, the downpour never ceased, not for one second. There was never a moment of silence with the rain splattering my bubble and the streams

LEFT
Laura Willamovsky in
Tamio's ofuro bath,
West Thurlow Island,
British Columbia,
October–November 1973

CENTRE
Tamio's dome,
West Thurlow Island,
British Columbia,
December 1973

RIGHT
Interior of Tamio's dome,
West Thurlow Island,
British Columbia,
December 1973

swelling and rushing with the unrelenting deluge. The lake that, in the summer, had been a good thirty feet from my home was now a scant foot away. It felt like the whole island was in constant motion. There were ten of us on the project, and we worked in the rain planting wild rice, clearing streams and attempting to rebuild a bridge on the road from Simmons to Hemming Lake, where some of the other members lived. Ken was obsessed with the bridge, which would have taken an experienced logging team a day to repair; for us, hauling in logs with the crummy winch was gruelling and dangerous work. If the steel cable ever snapped, it could easily maim or kill us. We were all relieved when the project ended with the bridge only partially repaired. I felt like I had been on location for the movie *The Bridge on the River Kwai*.

One morning, I awoke with the strange sensation that my world had changed. There was an eerie silence and a strange, new quality to the light. When my eyes fully opened, I saw that the protective plastic of my home was no more than a foot from my nose. Sometime during the night, the incessant rain had turned into incessant snow. I jumped up, fired up the airtight, grabbed a broom and jabbed furiously at the plastic to release the heavy layers that were threatening to bring my home down on my head. When my bubble—which had sagged like a grandmother's breast—was restored to its plump roundness, I realized that my time on Thurlow was at an end. I knew from the previous months of rain that the snow would be just as unrelenting, and I wasn't prepared to mount a twenty-four-hour snow patrol. I spent a day cleaning up and storing my tools and supplies under the house before flying to Campbell River.

My van needed a jump start, but once I was on the road, I stopped off at the nearest McDonald's for a Big Mac, large fries and shake. On the ferry, I had another hamburger along with their delicious clam chowder. By the time I arrived in Vancouver, my stomach, which had grown accustomed to a gentle, healthy diet on Thurlow, was in full revolt. I called up Pat to retrieve my goods and wound up living with her.

Pat had a lovely apartment walled with fragrant cedar, but it was too small for both of us. Strathcona itself was a great place to live, for it is one of the oldest and more interesting neighbourhoods in Vancouver. Centrally located, it was a residential area for waves of immigrants, starting with Italian, Chinese and Japanese before World War II and, more recently, Chinese from the mainland. Today Strathcona is known as the first local community to have stopped a major urban development plan. Under the banner of the Strathcona Property Owners and

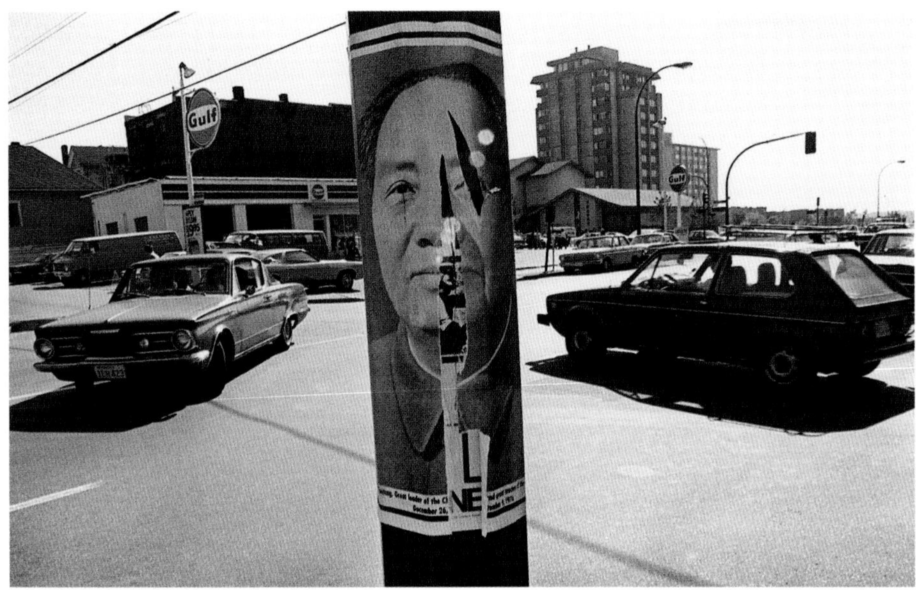

Tenants Association (SPOTA), the fractious Chinese community not only banded together to stop a proposed freeway that threatened to wipe out their neighbourhood but also managed to secure the allotted funds to improve the area. Pat and I went to the opening of their first housing project, a co-op of seven townhouses on Union Street, and little did I know that, in two years' time, I would be living in the demonstration unit that I was now admiring.

Pat knew the area well and had been actively involved with SPOTA, so she soon found a large house to rent a block up the street. I knew that I had finally broken free of Toronto, so with the help of my brother, I closed up my coach house studio and built my first West Coast studio in the basement of our rental home. When I packed my darkroom into my van at the beginning of the summer, I sensed that I was leaving the city for good, but I dared not state this openly lest the guardian spirits of Toronto punish me for this act of betrayal. I knew that I was now at a new beginning of my life.

One fine spring day, I received a letter from my mother. One of the first things I did after returning from Japan was call my mother so I could regale her with my new command of Japanese, but as usual, I got carried away. I started writing to her using the simpler syllabary of hiragana and katakana, and of course she would fire right back with her own letters, which would take me ages to decipher. This most recent

Corner of Pender Street
and Gore Avenue,
Chinatown, Vancouver,
British Columbia,
January 1977

letter had me totally befuddled (what the hell is "*jamu*"?) and when I growled in frustration, Pat suggested I walk up to Powell Street and seek help from one of the beautiful Japanese women at Language Aid for Immigrant Societies. "Beautiful women" was all I had to hear, so with letter in hand, I walked into the storefront operation a block from Main Street and was stunned by the sight of one of the most beautiful women I had ever seen sitting on the end of a ratty old couch like a serene Japanese princess. I walked to a desk at the back of the room and introduced myself to another quite beautiful, petite woman with long black hair. Michiko Sakata was her name, and in a pleasantly accented voice, she quickly translated my mother's letter—"*jamu*" turned out to be the homemade strawberry jam she was sending. Michiko was a gracious host, and after she served me green tea and cake, we talked for a long while. I mentioned that I had begun to learn the shakuhachi during my recent trip to Japan and was hoping to find a way to continue my studies. "You're in luck," she said. "Walk another block west on Hastings 'til you come to Tonari Gumi, where you will find Takeo Yamashiro. Take-chan is a wonderful guy and a real master of the shakuhachi."

I followed her instructions and entered my second storefront of the day, where I was greeted by the raucous sounds of a bilingual bingo game. A stout, beaming woman stood before a hopper of bouncing balls, shouting out, in a voice that needed no electrical amplification, "B *hachi*, B eighto." Staring intently at their cards were a group of old Japanese men and women sitting on the Salvation Army couches and chairs scattered throughout the large room. All around them darted a bevy of young men and women, filling up teacups and plates of Japanese sweets. The scene was oddly familiar, for it recalled our own communal gatherings at the old Masonic Temple in Chatham, and I could well imagine my own parents sitting comfortably in this group. The game ended when one white-haired *obasan* shouted out, "*Hai, bingo desu!*" In the ensuing silence, I walked to the back of the room, where I met Takeo Yamashiro, a handsome man with a megawatt smile who had the rare ability to focus in on the moment, so you were led to believe that you were the only reality in this universe. We talked for a long while, and he agreed to accept me as his student. Before I left, he introduced me to Jun Hamada, a Nisei from Brampton, Ontario, who had founded Tonari Gumi as a drop-in service centre for the Issei who had returned to the area after the war. I had just entered a world that would consume all my energy and bring closure to my life's journey.

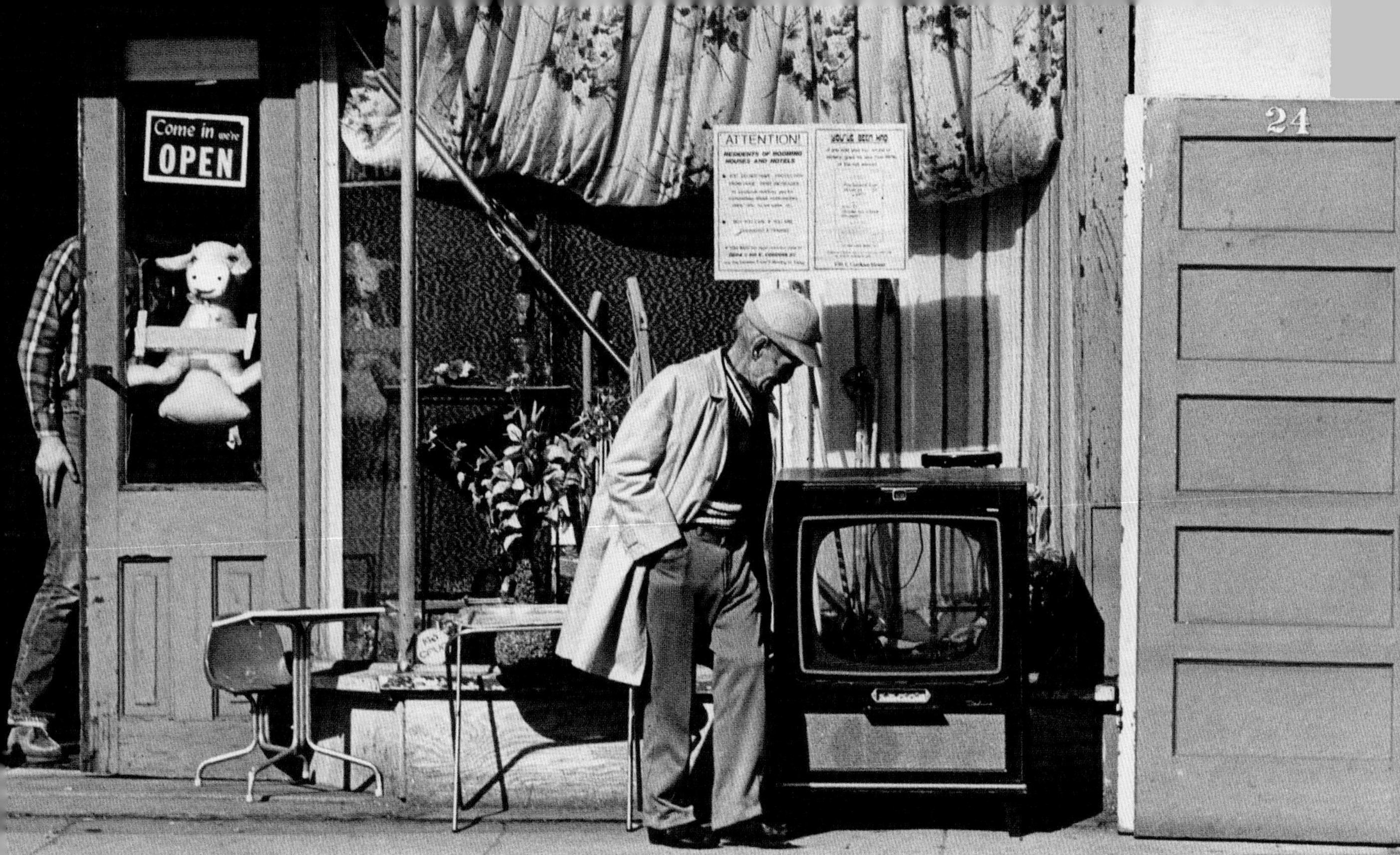

I developed a routine for my new life in Vancouver: morning coffee and crossword puzzle at the Lenity Café, followed by a visit to Language Aid to chat with Michiko or any of her gorgeous friends, and finally lunch at Tonari Gumi, where I would volunteer or simply hang out for the afternoon. One morning I was sitting on my favourite stool at the Lenity when Michiko rushed in and demanded we talk. We moved to a nearby table, and Michiko began her impassioned plea:

"You know, Tami-chan, I am Japanese, and before coming to Vancouver, I knew nothing about Japanese Canadians and their amazing history. But then I started Language Aid and began working with the Issei *ojisans* and *obachans* who tell me the stories of their lives and show me beautiful old photos. Everybody was so poor when they came to Canada. Women came as picture brides, expecting to live in the grand Vancouver Hotel, but instead were taken to dirty old shacks. The men who came and worked as fishermen, farmers or in logging camps got low pay, because white people don't like the Japanese. But Nikkei *gambaru* and life gets better. Little Tokyo is an exciting place with lots of stores, hotels, gambling dens, brothels and ofuro. They built language schools and Buddhist temples, and everybody came out to Powell grounds to

Powell Street,
Downtown Eastside,
Vancouver,
British Columbia,
March 1978

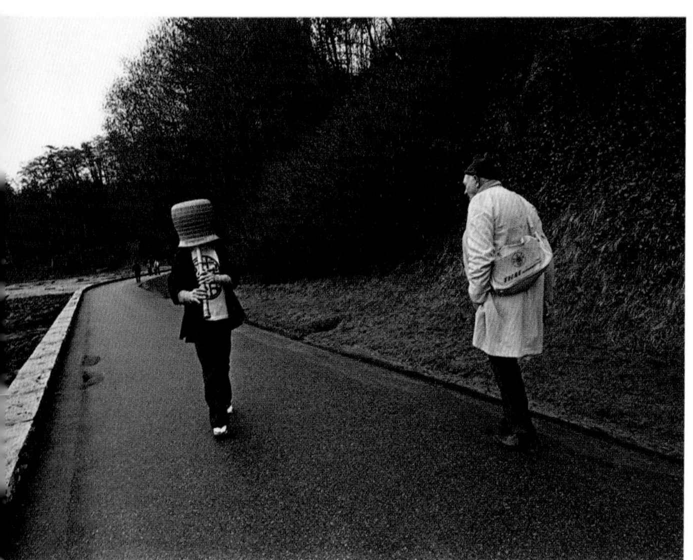

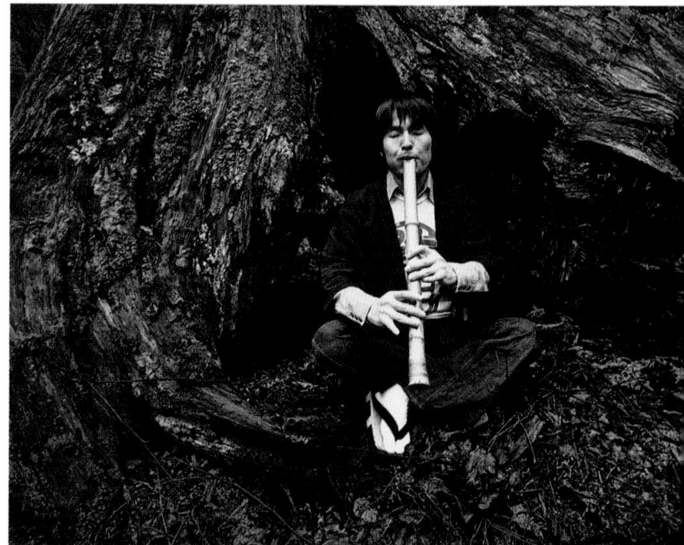

cheer for the Asahi baseball team. Then the war came, and the Nikkei lost everything and were put in camps. After the war, they were sent to Japan or else forced to move all across Canada. But nobody knows about this incredible history, and I think it's important to let everybody know what happened to the Nikkei. I want to start a Nikkei history project to make an exhibit and maybe a book, and since you are a photographer, I want you to help."

When Michiko finally wound down, I replied, "I'm sorry Mich-chan, but I'm much too busy right now, and besides, I have very little interest in the subject matter." I meant what I said, for ever since settling in Vancouver, I had, with Pat's help, managed to secure a number of hefty commissions from the newly elected New Democratic Party provincial government and the Vancouver Police Board. Undoubtedly my old friends would have accused me of selling out, but I'd never claimed to be artistically pure—it's just that I never could find anyone foolish enough to buy my brand of snake oil. I was relishing my newest persona as the hot new photographer in town, cashing fat cheques, matching wits with tough government ministers and grizzled police officers who were twice my size. I was also serious about not having any interest in Nikkei history, for the rejection of my own community was part and parcel of a total denial of my ethnic heritage. Besides, I had a negative view of contemporary Nikkei, formed one summer day when I happened to walk by Nathan Phillips Square in front of Toronto's magnificent city hall. It was multicultural week, and the stage was given over to a performance of classical Japanese *odori*. A thin, bespeckled Nisei man dressed in a happi coat was introducing a line of women dancers dressed in kimono. With a self-deprecating laugh, he admitted he knew little of classical Japanese art and that he could no longer speak the language of his parents, but the way he spoke indicated no regret or shame that he had lost this vital part of himself and important tool for communication. Rather it was a plea for acceptance—he had neutered himself so he could be part of the big, white world. Having just come from the hip, radical world of the 60s, I wanted no part of such an insipid and defeatist attitude.

Michiko, who was crestfallen by my response, said I should get back to being a real person and a real artist. I was greatly offended, and although I didn't say anything, I thought to myself, Who are you to tell me how to live my life? But if nothing else, Michiko was persistent, and she called a few days later to invite me to a dinner at the New Diamond restaurant in Chinatown to discuss the history project. There were ten of us at dinner. Most were young and casually dressed, except for one older man properly attired in a suit and tie. When I nudged Michiko to inquire about this oddity, she replied, "That's Gordon Kadota. He's a successful businessman and a leader in the Nikkei community." He was to play an important role in the coming events.

After dinner, Pat and I invited the others to our home, where we continued our discussions. I felt comfortable with this group. Some of them I knew from my recent involvement with the community, while the others, mostly Sansei, I felt were much like myself and a far cry from the typical, conservative Nikkei that I had grown to despise. In the end, we committed to the project, and I accepted the position of project director and curator of the proposed exhibition. Perhaps my decision to accept was due in part to the echo of Michiko's admonition to be true to myself, but most of all, it was because of my intuition that we were embarking on a critical mission that would alter and empower our lives.

We began work on the project immediately. We decided to use family snapshots to depict the history written in Issei and Nisei documents. While Michiko, Take and the other new immigrants solicited the support of the Issei, I retired to my basement studio to improvise a portable copy stand and to test various film/developer combinations to produce the best possible copy negatives. I decided at the outset that all the prints for the exhibition would be made from copy negs, for not only did I want to control the final quality and size of the prints, but

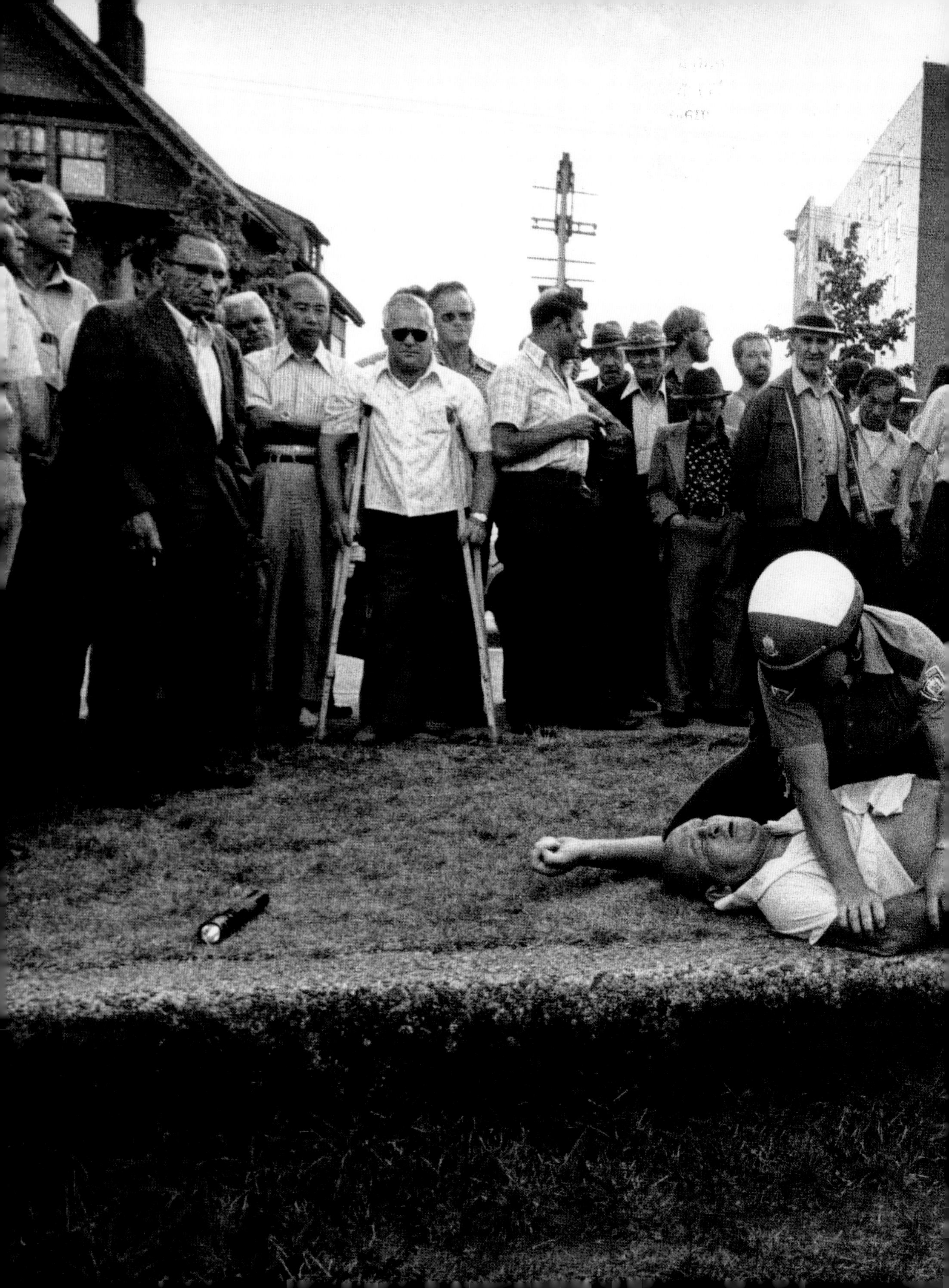

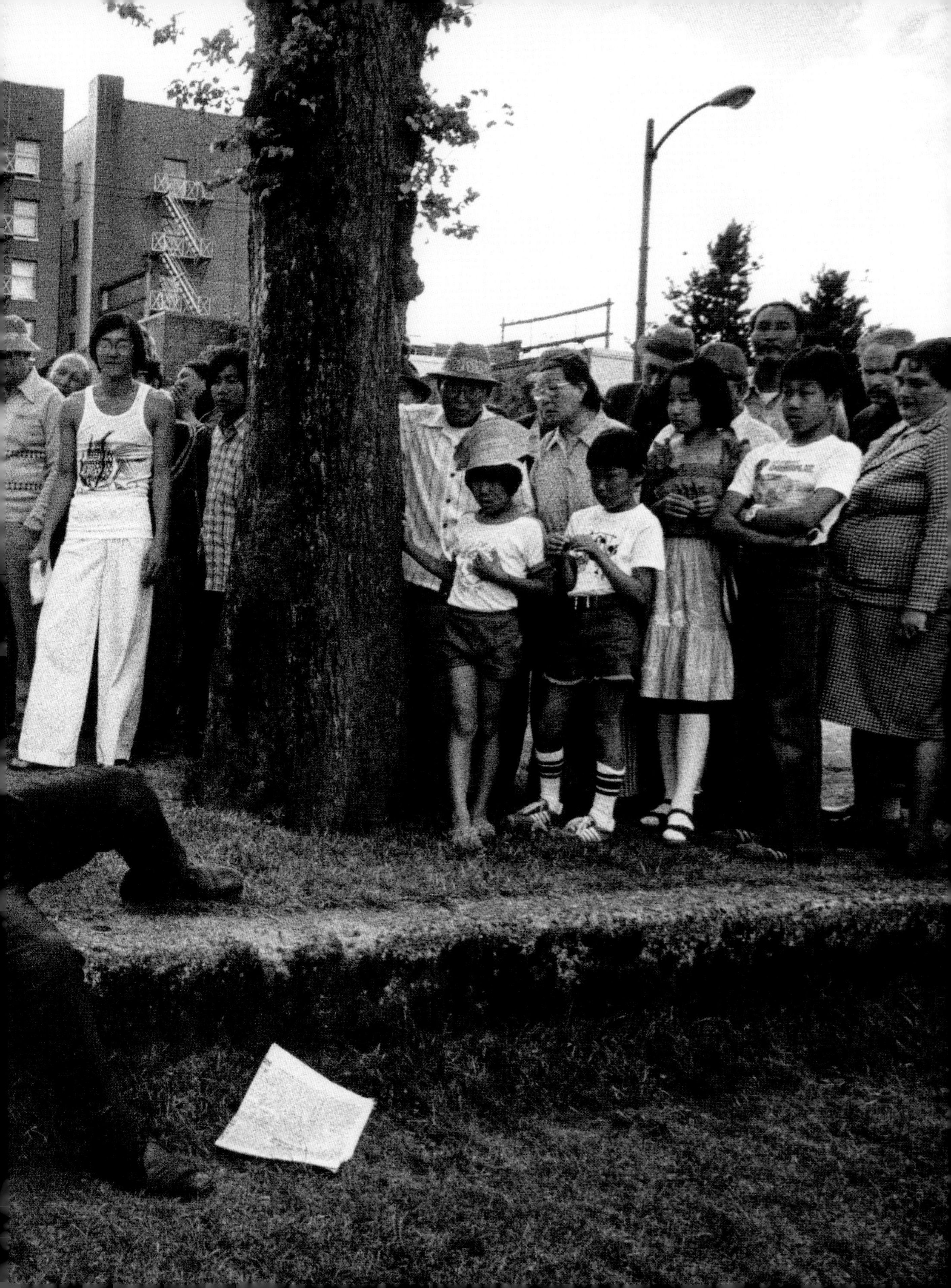

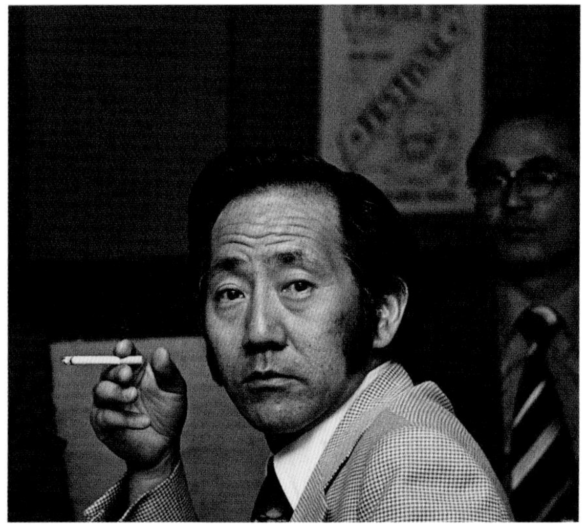

I also didn't want to risk damage or loss of the original material, the precious mementoes of the Issei. Once we'd gathered enough material, I mounted a mini exhibition at Tonari Gumi in order to introduce our project needs to the community. The afternoon event was well attended, and the Issei, particularly the women, had a great time pouring over the old photos. One group broke into gales of laughter when someone pointed at a figure and said, "Isn't that Kato-san? He was such a lady's man! And didn't he finally run off with that floozie from Fukuoka?" After that showing, photos and other historic material began to arrive in a steady stream.

I also managed to gain access to the extant public archives at the Royal BC Museum in Victoria, the UBC Special Collections and the superb Northeast Collections at the Vancouver Public Library. With our work expanding at an alarming rate, it became apparent that we would need a proper workspace. Fortunately, Pat, our administrator, had secured enough grant money to enable us to rent the third floor of an old building on Powell Street in the heart of the former Little Tokyo. Our project had a core membership of twelve, fairly evenly divided between new immigrants and Canadian-born, who were mostly Sansei, and, like myself, many of them had experienced the social and political tumult of the 60s. Randy Enomoto had been part of the student rebellion at UBC; Roy Miki was then a long-haired poet who would later transform himself into Dr. Miki, the well-dressed and articulate voice of the Redress Movement; Linda Uyehara Hoffman, a diminutive Sansei with a powerful voice reminiscent of Janis Joplin, had come to Vancouver with her husband, who was studying for a master's degree in creative writing at UBC. These three, alongside myself, were responsible for the English-language research and interviews and the writing of the exhibition text. Research and interviews in Japanese were left to the new immigrants: Michiko and her friend Maya Koizumi, a professional translator; Kuniko Yamamoto, a graduate architect; and Yuko Shibata, a UBC scholar who was the stunning beauty I saw on my first visit

PREVIOUS SPREAD
Powell Street Festival
coordinator Rick Shiomi
looks at disturbance,
Oppenheimer
Park, Vancouver,
British Columbia,
August 3–4, 1979

Gordon Kadota at
Koji's Restaurant on
Hastings Street during
the first Powell Street
Festival, Vancouver,
British Columbia,
June 10–11, 1977

to Language Aid. Assisting me with production were Marie Hora, a Sansei from Steveston; Noriko Hirota, an aspiring photographer from Japan; and Roger Thorn, an English immigrant who was a professional graphic designer and also brother-in-law to Pat. Administration of the project was in the hands of Pat and Dulce Oikawa, a student at Simon Fraser University.

Before beginning the project, most of us knew little of our history. The wartime uprooting of the Nikkei was never taught in our schools, and our parents, perhaps because of an unwarranted sense of shame or a desire to shield us from such painful and humiliating experiences, never spoke of the dark days of the war years. Given the corrosive racism of the post-war years, it was inevitable that we would maintain our parents' silence. Ironically, although I was a product of the 60s, an era in which every aspect of our present and past lives was brought under the most intense scrutiny, I had failed to use the brilliance of that period to illuminate my own history as an Enemy Alien. That appalling oversight was now to be redressed, for telling the story of our people in our own words was, as they say, an idea whose time had arrived.

Shaping our narrative from hidden truths unearthed from dusty archives and from the tales told to us by our elders was a process that began to transform our lives, both as individuals and as a collective. Due to his slightly rotund shape and phlegmatic demeanour, we affectionately called Randy Enomoto our Buddha, but any semblance of equanimity was shattered whenever he arrived back from the UBC Special Collections in a rage, sharing with us his latest discovery of yet another betrayal by racist politicians who had sought their final solution to the "Yellow Peril." Since I was still clinging to the last vestiges of my chauvinism, I resisted a demand by the women in our group to create a section of the exhibition devoted to the pioneer women of our community. Fortunately, the growing power of their sisterhood was not to be denied, for that section proved to be one of the most poignant in the entire exhibition. When we arrived at the war years, I argued that, since cameras were part of the long list of confiscated items, it would be more powerful to leave a photographic blank space for the period of evacuation and dispersal; but once again, saner heads prevailed. Using official archival photos, we were able to show, in stark visual detail, the immensity of the loss and suffering. These and other battles amongst us fought tooth and nail were rare, and they served only to bring us closer together and to add greater force and conviction to our narrative.

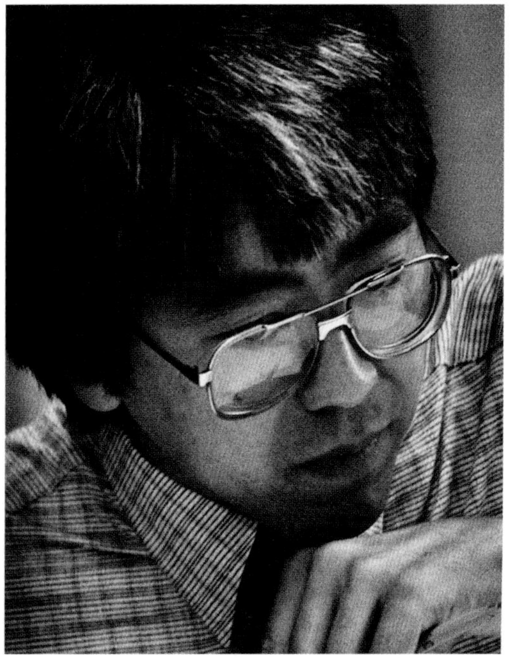

Not since my time with Snick had I felt such a bond with others, but my ties to my brothers and sisters in this new coalition were stronger and more intimate, for we were dealing with issues that went to the very core of our being.

I owed Pat a great deal—she had not only placed the project on a sound footing but also helped ease my entry into Vancouver. But I sensed that, to fully engage in my new reality, I would need a new beginning. I moved into the project workspace. My new home was essentially one long room with a bank of windows overlooking Powell Street at one end, and at the other, there was a bathroom with a shower and one other small room containing a salvaged mattress infested with lice that served as my bedroom. The Pacific Bakery occupied the first floor of our building, and at about eleven o'clock at night, the old European bakers would crank up the radiator and begin work. Soon blessed heat and the tantalizing aroma of baking bread would begin drifting up to our studio. A few hours later, after shutting off the heat, they would leave, and I would have to work in bone-chilling temperatures until the next evening.

Our group met almost daily, and our evening work parties began with food and ended with food. A donated hot plate, rice cooker and electric kettle were all we needed to prepare an exquisite meal with dishes that project members brought from their homes. Late at night, over a bowl of noodles at nearby Aki's or one of the surrounding Chinese restaurants, we would continue to debate the finer points of the show. Like Nikkei everywhere, our love of traditional food was a defining element in our growing sense of community.

One afternoon, I was sorting through a stack of photographs that Take had just brought over from Tonari Gumi when I came across one eleven-by-fourteen-inch sepia print showing a group of well-dressed men and women sitting around a long table. Although it was of no particular interest, there was something vaguely familiar about this image, which led me to study it more carefully. When I looked up, I

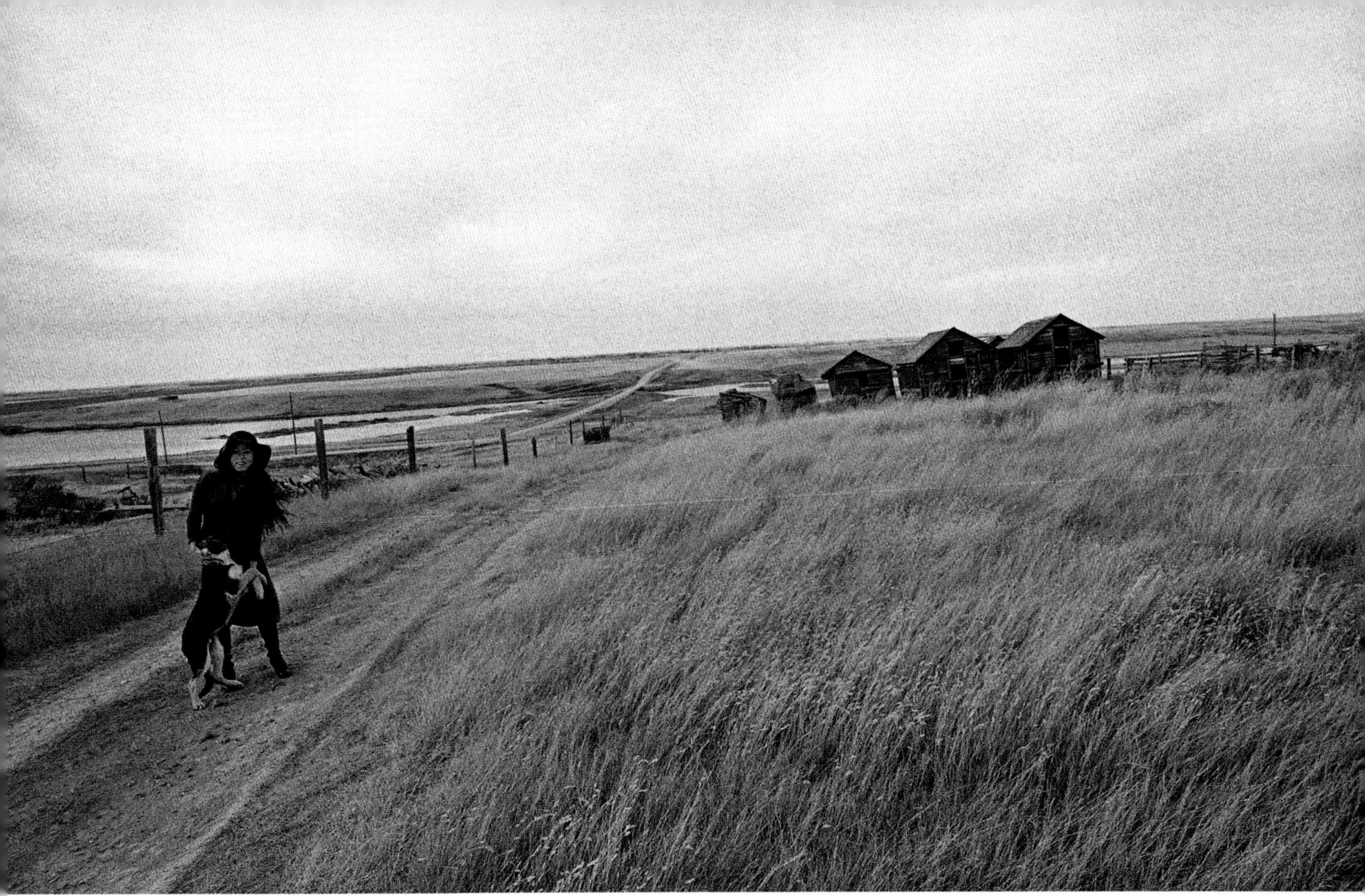

realized that the double doors and the arrangement of overhead pipes at the back of our studio was exactly the same as those in the photo. The moment was powerful and haunting. I could almost hear the voices of the people in the old photograph and the voice of my own father urging me to tell their stories and end the long silence of the Nikkei. It seemed that all the twists and turns of my life had conspired to bring me to this moment, and that whatever skills and strengths I had managed to garner along the way were powers bestowed upon me so I could complete this one mission.

In the fall of 1976, we put the last piece of glass into its frame and drove the completed exhibition, in a rented truck, to the H.R. MacMillan Planetarium and Museum, one of Vancouver's prime venues. The next morning, all of us gathered together to hang our work. It couldn't all fit into the spacious museum gallery, so Kuniko, our resident architect, had designed an additional wall made of fragrant cedar. That evening's opening was a gala affair and the social highlight of the year. The hundreds of guests were treated to the delicate creations of Ko-chan, who

Michiko Sakata on a research trip to Southern Alberta, near Taber, Alberta, October 1976

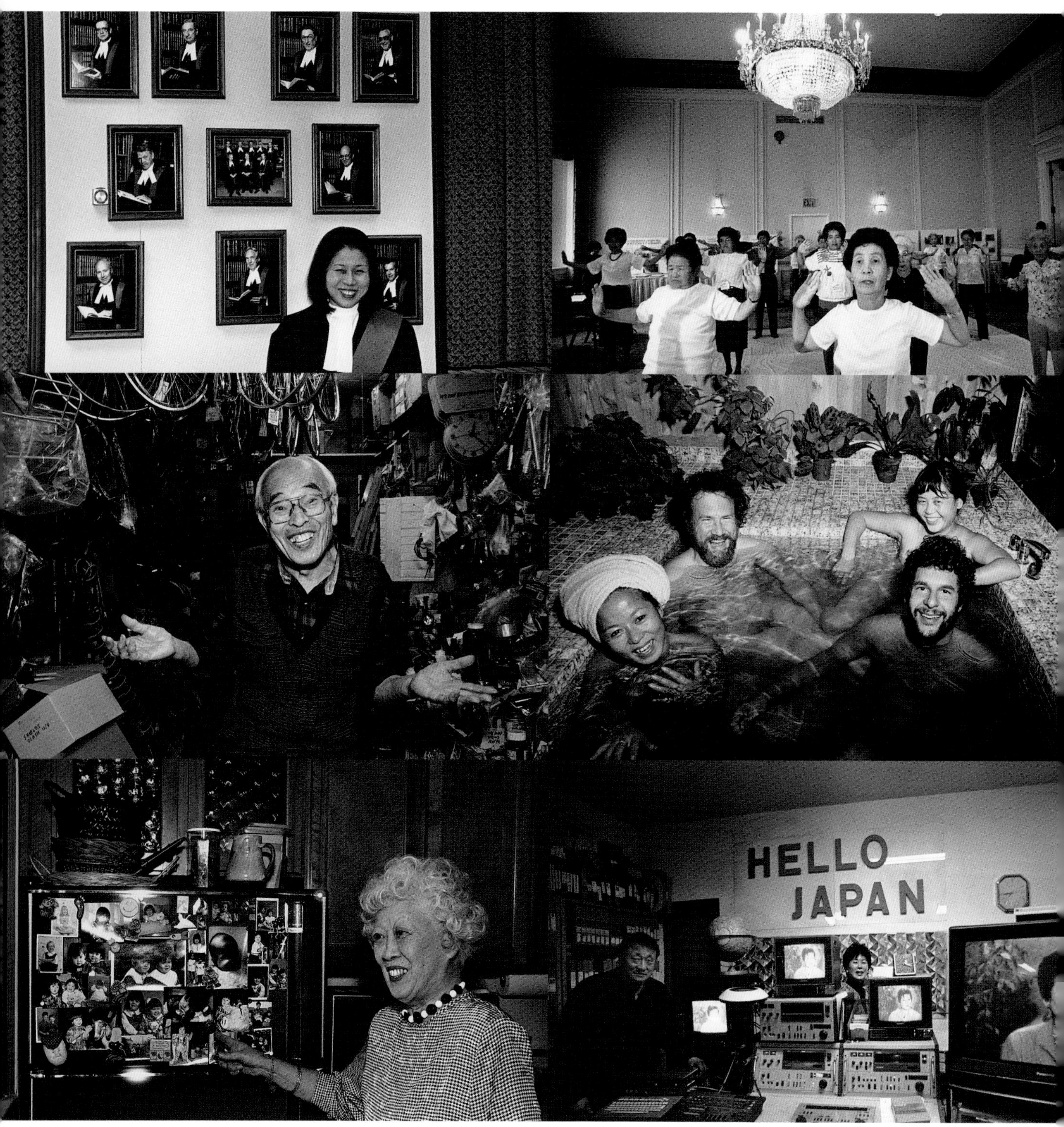

HELLO
JAPAN

singlehandedly began the sushi boom in Vancouver, and green tea and sweets served by Tonari Gumi volunteers. Michiko, Noriko and Yuko were stunning in their brightly coloured kimono, while Take and I, similarly dressed in elegant *hakama*, began the evening's festivities with a shakuhachi duet. After appropriate speeches by our community leaders, the Consul General of Japan and representatives from the three levels of government, we all gathered around a large wooden tub of sake, which we smashed open with ceremonial wooden mallets. *The Japanese Canadians: 1877–1976*, an exhibition that we had fought and laboured over for nearly two years, was now officially open.

What I remember most of that evening is the excitement, joy and, at times, sorrow on the faces of the Issei as they gathered around the panels and couldn't resist poking a finger at a glass-covered photo of themselves or a long-lost friend. In many ways, the exhibition was the story of their lives: a noble history of sacrifice, perseverance and courage that was worthy of public display and our supreme efforts as the exhibition's creators.

The exhibition itself began with the words "We came from an ancient land, with a dream of riches," in a flowing, handwritten script. Like a Greek chorus, this device was used at the beginning of each major section to emphasize that the narrative was derived not from some objective, scholarly viewpoint, but rather that it was a passionate tale told by those who lived through a near century of tumultuous history. Liberation theory states that one of the first steps to freedom is to write one's own story and reclaim history from the falsehood and self-serving rationalizations of the oppressor. The meticulously researched narrative text in the exhibition clearly stated that the rationale for the wartime treatment of the Nikkei was not a matter of national security nor due to the more benign reason of protecting them from an angry public, but rather it was the culmination of a long history of racist oppression that began with the arrival of the first Asian immigrants in Canada. One of the most common reactions to the exhibition amongst the general public was shock, especially when they read that the last parts of the War Measures Act, the enabling legislation that began the Nikkei evacuation, were not lifted until 1949, four years after the end of the war. And it wasn't until the following year that Japanese Canadians, along with Indigenous people, were allowed to vote in provincial elections. For many, these injustices, unthinkable in a democratic society, were not ancient history and had occurred well within the span of their own

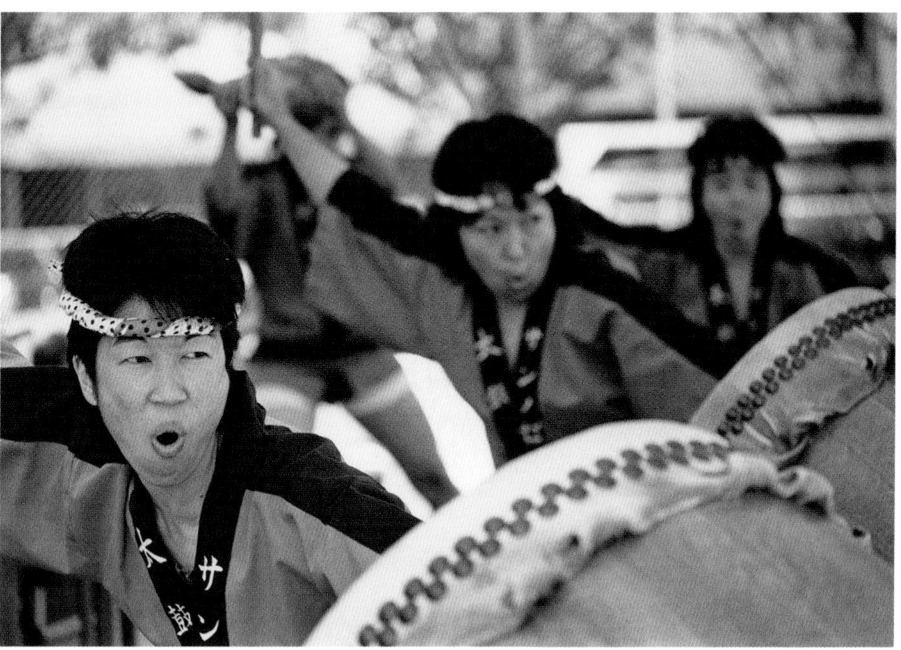

lives. By amending the historic record, our exhibition represented the opening salvo in the coming Nikkei battle for redress.

Shortly after the opening, I went back to the museum to take documentation slides of the exhibition to show to the Multicultural Secretariat, our main source of funds. I flew to Ottawa, and after the screening, the head of the agency stood up and said, "Thank God, we finally spent our money on something truly worthwhile." Their offer of support for any future projects would be needed, because soon after returning to Vancouver, our project received a request from an ad hoc national committee to coordinate plans for the upcoming celebrations marking the centennial of the arrival of the first Japanese immigrant to Canada. They were to sponsor two national projects. One was a touring stage show of traditional Japanese performing arts, and we were asked to become the second project, with the proviso that we include the postwar growth of Nikkei communities in other parts of Canada so that the exhibition could reflect the entire hundred-year history of Japanese immigration to the country. In the spring, I packed my copy stand into an old Salvation Army suitcase and travelled to Southern Alberta with Michiko. There we interviewed the Nikkei who had been sent to the area during the war to offset the labour shortage in the sugar beet industry. When we concluded our work, Michiko went back to Vancouver

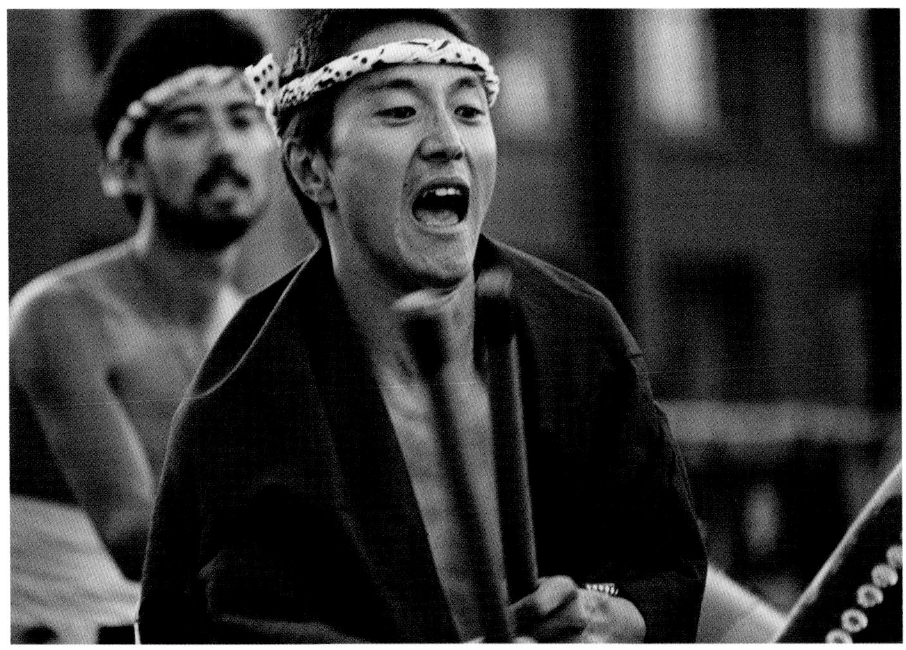

while I continued to cross the country, gathering more material from the other major centres of post-war Nikkei settlement in Winnipeg, Ottawa, Montréal, Toronto and, finally, my own hometown of Chatham.

When I returned to Vancouver, loaded down with boxes of taped interviews and rolls of exposed film, we began work on the final version of our exhibition. We had already successfully encapsulated most of our history, and it was a relatively simple matter of extending our design grid to encompass the last three decades of the Nikkei diaspora. In the fall, we all flew to Ottawa to mount our completed show, now titled *A Dream of Riches: The Japanese Canadians 1877–1977*, at the National Museum of Man. There were actually three versions of the exhibition: a version in English and French that would tour in Eastern Canada, an English-only version for the West, and a Japanese version to tour in Japan. In addition I had printed a fourth set of exhibition photos for publication purposes. Looking back, I find it hard to believe that I produced such a prodigious amount of work in such a short time, but back then, it all seemed to flow effortlessly. By the end of its tour schedule, *A Dream of Riches* was seen by countless thousands in over forty Canadian, American and Japanese venues.

Our project was only part of a larger renaissance occurring within the Nikkei community in the old Powell Street area. When the Canadian

John Greenaway
and Rick Shiomi,
Katari Taiko,
Powell Street Festival,
Vancouver,
British Columbia,
August 1–2, 1981

government ordered the evacuation of all Nikkei in late February 1942, the once-bustling *Nihonmachi* became a ghost town almost overnight, and bereft of its community, the area soon deteriorated into its present state—Vancouver's skid row. In the late 40s and early 50s, the Nikkei began trickling back to Vancouver. For many Nisei who had begun to gain acceptance—and given the opening of new opportunities in the East—the idea of returning to the poisonous racism of British Columbia was unthinkable. But for many Issei, the happy memories of Powell Street were too great to resist. However, when they returned, a few stores and restaurants, the old Japanese Language School and the Vancouver Buddhist Temple were all that remained of their lively pre-war community. Separated from their families and hampered by language, which prevented them from accessing essential services, many Issei were leading isolated lives of quiet desperation. A new coalition was forming to address their needs.

It began with Language Aid and then with Tonari Gumi, the real epicentre of the rebirth of the community. The catalyst for our awakening was the *Shin-Ijusha* (Japanese immigrants who arrived after 1967), who, like those of us who had come of age during the 60s, were the adventurous rebels of their own society: people like Michiko, who borrowed money from her older sister to buy a boat ticket to San Francisco in order to avoid a marriage arranged by her wealthy parents; or Take, who came to Canada knowing that life as a Japanese salaryman would destroy his irrepressible personality and his spiritual quest through music. With their quiet pride and unassuming sense of themselves as Japanese, they were like a beacon, drawing us, the Canadian-born, away from our alienation. Naomi Shikaze, from a farming family in Aldergrove, and her cousin Mayumi Takasaki, from the fishing village of Steveston, were typical of the young Sansei in the new coalition. They had gone on their pilgrimage to Japan and, on returning, discovered that Tonari Gumi was the perfect venue to continue their search for authenticity. With the immigrants acting as a bridge, a growing dialogue between the Nikkei generations allowed the young to weave together the lost threads of their history and heritage. It was an exciting time to be a Nikkei, because, like divergent streams in a vast watershed, all four generations—Issei, Nisei, Sansei and the *Shin-Ijusha*—were flowing into one mighty river.

We were all aware of the rapidly approaching Nikkei centennial, and Take came up with the idea of holding a festival in Oppenheimer Park, the old Powell Street grounds. He approached the Centennial Committee, who approved the project. The idea spread like wildfire, for we all

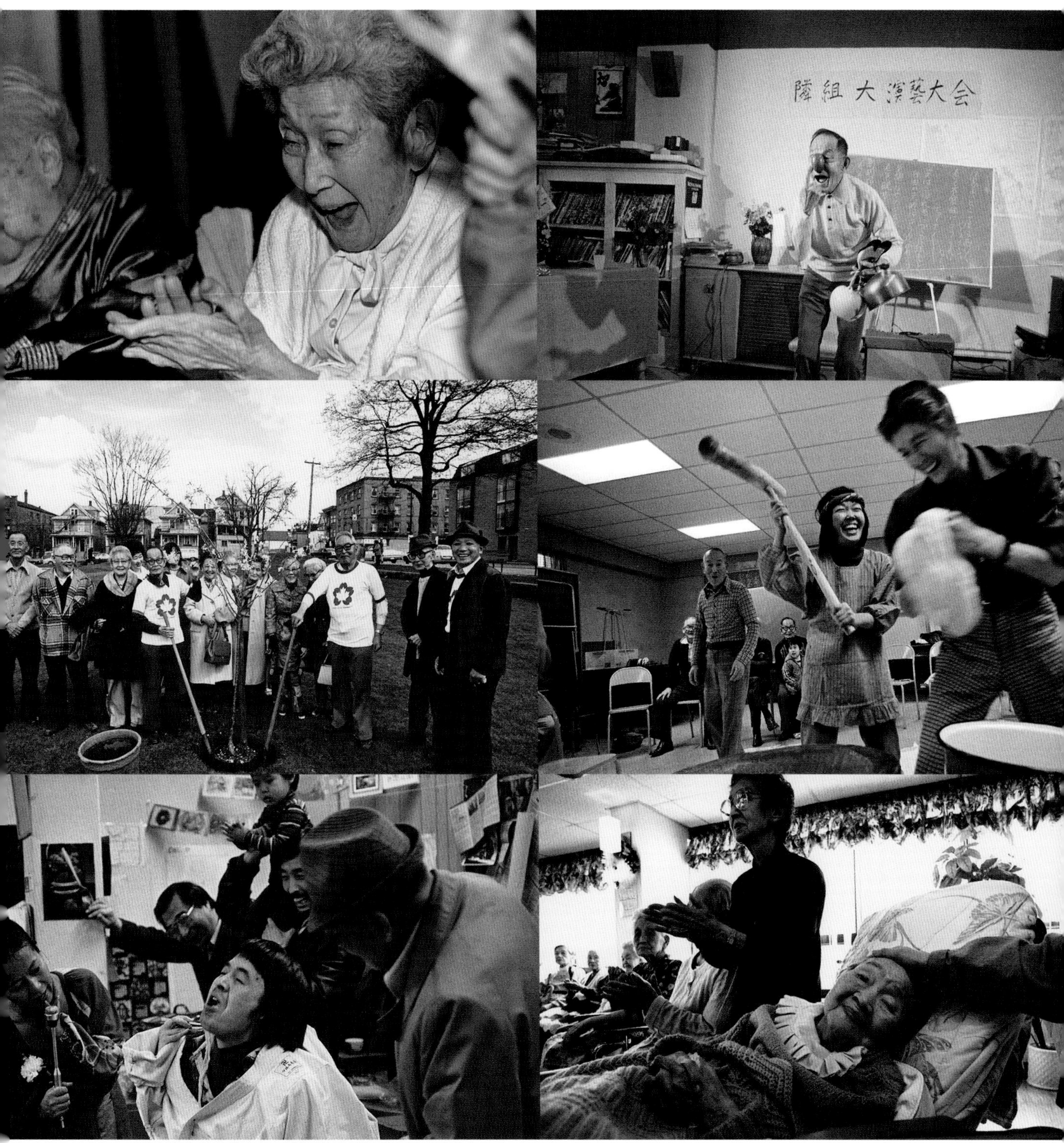

陸組 大演藝大会

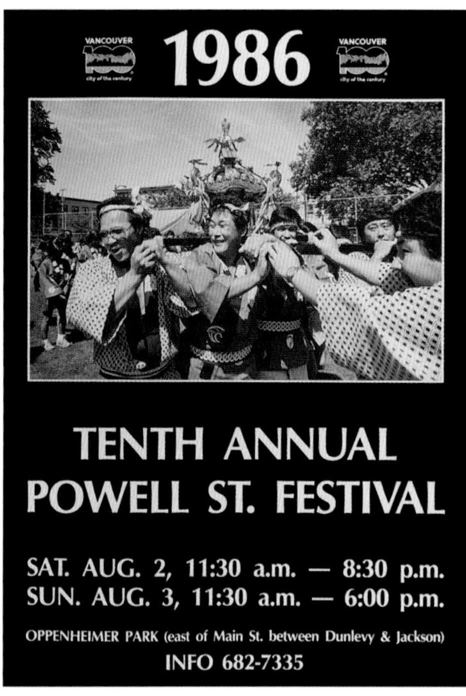

Promotional poster for the tenth annual Powell Street Festival, 1986

realized that a festival was the perfect means to express our joy in our growing community and the excitement of so many new discoveries. But the festival would be much more than just a big weekend gala party, for in choosing the old Powell Street grounds, we would also be making a political statement: that a new generation of Nikkei, proud and empowered, were reclaiming lost territory and asserting their rightful place in society.

As the sponsoring organization for the festival, Tonari Gumi secured a city grant and hired Rick Shiomi as festival coordinator. Rick was a young Sansei from Toronto who had recently become involved in the Vancouver community through his involvement in the international effort to support victims of Minamata disease in Japan. His mandate was to unite the community for the festival. Unfortunately, the Vancouver Nikkei community was deeply divided between the establishment of older Issei and Nisei and the new coalition that grew out of Language Aid, Tonari Gumi and the photo history project. The tension between these two factions would come to a head over the issue of the festival. When Michiko first began Language Aid, she tried to gain the support of the Vancouver Japanese Canadian Citizens' Association, a post-war national organization. But the board members were offended that an upstart outsider, an immigrant, would dare to suggest that the Issei—who were, after all, their own parents—were in need of assistance. When Jun and Take started Tonari Gumi, they wanted to get a feel for life on skid row, so they joined the lineup for a free lunch from the Franciscan Sisters of Atonement. They were spotted by a member of the nearby Buddhist temple, and word spread quickly that these beggars from Tonari Gumi were bringing eternal shame to the Nikkei community. Undoubtedly, the older establishment saw the new coalition as a bunch of dirty, dope-smoking hippies at best, and at worst, evil communists. And we, the hip, new generation, dismissed them as nothing more than stodgy roadblocks to the new world order. We were to pay dearly for our arrogance.

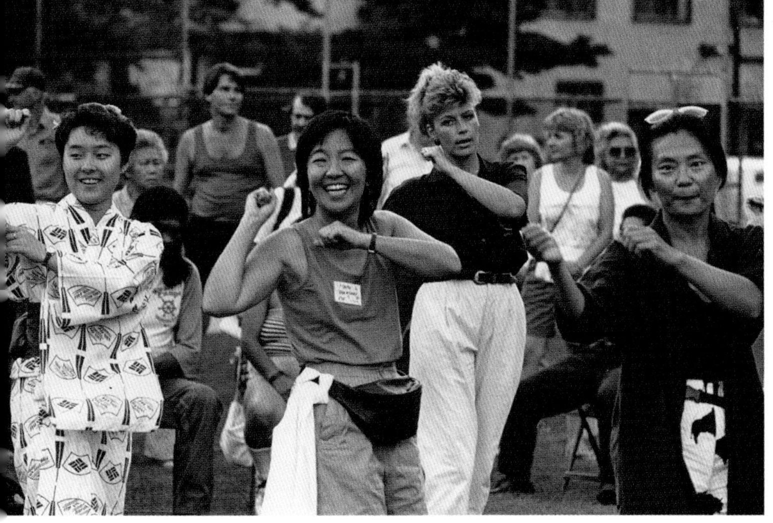

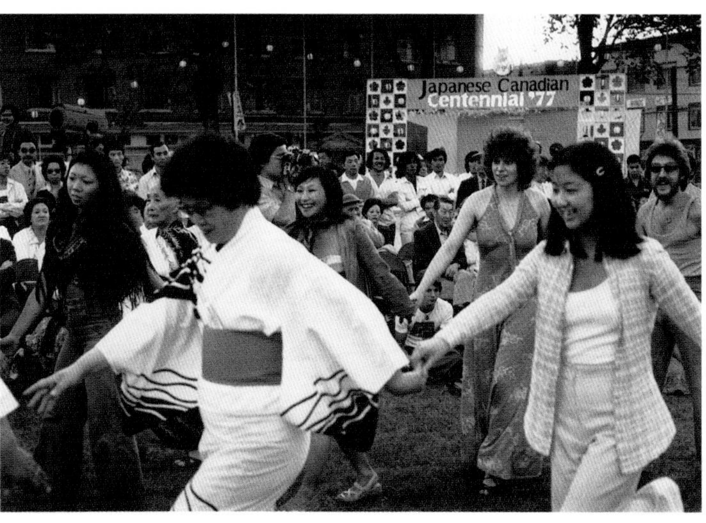

Rick had no idea what he had got himself into, and after a stressful month on the job, he had lost ten pounds from his already slender frame. I remember one particularly heated public meeting at the Japanese Language School, in which Tonari Gumi was castigated for daring to invite performers from Japan without first clearing it with the senior organizations. After the meeting, an angry kendo sensei, one of those macho Mishima wannabes, came up to our group and ridiculed Rick as being no better than an "Indian" who had abandoned his language and culture. Except for the obvious contempt, Rick had no idea what he was expressing. But I fired back that, if he was any example of Japanese manhood, I would much rather be an "Indian." Fortunately for me, Take intervened before we came to blows. We left the meeting with the depressing certainty that the Powell Street Festival was doomed to failure.

TOP
Mayu Takasaki and
Haruko Okano,
Bon Odori,
Powell Street Festival,
Vancouver,
British Columbia,
August 4, 1990

BOTTOM
Folk dance,
Powell Street Festival,
Vancouver,
British Columbia,
June 10–11, 1977

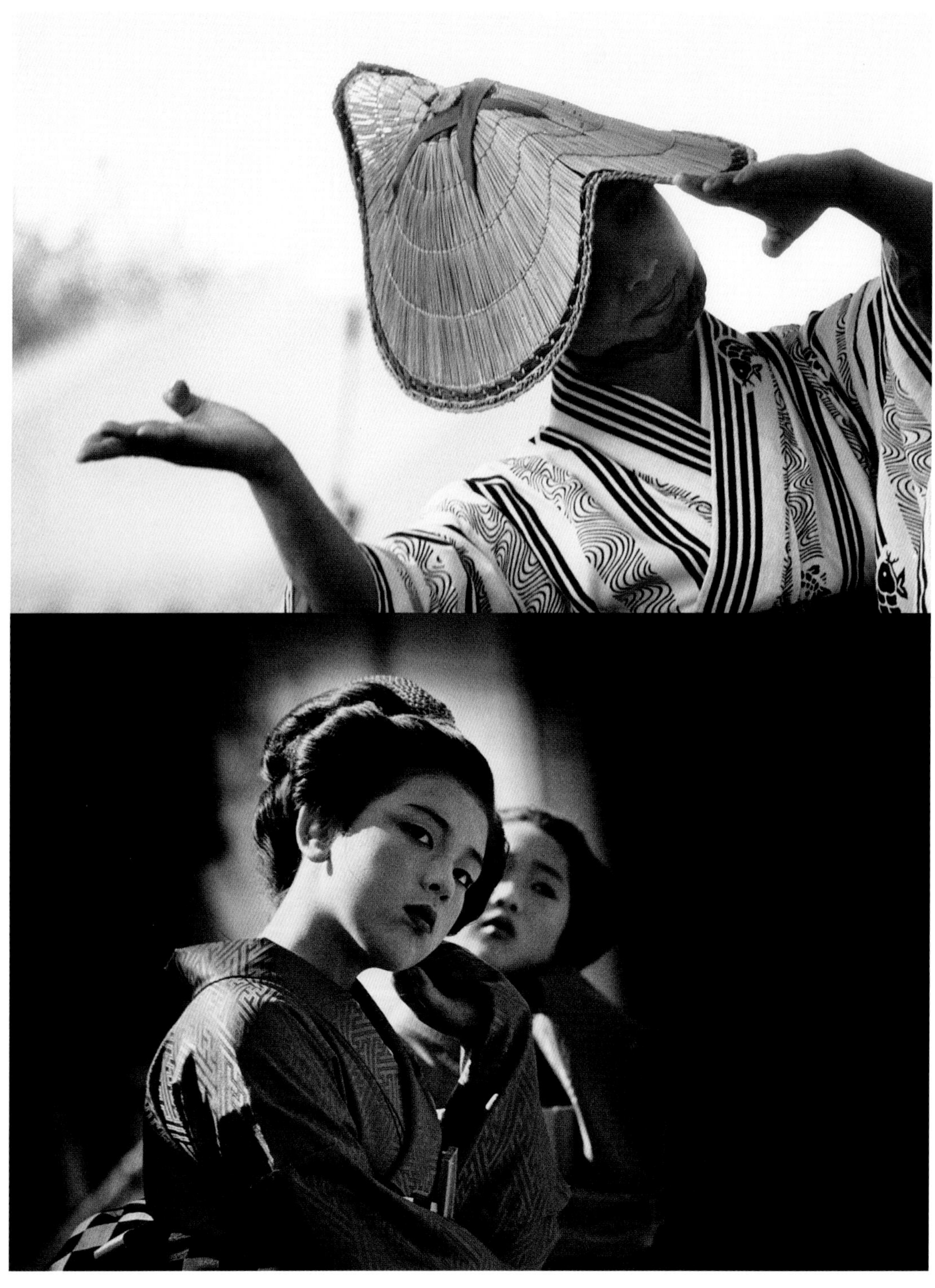

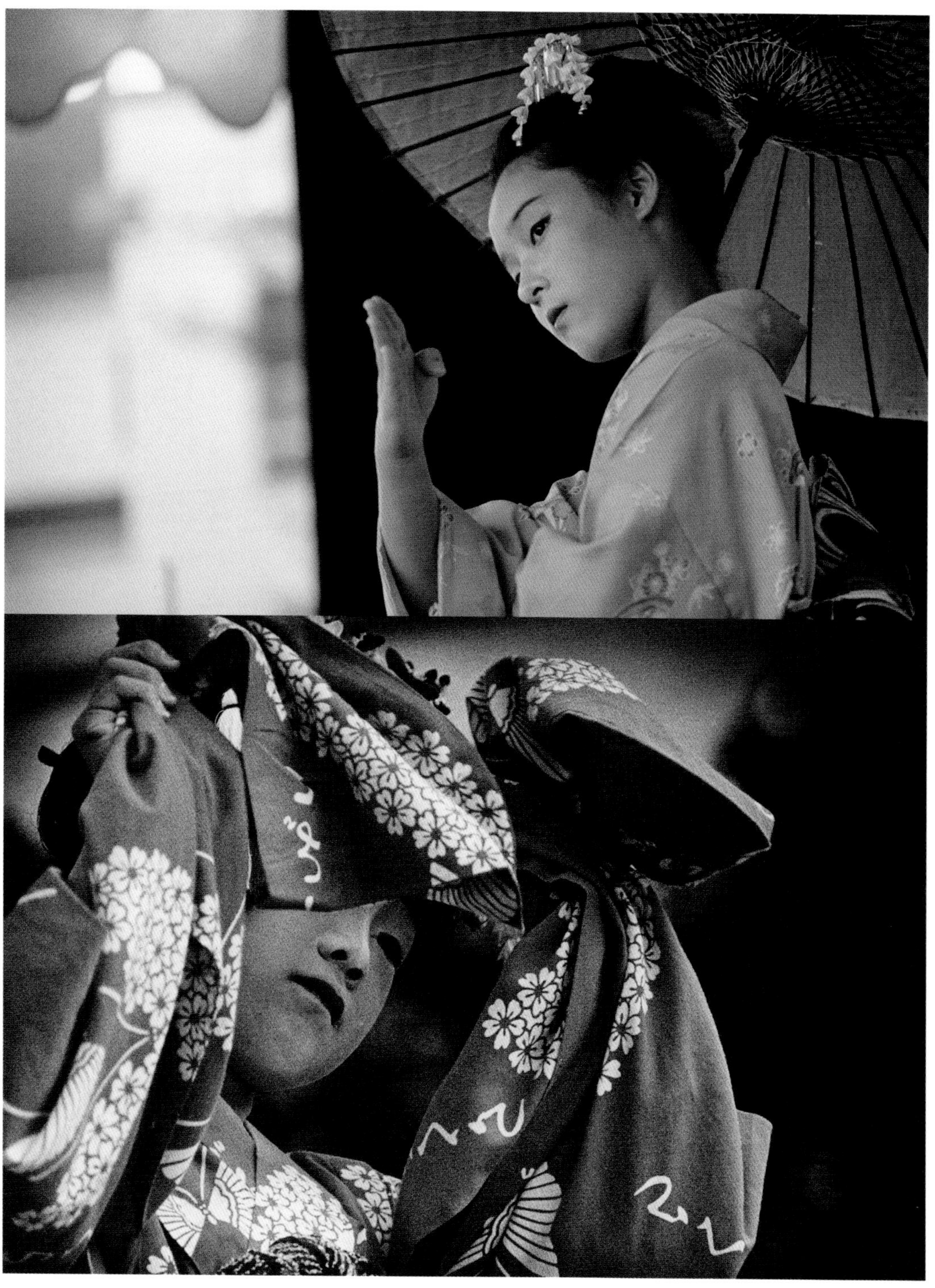

In desperation, Rick went to consult with Gordon Kadota at his downtown office. After listening to the young coordinator's tale of woe, Gordon picked up the phone and called one of his Nisei friends, a prominent member of the community. After inquiring about the state of his friend's health, his family and his business and commiserating over the sad state of their golf game and yet another abysmal season for the Canucks, he segued smoothly into the Powell Street Festival. "These kids," he said, "may be young and a bit brash, but they seem to be quite sincere. And since their hearts are in the right place and the festival is basically a great idea, perhaps we should all get behind them." For Rick, the conversation was a profound revelation, for he realized that the Nisei formed almost a closed society with its own rituals and language, and without those keys, he was hopelessly inadequate to the task at hand. However, Gordon continued to work the phones, and gradually the walls of resistance began to crumble.

Gordon reminds me of the cavalry in those old Westerns—riding in at the eleventh hour to save the defenders of the fort from being massacred by the Apache. He was a *Kika Nisei*, that is, someone who was born in Canada but spent most of his formative years in Japan. Prior to the outbreak of World War II, he accompanied his mother and two siblings to Japan. They were unable to return, and as the war intensified, the family moved to a small village in Tottori Prefecture to avoid the escalating American bombing. When Japan was finally defeated, the whole country braced for the arrival of the occupying army, which, according to wartime propaganda, would be made up of barbaric Americans who would shoot all the men, bayonet all the babies and rape all the women. In the little village in Tottori Prefecture, the elders met in a hastily called meeting to see if there was any way they could save their village. The principal of the local school spoke up and said that one of his pupils, a young child from Canada, might be able to intercede on their behalf. So, the next day, twelve-year-old Gordon led a contingent of village representatives to negotiate with the Americans, who, of course, turned out to be regular GIs, handing out K-rations to the adults and candy to the children.

Undoubtedly, there are those in the village who still believe that, on that day, Gordon saved them from a fate worse than death. The Kadota cavalry came again to the rescue in Vancouver, for Gordon not only saved the Powell Street Festival but was also instrumental in saving the publication of *A Dream of Riches* in its book form. Exhausted from a

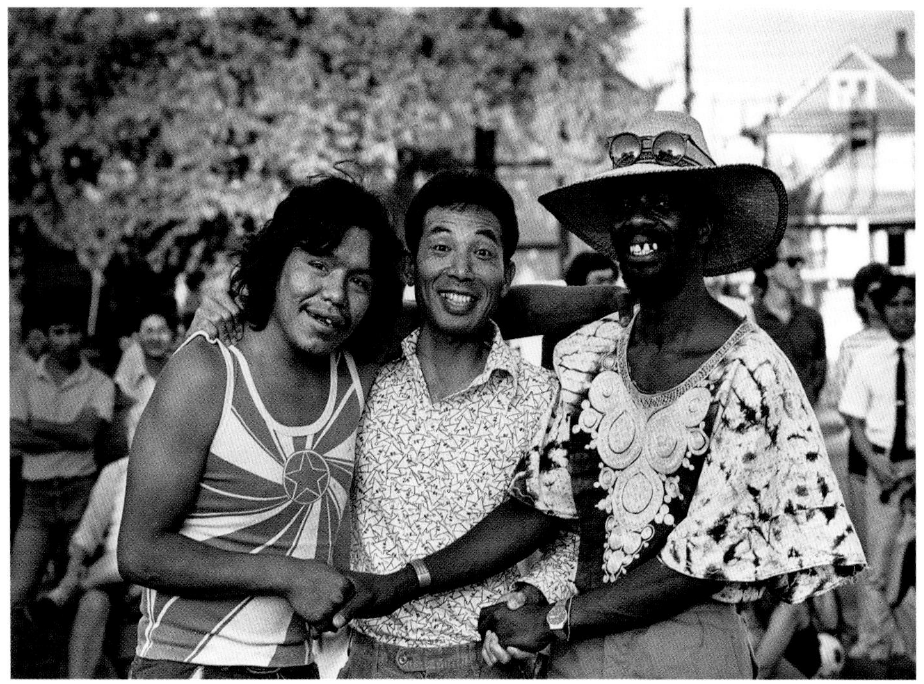

heavy tour schedule and having fallen into the costly pitfalls of trying to publish in three languages, we were nearly bankrupt when Gordon stepped in with the resources of his office and his business acumen to save the project. He was almost perfectly bilingual and bicultural, which allowed him to function just as easily with a group of Japanese businessmen, his Nisei peers, or the young rebels of the new coalition. He used that ability well.

Oppenheimer Park was only a stone's throw away from our project studio, and as the midsummer long weekend drew nearer, I often wandered over to watch the transformation of the park, once known as the Eastside Swamp, into a proper venue for the first Powell Street Festival. That spring, the Issei of Tonari Gumi had planted saplings of sakura, ornamental cherry trees purchased from Japan, as their centennial gift to the city and to future generations. With a generosity of spirit, they planted this living legacy as an affirmation of their cultural heritage and their allegiance to their adopted land. In the final week before the festival, an army of volunteers worked night and day to hang colourful centennial banners, erect tents, build two stages, and cobble together two-by-fours and stout bamboo poles for the many food and craft booths.

Audience,
Powell Street Festival,
Vancouver,
British Columbia,
August 4–5, 1984

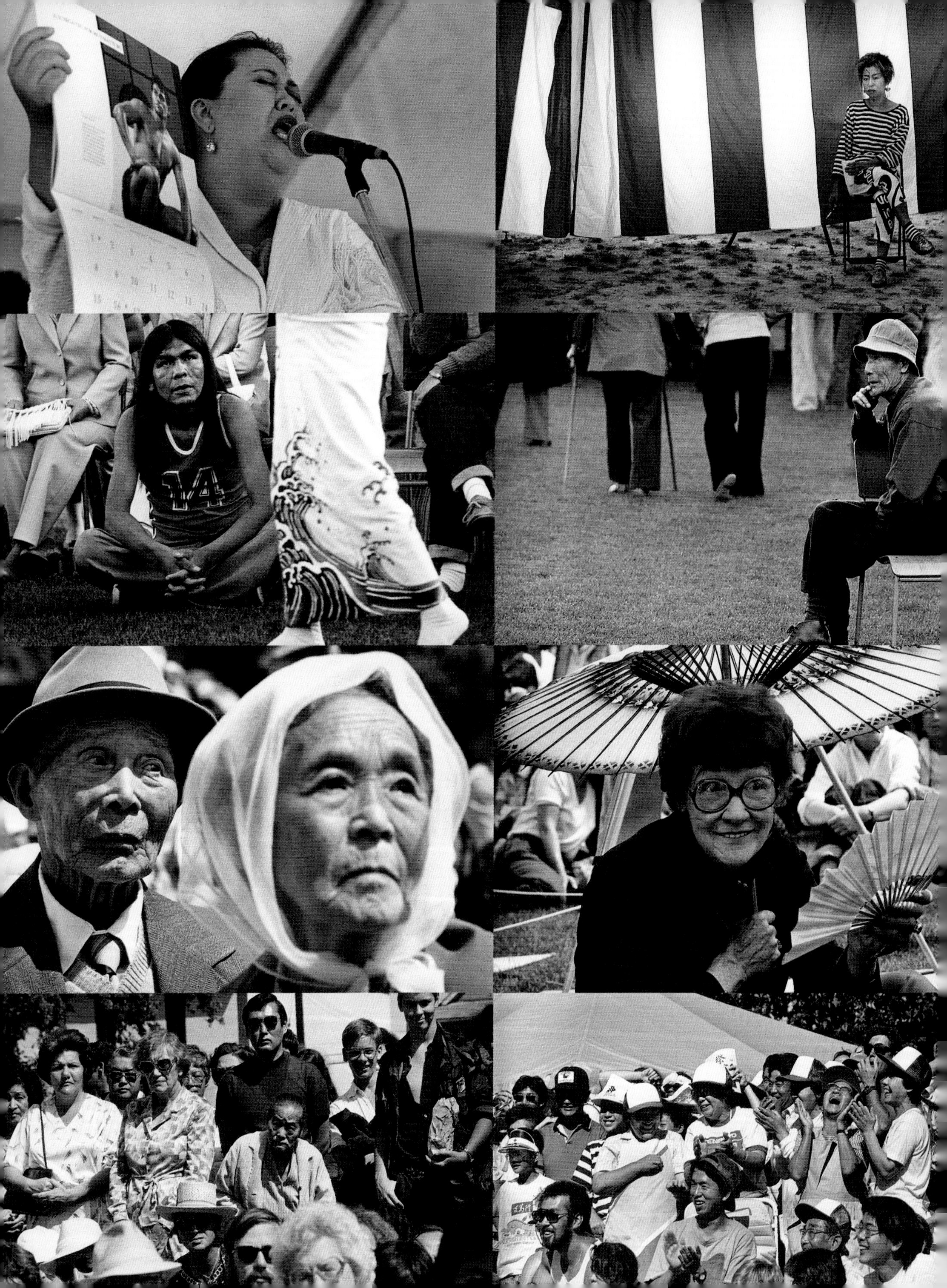

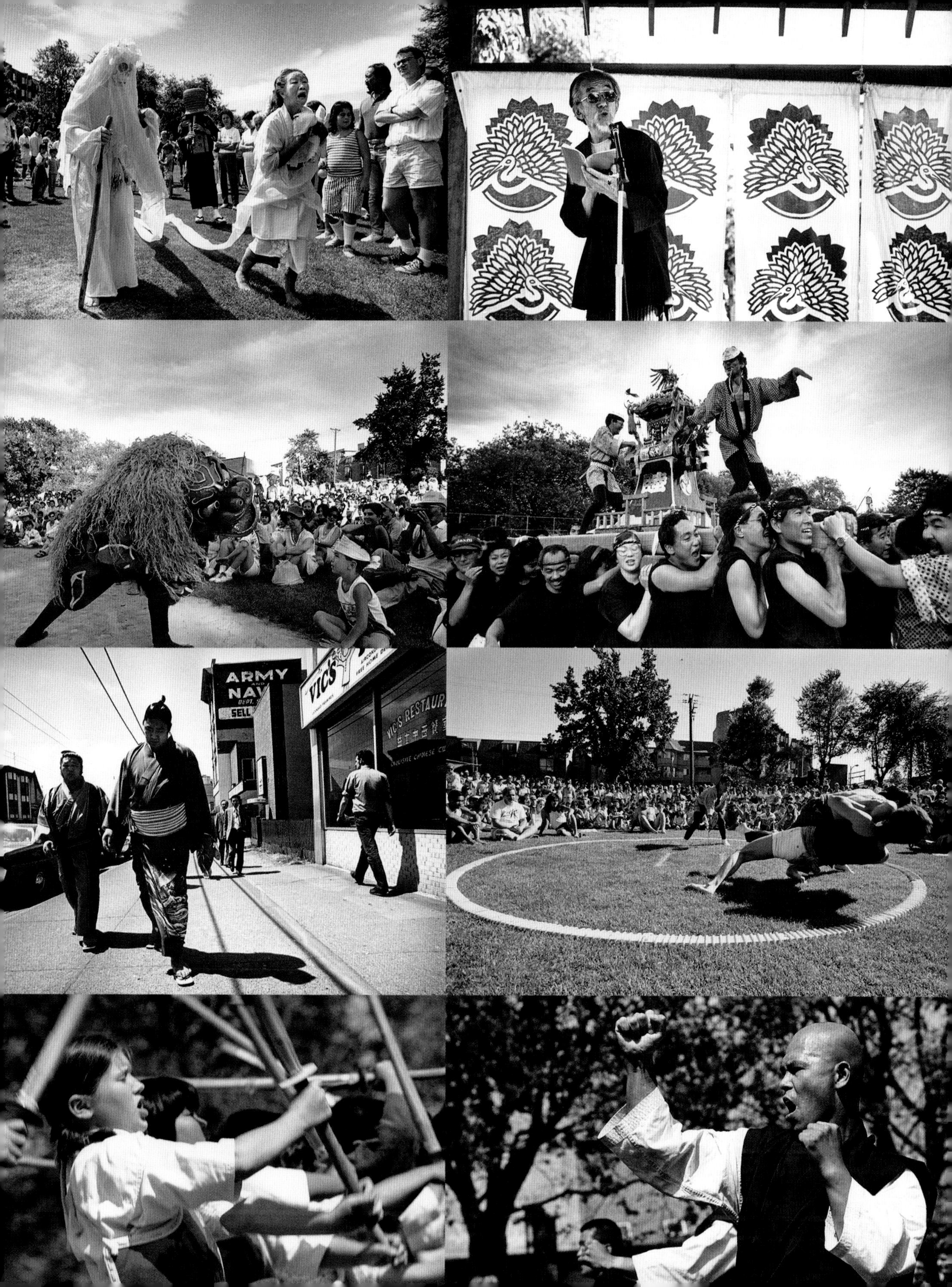

The first Powell Street Festival was blessed with the warmth of the summer sun, and the park overflowed with celebrants, many dressed in bright *yukata*. The visceral beat of the taiko drums, the soulful sounds of the shakuhachi and koto, the elegance of the *odori* dancers, the sakura saplings swaying in the gentle breeze; all these stirred a nearly forgotten communal memory. For the first time since the war years, the Nikkei from far and wide were reunited on the grounds where an earlier generation had come to enact its ancient rituals and acclaim its heroes. In the hundredth year since the arrival of the first Japanese immigrant to Canada, we were back on Powell Street—not as victims, but as proud victors over a century of racism that had sought our banishment from these lands.

After three decades of exile, I had found my way home.

PREVIOUS SPREAD

P.258 LEFT TO RIGHT, TOP TO BOTTOM

Amy Hill, Powell Street Festival, Vancouver, British Columbia, 1992; Audience for Frank Chickens, Powell Street Festival, Vancouver, British Columbia, August 4, 1991; Audience, Powell Street Festival, Vancouver, British Columbia, 1980; Oppenheimer Park, Powell Street Festival, Vancouver, British Columbia, 1980; Tonari Gumi seniors, Powell Street Festival, Vancouver, British Columbia, 1980; Oppenheimer Park, Powell Street Festival, Vancouver, British Columbia, 1980; Audience, Powell Street Festival, Vancouver, British Columbia, 1980; Audience, Powell Street Festival, Vancouver, British Columbia, 1980

P.259 LEFT TO RIGHT, TOP TO BOTTOM

Koko Kokubo, Bart Uchida, installation art, Powell Street Festival, Vancouver, British Columbia, July 31, 1988; Roy Kiyooka poetry reading, Powell Street Festival, Vancouver, British Columbia, July 30, 1988; Shi Shi Mai, Katari Taiko, Powell Street Festival, Vancouver, British Columbia, August 4, 1990; Omikoshi, Powell Street Festival, Vancouver, British Columbia, August 4, 1990; Sumo wrestlers visit Tonari Gumi, Powell Street Festival, Vancouver, British Columbia, June 10–11, 1977; Sumo wrestlers, Powell Street Festival, Vancouver, British Columbia, July 31, 1988; Kendo demonstration, Powell Street Festival, Vancouver, British Columbia, July 29–30, 1983; Martial art demonstration, Powell Street Festival, Vancouver, British Columbia, July 29–30, 1983

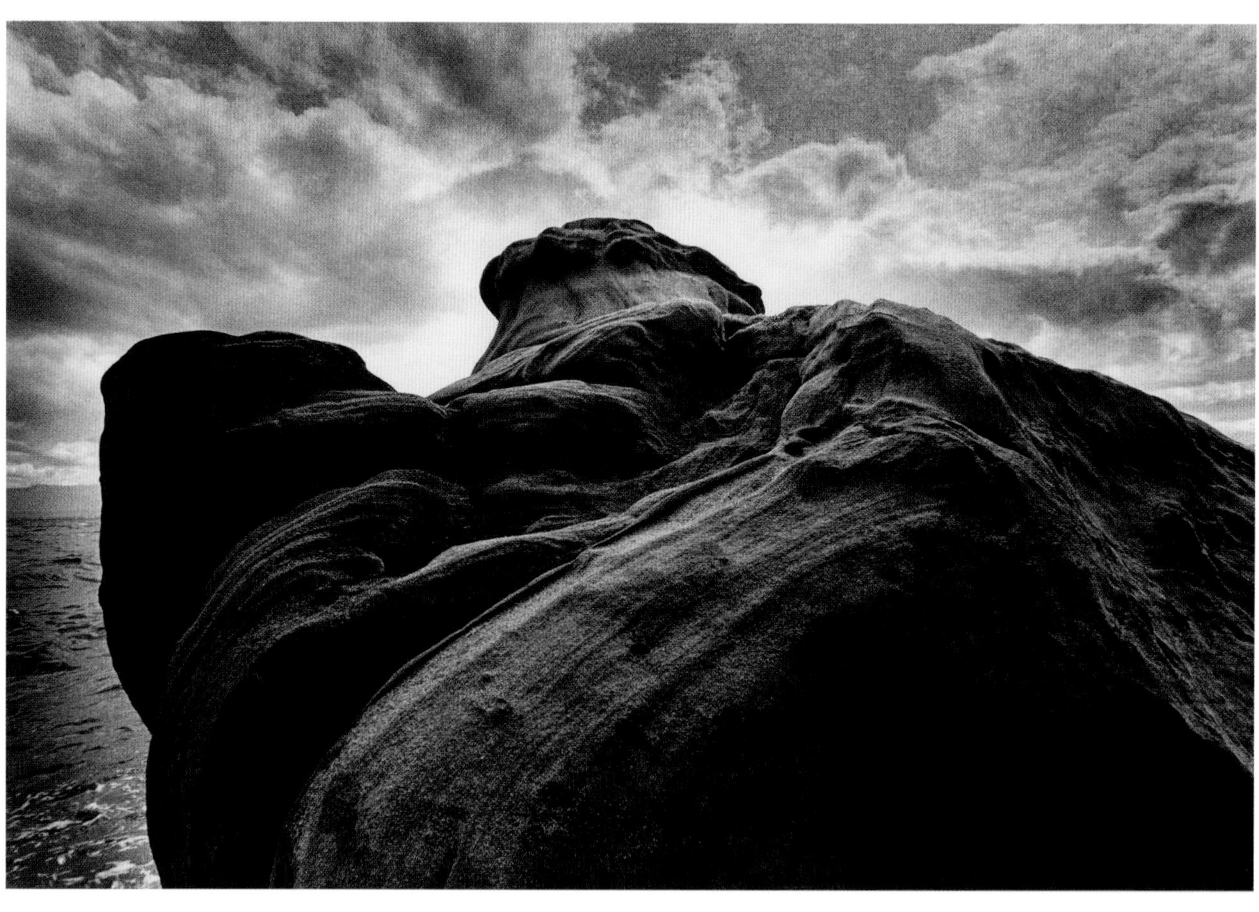

Hornby Island, British Columbia, July 1974

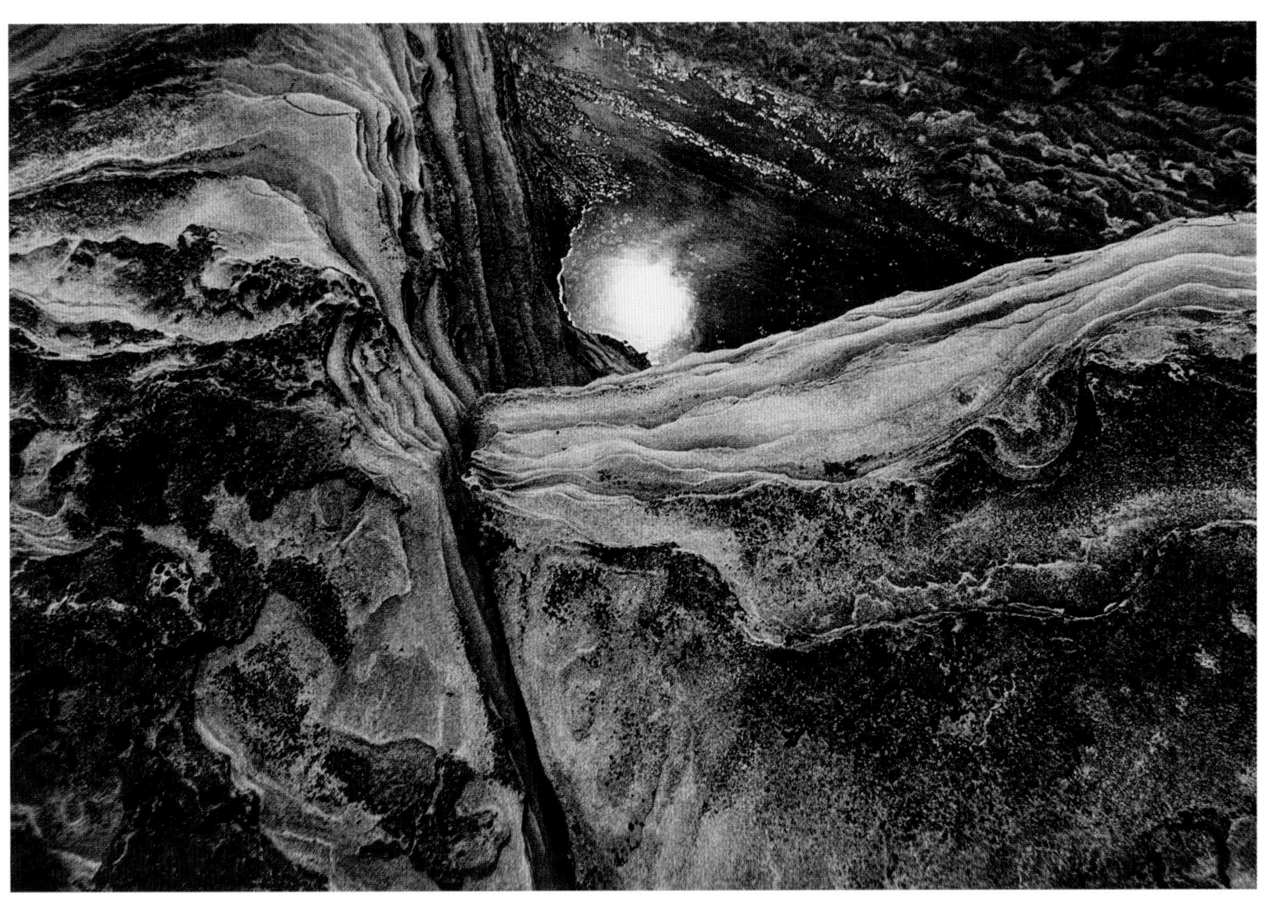

Hornby Island, British Columbia, July 1974

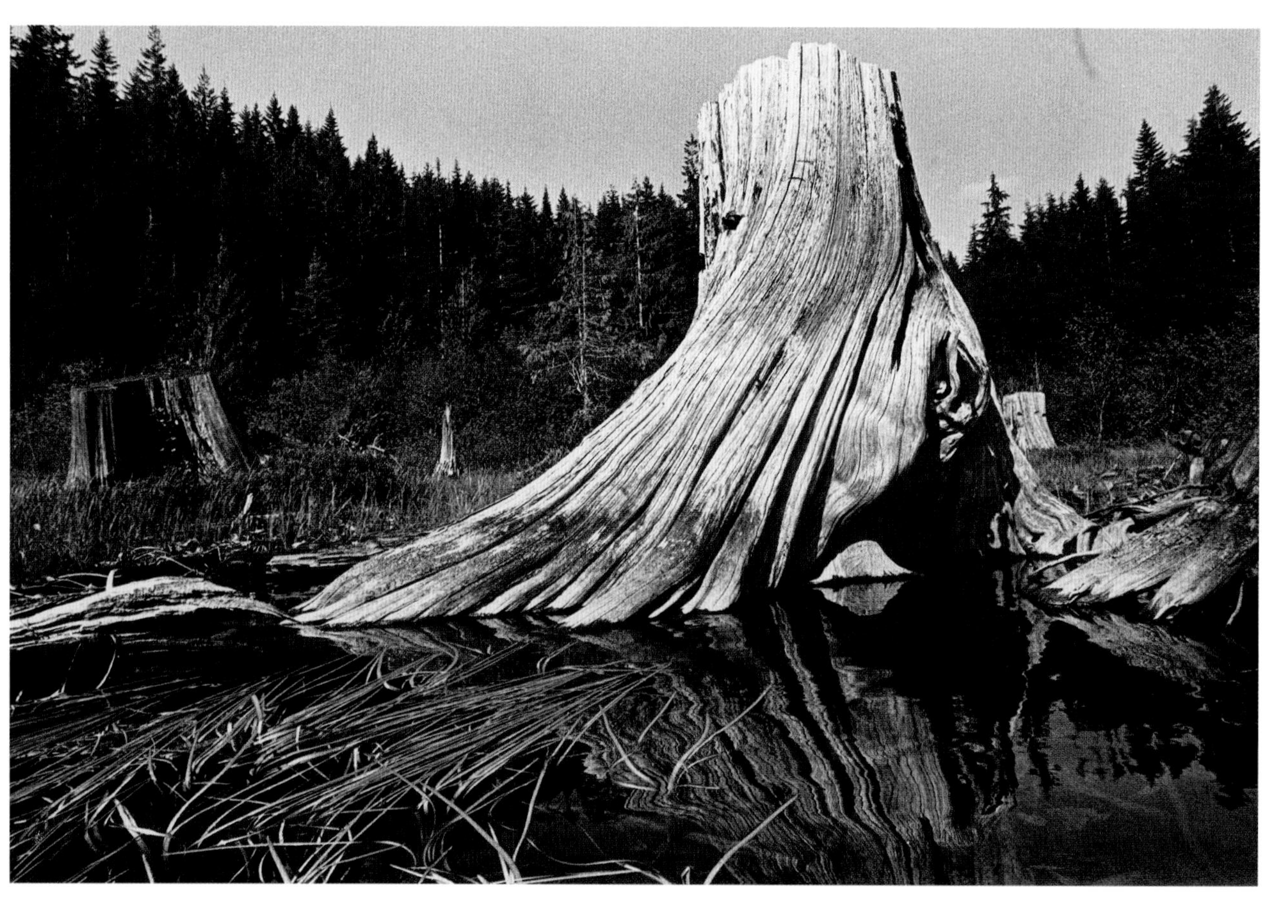

Thurlow Island, British Columbia, August 1974

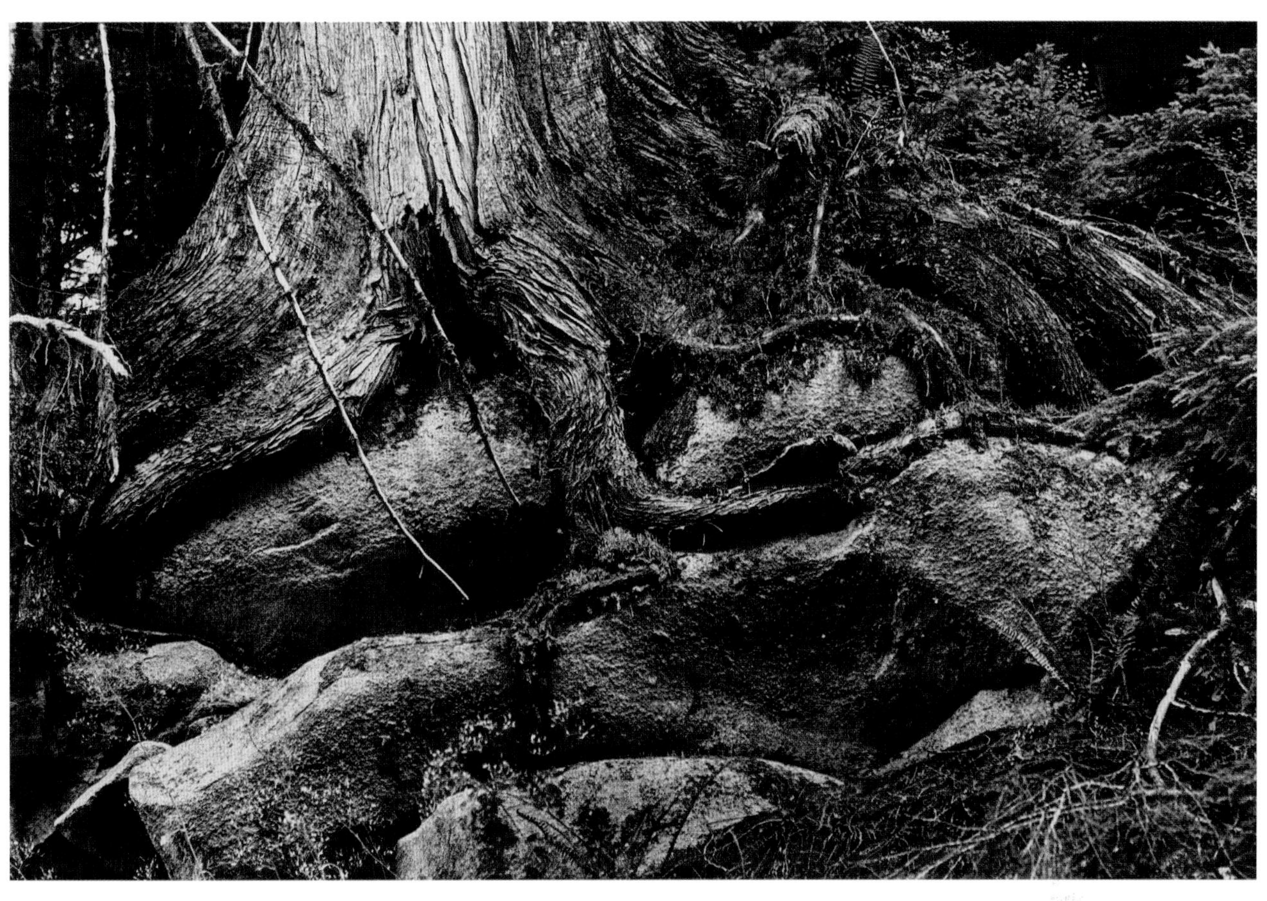

Thurlow Island, British Columbia, August 1974   265

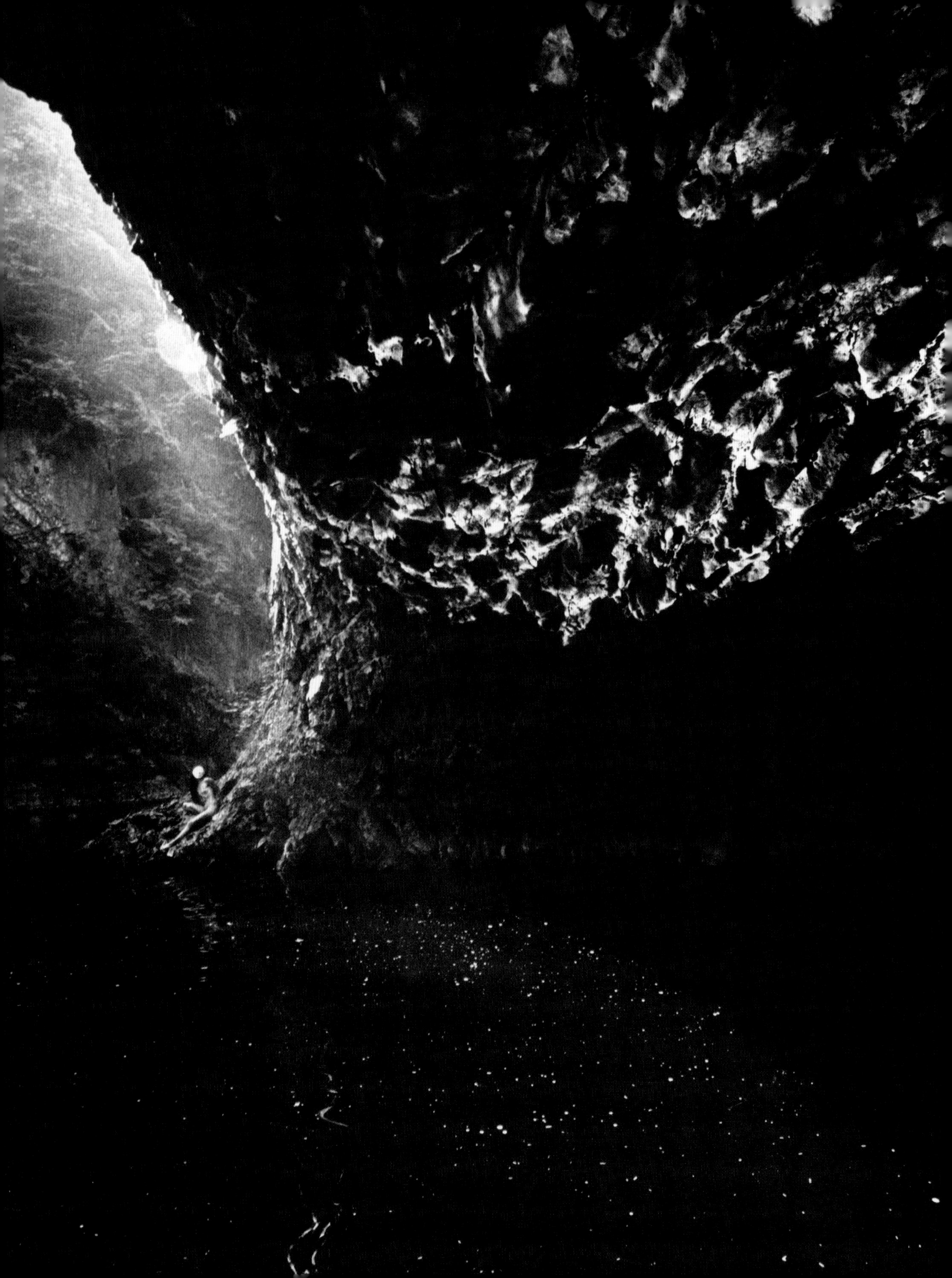

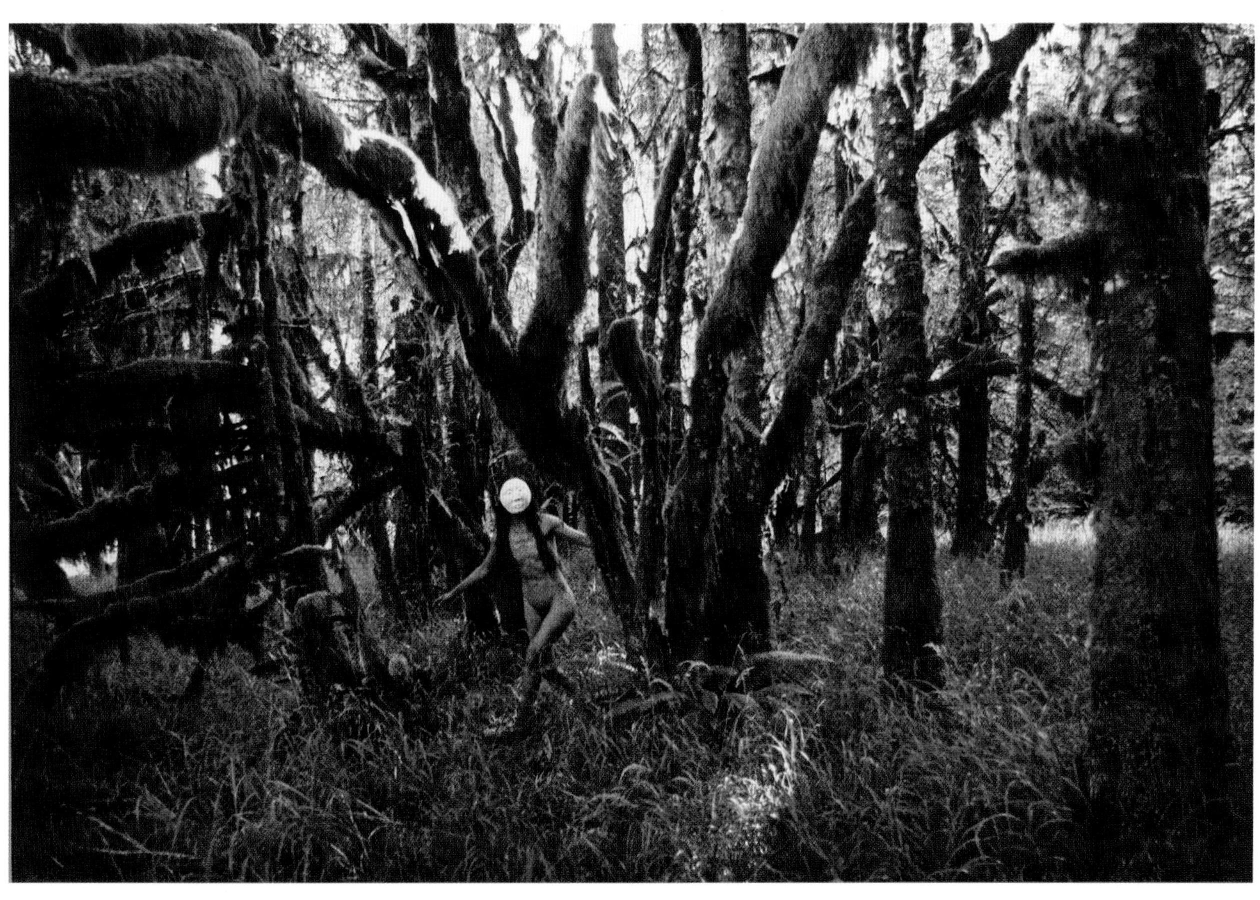

Nude Studies, Haruko, Quatsino Sound, Vancouver Island, British Columbia, August 1980   267

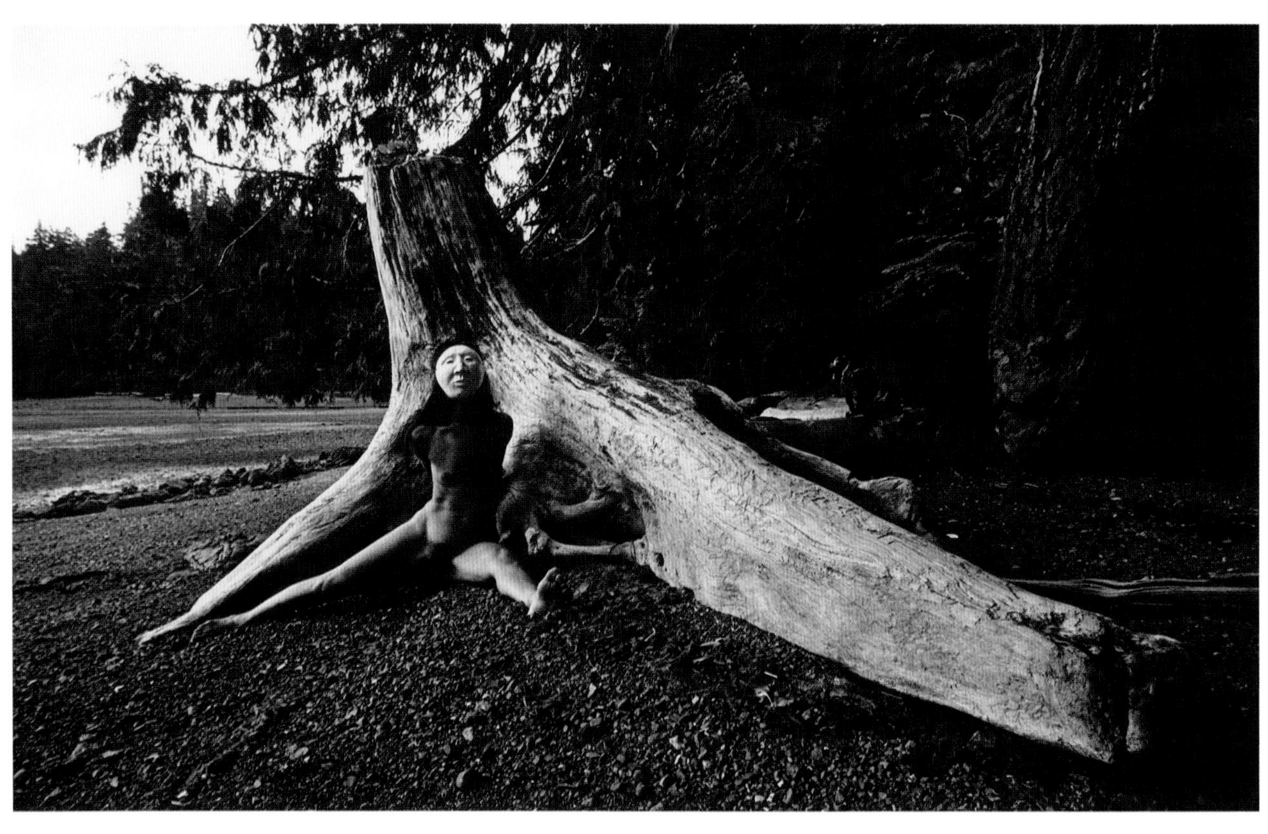

Nude Study, Haruko, Quatsino Sound, Vancouver Island, British Columbia, August 1980

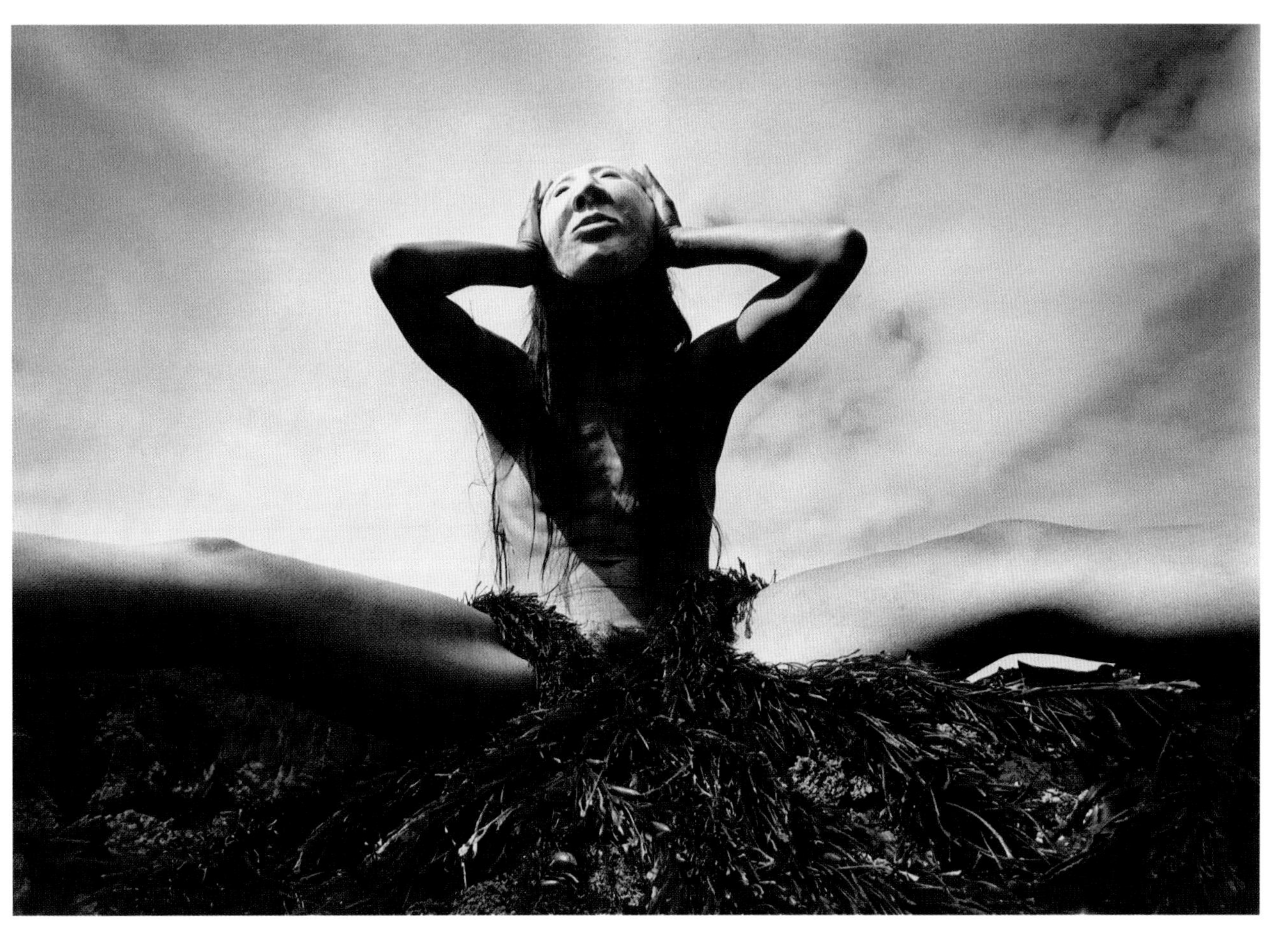

Nude Study, Haruko, Quatsino Sound, Vancouver Island, British Columbia, August 1980

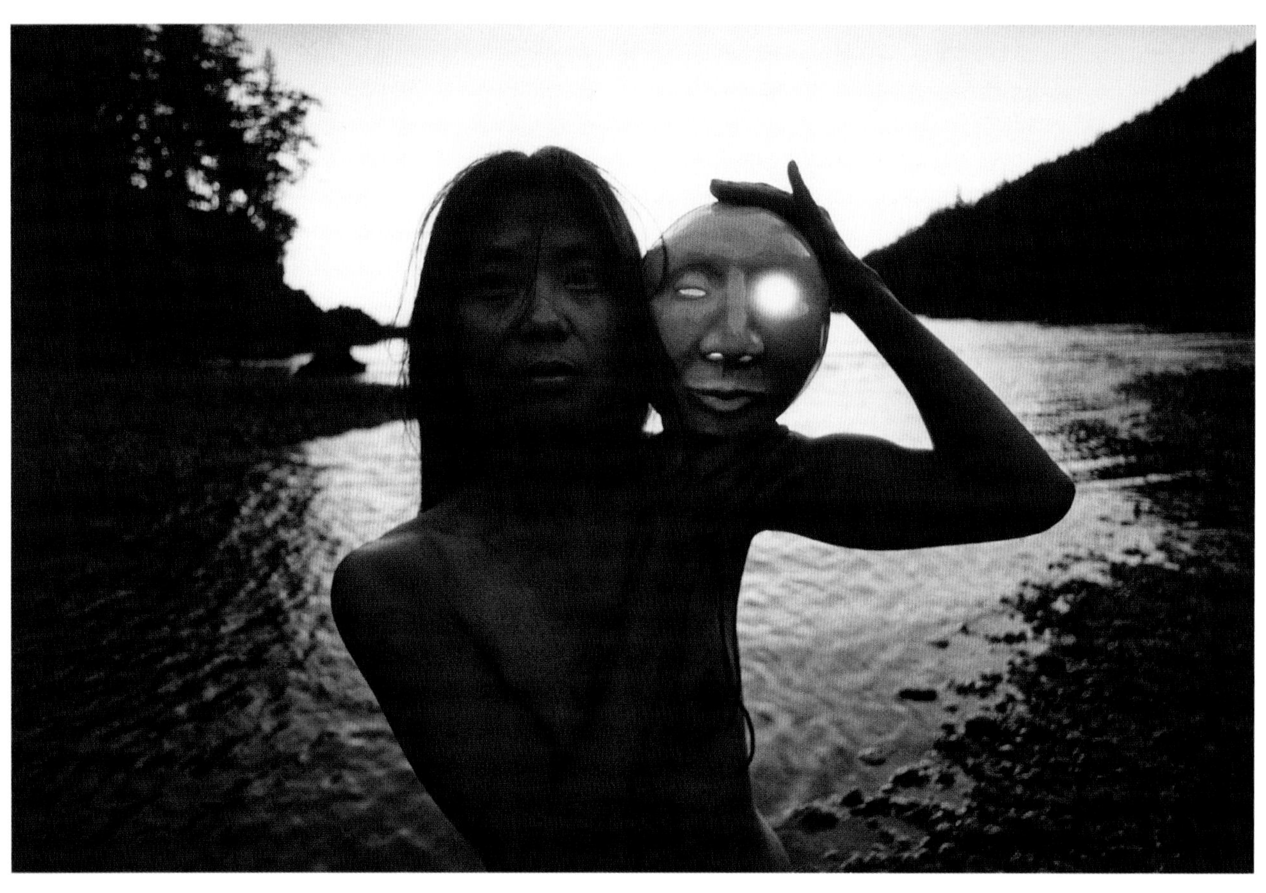

Nude Study, Haruko, Quatsino Sound, Vancouver Island, British Columbia, August 1980

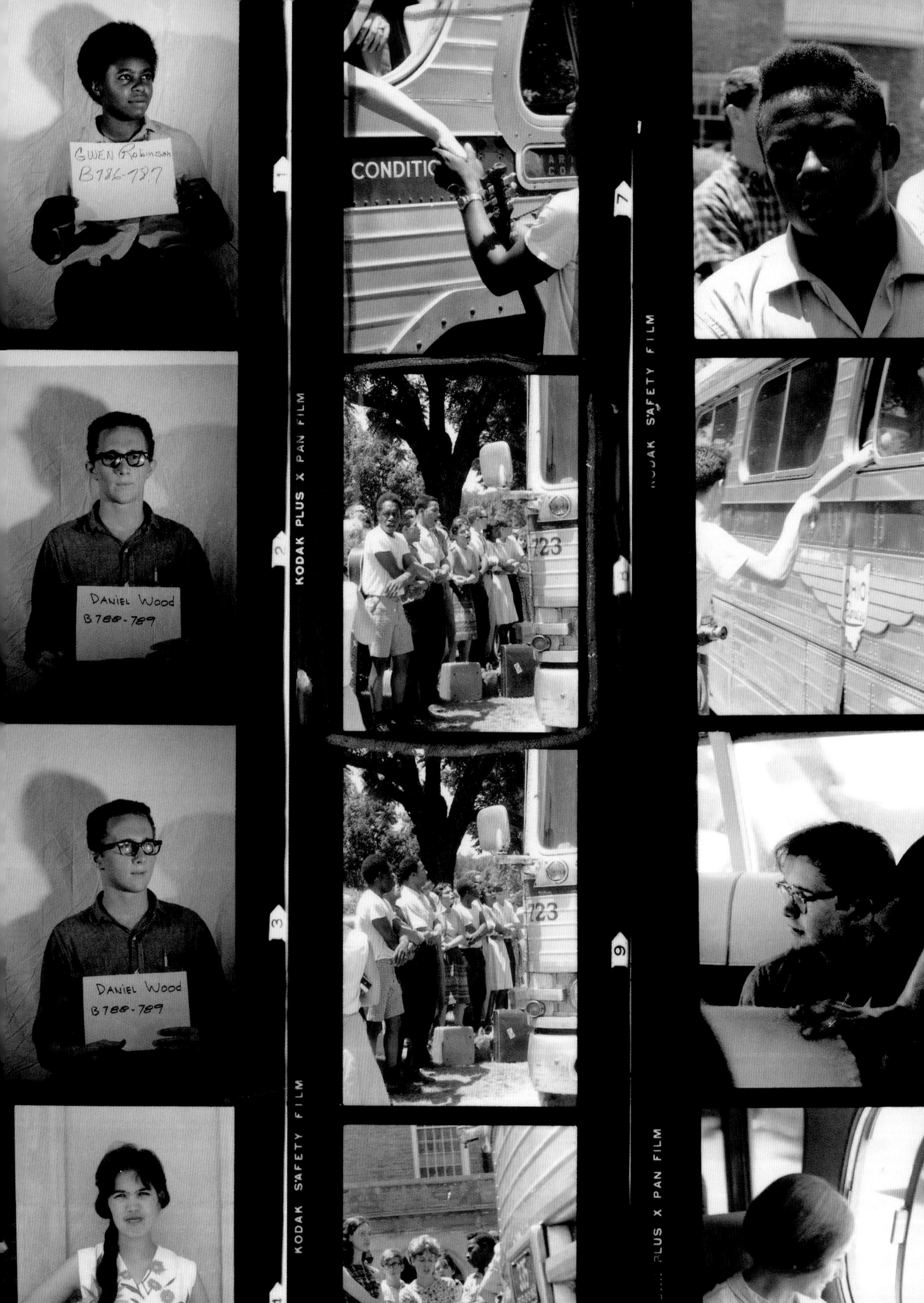

GWEN Robinson
B786-787
Daniel Wood
B788-789
Daniel Wood
B788-789
KODAK PLUS X PAN FILM
KODAK SAFETY FILM
CONDITIO
723
723

AFTERWORD (2008)

MY STORY ENDS RATHER abruptly, perhaps, at the first Powell Street Festival, and I feel compelled to provide you with an update. After the first festival, Rick Shiomi, with Mayu Takasaki's assistance, continued to nurse the event through its infancy until it was strong enough to stand on its own. Thanks to a policy they implemented after the first iteration, which relied heavily on performers from Japan, the festival is now a genuine expression of Nikkei arts and culture. I continued to photograph every year of the festival, and in 1992, I created the exhibition and book *Kikyō: Coming Home to Powell Street*.

Rick went on to become a writer, and his play *Yellow Fever*, set in the pre-war community of Little Tokyo, won an Obie Award. It's a murder mystery, and the inspiration for its chief protagonist, Sam Shikaze, is none other than Gordon Kadota. At the time of this writing, Rick is in Minneapolis, managing his own theatre company and taiko drum group.

As for Mayu, she suffered a more ignominious fate. A year after completing *A Dream of Riches*, I moved into a co-op townhouse in Strathcona on the edge of Chinatown, and since it was too large for one person, I offered to share it with Mayu. She readily agreed, which sent shock waves through her family in Steveston and our own community in Vancouver. The new immigrant women in particular were horrified that this sweet, innocent Sansei had fallen into the clutches of a dirty old man (namely, myself). Our relationship as roommates lasted about a week before we became lovers and partners in life. Our union has outlasted the marriages of all those naysayers, and we have become

Contact sheet of images taken during the second volunteer orientation session of Freedom Summer, Oxford, Ohio, June 22–27, 1964

pillars of society, which indicates the less-than-steady foundation of our community. Incidentally, our postal code has traditionally been the poorest area in all of Canada, and I would like to add that I have done more than my fair share in maintaining this dubious distinction.

Mayu is the perfect antidote to my basic nature as a curmudgeon. Without her gregarious and giving nature, our phone would not ring and few people would come to visit. Which is not to say she is a Pollyanna—Mayu is also a very smart and demanding woman, and her refusal to accept anything but the best during the early years of the Powell Street Festival earned her the acronym "DOB": "dirty old bitch." Mayu also got to experience life with the Doukhobors when she and her drum group, Katari Taiko, were invited on a tour of the old Russian communities in the Kootenay Valley. She performed in the same community hall in Brilliant where I once gave a speech in Russian, and she returned with the same love for the gentle people and their sumptuous food.

We still live in the same townhouse. Our immediate neighbours to the left are Take Yamashiro and his wife Sumi. On most summer mornings, I am awakened not by the cacophony of my Casio, but by the ethereal sounds of the shakuhachi drifting through my open window. Like myself, Take is an avid gardener, and we regularly meet out back to discuss the vagaries of our vegetables. Take's latest solution to his undersized strawberries was to rip out all the obstructing leaves: "They're not getting enough sun." He has never been clear on the concept of photosynthesis.

I took one last stab at the deer sequence. My partner in this adventure was Haruko, a young Sansei and a powerful artist in her own right. Armed with the old Winchester 30-30 borrowed from Ken Drushka and dramatic masks created by Haruko, we scoured the length of Quatsino Sound, from the open ocean to Winter Harbour, in our borrowed skiff. It's fortunate that we failed in this mission, for the area is not as remote as I had thought, and I undoubtedly would have been caught and fined for shooting a deer out of season. I doubt that the judge would have looked kindly on my only defence—artistic licence.

These days, I lead a quiet, contemplative life. I play mediocre tennis, grow my own vegetables and cook. My great pleasure is to go out my back door, pick the fruits of my labour and prepare a fine meal for family and friends. The pleasure I get and give from this simple exercise is immediate and visceral, with none of the ambiguity and angst of art. If I had my life to live over again, I would centre it around food. At one of our last family gatherings, my late Uncle Yoshimaru told me that, when we first moved to Chatham, an entrepreneur wanted to open up a Japanese restaurant in Toronto and offered the job of cook and manager to my father. I wonder how different my life would have been had he accepted this offer. I could have been a celebrity chef with my own program on the Food Network, or more realistically, perhaps, I might be slinging teriyaki burgers at some fast-food joint on Hastings Street or serving up Japadogs—they actually exist—from my cart on Burrard.

Perhaps it was the election of President Barack Obama that reminded me I was once a part of the process that led to this historic moment, which may herald the dawn of a new American era. When Obama was elected, I called Ed Nakawatase in Philadelphia. After leaving the Movement, Brother Ed went to work for the American Friends Service Committee. One day, out of the blue, he called to say he would be coming to Seattle and asked if I could come down to meet him. Since that day, our friendship has continued to grow, with several exchanges of visits and a steady flow of emails. After the previous elections and especially after the ill-fated re-election of George W. Bush in 2004, Ed would call to lament the fate of his nation and half-jokingly inquire about the possibility of seeking political asylum in Canada. I told Ed that it would be an exciting time to be in America. Canada's political leaders are not especially evil, and the amount of damage they can cause is limited by our parliamentary system, their own anemic imagination and the fact that Canada is not a superpower. The only real danger they pose is boring us to death. Incidentally, Brother Ed's fertile imagination came up with the first working title of this narrative: *Soul on Rice*.

I'd like to end my narrative by going back to the beginning. I have just returned from Snick's fiftieth anniversary reunion on the campus of Shaw University in Raleigh, North Carolina. Students gathered there in 1960 to form the Student Nonviolent Coordinating Committee. In 2010, I met old friends whom I hadn't seen in over four decades. Although our hair was greyer and our bodies a little less agile, we hugged and carried on as if we'd parted only yesterday. John Lewis, the "conscience of the Congress," was in fine form, regaling us with humour, grace and gratitude. He was back in the bosom of his family, the band of brothers and sisters that was Snick. Julian Bond, his voice still like liquid honey, reviewed the history of Snick and how it became the vanguard of the Movement that inspired an entire generation of youth, who shook the very foundations of America and the world. The Freedom Singers, the power of their voices undiminished by the years, sang the songs that sustained us through the darkest nights of terror and spread the gospel of the Movement throughout the world. To think that I was once a part of all that is incredible, humbling and glorious.

One of the last items on the agenda of the five-day reunion/conference was the introduction of the children of Snick veterans. These beautiful and vibrant young men and women, with their impressive lists of credentials, seemed well on their way to taking over the educational, legal and artistic life of the nation. Bob Moses, looking more and more like Buddha, was there, gently urging his young disciples—members of the Algebra Project and the Young People's Project in Mississippi—to continue the conference. Take note America: they have snatched the torch from our hands and are organizing the next phase of the struggle in your backyard. We will not be moved, and we shall overcome.

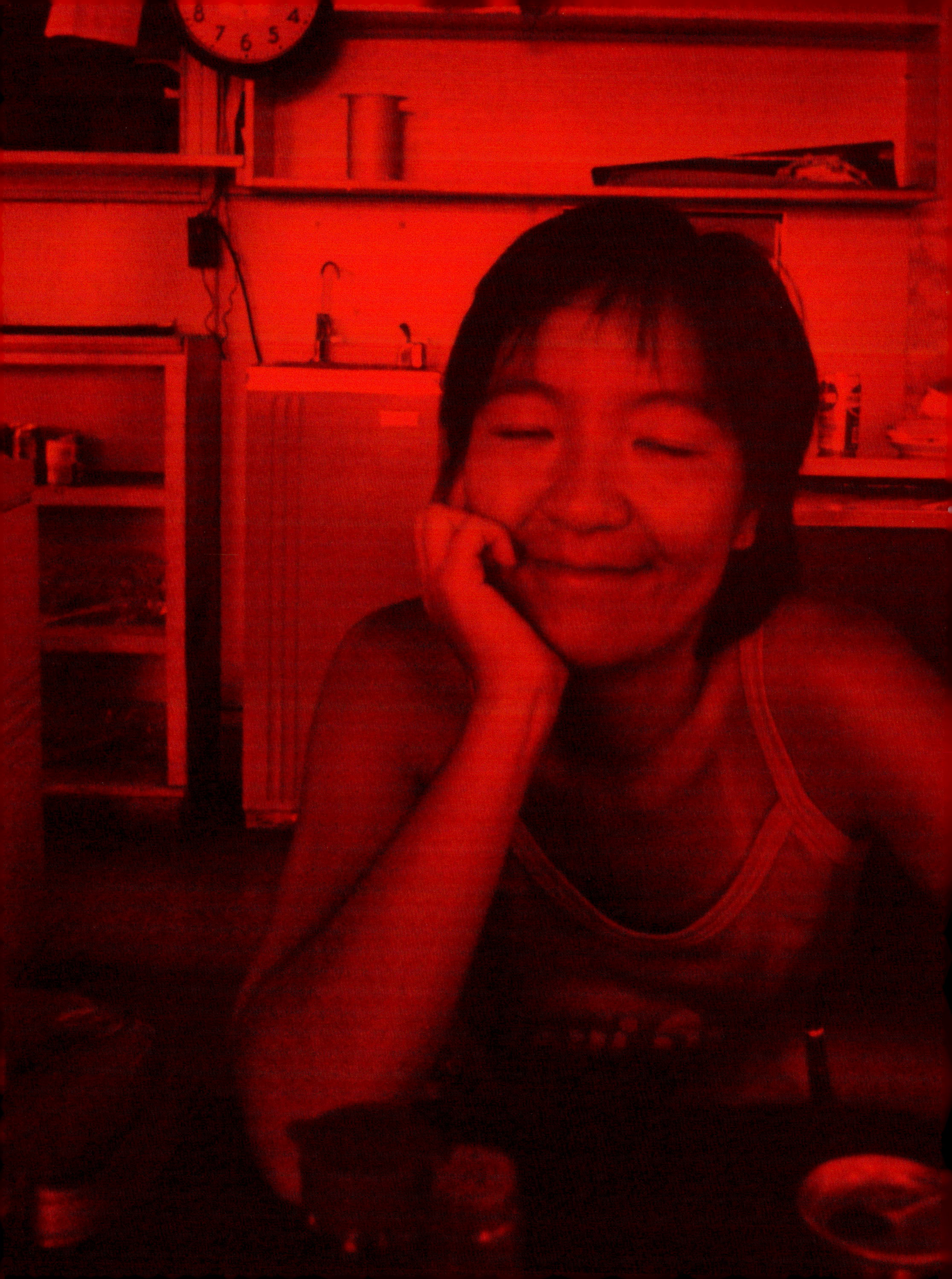

MAYUMI TAKASAKI IN CONVERSATION WITH PAUL WONG

The following conversation between Mayumi Takasaki and Paul Wong was recorded in Vancouver on November 28, 2024, and has been edited for clarity and length.

Paul Wong: Tell me about yourself and your relationship with Tamio Wakayama.

Mayumi Takasaki: I'm a third-generation Japanese Canadian. I was born in Vancouver and raised in Steveston, British Columbia, and I have lived in the Strathcona neighbourhood of Vancouver for forty-five years. Tamio was my partner for forty years. I met him in 1977, shortly after I returned from Japan, where I lived for two and a half years after I finished university. When I came back to Vancouver, I started working at Tonari Gumi, the Japanese Community Volunteers Association. It's primarily a social service agency for Japanese Canadian senior citizens but also for anyone who speaks Japanese and needs assistance. At the time, Tamio was just finishing up the *A Dream of Riches* photo exhibit project, and we were all gearing up for the very first Powell Street Festival in 1977. The group who worked on *A Dream of Riches* and the Powell Street Festival all hung out at Tonari Gumi.

PW: When did you start your activism within the Japanese Canadian community?

MT: While at the University of British Columbia (UBC), I met Ron Tanaka—a Japanese American who graduated from the University of California, Berkeley, who had come to UBC to teach English in the late 1960s. He gathered young Asian Canadians to teach us about the Asian American movement and its relationship to the Civil Rights Movement and Black history. We were inspired to form the Asian Canadian Coalition—a group where we discussed self-determination and the importance of returning to our communities and learning about our histories. Ron was a photographer, and his wife was skilled in darkroom techniques. He let us use his cameras and sent us off to photograph our communities.

For example, I went home to Steveston and photographed the bazaars at the Steveston Buddhist Temple and the Japanese Canadian fishermen on the wharf. We used photography to learn about our communities and family histories. In 1972, we held an exhibition at the UBC Student Union Building titled *The Asian Canadian Experience*. Through this project, we Sansei realized that many of us knew very little about our own Japanese Canadian history. We had heard stories about the internment camps from our parents, but we didn't understand the whole history because it wasn't taught in schools. We researched in UBC's Special Collections and through our own family albums to produce the exhibition, which featured contemporary and historical photographs of our families and community.

At the time of graduation, I was living with four other Japanese Canadian women, and we wanted to see what it would be like to live in Japan as Japanese Canadians. We were curious about our cultural heritage and what it would be like to live in a place where we were the majority, where we could walk into a room and not stand out.

PW: So you and Tamio were in Japan around the same time?

MT: I was in Japan from 1974 to 1977. Tamio was there earlier, from 1969 to 1970 on a Canada Council grant. It was different for him—he was there for a set period of time. He had a host family in Tokyo and travelled the country taking photographs.

The other women and I rented small apartments or little houses; we taught English and had everyday lives, going to language school and other classes like martial arts, cooking, ikebana, tea ceremony.

PW: What do you think of Tamio's photographs of his time in Japan?

MT: There's a dichotomy: there are the artistic photographs and then there are the photographs where he is searching for a connection. There are a lot of art photographs: the mannequin drinking Coke, the people walking down a stairwell, the crying Kewpie dolls. But my favourite picture from his time in Japan is of the two elderly gentlemen walking down a country path—I have relatives who look exactly like them.

Tamio's art photographs of Japan are detached, whereas his photographs like the one of those two old men evince an emotional connection. They're more akin to the pictures that he took of the of people in the American South. When he was photographing in the South, it wasn't to make art. It was to convey a message, tell a story. The photographs were taken for a purpose. He was Tamio Wakayama, Student Nonviolent Coordinating Committee (SNCC) worker, Civil Rights activist. Afterward, he became a "Canada Council for the Arts" photographer. I think he struggled to be recognized as an artist and not just as a Civil Rights activist.

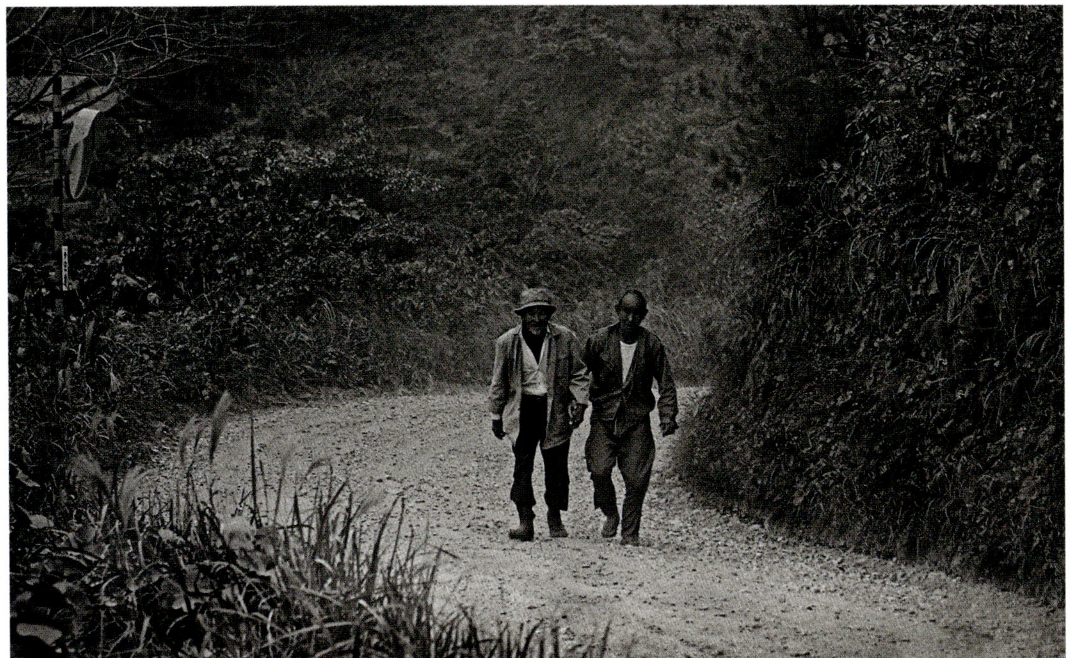

Two old friends, Shiida, Fukuoka, Japan, November 1969

PW: What is Tamio's legacy with SNCC?

MT: My one regret is that I never went with him to any SNCC events, like reunions and Freedom Summer gatherings. I always encouraged him to go, because I knew that it was such an important part of his life and that he loved those people dearly. My friend Kathy Shimizu attended SNCC's fiftieth reunion with him at Shaw University in Raleigh, North Carolina, in 2010 and said it was amazing to see Tamio embraced by the SNCC community. They were all so happy to see him.

PW: What were his favourite photographs from that period?

MT: I think there are three or four photographs that he really loved: the *Delta* photograph (pp. 110-11)—the big image of the house with the gnarly tree—represented to him the beauty of the South. He loved the *Super SNCC* photograph with the little boy (cover). Most people see the boy as Superman, but he was "Super SNCC"—the SNCC activists were the heroes to him. The *Freedom cross* was another one of his favourites, because it was his most published photograph (pp. 120-21). And then the beaming lady (p. 115). He loved that picture.

PW: What was it like to live with Tamio and have his darkroom in your home?

MT: Tamio's darkroom was in the basement, right below the living room, so I could hear everything. I could hear the timer: tick,

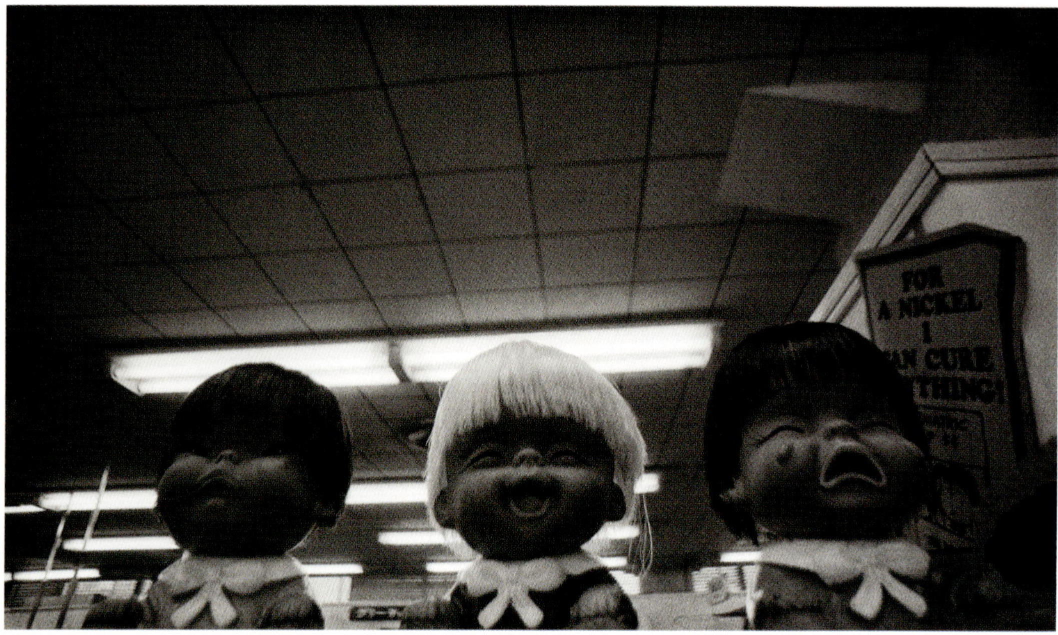

Dolls in department store, Tokyo, Japan, 1969

tick, tick, tick, tick. I could hear the light switch go on and off. It was a constant. It was almost like I was in the darkroom with him. He could be moody when he was working on something, so I gave him space to do his work. There were times when he was working on something and our entire kitchen table was covered with prints that he was getting ready to spot. And I would say, "Where are we going to eat dinner?" Because I used to take pictures, I knew how to spot, so I would spot prints for him if he was in a rush.

PW: Aside from spotting, were you involved in his photography projects?

MT: Not really. I was involved in his writing projects simply because he was a terrible speller and he needed me to proofread. With his photo projects, he was very clear in his vision.

PW: What was Tamio's contribution to the Japanese community? How was he perceived?

MT: *A Dream of Riches*, the exhibition and the book, were important milestones for the community. It was our community acknowledging our history in a visual form. He was seen as the coordinator of that exhibition and was respected for being part of the team that put it together. The community across Canada was appreciative. Later on, he moved into the Redress Movement, not just as a photographer but also as an activist.

PW: Was *Kikyō: Coming Home to Powell Street* (1992) a highlight of his photography career?

MT: *Kikyō* was a project that Tamio wanted to do; it was a career highlight because he was able to tell a story without any rules or guidelines. *A Dream of Riches* was a historical project using primarily archival photographs. They were images that he chose, not ones that he took. With *Kikyō*, he was able to tell the story of the Festival through his own eyes.

PW: How did he make a living?

MT: That was a big question for all his friends and family. They never understood how he survived. He would sell the odd print or get hired to document a project. For a time, he provided the Powell Street Festival with fifty prints every year and was paid ten dollars a print. There was a period in the 1980s when he was paid well to be the locations coordinator for Japanese film shoots in Canada. He was always very frugal, very careful.

He was also involved in things like the Greater Vancouver Japanese Canadian Citizens' Association *Bulletin*. Tamio edited *The Bulletin* for a few years, and he photographed community events and published them in the newsletter. At some point, it was just expected that he would be at events, documenting the community. I don't know if our community—or communities in general—recognize the importance of the photographers who capture and preserve everything. Don Rosenbloom, Michiko Sakata's ex-partner, said: "Your community is lucky to have somebody here who has taken all these photographs for all these years."

PW: Did he come to terms with being born and branded an Enemy Alien?

MT: I think working on *A Dream of Riches* helped him reclaim his history, as did being a part of the Japanese Canadian community in Vancouver. Redress was also significant, because the whole process is based in standing up for your rights and for what you are owed as a community. So yes, I believe he was at peace with it.

PW: You worked with Tamio to organize his archives for Stanford University, and you continue to contribute to his legacy. What would Tamio think about all this?

MT: In 2025, it will be ten years since we started the journey with Stanford University. He would be happy that the collection is finally being acquired by Stanford. It took us a year to process and document all the prints. It was good for him, because he had the opportunity to see the whole span of his work.

He wanted to publish his memoir; he had selected all the photographs for it. After he finished working on the exhibition and publication *This Light of Ours: Activist Photographers of the Civil Rights Movement* (2011), he contacted the University Press of Mississippi, and he was disappointed that they never got back to him. They responded after he died to say that they might be interested in publishing the memoir. Knowing that they were interested would have made him happy. So this book would make him very happy.

I never liked the title, *Soul on Rice*, because I thought it was silly. But he loved it, and everybody at SNCC laughed when he mentioned it to them. He would get on his bicycle with a thermos of coffee and go to the park to write in his godawful handwriting that no one could read. He would come home and transcribe it onto the computer.

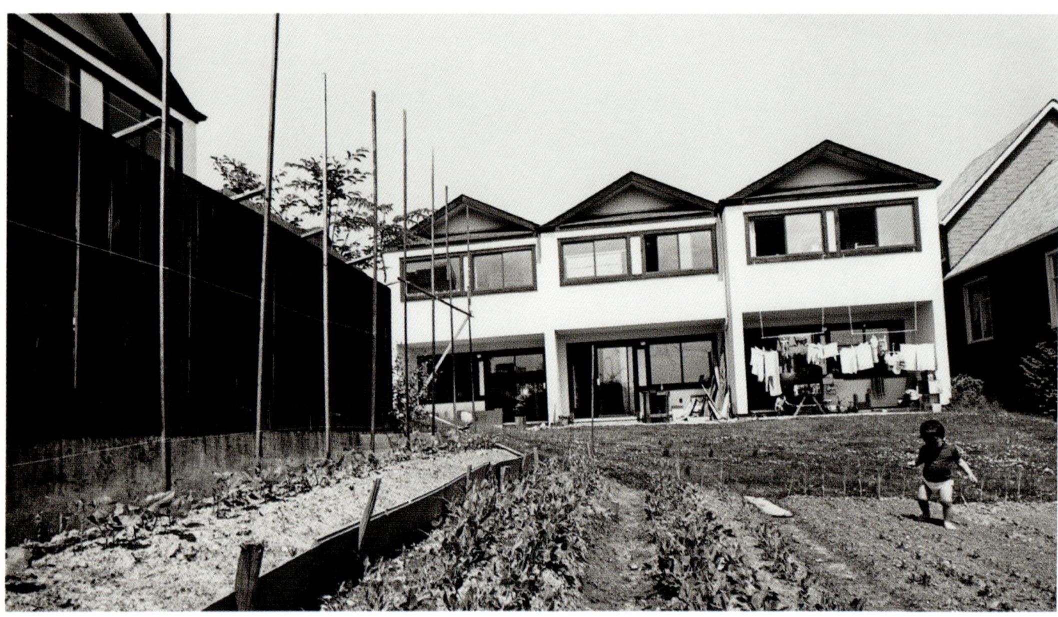

Co-op garden, 730 Union Street, Vancouver, May 20, 1979

He never asked me to read it, and I've never read the whole thing. I have read parts; I know many of the stories. I figured if he wanted me to read it, he would have given it to me to read.

PW: What is your favourite memory of Tamio?

MT: In recent years, the joy he took in cooking. I have a picture of him when he barbecued his first turkey, and it was pure joy on his face. He really cared for my grandmother. She claimed to be hard of hearing, and Tamio's voice was deep, and he didn't speak very loudly. Yet they would sit together and chortle away for long periods. I like that memory of them.

When he was sick, just before he died, he spent about two weeks in and out of bed. We didn't know what was wrong. But I think perhaps he knew that he was dying, as he spent most of that time reflecting on his life. Muhammad Ali was one of Tamio's heroes, and he loved the phrase "Float like a butterfly, sting like a bee." He said, "My mind is like a butterfly. My mind is just flitting from place to place in my life." He realized how fortunate he was to have experienced all that he had. In his memoir, he talks about appreciating that he had been part of the most amazing and beautiful time in American history, though it was his experience of an ugly period in history that shaped him. He came full circle: being a SNCC photographer, his time in Japan, the series of nudes, being part of the redress community, documenting the Japanese Canadian community. He came back to that time with SNCC; he was really grateful for that shining moment. And, at the end, I'd like to think that he was at peace with his life.

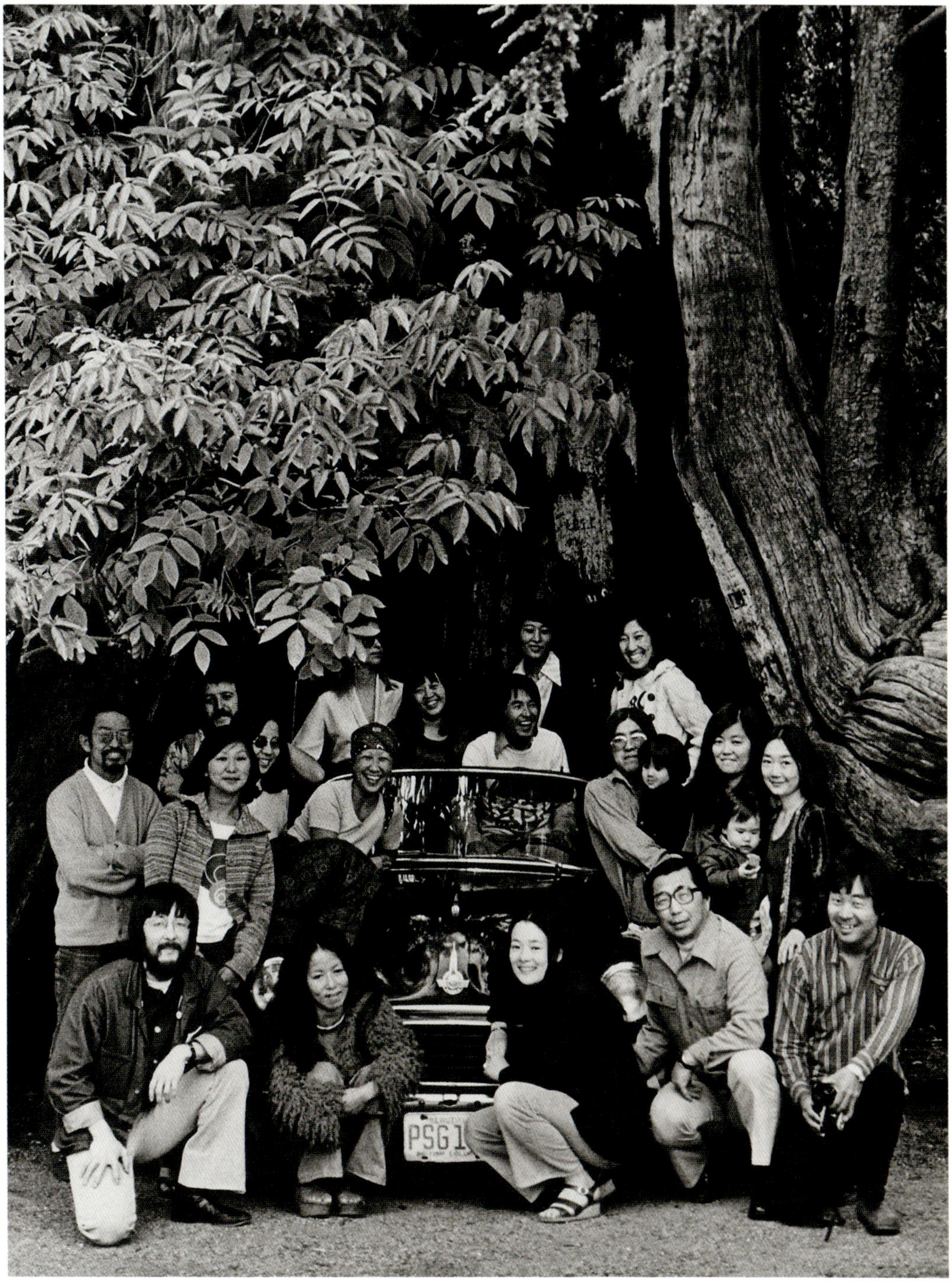

Japanese Canadian Centennial Project (JCCP) members in front of a hollow tree in Stanley Park, Vancouver, British Columbia, June 1976

CONTRIBUTOR BIOGRAPHIES

Eva Respini is Interim Co-Chief Executive Officer and Curator at Large at the Vancouver Art Gallery, working to shape and drive the vision of the Vancouver Art Gallery's curatorial program along with the Gallery team. Respini served as the curator and co-commissioner for the 2022 US Pavilion's presentation of Simone Leigh at the fifty-ninth International Art Exhibition of La Biennale di Venezia. She organized the highly successful mid-career survey of Simone Leigh's work, which opened at the ICA/Boston in April 2023, and will tour across the United States through 2025. Previously she worked as a curator in the photography department at the Museum of Modern Art, New York, for a decade. She has edited and contributed to numerous publications, and her work appears in various museum publications and periodicals.

Mayumi Takasaki is a third-generation Japanese Canadian. Since the 1970s, she has been involved with the Japanese Canadian community in Vancouver, with the Powell Street Festival and Tonari Gumi (the Japanese Community Volunteers Association)—a social service agency for Japanese Canadian senior citizens. She is also a founding member of Katari Taiko, the first taiko group in Canada.

Paul Wong is an award-winning artist and independent curator known for pioneering early visual and media art in Canada. He is the artistic director of On Main Gallery and the co-founding director of the VIVO Media Arts Centre, a major Vancouver-based video production and distribution centre. Wong's honours and awards include the Canada Council Bell Canada Award in Video Art (1992), a Governor General's Award for Visual and Media Arts (2005), the Audain Prize for Lifetime Achievement (2016), an Honorary Doctor of Letters from Emily Carr University of Art + Design (2023), and the Fire Horse Award (2024) from the Toronto Reel Asian International Film Festival.

ACKNOWLEDGEMENTS

The making of this book and exhibition has required the expertise and collaboration of a great many sets of eyes, my thanks and gratitude to the incredible team of people who have contributed to this project. Mayumi Takasaki for trusting me with Tamio's story, his archive and his legacy. Your assistance, detailed knowledge and friendship have been invaluable. Cindy Mochizuki for making the insightful documentary film *Between Pictures: The Lens of Tamio Wakayama*.

Senior Curator Diana Freundl for believing in the project and steering it through the Vancouver Art Gallery; former Curatorial Assistant Joanne Chung, who spent a year working alongside me as we poured our hearts out looking through the thousands of pictures; former CEO Anthony Kiendl for supporting this initiative from the start; and Director of Publishing Stephanie Rebick with Natalia Camacho and Anna Luth for overseeing the complex coordination, keeping us all focused and on track and bringing on the co-publishers Figure 1. Interim CEO & Curator at Large Eva Respini for your elucidating essay "A Revolution of the Self" and to the vast experience of photographer Ian Lefebvre for processing all the images.

A special shout-out to Brian Howell for your passion for Tamio's photography and dedication to digitizing the 35mm negatives and producing the very best possible prints. Linda Uyehara Hoffman for working on the memoir. Debbie Cheung for the exceptional design of this memoir and photography art book.

Also, appreciation to Lisa Uyeda, Daien Ide and Director/Curator Sherry Kajiwara at the Nikkei National Museum & Cultural Centre for your generous access and help researching your archives, and my studio assistant Christian Y. Jones for assistance throughout the process.

Tamio thank you for leaving us with your words, memories and pictures. I hope that we have done you proud.

Peace Out, Paul Wong

PHOTO CREDITS

Cover: Boys playing in Vine City, Atlanta, Georgia ("Super Snick"), July 7, 1964; **2:** A sharecropper shakes hands with a volunteer on a voter registration drive, Mississippi, December 1964; **13 (background):** Vancouver Art Gallery Photography Archives; **13 (foreground):** Nikkei National Museum & Cultural Centre, 2001.3.68; **14:** Vancouver Art Gallery; **19:** Library of Congress, Prints and Photographs Division, LC-DIG-ppmsca-98857; **20:** © Danny Lyon/Magnum Photos; **21:** Library of Congress, Prints and Photographs Division, LC-USZC4-4832; **22:** Courtesy of the Daido Moriyama Photo Foundation; **24–25:** Audience, Powell Street Festival, Vancouver, BC, August 5, 1989; **28:** Nikkei National Museum & Cultural Centre; **31:** Vancouver Public Library, Historical Photography Collection, VPL 14920; **33 (background):** Nikkei National Museum & Cultural Centre, 2002.10.9.b; **33 (foreground left):** Nikkei National Museum & Cultural Centre, 2010.80.3.3; **33 (foreground right):** Courtesy of Mayumi Takasaki; **35 (top row):** Nikkei National Museum & Cultural Centre, 2002.10.9; **35 (middle row):** Nikkei National Museum & Cultural Centre, 2010.80.3.3; **35 (bottom row):** Courtesy of Mayumi Takasaki; **40:** Nikkei National Museum & Cultural Centre, 2010.23.2.4.96; **44 (bottom):** Nikkei National Museum & Cultural Centre, 2010.23.2.4.527; **48 (right):** Nikkei National Museum & Cultural Centre, 2010.23.2.4.733; **50:** Nikkei National Museum & Cultural Centre, 2010.23.2.4.538; **180:** Vancouver Art Gallery; **252:** Vancouver Art Gallery; **Endpapers:** Details of Tamio Wakayama's handwritten memoir *Soul on Rice*

Published in conjunction with the exhibition
Enemy Alien: Tamio Wakayama, organized by the
Vancouver Art Gallery as an initiative of the Centre
for Global Asias, guest curated by Paul Wong with
Joanne So Jeong Chung, former Curatorial Assistant,
and Anna Luth, Curatorial Assistant, and presented
from October 3, 2025, to February 22, 2026.

Editor: Paul Wong
Publication coordination: Stephanie Rebick
Copyeditors: Linda Uyehara Hoffman, Kate Woolf
Proofreaders: Julia Monks, Natalia Camacho H.
Design: Debbie Cheung
Digital image preparation: Brian Howell; Ian
Lefebvre and Kyla Bailey, Vancouver Art Gallery

Printed in China in 2025 by Shenzhen Reliance
Printing Co., Ltd.

All photographs are by Tamio Wakayama and are
courtesy of the Estate of Tamio Wakayama, unless
otherwise noted.

**Library and Archives Canada Cataloguing in
Publication**

Title: Enemy alien : Tamio Wakayama.
Other titles: Enemy alien (Vancouver, B.C.) |
Tamio Wakayama
Names: Container of (work): Wakayama, Tamio,
1941-2018. Photographs. Selections. | Vancouver Art
Gallery, host institution, publisher.
Description: Essays by Paul Wong and Eva Respini.
Identifiers: Canadiana 20250198908 | ISBN
9781927656754 (softcover)
Subjects: LCSH: Wakayama, Tamio, 1941-2018—
Exhibitions. | LCGFT: Exhibition catalogs.
Classification: LCC TR647 .W257 2025 |
DDC 779.092—dc23

ISBN 978-1-927656-75-4 (Vancouver Art Gallery)
ISBN 978-1-77327-280-1 (Figure 1 Publishing)

Publication Support:
The Pamela and Dave Richardson Family
The Jack and Doris Shadbolt Endowment for
Research and Publications

The Vancouver Art Gallery is a not-for-profit
organization supported by its members, individual
donors, corporate funders, foundations, the City of
Vancouver, the Province of British Columbia through
the British Columbia Arts Council, and the Canada
Council for the Arts.

Vancouver Art Gallery
750 Hornby Street
Vancouver, BC
V6Z 2H7 Canada
vanartgallery.bc.ca

Figure 1 Publishing Inc.
Vancouver, BC Canada
figure1publishing.com

The Vancouver Art Gallery respectfully
acknowledges its location on the traditional,
ancestral and unceded territories of the
xʷməθkʷəy̓əm (Musqueam), Sḵwx̱wú7mesh
(Squamish) and səlilwətaɬ (Tsleil-Waututh) peoples,
and honours the Indigenous stewards of the land
whose rich cultures are fundamental to artistic life
in our province and the work of the Gallery.

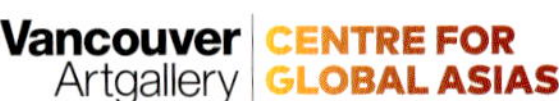
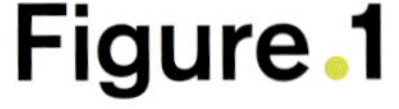

The Fest. Powell St. Festival

OUTLINE

- Trace own history back to Oppenheimer & Powell St

- Old adage — an idea whose time has finally come

- '77 Centennial celebration. local project — Apex renaissance in the Nikkei community — children of the ... used coming up in ... on Powell St to explore and reclaim their past

- I take it as I under aegis of ... ... It seized the application for grant to city to hold of Festival in Oppenheimer Park

- City recognition of the idea thanks to the good works done by both ... Nikkei community, all coming ... as well as the respected national ... institutions of JCCA, the Buddhist Church, Japanese Language School.

- Hired ... Shiomi who had been perpetually involved with the community ... city work supporting the ... project

okely his best defence was a stout offense. I
fired back with "any nigger who the fuck you
callin white. Stokely you is not only colored but
you is colored blind. (I definitely meant white that
day). And don't give none of this shit about how
you is descended from of the great chieftains of Africa
cause... your great great great grandmother was ...
through the streets with tampons in ancestors in
safari were ...

The next day I began to
move the film from my own
store of the first project. It was
an unusually hot day and Folleeln
stepped into the bedroom to offer
me a cooling drink laced
with a slow & creadown cuspid.
Some a lot of ... I had
a violent reaction. It only takes
a smell around ... up my heart
rate and to turn my body bristle red,
nausea and a splitting headache was
soon to follow. I had reached the first
stage and I went out to cool down
on the front steps. I was greeted
Woute berg came by and was amused
by my suddenly transformation from
mellow yellow to fire engine red.
He called out to others to come out b
to witness this spectacle. Stokely
Carmichael count out was one of them.
I had been warned to be wary of
Stokely as his white baiting when
he would leave on on any circleness
to ferret out any signs hints of
paternalistic. No cooler, liberal, am
I'd always liked Stokely for his uneasy
energy and the passion of his radical
ideas. ... with ... to form his challenge